THE ENFORCEMENT OF EU FINANCIAL LAW

This book focuses on the enforcement of EU financial law on the national and supra-national levels. Emphasis is laid on the interaction between the EU and national levels (vertical interaction), as well as between private, administrative and criminal law (horizontal interaction). The book takes a multi-jurisdiction and inter-disciplinary approach and covers a range of issues that are highly topical, such as the new EU Anti-Money Laundering regime, and the ReNEUAL model for administrative law.

With contributions by leading academics and senior members of EU and national institutions, the book will be of interest to professionals dealing with financial law in their daily practice such as lawyers, bankers, policy makers and officers at supervisory authorities, but also to academics interested in fundamental questions of interaction between legal systems.

Hart Studies in Commercial and Financial Law: Volume 8

Hart Studies in Commercial and Financial Law
Series Editors: John Linarelli and Teresa Rodríguez de las Heras Ballell

This series offers a venue for publishing works on commercial law as well as on the regulation of banking and finance and the law on insolvency and bankruptcy. It publishes works on the law on secured credit, the regulatory and transactional aspects of banking and finance, the transactional and regulatory institutions for financial markets, legal and policy aspects associated with access to commercial and consumer credit, new generation subjects having to do with the institutional architecture associated with innovation and the digital economy including works on blockchain technology, work on the relationship of law to economic growth, the harmonisation or unification of commercial law, transnational commercial law, and the global financial order. The series promotes interdisciplinary work. It publishes research on the law using the methods of empirical legal studies, behavioural economics, political economy, normative welfare economics, law and society inquiry, socio-legal studies, political theory, and historical methods. Its coverage includes international and comparative investigations of areas of law within its remit.

Volume 1: The Financialisation of the Citizen: Social and Financial Inclusion through European Private Law
Guido Comparato

Volume 2: MiFID II and Private Law: Enforcing EU Conduct of Business Rules
Federico Della Negra

Volume 3: Reforming Corporate Retail Investor Protection: Regulating to Avert Mis-Selling
Diane Bugeja

Volume 4: The Future of Commercial Law: Ways Forward for Change and Reform
Edited by Orkun Akseli and John Linarelli

Volume 5: The Cape Town Convention: A Documentary History
Anton Didenko

Volume 6: Regulating the Crypto Economy: Business Transformations and Financialisation
Iris H-Y Chiu

Volume 7: The Future of High-Cost Credit: Rethinking Payday Lending
Jodi Gardner

Volume 8: The Enforcement of EU Financial Law
Edited by Jan Crijns, Matthias Haentjens and Rijnhard Haentjens

The Enforcement of EU Financial Law

Edited by
Jan Crijns
Matthias Haentjens
and
Rijnhard Haentjens

• HART •
OXFORD • LONDON • NEW YORK • NEW DELHI • SYDNEY

HART PUBLISHING

Bloomsbury Publishing Plc

Kemp House, Chawley Park, Cumnor Hill, Oxford, OX2 9PH, UK

1385 Broadway, New York, NY 10018, USA

29 Earlsfort Terrace, Dublin 2, Ireland

HART PUBLISHING, the Hart/Stag logo, BLOOMSBURY and the Diana logo are trademarks of Bloomsbury Publishing Plc

First published in Great Britain 2022

A catalogue record for this book is available from the British Library.

Library of Congress Cataloging-in-Publication data

Names: Crijns, J. H. (Jan Herman), editor. | Haentjens, Matthias, editor. | Haentjens, Rijnhard, editor.

Title: The enforcement of EU financial law / edited by Jan Crijns, Matthias Haentjens, and Rijnhard Haentjens.

Other titles: Enforcement of European Union financial law

Description: Oxford, UK ; New York, NY : Hart Publishing, an imprint of Bloomsbury Publishing, 2022. | Series: Hart studies in commercial and financial law ; volume 8 | Includes bibliographical references and index.

Identifiers: LCCN 2022014184 (print) | LCCN 2022014185 (ebook) | ISBN 9781509959747 (hardback) | ISBN 9781509959785 (paperback) | ISBN 9781509959761 (pdf) | ISBN 9781509959754 (epub)

Subjects: LCSH: Finance—Law and legislation—European Union countries. | Financial services industry—Law and legislation—European Union countries. | Financial institutions—Law and legislation—European Union countries. | Securities—European Union countries. | Money laundering—Law and legislation—European Union countries—Criminal provisions. | Administrative law—European Union countries. | International and municipal law—European Union countries.

Classification: LCC KJE2188 .E54 2022 (print) | LCC KJE2188 (ebook) | DDC 346.24/082—dc23/eng/20220526

LC record available at https://lccn.loc.gov/2022014184

LC ebook record available at https://lccn.loc.gov/2022014185

ISBN: HB: 978-1-50995-974-7
ePDF: 978-1-50995-976-1
ePub: 978-1-50995-975-4

Typeset by Compuscript Ltd, Shannon

To find out more about our authors and books visit www.hartpublishing.co.uk. Here you will find extracts, author information, details of forthcoming events and the option to sign up for our newsletters.

PREFACE

In response to the global financial crisis of 2008, the European Banking Union was created, which was a major legislative operation. The introduction of the Banking Union resulted in dramatic changes to the organisation of financial regulation and supervision in the EU. Whilst the European Banking Union has not yet been fully completed, the European Commission has already proposed and implemented a host of new legislative instruments to regulate financial markets. These include the Capital Markets Union 2020 Action Plan which, amongst other objectives, aims to support a green and digital economic recovery after the economic crisis caused by the COVID-19 pandemic.

Virtually all these new EU regulations require enforcement. However, as a ramification of what is known as the national procedural autonomy principle, the EU legislator generally is reluctant to regulate enforcement at the national level. Consequently, if enforcement is not conferred to the EU level, the EU legislature often does not prescribe whether enforcement should take place through national criminal, administrative or private law. This results in both practical and fundamental questions for the legal practitioner and the academic.

This book focuses on the enforcement of EU financial law on the national and supranational levels. Emphasis is placed on the interaction between the EU and national legal systems, and, more specifically, on the interaction between the EU and the national levels of the 27 Member States (vertical interaction) and between private, administrative and criminal law (horizontal interaction). Moreover, enforcement is understood in a broad sense, so that it covers not only the *ex post* implementation of hard law, but also *ex ante* 'guidance' of market participants.

The above already indicates that the book will not be confined to a specific area of law, but integrates private law, administrative law and criminal law. The integrated approach is also expressed in the form of the book, which consists of contributions from authors from various jurisdictions, and from both practice and academia. Thus, the book covers a wide range of issues that we believe are highly topical and at the epicentre of current debate. It will, inter alia, discuss procedural aspects of enforcement, new EU Anti-Money Laundering regulatory bodies and instruments, and the (sometimes tense) relationship between enforcement and fundamental principles of law.

We hope that the book will be of interest to professionals dealing with financial law in their daily practice, but also for academics interested in fundamental questions of interaction between legal systems. Whilst the conclusions reached may be based on EU law and certain specific national jurisdictions, we truly hope they may also be of broader value and show the breadth and width of law enforcement in financial markets.

We find it important to stress here that where our contributors are affiliated to non-academic governmental and commercial institutions (and virtually all of them are), the views and opinions expressed in their contributions are personal and do not bind in any way these non-academic governmental and commercial institutions. Thus, the following chapters do not bind in any way the Single Resolution Board, NautaDutilh, Stibbe, or Wladimiroff Advocaten.

Finally, we are most grateful to Hart Publishing, and especially to Roberta Bassi, for their fantastic support and encouragement. This was the basis of the entire project. Similarly, thanks go to the Stichting voor Strafrechtelijk Onderzoek (Foundation for Academic Research in Criminal Law) for its generous financial support. We are also greatly indebted to our contributors, who agreed not only to write their contributions but also to participate in our seminar. We know we have tested their patience and are very grateful for them not to have abandoned ship midway. We are also thankful to the commentators who gracefully agreed at short notice to read and comment on our draft chapters. Special thanks here are due to Dr Marnix Wallinga, Prof Bart Joosen and Prof Matthijs Nelemans, as we have benefited greatly from their pertinent remarks. This book would certainly never have been finished if we could not have counted on Marijke Veerman LLM at Leiden Law School to steadily guide us throughout the process with her impressive organisational talent. Florine Mars was invaluable when under great time pressure she took care of the texts and crafted them into a publishable manuscript. Many thanks.

Please note that legal research for this book has been concluded on 1 January 2022. Later developments could only sporadically be taken into account.

Jan Crijns, Matthias Haentjens and Rijnhard Haentjens
Leiden, The Hague and Amsterdam
January 2022

TABLE OF CONTENTS

LIST OF CONTRIBUTORS

Editors

Jan Crijns is Professor of Criminal Law and Criminal Procedure at Leiden University, the Netherlands and a deputy judge in the Hague Court of Appeals.

Matthias Haentjens is Professor of Private Law, specialising in financial law, at Leiden University, the Netherlands and a deputy judge in the Court of Amsterdam.

Rijnhard Haentjens is Emeritus Professor of Financial Criminal Law at the University of Amsterdam, the Netherlands and former vice-president at the Amsterdam Court of Appeals. His chamber specialised in financial-economic criminal law.

Contributors

Silvia Allegrezza is Associate Professor of Criminal Law at the Faculty of Law, Economics and Finance at the University of Luxembourg.

Daan Doorenbos is Professor of Corporate Criminal Law at Radboud University Nijmegen, the Netherlands, and partner at law firm Stibbe in Amsterdam, the Netherlands.

Bart Joosen is Professor of Financial Supervision Law at the VU University Amsterdam, the Netherlands. He is a board member of the ZIFO Institute for Financial and Corporate Law Amsterdam of that university.

Joost Nan is Professor of Criminal Law and Criminal Procedure, in particular financial-economic law, at the Erasmus School of Law in Rotterdam, the Netherlands. He is also a criminal defence lawyer in Supreme Court cases with Wladimiroff Advocaten in The Hague, the Netherlands.

Saskia Nuijten is Associate Partner at the international law firm NautaDutilh in Amsterdam, the Netherlands.

Jouke Tegelaar is a PhD candidate at the Hazelhoff Center for Financial Law at Leiden University, the Netherlands and a member of the Young Researchers Group at the European Banking Institute.

Karl-Philipp Wojcik is the General Counsel to the EU Single Resolution Board in Brussels and a lecturer at the Faculty of Law of the University of Bonn, Germany and the European College of Parma Foundation, Italy.

Eddy Wymeersch is Emeritus Professor at the University of Ghent, Belgium and former Chairman of the Committee of European Securities Regulators (CESR) and of the European Regional Committee of IOSCO. He also was Chairman of the Belgian Commission Bancaire, Financière et des Assurances (CBFA).

LIST OF ABBREVIATIONS

ABoR	Administrative Board of Review
ACPR	Autorité de contrôle prudentiel et de résolution
AFM	Autoriteit Financiële Markt
AG	Aktiengesellschaft
AIF	Alternative investment fund
AIFMD	Directive 2011/61/EU of the European Parliament and of the Council of 8 June 2011 on Alternative Investment Fund Managers and amending Directives 2003/41/EC and 2009/65/EC and Regulations (EC) 1060/2009 and (EU) 1095/2010
AML	Anti-money laundering
AMLA	Anti-Money Laundering and Terrorist Financing Authority
AML Directive	Directive (EU) 2015/849 of the European Parliament and of the Council of 20 May 2015 on the prevention of the use of the financial system for the purposes of money laundering or terrorist financing, as amended by Directive (EU) 2018/843 of the European Parliament and of the Council of 30 May 2018
AMLTF	Anti-money laundering and terrorist financing
AT1	Additional Tier 1
BRRD	Directive 2014/59/EC of the European Council of 15 May 2014 establishing a framework for the recovery and resolution of credit institutions and investment firms and amending Council Directive 82/891/EEC, and Directives 2001/24/EC, 2002/47/EC, 2004/25/EC, 2005/56/EC, 2007/36/EC
CA	Competent authority
CEAOB	Committee of European Auditing Oversight Bodies
CEBS	Committee of European Banking Supervisors

CEIOPS	Committee of European Insurance and Occupational Pensions Supervisors
CESR	Committee of European Securities Regulators
CET1	Common Equity Tier 1
CFT	Combatting the financing of terrorism
Charter	Charter of Fundamental Rights of the European Union
CISA	Convention Implementing the Schengen Agreement
CNCM	Comisión Nacional de los Mercados y la Competencia
CRA Regulation	Regulation (EU) No 462/2013 of the European Parliament and of the Council of 21 May 2013 amending Regulation (EC) No 1060/2009 on credit rating agencies
CRD IV	Directive 2013/36/EU of the European Parliament and of the Council of 26 June 2013 on access to the activity of credit institutions and the prudential supervision of credit institutions and investment firms, amending Directive 2002/87/EC and repealing Directives 2006/48/EC and 2006/49/EC
CRD V	Directive (EU) 2019/878 of the European Parliament and of the Council of 20 May 2019 amending Directive 2013/36/EU as regards exempted entities, financial holding companies, mixed financial holding companies, remuneration, supervisory measures and powers and capital conservation measures
CRR	Capital Requirements Regulation; Regulation (EU) No 575/2013 of the European Parliament and of the Council of 26 June 2013 on prudential requirements for credit institutions and investment firms and amending Regulation (EU) No 648/2012
CRR2	Amended Capital Requirements Regulation; Regulation (EU) 2019/876 of the European Parliament and of the Council of 20 May 2019 amending Regulation (EU) No 575/2013 as regards the leverage ratio, the net stable funding ratio, requirements for own funds and eligible liabilities, counterparty credit risk, market risk, exposures to central counterparties, exposures to collective investment undertakings, large exposures, reporting and disclosure requirements, and Regulation (EU) No 648/2012
DNB	De Nederlandsche Bank

EAW FD	Council Framework Decision 2002/584 JHA on the European arrest warrant and the Framework Decision
EBA	European Banking Authority
ECB	European Central Bank
ECHR	European Convention on Human Rights
ECJ	Court of Justice of the European Union
ECN	Enhanced capital notes
ECtHR	European Court of Human Rights
EIOPA	European Supervisory Authority for Insurance and Company Pensions
EPPO	European Public Prosecutor Office
ESA	European Supervisory Authorities
ESA Regulation	Regulation (EU) No 1093/2010 of the European Parliament and of the Council of 24 November 2010 establishing a European Supervisory Authority (European Banking Authority), Regulation (EU) No 1095/2010 of the European Parliament and of the Council of 24 November 2010 establishing a European Supervisory Authority (European Securities and Markets Authority) and Regulation (EU) nr. 1094/2010 of the European Parliament and of the Council of 24 November 2010 establishing a European Supervisory Authority (European Insurance and Occupational Pensions Authority)
ESCB	European System of Central Banks
ESFS	European System of Financial Supervision
ESMA	European Securities and Markets Authority
ESRB	European Systemic Risk Board
EU	European Union
FATF	Financial Action Task Force
FD	Framework Decision
FIU	Financial Intelligence Unit
FSA	Financial Services Authority
GDP	Gross domestic product

GDPR	Regulation (EU) 2016/679 of the European Parliament and of the Council of 27 April 2016 on the protection of natural persons with regard to the processing of personal data and on the free movement of such data, and repealing Directive 95/46/EC (General Data Protection Regulation)
IFIAR	International Forum of Independent Audit Regulators
ISA	International Standards on Auditing
ITS	Implementing Technical Standards
JST	Joint Supervisory Team
KAM	Key audit matters
KYC	Know Your Customer
LBG	Lloyds Banking Group
LEA	Law enforcement agencies
LSI	Less significant institution
MAR	Market Abuse Regulation; Regulation (EU) No 596/2014 of the European Parliament and of the Council of 16 April 2014 on market abuse (market abuse regulation) and repealing Directive 2003/6/EC of the European Parliament and of the Council and Commission Directives 2003/124/EC, 2003/125/EC and 2004/72/EC
MiFID II	Directive 2014/65/EU of the European Parliament and the Council of 15 May 2014 on markets in financial instruments and amending Directive 2002/92/EC and Directive 2011/61/EU
MiFIR	Regulation (EU) No 600/2014 of the European Parliament and of the Council of 15 May 2014 on markets in financial instruments and amending Regulation (EU) No 648/2012
MREL	Minimum Requirement for Eligible Liabilities and Own Funds
NCA	National competent authority
NV	Naamloze Vennootschap
OLAF	European Anti-Fraud Office (*Office européen de lute antifraude*)
PIE	Public interest entity

PRA	Prudential Regulation Authority of England
PRIIPS Regulation	Regulation (EU) No 1286/2014 of the European Parliament and of the Council of 26 November 2014 on key information documents for packaged retail and insurance-based investment products (PRIIPs)
Q&As	Questions and Answers
ReNEUAL	Research Network on EU Administrative Law
RTS	Regulatory Technical Standards
SA	Société Anonyme
Short Selling Regulation	Regulation (EU) No 236/2012 of the European Parliament and of the Council of 14 March 2012 on short selling and certain aspects of credit default swaps
SI	Significant institution
Solvency II	Directive 2009/138/EC of the European Parliament and of the Council of 25 November 2009 on the taking-up and pursuit of the business of Insurance and Reinsurance
SREP	Supervisory Review and Evaluation Process
SRF	Single Resolution Fund
SRM	Single Resolution Mechanism
SRM Regulation	Regulation (EU) No 806/2014 of the European Parliament and of the Council of 15 July 2014 establishing uniform rules and a uniform procedure for the resolution of credit institutions and certain investment firms in the framework of a Single Resolution Mechanism and a Single Resolution Fund and amending Regulation (EU) No 1093/2010
SSM	Single Supervisory Mechanism
SSM Regulation	Council Regulation (EU) No 1024/2013 of 15 October 2013 conferring specific tasks on the European Central Bank concerning priorities relating to the prudential supervision of credit institutions
STR	Suspicious Transaction Report
TFEU	Treaty on the Functioning of the European Union
UCITS	Undertaking for Collective Investment in Transferable Security

UCITS IV	Directive 2009/65/EC of the European Parliament and of the Council of 13 July 2009 on the coordination of laws, regulations and administrative provisions relating to undertakings for collective investment in transferable securities
VAT	Value-added tax
Winding Up Directive	Directive 2001/24/EC of the European Parliament and of the Council of 4 April 2001 on the reorganisation and winding up of credit institutions

TABLE OF CASES

International

European Court of Human Rights

The Court of Justice of the European Union

The General Court of Justice of the European Union

The Netherlands

Dutch Supreme Court

Board of Appeals for Business

Court of First Instancc

France

Conseil d'État

United Kingdom

Court of Appeal

TABLE OF STATUTES

International Legislation

Domestic Laws

France

The Netherlands

United States of America

1

Enforcement of EU Financial Regulation and Investor Protection

MATTHIAS HAENTJENS, RIJNHARD HAENTJENS AND JAN CRIJNS

1.1. Enforcement of Financial Regulation

Enforcement is a critical element of financial law – and, indeed, all law. Whether enforcement or coercion also is a *necessary* element of law is a fundamental question that is currently under debate in legal theory. In other words, can law be called 'law' without its coercive function? As explained by Schauer, it was the legal theorist Jeremy Bentham who argued in 1793, and his disciple John Austin after him in 1832, that law cannot exist without coercion. This view was subsequently challenged by HLA Hart, who argued that whilst enforcement is an important and usually present element of law, it is not a necessary element of it. Hart's view has become widely adopted, but has recently been challenged by Schauer, who thus returns to Bentham's theory.[1]

This book is about enforcement, but does not pretend to solve the philosophical debate just summarised. It does work, however, on the premise that enforcement is a critical (if not necessary) element of law, and of financial law more specifically. With financial law, we mean the set of rules (ie the regulation) that concerns financial markets and the activities of financial institutions. Thus, this book covers both non-financial companies where these are active on the financial markets (eg, when they issue exchange-traded capital instruments), and financial institutions such as banks, investment firms, central counterparties and insurance companies. In the EU, the regulation of financial markets and financial institutions has been increasingly formulated and enacted on the supranational level. This development results in various difficulties, which are further investigated in the following chapters.

Enforcement is a critical element of law. This is especially true for financial law, which generally accepts that regulation – and therefore also the enforcement of such regulation – is of critical importance. An impressive amount of scholarly literature has been published on the topic of regulation as a means to order financial

[1] F Schauer, *The Force of Law* (Harvard University Press, 2015) IX.

markets, especially in the field of law and economics. From this perspective, regulation is seen as a means to enhance (market) efficiency.[2] Financial regulation is therefore considered a function of efficiency, and fairness plays a only secondary role. Thus, fairness is considered to be merely conducive to efficiency or may even be detrimental to it. We, however, would think that fairness is and should be an objective of all law, at least on a par with efficiency. This, of course, is not a radical or new position, but seems to have been marginalised since the rise of the law and economics movement, and Kaplow and Shavell's seminal work on fairness and welfare is but one, albeit important work in this respect.[3]

The subordinated position of fairness as an objective of financial law can especially be observed in EU financial regulation. This is understandable because as a constitutional matter, EU instruments must always be grounded in treaties, which historically have mainly focused on economic objectives. The Prospectus Regulation,[4] for instance, has investor protection as one of its main objectives, and Recital (10) reads: 'The obligation to publish a prospectus should apply to both equity and non-equity securities offered to the public or admitted to trading on regulated markets in order to ensure investor protection'. This would suggest some notion of fairness, yet the instrument is grounded on the constitutional objective of 'the establishment and functioning of the internal market' (Article 114(1) Treaty on the Functioning of the EU (TFEU)) and is mainly presented in economic terms. Recital (7), for instance, reads: 'The aim of this Regulation is to ensure investor protection and market efficiency, while enhancing the internal market for capital'.

In any event, enforcement of financial regulation is of critical importance for the effectiveness of such regulation and, therefore, of critical importance for the realisation of all regulatory goals, such as investor protection, consumer protection, financial stability, competition and the prevention of crime.[5] Regulation without enforcement has little value and perhaps does not even merit the name. However, there is good reason to believe that (the realisation of) some regulatory goals are better served by some forms of enforcement than others. For instance, enforcement through private law, or, more specifically, through tort law litigation in which damages may be awarded for violations of financial regulation, will probably better serve investor protection than financial stability, because such enforcement through private law necessarily happens *ex post*. In other words, enforcement of financial regulation through tort law is reactive rather than preventive, and may therefore better compensate investors who suffered damages than prevent the

[2] See, eg J Armour et al, *Principles of Financial Regulation* (OUP, 2016) 53 ff.

[3] L Kaplow and S Shavell, *Fairness versus Welfare* (Harvard University Press, 2002).

[4] Regulation (EU) 2017/1129 of the European Parliament and of the Council of 14 June 2017 on the prospectus to be published when securities are offered to the public or admitted to trading on a regulated market, and repealing Directive 2003/71/EC [2017] OJ L 168/12.

[5] Armour et al, *Principles* (2016) 61–72. The regulatory goals mentioned here can also be seen as (general) principles that form the basis of (concrete) legal norms. See, eg K Broekuizen, 'Rechtsbeginselen van Financieel Toezicht', *Rechtsgeleerd Magazijn THEMIS 2016-6*, 311 and 316 ff.

materialisation of risks to financial stability. This is not to say, of course, that such *ex post* private law enforcement may not have preventive effects (which it certainly has), but this effect is indirect at best. The same would be true for most forms of criminal enforcement, where sanctions are administered *ex post*, but which are generally believed to also have preventative effects. On the other hand, criminal law enforcement generally is not aimed at the compensation of damages, such as those suffered by investors. In contrast, enforcement through administrative law, or more specifically, through administrative procedures that require prior authorisation from a financial supervisory authority, will probably more directly serve goals of financial regulation such as financial stability. Again, this is not to say that *ex ante* administrative law enforcement may not serve also other policy goals such as investor protection (which in many cases it most certainly has). This shows that the legal distinction between private law, criminal law and administrative law is important when considering the enforcement of financial law and its effects on the realisation of the policy goals of financial regulation.

In this book, we understand enforcement (of financial law) in a broad sense. First, and as illustrated already above, we qualify as 'enforcement' not only *ex post* actions to correct violations of regulation (such as by tort litigation or the imposition of an administrative or criminal fine), but also *ex ante* actions to prevent such violations from happening (such as by prior authorisation). Second, not only do we qualify 'enforcement' if and when it is performed by government authorities such as financial supervisory authorities or the public prosecution office, but also when performed by private parties such as investors or banks, for instance through civil litigation. Such civil litigation may result in damages awarded or the nullification of a contract, which may also be a means to enforce norms of financial law. In his chapter, Wymeersch maps the breadth and width of the various forms of enforcement of EU financial law and its consequences under national law(s), while Joosen zooms in on the consequences of *ex ante* administrative enforcement for private law.

Thus, the enforcement of financial law may be performed through all branches of law that are traditionally distinguished, viz administrative, criminal and private law. It may perhaps persuasively be argued that these branches are indeed distinguishable only because they differ in their means of enforcement, and in most jurisdictions, these three branches of law are litigated before specialised courts under specialised rules of procedure. For instance, norms of financial law that require an investment firm to treat their customers fairly may be enforced through administrative law, for instance by the imposition of a fine when this norm is violated – which fine may be challenged before an administrative court (which will be the topic of chapters five and six by Nuijten and Tegelaar, respectively) – but also through private law, for instance by having the investment firm to pay the damages that follow from such violation to aggrieved customers – which may be ordered by a civil court (covered by Wojcik in chapter three). Courts in several jurisdictions, however, have struggled with the question whether violations of administrative norms of financial law can (also) be sanctioned under private law

(Dutch law: yes; German law: no).[6] The same is true regarding the horizontal relationship between national administrative law and criminal law, as shown in chapters eight and nine by Nan and Haentjens, respectively, which discuss the *nemo tenetur* and *ne bis in idem* principles. But it may become even more problematic when financial regulation is enacted at the supranational level (vertical dimension). In particular, the supranational or vertical dimension may represent a high degree of complexity as regards the enforcement of financial law, which is especially acute in the EU.

First, because under EU law the vertical dimension also involves enforcement of EU law vis-à-vis the Member States, ie enforcement where the 'recipient' or subject of the enforcement action is not a natural person or corporate entity, but a national government body. More concretely, in the EU context, enforcement of financial law also means the manners in which national authorities can be forced to comply with EU law. As will be explained by Wojcik in his chapter, such enforcement can be initiated by the EU Commission or by the European Supervisory Authorities.

Second, the vertical dimension of enforcement of financial law is highly complex in the EU, because as matter of principle, EU law is agnostic to the form of enforcement, or may prescribe a means of enforcement which derogates from national law(s). The root of the this complexity is to be found in the clash between the EU principles of national procedural autonomy, on the one hand, and effectiveness and equivalence on the other. First, the principle of national procedural autonomy means that as a matter of principle, the EU may not prescribe how a Member State's rules of procedure, its court system and thus its means of enforcement are to be organised. Thus, the EU legislator generally is reluctant to regulate enforcement at the national level, but limits itself to formulating (sometimes highly specific) norms, which are then left to to be enforced nationally. Consequently, if enforcement is not explicitly regulated at the EU level, the EU legislature often does not prescribe whether enforcement should take place through national criminal, administrative or private law. On the other hand, the principles of effectiveness and equivalence mean that whatever form national implementation and enforcement of EU law may take, EU norms must be effectively applied (effectiveness), so that such EU law is no less effective than the national law that may apply (equivalence).

A relatively recent example of this clash is Case C-679/18 *OPR-Finance v GK*, ECLI:EU:C:2020:167. This case concerned the Consumer Credit Directive,[7] which, in short, requires the lender/creditor to assesses a consumer's creditworthiness before the conclusion of the credit agreement (Article 8(1)). Pursuant to

[6] See OO Cherednychenko and M Andenas (eds), *Financial Regulation and Civil Liability in European Law* (Edward Elgar Publishing, 2020).

[7] Directive 2008/48/EC of the European Parliament and of the Council of 23 April 2008 on credit agreements for consumers and repealing Council Directive 87/102/EEC [2008] OJ L 133/66, and corrigenda [2009] OJ L 207/14, [2010] OJ L 199/40 and [2011] OJ L 234/46.

Article 23, Member States are free to organise the enforcement of this norm, provided 'The penalties … be effective, proportionate and dissuasive'. Under Czech law, Article 8 is to be enforced under private law, more specifically by requiring a consumer to raise the objection of nullity of the credit agreement. Additionally, under Czech administrative law, a credit institution can be fined should credit be granted without compliance with the obligation to assess the creditworthiness of the consumer. In a preliminary procedure, the Czech court asked, inter alia, whether these enforcement matters would be sufficiently 'effective' and, if not, what the consequences would be.

The ECJ reiterated, first, that from the principle of 'sincere cooperation' as codified in Article 4(3) of the Treaty of the EU, it follows that,

> while the choice of penalties remains within their discretion [ie the principle of procedural autonomy], Member States must ensure in particular that infringements of EU law are penalised under conditions, both procedural and substantive, which are analogous to those applicable to infringements of national law of a similar nature and importance [ie the principle of equivalence] and which, in any event, make the penalty effective, proportionate and dissuasive [ie the principle of effectiveness] (at [25]).

The Court proceeded to observe that it had no reason to suspect a violence of the principle of equivalence (at [33]), but that the principle of effectiveness would preclude the condition that the penalty of nullity of the credit agreement would have to be raised by the consumer within a limitation period of three years as was the case under current Czech law (at [36]), also because the possible sanction under administrative law would not help the consumer (at [38]). In this case, the (violation of the) principle of effectiveness therefore trumped the principle of procedural autonomy in that the Court concluded that the sanction under private law was insufficient, and therefore should be changed.

This 'vertical complexity' is one of the main issues that this book seeks to investigate, and as such the following paragraphs will, by way of introduction, look at how the EU creates financial regulation and organises financial supervision. This will be followed by an example of how a specific policy goal of financial regulation, viz investor protection, is addressed by EU regulation, and how such EU regulation has organised its enforcement on the national level.

1.2. EU Financial Regulation[8]

In 2000, there was concern that the creation of a single European market for financial services had not materialised as planned, and that the process of creating EU financial legislation was slow and rigid. The European Council therefore entrusted Alexandre Lamfalussy and a group of 'wise men' with assessing the efficiency of

[8] This paragraph and the following have been partly based on M Haentjens and P De Gioia Carabellese, *European Banking and Financial Law*, 2nd edn (Routledge, 2020).

the legislative progress in the securities sector. When it was published in 2001, the group's final report contained a set of recommended guidelines conducive to a more efficient law-making process.[9] The EU legislature has embraced the recommended process, which is now commonly referred to as the 'Lamfalussy process', and has been adhered to ever since, not only in the securities sector, but for all EU financial law.

In brief, the Lamfalussy process recommends the following four levels of regulation:[10]

(1) Framework principles (and only framework principles) should be laid down in Directives or Regulations (Level 1). Under current EU law, directives and regulations in the field of financial law will commonly be based on Article 114 of the TFEU.[11] This provision prescribes that for statutes which have as their object the establishment and functioning of the internal market, the 'ordinary legislative procedure' must be followed, which means that these statutes are to be adopted by the European Parliament and Council, based on a proposal made by the Commission.[12]
(2) Additional, more technical, legislation should be adopted and updated by the Commission with the help of consultative bodies (Level 2). The purpose of this level of regulation is to fill in the details left open by Level 1 regulation.
(3) National supervisors should work together in committees to advise the Commission in the adoption of Level 1 and 2 acts, and to issue guidelines on the implementation of the rules, so that 'consistent implementation and enforcement' can be ensured (Level 3).
(4) The Commission should be effective in ensuring the correct enforcement of EU rules by national governments (Level 4).

The interaction between Level 1 and Level 2 of the Lamfalussy Report is fundamental and deserves further explanation. As stated above, a Level 1 instrument (a directive or regulation) is proposed by the Commission and adopted by the European Parliament and Council. This is a time-consuming and complex process. On the other hand, Level 2 instruments, the delegating and implementing acts (which can also be either directives or regulations) in which more detailed norms are provided, are adopted by the Commission (or, sometimes, the

[9] Final Report of the Committee of the Wise Men in the Regulation of European Securities Markets, Brussels, 15 February 2001, available at esma.europa.eu/sites/default/files/library/2015/11/lamfalussy_report.pdf.

[10] See also, eg 'Regulatory process in financial services', available at ec.europa.eu/info/business-economy-euro/banking-and-finance/financial-reforms-and-their-progress/regulatory-process-financial-services/regulatory-process-financial-services_en.

[11] See, eg, the Prospectus Regulation (n 4).

[12] See Art 289(1) TFEU. More specifically, in the ordinary legislative procedure, the European Parliament needs a majority of the votes cast during the first reading (Art 231 TFEU) and a majority of component members during the second reading (Art 294(7) TFEU). The Council votes by using qualified majority voting (Art 16(3)-(4) TEU and 238 TFEU).

Council[13]) only. This means that detailed statutes now need not be adopted by the full EU legislature, but the process has also been criticised for being technocratic and undemocratic.

For the enforcement of financial law, the Level 3 committees referred to above, ie the national supervisors working together to advise the Commission, are of special importance. These committees have been organised per sector: the Committee of European Banking Supervisors (CEBS) for the banking sector; the Committee of European Insurance and Occupational Pensions Supervisors (CEIOPS) for the insurance and pension fund sector; and the Committee of European Securities Regulators (CESR) for the securities markets sector. As a result of the implementation of the de Larosière Report, which is discussed below, these three committees have been succeeded by three European Supervisory Authorities (ESAs). The ESAs continue to consist of the cooperating national supervisors, but with more autonomous powers, and have been renamed the European Banking Authority (EBA), European Insurance and Occupational Pensions Authority (EIOPA) and European Securities and Markets Authority (ESMA), respectively. The ESAs function as consultative bodies at the second level, and are empowered to issue Regulatory Technical Standards (RTSs) and Implementing Technical Standards (ITSs), as well as non-binding guidelines and recommendations. RTSs and ITSs must subsequently be adopted by the Commission and serve as detailed implementation norms of the second level. On the third level, the same ESAs now may issue recommendations and guidelines for consistent EU supervision, which is discussed in the next section.

1.3. EU Financial Supervision

Enforcement of financial law has a complex but important relationship with supervision. This is especially true where financial law is considered a part of, and enforced through, administrative law (although a similar argument could be made for private and criminal law enforcement). Thus, supervision and enforcement may either be seen as substituting each other (if there is adequate supervision, enforcement is not needed) or complementing each other (adequate supervision can only exist if there is credible enforcement).[14] Consistent with the holistic view of enforcement embraced throughout this book, we do not believe these views are necessarily contradictory, but rather shed light on a complex relationship from different angles, the complexity of which is exacerbated by the supranational dimension present in the EU.

Regarding financial supervision organised at the EU level, it is remarkable how the EU regulation of financial services, the creation of a single market for the

[13] See Art 291 TFEU.

[14] Armour et al (n 2) 579.

European financial sector and thus the liberalisation of European financial markets progressed significantly as early as the 1970s, whilst the integration of EU financial supervision has remained absent or at least remained far less advanced. This discrepancy may have been a contributory factor to the depth and scope of the financial crisis of 2007/08 in the EU, so that in October 2008, Jacques de Larosière de Champfeu was to chair a group of experts to devise practical proposals in the area of financial regulation and supervision. The de Larosière Report essentially emphasised three steps to guard against the likelihood of a future collapse: (a) a new regulatory agenda; (b) a stronger coordinated supervision; and (c) effective crisis management procedures.[15]

Significantly, the de Larosière Report did not recommend structurally amendment of the current regulatory architecture, as explained above. Rather, it provided the legislator with important pointers on norms and principles that should be promoted as regards various categories of financial institutions. It found that EU Member States were afforded a significant degree of discretion over the extent to which they could implement and enforce Directives, such 'options [led] to a wide diversity of national transpositions related to local traditions, legislations and practices'.[16] The reason for this lack of harmonisation was the vagueness which characterised directives at the first level of regulation, where the national legislator had at his/her disposal a multitude of options so that it became very difficult, if not impossible, to 'impose a single solution' at the third level.[17] The de Larosière Report therefore proposed that future legislation should be based, wherever possible, on regulations rather than on directives, and that when directives are used, the legislator 'should strive to achieve maximum harmonisation of the core issues'.

In providing instances of where the European legislature has implemented the de Larosière Report's call for a greater degree of harmonisation, we limit ourselves to the following. The European regime for (national) deposit guarantee schemes was previously based on a minimum harmonisation directive, which thus left a certain amount of discretion to each country on the level of protection afforded to the depositor.[18] Since the de Larosière Report, this directive has been replaced by a maximum harmonisation directive that significantly curtails, if not entirely removing, this discretion.[19] As examples of directives that have been replaced (in part) by regulations since the de Larosière Report, reference can be made to the Market Abuse Directive, the Prospectus Directive and the Banking Directive, which have (in part) been replaced by, respectively, the Market Abuse Regulation,

[15] J de Larosière, The High-Level Group on Financial Supervision in the EU' (25 February 2009), available at ec.europa.eu/economy_finance/publications/pages/publication14527_en.pdf.

[16] ibid 27.

[17] ibid.

[18] Directive 94/19/EC of the European Parliament and of the Council of 30 May 1994 on deposit-guarantee schemes [1994] OJ L 135/5.

[19] Directive 2009/14/EC of the European Parliament and of the Council of 11 March 2009 amending Directive 94/19/EC on deposit-guarantee schemes as regards the average level and the payout delay [2009] OJ L 68/3.

the Prospectus Regulation and the Capital Requirements Regulation.[20] Also, where no instrument of harmonisation was previously found, regulations such as the Regulation on Central Securities Depositories have been adopted.[21]

Perhaps most significantly, de Larosière Report led to important changes in the sphere of financial supervision. First, the de Larosière Report has resulted in the creation of a European System of Financial Supervision (ESFS), the purpose of which is to ensure the coordinated supervision of the Union's financial system. The ESFS consists of the three ESAs referred to above: the EBA (previously located in London, but now relocated to Paris); ESMA (Paris); and EIOPA (Frankfurt).[22] As stated above, in these authorities the relevant national supervisors participate and it is therefore the national supervisory authorities that remain chiefly responsible for financial supervision in the EU. Yet, unlike their predecessors, the ESAs have become empowered to issue binding RTSs and ITSs (which ultimately need to be enacted by the Commission), as well as non-binding guidelines and recommendations. Moreover, ESMA has become responsible for the direct supervision of two specific categories of financial institutions, viz credit rating agencies and trade repositories.

In addition, following the Lamfalussy Report, a European Systemic Risk Board (ESRB) was created, which now forms part of the ESFS. This ESRB is

> responsible for the macro-prudential oversight of the financial system within the Union in order to contribute to the prevention or mitigation of systemic risks to financial stability in the Union that arise from developments within the financial system and

[20] Directive 2003/6/EC of the European Parliament and of the Council of 28 January 2003 on insider dealing and market manipulation [2003] OJ L 96/16); Directive 2003/71/EC of the European Parliament and of the Council of 4 November 2003 on the prospectus to be published when securities are offered to the public or admitted to trading and amending Directive 2001/34/EC [2003] OJ L 345/64; Directive 2006/48/EC of the European Parliament and of the Council of 14 June 2006 relating to the taking up and pursuit of the business of credit institutions (recast) [2006] OJ L 177/1. These are repealed by Regulation (EU) 596/2014 of the European Parliament and of the Council of 16 April 2014 on market abuse (market abuse regulation) and repealing Directive 2003/6/EC of the European Parliament and of the Council and Commission Directives 2003/124/EC, 2003/125/EC and 2004/72/EC; Regulation (EU) 2017/1129 of the European Parliament and of the Council of 14 June 2017 on the prospectus to be published when securities are offered on the public or admitted to trading on a regulated market, and repealing Directive 2003/71/EC; and Regulation (EU) 575/2013 of the European Parliament and of the Council of 26 June 2013 on prudential requirements for credit institutions and investment firms and amending Regulation (EU) 648/2012, respectively.

[21] Regulation (EU) No 909/2014 of the European Parliament and of the Council of 23 July 2014 on improving securities settlement in the European Union and on central securities depositories and amending Directives 98/26/EC and 2014/65/EU and Regulation (EU) No 236/2012 [2014] OJ L 257/1.

[22] See, respectively, Regulation (EU) 1093/2010 of the European Parliament and of the Council of 24 November 2010 establishing a European Supervisory Authority (European Banking Authority), amending Decision 716/2009/EC and repealing Commission Decision 2009/78/EC [2010] OJ L 331/12; Regulation (EU) 1095/2010 of the European Parliament and of the Council of 24 November 2010 establishing a European Supervisory Authority (European Securities and Markets Authority), amending Decision 716/2009/EC and repealing Commission Decision 2009/77/EC [2010] OJ L 331/84); and Regulation (EU) 1094/2010 of the European Parliament and of the Council of 24 November 2010 establishing a European Supervisory Authority (European Insurance and Occupational Pensions Authority), amending Decision 716/2009/EC and repealing Commission Decision 2009/79/EC [2010] OJ L 331/48.

taking into account macroeconomic developments, so as to avoid periods of widespread financial distress.[23]

Thus, when looking at the European supervisory landscape from a more abstract perspective, it can be concluded that it presents a diverse view. On the one hand, the supervisory landscape is organised along sectoral lines, where EBA is responsible for supervision of the banking sector, EIOPA for the insurance and pension fund sector, and ESMA for the securities markets sector. This supervisory design is called sectoral or institutional supervision. On the other hand, the ESRB has been created specifically for macro-prudential oversight of the financial system. This is called objectives or goal-based supervision.

Also on the national level, the same diversity in supervisory architecture can be discerned. In some Member States, the supervisory architecture is mainly objective- or goal-based. In the UK and the Netherlands, for example, there are separate supervisory authorities for prudential supervision and for conduct supervision. The authority for prudential supervision focuses on the (financial) soundness and viability of financial institutions, whilst the authority for conduct supervision focuses on the behaviour of the same. In other Member States, supervision is mainly organised along sectoral or institutional lines: in France and Italy, there is a separate supervisory authority for the banking and insurance sector, and one for the securities markets. This model is also called the Two Agency Model.[24] As a third model to organise supervision (not found at the EU level), there can be one single supervisory authority for the entire financial sector. This model is called a unified or integrated model. In some Member States, such as Ireland, the local central bank performs this role, while in others, such as Germany, there is a separate, single financial supervisory authority. The introduction of the European Banking Union in 2012 has further complicated the diverse landscape as just discussed, for it made the ECB responsible for prudential oversight of the banking sector and for direct oversight of the most significant credit institutions in the EU.

1.4. Example: Investor Protection

We will now consider an example of how a specific policy goal of financial regulation, viz investor protection, is addressed by EU regulation, and how such EU regulation has organised its enforcement. Investor protection, as discussed above, is a policy goal of financial regulation that is critically important from both an economic perspective (welfare) and a normative one (fairness), and the EU legislator has enacted an impressive amount of regulation to address the issue.

[23] Art 3 Regulation (EU) 1092/2010 of the European Parliament and of the Council of 24 November 2010 on European Union macro-prudential oversight of the financial system and establishing a European Systemic Risk Board [2010] OJ L 331/1.

[24] See, eg, D Calvo, J Crisanto, S Hohl and O Gutiérrez, 'The BIS Report Financial supervisory architecture: what has changed after the crisis?' (April 2018), available at bis.org/fsi/publ/insights8.pdf.

Investor protection and its regulation can therefore be analysed from various angles. In this section we will categorise the most relevant EU instruments of regulation by whom or what the relevant regulation aims to protect against.

First, the EU legislator has traditionally sought to protect investors against the *issuers* of the financial instruments they acquire. More specifically, various EU instruments seek to protect investors against misleading information of the issuing institutions so that they can make informed decisions when acquiring financial instruments, and so as to ensure market confidence. First, Article 11(2) (first sentence) of the Prospectus Regulation (EU) 2017/1129 already cited, requires Member States to enforce the norms of this regulation, ie to sanction the violations of its norms, through private law: 'Member States shall ensure that their laws, regulations and administrative provisions on civil liability apply to those persons responsible for the information given in a prospectus'. Thus, the Prospectus Regulation makes inroads into national procedural autonomy and prescribes the branch of law through which enforcement must be effectuated on the national level. This is similar to the PRIIPs Regulation,[25] which prescribes in its Article 11(2): 'A retail investor who demonstrates loss resulting from reliance on a key information document … may claim damages from the PRIIP manufacturer for that loss in accordance with national law'. This again represents a requirement, in a regulation, that national private law must facilitate *ex post* enforcement of information requirements. Somewhat differently, the Transparency Directive,[26] which also regards the provision of information by issuing entities, provides in Article 28(1):

> Without prejudice to the powers of competent authorities in accordance with Article 24 and the right of Member States to provide for and impose criminal sanctions, Member States shall lay down rules on administrative measures and sanctions applicable to breaches of the national provisions adopted in transposition of this Directive and shall take all measures necessary to ensure that they are implemented. Those administrative measures and sanctions shall be effective, proportionate and dissuasive.

Whilst this Article 28(1) seems relatively agnostic to the manner of enforcement on the national level, Article 28a and 28b Transparency Directive specify that 'competent authorities' must have the power to impose, under (national) administrative law, at least public statements indicating the natural person or the legal entity responsible and the nature of the breach, orders requiring the natural person or the legal entity responsible to cease the conduct constituting the breach and to desist from any repetition of that conduct, and fines. Furthermore, the

[25] Regulation (EU) 1286/2014 of the European Parliament and of the Council of 26 November 2014 on key information documents for packaged retail and insurance-based investment products (PRIIPs) [2014] OJ L 352/1.

[26] Directive 2004/109/EC of the European Parliament and of the Council of 15 December 2004 on the harmonisation of transparency requirements in relation to information about issuers whose securities are admitted to trading on a regulated market and amending Directive 2001/34/EC [2004] OJ L 390/38.

Transparency Directive explicitly allows Member States to also impose criminal sanctions.

Second, it is a settled tradition to protect investors against impropriate behaviour *from each other* under market abuse regulations. The enforcement of the norms codified in the Market Abuse Regulation[27] is similar to the Transparency Directive, which states in Article 30(1):

> Without prejudice to any criminal sanctions and without prejudice to the supervisory powers of competent authorities under Article 23, Member States shall, in accordance with national law, provide for competent authorities to have the power to take appropriate administrative sanctions and other administrative measures in relation to at least the following infringements.

Also in Article 23, an extensive list of administrative sanctions follows that must be exercised under national laws. The reference, in Article 30, to the enforcement of the norms of the Market Abuse Regulation by criminal sanctions implies a dual structure of enforcement, viz both under criminal and administrative law. The criminal enforcement of market abuse norms is further elaborated in the Market Abuse Directive,[28] which establishes 'minimum rules for criminal sanctions for inside dealing, for unlawful disclosure of inside information and for market manipulation to insure the integrity of financial markets in the Union and to enhance investor protection and confidence in those markets' (Article 1). Article 7(1) stipulates criminal penalties for natural persons: 'Member States shall take the necessary measures to ensure that offences referred to in Articles 3 to 6 are punishable by effective, proportionate and dissuasive criminal penalties'. Article 7(2) and (3) provides maximum terms of imprisonment: at least four and two years, respectively. Moreover, the Directive points at the necessity to make punishable inciting, aiding, attempt of and abetting the described behaviour. Thus, the EU legislator has prescribed the enforcement of market abuse rules both under administrative and criminal law, which is to be organised under national laws, and is further discussed in the chapter by Doorenbos.

Third, investors are typically to be protected against impropriate behaviour of *investment firms*, for instance where these firms advise investors or manage their portfolios. Importantly, Article 68 (last sentence) of the Markets in Financial Instruments Directive (MiFID) II[29] provides that

> Member States shall ensure that mechanisms are in place to ensure that compensation may be paid or other remedial action be taken in accordance with national law for any

[27] Regulation (EU) 596/2014 of the European Parliament and of the Council of 16 April 2014 on market abuse (market abuse regulation) and repealing Directive 2003/6/EC of the European Parliament and of the Council and Commission Directives 2003/124/EC, 2003/125/EC and 2004/72/EC [2014] OJ L 173/1.

[28] Directive 2014/57/EU of the European Parliament and of the Council of 16 April 2014 on criminal sanctions for market abuse (market abuse directive) [2014] OJ L 173/179.

[29] Directive 2014/65/EU of the European Parliament and of the Council of 15 May 2014 on markets in financial instruments and amending Directive 2002/92/EC and Directive 2011/61/EU [2014] OJ L 173/349.

> financial loss or damage suffered as a result of an infringement of this Directive or of Regulation (EU) No 600/2014.

This provision is generally understood as a requirement for national laws to have effective sanctions available for investors under private law. In addition, Article 70 MiFID II is similar to the Transparency Directive, in that it also requires Member States to 'lay down rules on and ensure that their competent authorities may impose administrative sanctions and measures applicable to all infringements of this Directive or of Regulation (EU) 600/2014', and continues to list a host of administrative measures that must be implemented into, and enforced under, national administrative law(s). Article 75(1) MiFID II further limits Member States' national procedural autonomy, requiring them to 'ensure the setting-up of efficient and effective complaints and redress procedures for the out-of-court settlement of consumer disputes concerning the provision of investment and ancillary services provided by investment firms'.

Fourth, investors must also be protected against the *investment firm(s)* holding their assets, so that a possible investment firm's insolvency would not lead to a loss for the investors. Article 16(8) of MiFID II therefore provides that

> An investment firm shall, when holding financial instruments belonging to clients, make adequate arrangements so as to safeguard the ownership rights of clients, especially in the event of the investment firm's insolvency, and to prevent the use of a client's financial instruments on own account except with the client's express consent.

This is apparently a norm of private law, and is supplemented in the Alternative Investment Fund Managers Directive[30] and the Undertakings for Collective Investment in Transferable Securities Directive,[31] both of which require, in short, that investment funds appoint a depositary, and that this depositary

> be liable to the AIF or to the investors of the AIF, for the loss by the depositary or a third party to whom the custody of financial instruments held in custody in accordance with point (a) of paragraph 8 has been delegated. … The depositary shall not be liable if it can prove that the loss has arisen as a result of an external event beyond its reasonable control, the consequences of which would have been unavoidable despite all reasonable efforts to the contrary. The depositary shall also be liable to the AIF, or to the investors of the AIF, for all other losses suffered by them as a result of the depositary's negligent or intentional failure to properly fulfil its obligations pursuant to this Directive.

This Article 21(12) AIFMD, which is similar to Article 24(1) UCITS IV, clearly serves to enforce the norms that a depositary must comply through national private law.

[30] Directive 2011/61/EU of the European Parliament and of the Council of 8 June 2011 on Alternative Investment Fund Managers and amending Directives 2003/41/EC and 2009/65/EC and Regulations (EC) 1060/2009 and (EU) 1095/2010 [2011] OJ L 174/1.

[31] Directive 2009/65/EC of the European Parliament and of the Council of 13 July 2009 on the coordination of laws, regulations and administrative provisions relating to undertakings for collective investment in transferable securities (UCITS IV) [2009] OJ L 302/32.

Fifth and finally, investors may be protected against *credit-rating agencies* that mislead investors by providing false information regarding financial instruments or issuing entities. For the enforcement of the norms that credit-rating agencies must comply with, the EU legislature has chosen, interestingly and exceptionally, for *ex post* enforcement through private law as codified in Article 35a(1) of the CRA Regulation:[32]

> Where a credit rating agency has committed, intentionally or with gross negligence, any of the infringements listed in Annex III having an impact on a credit rating, an investor or issuer may claim damages from that credit rating agency for damage caused to it due to that infringement. An investor may claim damages under this Article where it establishes that it has reasonably relied, in accordance with Article 5a(1) or otherwise with due care, on a credit rating for a decision to invest into, hold onto or divest from a financial instrument covered by that credit rating.'

This is exceptional, as virtually no other European instrument provides for a ground for civil lability in a regulation, and can therefore be invoked directly, ie without first having to be implemented into national private law.

1.5. Conclusions

The preceding paragraphs, and the example of how EU financial regulation seeks to effectuate investor protection through enforcement on the national level, illustrate the complexity of the vertical interaction between the supranational (ie at the EU level) and the national level. Notably, it has been shown how various EU regulatory instruments aim to achieve the same policy goal of investor protection, but differ substantially in the ways they organise the enforcement of the norms that these regulatory instruments contain. Without much exaggeration, it can be concluded that there are almost as many enforcement regimes as there are regulatory instruments. This complexity is exacerbated by the differences that exist at the national level where it regards the horizontal interaction between the different branches of law. As already stated above, Dutch law, for instance, has a fundamentally different view to German law on the question whether violations of administrative norms of financial law can (also) be sanctioned under private law. In practice this extreme complexity is probably detrimental to the efficiency of the enforcement and thus of the regulations themselves, and of the norms these regulations contain.

On the one hand, the obvious solution to the variety and complexity observed would be a more coherent legislative approach and a radical centralisation of regulation and enforcement at the EU level. Various academic publications, however, have brought to light the numerous practical and theoretical difficulties that follow from, for instance, Article 35a of the CRA Regulation, which exceptionally provides

[32] Regulation (EC) 1060/2009 of the European Parliament and of the Council of 16 September 2009 on credit rating agencies [2009] OJ L 302/1.

a ground for civil lability that can be invoked directly, ie without first having to be implemented into national private law.[33] Without a general EU private law, it seems, the complexity observed cannot be solved by more centralised private law enforcement. As Nuijten shows in her chapter, the same argument can be made for administrative law enforcement. Until the introduction – if ever – of such general laws on the supranational level, one will probably have to (continue to) rely the principles of equivalence and effectiveness so as to ensure effective enforcement of financial law at the national level(s).

The immediate future will inevitably test the resilience of the system as we have set it out. For instance, it may be expected that the further integration of the internal market will continue to give rise to multi-jurisdictional collective actions, in which investors from various jurisdictions seek damages from issuers under private law. The *VEB/BP* case[34] may be illustrative of this development. In same vein, the EU is expected to make substantial progress in addressing financial crime, which until now has been largely left to the Members States, so that fundamental changes may be expected in relation to the interaction between EU norms and national criminal enforcement. Moreover, the significant increase in sustainable finance regulation, including the recently enacted Disclosure Regulation,[35] will also require robust enforcement mechanisms across the EU. Finally, the enormous increase in the volume and value of crypto-assets as a form of capital may require a supranational approach with effective ways of enforcement.[36] We do hope that the following chapters will inspire the reader and provide the tools to effectively engage with these challenges, which concern one of the most critical elements of our present-day societies: the financial markets.

[33] See, eg, DJ Verheij, 'Credit rating agency liability in Europe. Rating the combination of EU and national law in rights of redress', dissertation (Leiden, 2021).

[34] Case C-709/19 *Vereniging van Effectenbezitters v BP plc*, ECLI:EU:C:2021:377. This development may be further stimulated by the (procedural) facilitation of collective actions in several jurisdictions. See, eg the introduction, in the Netherlands, of the Wet afwikkeling massaschade in collectieve actie (Act on the settlement of damages in collective actions) as of 1 January 2020, and on a European level, Directive (EU) 2020/1828 on representative actions for the protection of the collective interests of consumers [2020] OJ L 409/1.

[35] Regulation (EU) 2019/2088 of the European Parliament and of the Council of 27 November 2019 on sustainability-related disclosures in the financial services sector [2019] OJ L 317/1.

[36] See, eg the Proposal for a Regulation of the European Parliament and of the Council on Markets in Crypto-assets, and amending Directive (EU) 2019/1937 COM/2020/593 final, and especially Art 63(1).

2

The Implementation and Enforcement of European Financial Regulation

EDDY WYMEERSCH

2.1. Introduction

Financial institutions are subject to a complex body of rules and regulations, governing the institution itself, its organisation and its activities, and as entities supervised by public interest supervisory bodies, their relationship with these bodies, and their relations with their clients, including with the financial markets and the overall business context. This complexity is the result of several factors, partly due to the central function of financial institutions in our societies, where public and private interests converge. But it is also due to the diversity of the services offered, covering so many aspects of life, driven by public confidence in their effectiveness, related to the solvency of the institutions and their awareness of their responsibility for the general interest and the ensuing duties. These objectives are pursued by numerous laws and regulations on banking[1] and other financial transactions, as adopted by the national legislators and authorities.

This chapter analyses the drivers behind the application of these rules, regulations and other instruments. It seeks to give an overview of the instruments used to have these rules 'implemented', and where needed, 'complied' or 'enforced'.

2.2. National Rules and EU Rules as Applicable to Financial Institutions and Transactions

There are two basic levels of regulation: the applicable law is national, on which an additional layer – the European one – is superimposed, or – to be more precise – integrated. The outcome is a single system, fed by two streams, with differening

[1] *Brevitatis causa* we have used the term 'banking' rather than 'credit institution' as used in the European regulation.

intensity according to the volume of business. Clear examples of this phenomenon can be found in the relation between national company law and financial regulation, or to the rules applicable to financial products or services, and contract law. In both cases, national law will apply, but respect must be given to the applicable conditions imposed by European law.

Fundamentally, products or services are governed by national private law, especially contract law, including their characteristics and the conditions of their validity; these are financial 'products' or 'contracts'. Insolvency of financial institutions was also entirely governed by national laws, but since Directive 2014/59/EC of the European Council (BRRD) and Council Regulation (EU) No 806/2014 of 15 July 2014 on the Single Resolution Mechanism (SRM), the European regulatory framework has largely taken over, certainly for the large institutions.[2] This analysis implies that the validity of certain legal acts, eg contracts, may depend on national law, for essential questions such as their validity, and on EU rules, for specific features. This regime also extends to the conditions under which the financial products or services are offered. The characteristics of shares and bonds are fundamentally defined in national law, although their circulation as dematerialised securities is rooted in EU regulation.[3] However, for some products, EU law is more predominant: this is the case for investment funds, securitisation products, derivatives, but also for several insurance-based products.

This short introduction points to the need to pursue adequate integration of the two levels in the legal systems: often, the EU legal act itself will indicate that legally it is fully embedded in the national system, and that the latter will give priority to it.[4] In other cases the EU rule provides that it applies 'notwithstanding different rules in the national system', eg even in the case of derogatory agreements of the parties. Thirdly there are the cases where the precedence is being determined by the legal system, whether that be the national one, or the European one, and a balance has to be struck between both. The final objective is a well-functioning financial system meeting the fundamental objectives of financial stability and fairness.

The integration of national legal instruments in the context of the application of EU rules takes place under the watchful eye of the European authorities,

[2] S Allegrezza (ed), *The Enforement Dimension of the Single Supervisory Mechanism* (Kluwer Cedam, 2020); TMC Arons, 'Judicial Protection of Supervised Credit Institutions in the European Banking Union' in D Busch and G Ferrarini, *European Banking Law*, 2nd edn (OUP, 2020) 110 ff.

[3] eg a consumer contract may be vitiated because of fraud, or lack of agreement, but also non-respect of the rules on consumer credit or investor protection. For company law aspects see: Directive 2017/1132 of the European Parliament and of the Council of 14 June 2017 relating to certain aspects of company law [2017] OJ L 169/46.

[4] This is the case for the regulations, eg CRR (Regulation (EU) No 575/2013 of the European Parliament and of the Council of 26 June 2013 on prudential requirements for credit institutions and investment firms and amending Regulation (EU) No 648/2012 [2013] OJ L 176/1); see Arts 4(3) and 9(11) SSM Regulation (Council Regulation (EU) No 1024/2013 of 15 October 2013 conferring specific tasks on the European Central Bank concerning policies relating to the prudential supervision of credit institutions [2013] OJ L 287/63).

ensuring that national law and the corresponding practice conform to EU law, thereby giving precedence to EU law.[5] This approach is a logical outcome of the use of EU law as a tool for integrating the EU financial system, thereby guaranteeing the level playing field and conferring uniform protection to all European citizens.[6] Precedence of EU law can only be accepted after a detailed analysis of the EU formal regulation, as compared with the applicable national rule, and taking into account general principles such as the proportionality principle[7] or the overall objectives of the regulatory system, among which the protection of the investors, or the avoidance of systemic risk.

The precedence or priority rule of European law relates to all European acts provided these have binding force, and create priority over all national acts, including constitutions and decisions of the judiciary. Precedence of EU law therefore leads to the predominance of the EU legal and institutional order, implying its equal application throughout the EU. European Treaties, directives and regulations, and other instruments provide that they are binding for those addressed.[8] Other soft law instruments, such as decisions, recommendations, guidelines and general instructions,[9] Questions and Answers (Q&As), Communications, conclusions, resolutions, and Green and White Papers are increasingly used: their binding character varies.

Apart from legal priority, in practice, there is also 'factual priority' which is based on a wider analysis of the interests at stake, balancing the non-binding opinion of the supervisory authority against the formal formulation of the rule, both contributing to the framing of the supervisory regime. Often, financial institutions will prefer to follow the opinion of the authority, rather than engage in a long-term and costly debate with the relevant administrative or judicial decision-making bodies. This observation indicates that beyond the legal precepts, there are important factual forces impacting the implementation and enforcement of financial regulation.

The activity of financial institutions in the EU may also be affected by decisions of foreign financial supervisory authorities, based on their domestic regulation, but enforceable in the EU through different channels, often merely on a de facto basis from an EU perspective.[10] In the EU, the recognition of the equivalence of non-EU regulatory regimes has allowed to streamline this process and grants free access to the EU markets for institutions or products that meet the same or

[5] Case C-6/64 *Costa v Enel*, ECLI:EU:C:1964:66. It was explicitly adopted in several ECJ cases such as Case C-26/62 *Van Gend en Loos*, ECLI:EU:C:1963:1; Case C-106/77 *Simmenthal*, ECLI:EU:C:1976:49; Case C-106/89 *Marleasing*, ECLI:EU:C:1990:395. See PP Craig, 'The Legal Effect of Directives: Policy, Rules and Exceptions' (2009) 34 *European Law Review* 349.

[6] This does not put an end to the precedence of the EU provision with respect to extra-EU relations: see Case C-106/77 *Simmenthal*, ECLI:EU:C:1976:49.

[7] The principle was laid down in Art 17 of the Treaty of Lisbon but was first formulated in the EU case law.

[8] Art 288 TFEU.

[9] As mentioned in Art 6(5) SSM Regulation for the LSI regime.

[10] See eg de facto application of US money laundering rules.

equivalent requirements. Equivalence would allow for reciprocity of both the national and the foreign legal order and opens the door to equal implementation in both of them.[11]

2.3. The Impact of National Company Law on EU Banking Law

The two-level system of rules in the banking field – national versus European – can be illustrated by analysing the relationship between company law and financial regulation.

The entities active in the financial services field are organised, as legal entities, according to national law, mostly company law. Companies limited by shares (such as NV, AG, SA) are the most frequently used. Most legal systems do not accept individuals to carry on the banking business in their own name, but this is different for investment services.[12]

The application of national company law is left to the preferences of the founding partners: there is no mandatory legal company format, nor an *ex ante* screening of future companies as such, nor is there a 'company law commission' guaranteeing that companies are validly organised and conform to their national company law. Also, there are no European regulations directly addressing company law: in company law, only harmonisation directives have been adopted, resulting in the Member States – represented in the Council and the European Parliament – keeping strong control over the adopted national solutions. These directives have to be transposed into the national legal systems, thereby becoming national law. The European Commission will closely monitor the transposition of directives into the national legal systems. Enforcement mechanisms including fines may be applied.[13] Also, shareholders who disagree with divergent transposition in national company law may call on the European authorities to mandate a conforming formulation being adopted, and fines may be imposed. The same principle may apply to violations of EU banking law, at least if the latter is laid down in European directives; liability sanctions will be governed by national laws, but EU administrative fines may be imposed for violations.

A similar relationship occurs in the financial field where the main directive for financial institutions – the Capital Requirements Directive (CRD IV) contains

[11] On equivalence see E Wymeersch, 'Brexit and the equivalence of regulation and supervision' (2017) EBI Working Papers No. 15, available at papers.ssrn.com/sol3/papers.cfm?abstract_id=3072187.

[12] See the Art 4 MiFID I (Directive 2014/65/EU of the European Parliament and of the Council of 15 May 2014 on markets in financial instruments and amending Directive 2002/92/EC and Directive 2011/61/EU [2014] OJ L 173/349).

[13] Commission imposes fines for non-implementation: ec.europa.eu/info/law/law-making-process/applying-eu-law/infringement-procedure_en.

numerous provisions – on governance, on capital or own funds, on disclosures, on risk, profit distribution, etc – specifying matters of company law. Most of these provisions of the banking directives or regulations are more specific than the relevant national company law provisions and will generally therefore have precedence over the latter: the banks' minimum capital is much higher than a regular company's minimum capital. Other examples of precedence can be found in the field of authorisation of a bank by the banking supervisors; where, under national company law, companies are freely created, banking law imposes a strict authorisation regime. In these matters, the banking supervisors will claim leadership and hence precedence of the banking regulations.

2.4. The Implementation of the Banking Regulatory System

Depending on the company's sector of activity, its board's operation will in many respects be governed by sectoral regulation, in this case banking regulation. This is especially the case for the entire financial field, where – apart from banking – comparable regulations and requirements apply to the activity – and products or services – in most other subsectors, such as investment firms, investment funds, insurance companies and even for different investment products, especially as in these the public interest may equally be involved.[14]

The financial services field is regulated by an impressive body of EU and international legal provisions, many of which are implemented in national law and regulations. Generally the implementation of this body of rules and its two-layered structure – EU and national law – presents similarities with other bodies of law, but an essential difference is that external public oversight is exercised by the financial authorities mainly on the implementation of the EU provisions, and therefore focuses on the activity actually developed by these institutions on the basis of the EU provisions. This oversight or supervision is also exercised at two levels, for the national provisions, by the national supervisory authorities (NCAs), and by the European central authorities, especially the European Central Bank (ECB), or by the European Supervisory Authorities (ESAs), who coordinate the activities of the national supervisors. Here, the relationship between national law and European law is one of coexistence, not of integration, as is the case with company law.

[14] This would relate to investor or consumer protection, product safety. The interaction with private law can be illustrated by several ECJ cases dealing with consumer relations: see eg Case C-609/19 and Joined Cases C-776/19 to C-782/19 *BNP Paribas Personal Finance*, ECLI:EU:C:2021:469, referring 'to a significant imbalance in the parties' rights and obligations'; see also Joined Cases C-698/18 and C-699/18 *Raiffeisen Bank*, ECLI:EU:C:2020:537.

2.4.1. Instruments for the Implementation of Banking Regulation

This chapter aims to identify the methods and instruments used to ensure the implementation of the complex body of regulations in the actual banking and regulatory practice.

Compliance with the rules applicable to financial sector activity is first and foremost the result of the voluntary action of the financial institutions themselves in order to maintain their business licence and their business reputation. The authorisation of a bank is a substantial element of its lawful existence and an essential condition for obtaining the confidence of clients and official recognition in its the relations with other institutions. These objectives are pursued internally, for example by requiring a governance system which is likely to deliver the objectives of high-level expertise at the board level, high technical specialisation at executive levels, and an adequate internal organisation that is able to reach the stated objectives. The supervisory authorities will monitor whether these conditions are fulfilled, vetting board members and top executives, and scanning the quality and robustness of the overall organisation.[15] Internal supervisory oversight takes place in several segments, especially with respect to risk assessment or accounting. From both sides – from the bank's and from the supervisory side – these are fundamental techniques to ensure the adequate implementation of this building block of banking legislation and contribute strongly to the quality of bank management.

Supervisory follow-up is an integral part of the implementation of regulations: it takes place through different instruments and covers all relevant fields, such as assessment or accounting. Monitoring by the supervisory authorities is undertaken throughout the entire organisation[16] using the different methods analysed in the ECB's supervisory measures,[17] peer reviews, or comparative questionnaires. From the supervisory angle, investigations by the supervisory authorities lead to verifying correct implementation, investigating infringements, and in case of serious violations, imposing (sometimes hefty) fines.[18]

Inevitably, differences in interpretation arise when the same provisions have to be applied at several levels of competence. With respect to conflicts between national and European laws and their respective interpretations, differences of views may be submitted to the national judiciary when involving national law, or to the Union courts when EU law is involved. These cases are brought by individual

[15] 'Fit and proper' is the catchword for the conditions which board members and top managers must fulfil.

[16] See eg EBA, 'Risk Assessment of the European Banking System' (December 2020); ECB, 'Assessment of risks and vulnerabilities for 2021' (28 January 2021), mentioning inter alia COVID-19, the uncertain macro-economic situation and credit risk.

[17] www.bankingsupervision.europa.eu/banking/tasks/measures/html/index.en.html, very much addressed to concrete measures.

[18] See ECB, 'Sanctions, As Supervisory Practice', available at www.bankingsupervision.europa.eu/banking/tasks/sanctions/html/index.en.html. See for the list: 'Sanctions imposed by the ECB', available at www.bankingsupervision.europa.eu/banking/sanctions/html/index.en.html. See also chapter 5.

parties disagreeing with the decision of their national or European supervisor, by national governments or by the Union bodies – especially the Commission – acting against supervisory decisions by EU authorities.

The ECJ decisions in this field constitute hallmarks in the development of banking law, but also in EU law in general. These cases demonstrate that European financial law not only deals with the EU regulatory financial provisions and their interpretations, but also with their interaction with national law, especially with the general principles of national or EU law, or with specific bodies of law such as company law, or contract law.[19]

2.4.2. Internal Company Monitoring

In the field of financial regulation – specifically banking regulations – several legal provisions aim to organise and monitor the activity of the bank from the inside. This internal organisation is installed by the bank's leadership taking into account both the rules of company law and the applicable provisions of financial regulation. An important function of the banks' management is monitoring the activity of the bank, for which several directive provisions require conditions of expertise, integrity and independence of mind.[20] The exercise of effective management functions is overseen not only by the board, but also by several board committees. They address core management functions such as accounting, auditing and reporting, especially for risk-intensive activities; three of those most discussed are money laundering, IT risks or excessive risk-taking. Other board committees prepare the highest nominations in the bank: the nomination committee selects board and executive members of the management, able to cope with today's needed professionalism and expertise – eg on information technology. A board remuneration committee will prepare the board's decisions on the remunerations of the members of management, to be adapted on an annual basis, considering the business results of the entity and the assessments of the individual members.[21] Each of these committees contain one or several independent board members, ensuring objective decision-making.[22] In direct contact with the bank's leadership, they ensure the effective implementation of the relevant EU regulatory provisions, and the agreed policies. This decision-making structure is a central instrument for the implementation of the financial regulatory regime.

The legal department exercises a transversal function in keeping these different bodies informed about often critical developments in the legal field, but

[19] Among which human rights, contract law, administrative law, criminal law and other branches of national law.

[20] See Art 91 CRD IV (Directive 2013/36/EU of the European Parliament and of the Council of 26 June 2013 on access to the activity of credit institutions and the prudential supervision of credit institutions and investment firms, amending Directive 2002/87/EC and repealing Directives 2006/48/EC and 2006/49/EC [2013] OJ L 176/338). They shall act: 'with honesty, integrity and independence of mind', see under (8).

[21] See Art 95 CRD IV and the remuneration policies Art 92.

[22] See for the Belgian case: the majority of the members of the audit committee are independent.

also advising them on the decisive actions to be undertaken with respect to the weaknesses to which the risk department has drawn their attention. The legal department may suggest alternatives to existing regulatory risks. Its function is an all-encompassing component in the implementation of the legal system on which the safety of the banking activity is based.

2.4.2.1. *The Governance of Banks*

Banks are led by a board of directors, its members being appointed according to national company law. EU banking regulation does not give any information on how directors are to be appointed: this is left to national company law. In several jurisdictions, company law provides that the board of directors should be overseen by a supervisory board, whose position is outlined in applicable company law provisions. The board will also oversee the activities of the specialised committees such as the nomination, audit, risk and other committees, about which more hereafter. The banking supervisors will review these documents, and, where indicated, add their express recommendations.[23]

The board of directors is the decision-making body in the bank, as has been stated in the Companies Act: it will decide the economic objectives of the bank and how these are to be achieved. These tasks have been defined in the directive – mainly CRD IV and V but also SSM and SRM regulations – and consist of assuming the overall responsibility of the bank's activities, developing and overseeing the strategic objectives, the risk strategy, and the internal governance.[24] The board is also responsible for the integrity of the accounting and financial reporting system. It must exercise effective oversight over senior management.

The European regulation develops in detail these governance requirements, dealing with the structure of the advisory bodies and their tasks.[25] Their governance will be detailed in internal statements, in which the board will develop its internal governance charter, which will analyse the role of the advisory committees. The banking supervisors will review these documents, checking whether they meet the supervisors' expectations, and where applicable, add their express recommendations.

Board members must be of 'sufficiently good repute' and possess the necessary skills, knowledge and experience, essential conditions for correct implementation of the regulations.[26] Banking supervisors exercise close supervision on

[23] Recommendations on internal bodies are detailed in EBA, 'Guidelines on internal governance under Directive 2013/36/EU' (26 September 2017). See specifically the EBA Guidelines compliance table, EBA/GL/2017/11, pointing to diversity.

[24] CRD IV does not assign this function to any organ within the company: it is for 'the bank' to decide.

[25] See in general: KJ Hopt, 'Corporate Governance of Banks and Financial Institutions: Economic Theory, Supervisory Practice, Evidence and Policy' (2021) 22 *European Business Organization Law Review* 13.

[26] See Art 91 CRD IV referring to the EBA Guidelines. These are the well known 'fit and proper' conditions.

these qualities, often on the basis of initial or subsequent personal interviews. To concentrate on their banking activities, members of boards are restricted in the number of directorships they may hold in other organisations. This would also avoid some conflicts of interest.[27] With respect to most of these elements, the European Banking Authority (EBA) has issued detailed guidelines,[28] in some cases jointly with the European Securities and Markets Authority (ESMA).[29] The national competent authorities (NCA) and the financial institutions are not, strictly speaking, bound to implement the guidelines: banks 'shall make every effort to comply',[30] which means they are binding on a 'comply-or-explain' basis, NCAs informing the ESA on the reasons for not implementing.[31] Most banks have developed their own governance codes.[32] They are publicly accessible, allowing for some external insight.

2.4.2.1.1. Board Advisory Committees

The board of directors is assisted by various advisory committees in charge of further implementing governance related tasks. Several of these have been mandated in the CRD IV and are strong levers for implementing the related requirements.

The Nomination Committee

Significant institutions shall install a nomination committee composed of non-executive members in charge of identifying candidates for appointment to the board of directors. This committee will evaluate the skills, experience and knowledge of the candidates and advise on candidates for the board, including its executive members. It will annually assess the structure and size of the body, as well as the individual members of the management. In practice, the activities of this committee often extend to the remuneration of the board members and executives.

The proposals developed by the nomination committee will be submitted to the supervisory authority to assess whether it agrees with the committee's evaluation

[27] Conflicts of interest are monitored by adopting measures in the field of remuneration. See Art 91 CRD IV.

[28] See Compliance with EBA regulatory products – EBA guidelines and recommendations, 'Guidelines on internal governance under Directive 2013/36' EBA/GL/2017/11 (26 September 2017). Conflicts of interest are monitored by adoption measures in the field of remuneration; BCBS, 'Corporate governance principles for banks' (July 2015), available at bis.org/bcbs/publ/d328.htm.

[29] Art 91(12) CRD IV; See EBA, 'Regulation and Policy – Single Rulebook; Joint ESMA and EBA guidelines on the suitability of members of the management body' EBA-GL-2017-12.

[30] Art 16 EBA Regulation (Regulation (EU) No 1093/2010 of the European Parliament and of the Council of 24 November 2010 establishing a European Supervisory Authority (European Banking Authority), amending Decision No 716/2009/EC and repealing Commission Decision 2009/78/EC [2010] OJ L 331/12).

[31] The European Parliament, the Council and the Commission will also be informed.

[32] Being inspired by the 2015 Basel Committee Guidelines for corporate governance principles for banks.

of the candidates as meeting the requirement of 'fit and proper'. The NCAs draft detailed guidelines are useful to assess the elements to be considered to determine whether a candidate meets the criteria as laid down in the Directive.[33] They must be interviewed and submit information at the request of the authority. To test whether the candidate has a 'proper' profile, information on financial antecedents – both personal as professional – will be considered. It would be inappropriate for the authority to collect information from third parties, except with the candidate's consent. The vetting of candidates is a process in which the financial supervisory authority exercises more than marginal control. Its approval is the decisive moment of the effective appointment to the board, to be ratified by the company.

The committee prepares the board's annual assessment of the members and executives, allowing it to suggest certain improvements.

The Risk Committee[34]

It is mandatory for financial institutions to install a specialised risk committee, composed of executive and non-executive members, in charge of assessing and following up on the risk strategy, the risk profile and risk tolerance of the entity.[35] This is a core function in the identification and implementation of the relevant risk standards. The committee advises the management on the risk appetite and strategy of the institution and oversees the effectiveness of management's oversight on the different types of risk, including reputational risk, conduct risk, legal risk and macroeconomic risks. Its members should have the appropriate knowledge, skills and expertise to fully understand and monitor the risk profile, strategy and risk appetite. In addition, these financial institutions should organise a separate department, headed by a chief risk officer, with distinct responsibilities, as the risk management function is independent from the operational side.

The Audit Function and the Audit Committee

The financial statements of a financial institution are essential management tools, to be prepared in compliance with the accounting rules for banks, and closely followed up by the financial supervisors. This function is delegated to executive directors with expertise in accounting and is exercised by the Audit Committee. These requirements are closely followed up by the supervisory authorities.[36]

Private entities are required to appoint an external auditor; in public interest companies he will be a leading expert in auditing, often a partner in one of

[33] See EBA/GL/2017/12 Joint ESMA and EBA guidelines on the assessment of the suitability of members of the management body and key function holders under Directive 2013/36 and Directive 2014/654 (26 September 2017).

[34] See Art 16 EBA Regulation. EBA Compliance with EBA regulatory products, with a list of applicable guidelines and recommendations. Also: in the EBA Annual reports. See for the list of 'comply or explain' responses, ECB Compliance with EBA guidelines and recommendations.

[35] Art 76 CRD IV allows to combine audit and risk committee.

[36] See EBA, 'Accounting and auditing' (November 2018), available at www.eba.europa.eu/regulation-and-policy/accounting-and-auditing; ECB, 'Guide to internal models', mainly dealing with internal models'; and on internal audit, 33.

the leading audit firms in the state where the bank is located.[37] The scope of this requirement differs according to the applicable national law.[38] With respect to banking institutions the requirement is laid down in Directive 2014/56 of 16 April 2014, which also describes their functions for the 'public interest entities' (PIEs).[39] The Directive also prescribes the constitution of an audit committee for the PIEs, composed of non-executive directors, contributing to the direct dialogue with the board on audit and risk issues.[40] For less significant institutions (LSIs), the audit committee and the risk committee may form a combined committee.[41]

The oversight on the bank's accounting and financial reporting is generally delegated to the audit committee, mandatory for all public interest entities and mostly composed of independent directors.[42] It is attended by the group chief auditor. This committee will supervise the financial reporting process, the effectiveness of internal control procedures and related control functions, with special attention to their integrity.

The statutory auditor has an intimate knowledge of the activity of the audited entities and its subsidiaries. He will be able to ascertain whether the entity has applied the legal requirements applicable to it, and identify possible shortcomings or defects. The statutory auditor will independently review the bank's activity and the reporting by the accounting department of the bank, giving 'reasonable assurance' as to the quality of the information, presented as being 'true and accurate' and having been prepared in accordance with the International Standards on Auditing (ISAs) as declared applicable in the jurisdiction competent for the audited institution.[43] The statutory auditor should report to the audit committee about his review and about the findings he has made. He further reports to the board, who will draw the necessary management conclusions. Elements of his report, and especially its conclusion, will be published along with the financial statements and should contribute to the confidence of shareholders, financial markets, rating agencies, and of other interested parties.[44]

[37] See SB Harris, 'Audit industry concentration and potential implications' (Public Company Accounting Oversight Board, December 2017), available at pcaobus.org/news-events/speeches/speech-detail/audit-industry-concentration-and-potential-implications_674.

[38] See eg for the French regime: Code de Commerce, L 820-1.

[39] The PIEs are defined by Directive 2014/56/EU of the European Parliament and of the Council of 16 April 2014 amending Directive 2006/43/EC on statutory audits of annual accounts and consolidated accounts [2014] OJ L 158/196, being defined as inter alia the central banks, the post giro institutions and public financial institutions. The banking supervisor has to approve the designation of the auditor.

[40] See Art 41 Directive 2006/43/EC of the European Parliament and of the Council of 17 May 2006 on statutory audits of annual accounts and consolidated accounts, amending Council Directives 78/660/EEC and 83/349/EEC and repealing Council Directive 84/253/EEC [2006] OJ L 157/87 describing the main functions of the committee.

[41] See Art 6(3)–(4) CRD IV.

[42] See Art 41 Directive 2006/43/EC on audit committee, Art 42 Directive 2006/43/EC on the statutory auditors; see also: Regulation (EU) No 537/2014 of the European Parliament and of the Council of 16 April 2014 on specific requirements regarding statutory audit of public-interest entities and repealing Commission Decision 2005/909/EC [2014] OJ L 158/77.

[43] The international audit standards can be declared applicable in the EU in accordance with Art 26(2) Directive 2006/43/EC.

[44] Elements of these reports will be of interest to the organisations pursuing sustainability objectives.

The statutory auditor also has the duty to report to the supervisory authorities about the outcome of his investigations and oversight, or report back on observations formulated by the supervisory bodies. They will pay special attention to key audit matters (KAM), as formulated by the auditor[45] and to possible violations of laws and regulations which may seriously affect the financial situation of the institution, its business activity or its administrative and accounting organisation.[46]

The statutory auditor is not expected to systematically investigate the bank to detect non-compliance with all laws or regulations. This would change the substance of his mission, which would then be transformed into a 'forensic' audit mandate, responsibilities and means.[47] Therefore, the international standard on auditing ISA 250[48] states that he is only held to obtain 'reasonable assurance' that the financial statements are, generally spoken, free from fraud and error. But he should remain alert and maintain professional scepticism. The formal duties of auditors in combatting illegal conduct are an important contribution to the effective application of many criminal laws, eg on fraud or money laundering. The auditor who has been made aware of non-compliance or suspected non-compliance with laws and regulations ('Noclar') has a duty to further investigate the facts, and in the absence of appropriate redress by the management, to inform the supervisory authorities.[49] A comparable provision has been included in the CRD IV: the statutory auditor should inform the competent authorities of any material breach of the laws and regulations. This obligation goes into the direction of a whistleblowing regime, but the related duty is part of the legal position of the statutory auditor.

External oversight of the activities of the auditor is exercised in accordance with the European regulation by the local audit regulator. The national auditor supervisory bodies cooperate at the EU level in the Committee of European Auditing Oversight Bodies (CEAOB).[50] The legal position of the auditors and the conformity of their auditing activity is verified in accordance with the European regulation[51]

[45] ISA 701, being points of special interest which in the auditor's view are of most significance in the audit. They may refer to higher risks of material misstatement, matters of significant management judgement, or significant events or transactions during the period under review.

[46] Recital 33 CRD IV.

[47] See eg the Institute of Fraud Auditors, ifabelgium.be; ACCA, 'Forensic Auditing', available at accaglobal.com/an/en/student/exam-support-resources/professional-exams-study-resources/p7/technical-articles/forensic-accounting.html.

[48] See: iaasb.org/publications/isa-250-revised-consideration-laws-and-regulations-audit-financial-statements-13.

[49] On the Noclar international ethics standard, nr 360, see: E Wymeersch, 'Noclar or how Accountants deal with Suspected or Occurred Breaches of the Law' (2016) Universiteit Gent, Working paper series, Working paper No 2016-05, available at papers.ssrn.com/sol3/papers.cfm?abstract_id=2845282.

[50] See the Committee of European Auditing Oversight Bodies, or the CEAOB, available at ec.europa.eu/info/business-economy-euro/banking-and-finance/regulatory-process-financial-services/expert-groups-comitology-and-other-committees/committee-european-auditing-oversight-bodies_en.

[51] See Directive 2006/43/EC, esp Art 29, and further on quality assurance; Reg 537/2014.

by the national oversight body to which the auditor is professionally accountable. At the worldwide level, the oversight bodies cooperate within the International Forum of Independent Audit Regulators[52] (IFIAR),[53] which undertakes reviews of the largest international audit firms. IFIAR's findings are confidential, but its published summaries point to the need for a close follow-up.[54]

The auditors deliver an essential service in guaranteeing the quality of the banks' accounting and reporting. Indirectly their reviews will also contribute to the right application of accounting and auditing standards as well as prudential rules, as both regulatory infringements and negative financial developments must be identified by the auditor as part of his revision of the accounts. Audit failures may have dramatic consequences for the audited companies and their market position.

2.4.2.1.2. The Role of the Shareholders

The position of the shareholders in the organisation and functioning of the bank also deserves attention. To a large extent their position is determined by company law and is identical to that of any other company. Their contribution to the bank policies and actions will be part of the collective action in the general meeting, and their individual position will remain largely untouched by financial regulation. Their monitoring role may in some cases be very active, especially when deciding on the appointments in the board, discussing the annual reports and financial statements, criticising the bank's management, its business policy or its distribution policy, and deciding on the manager's remuneration in line with regulatory guidelines.[55]

These monitoring actions take place within the framework of the company law rules, in the general meeting or outside, as adapted to the applicable banking regulation. The press will report on these discussions, adding to pressures which shareholders – and the public opinion – will exercise on the bank' management in urgent cases. The general meeting may decide without the supervisory authorities being informed beforehand. If necessary, the authorities will then be called upon to adopt urgent measures.[56]

[52] See 'Annual Report 2019', available at ifiar.org/?wpdmdl=11085.

[53] Independent Forum of Independent Audit Regulators, with an overview of inspection findings in PIEs.

[54] Independent Forum of Independent Audit Regulators, with an overview of inspection findings in PIEs; see: 'Annual Report 2019' (n 52).

[55] The EBA has issued 'Guidelines on sound remuneration policies under Articles 74(3) and 75(2) of Directive 2013/36/EU and disclosures under Article 450 of Regulation (EU) No 575/2013, of 27 June 2016, EBA/GL/2015/22'. EBA has launched a consultation of revised guidelines on sound remuneration policies (29 October 2020). See the surveys on the implementation of the guidelines, available at eba.europa.eu/sites/default/documents/files/documents/10180/106961/1aa3364a-f7c5-4ada-9c2b-798b0783557a/Implementation-survey-on-CEBS--Guidelines-on-Remuneration--final-.pdf?retry=1.

[56] This case has to be distinguished from the emergency measures under Art 18 of the EBA Reg, relating to crises which may jeopardise the orderly functioning and integrity of the capital markets.

Qualifying Shareholders

From the regulatory angle, financial regulation deals with larger shareholders in the bank, whose actions may have a direct influence on the bank's affairs, its continuity and risk profile, structure and top management. This is especially the case for the qualifying shareholders, which have to obtain an authorisation from the supervisory authority either at the initial foundation of the bank, or later upon their entry in the share ownership. The supervisor will check the 'suitability' of this shareholder[57] – the identity which must be communicated to the supervisor – to verify whether this person might be 'likely to operate to the detriment of the prudent and sound management of the institution' or possibly affect the stability of the bank.[58] If no shareholder is a suitable 'qualifying shareholder', the 20 largest shareholders will be assessed on the same basis.[59] This information has to be updated annually for publicly listed banks. The annual review is an important safeguard to avoid controversial initiatives from shareholders from the prudential point of view.

With respect to admitting 'qualifying' institutions in a single supervisory mechanism (SSM) bank, the assessment takes place in two stages: first, the NCA will make the initial assessment and send over a draft to the ECB; secondly, the ECB will make a final assessment. The decision of the ECB is the effective one and can be subject to certain conditions. In the absence of agreement, the candidate can submit its case to the administrative board of review (ABoR), which will submit its opinion to the ECB board. This procedure is applicable in case of mergers, and in any event if a new party qualifies as a qualifying shareholder.[60] If not, the procedure would not apply and the NCA as supervisor for the merged or absorbing entity will refuse the authorisation.[61]

The attitude for the supervisory authorities may become stricter if the influence exercised by the persons who acquired a qualifying holding is likely to 'operate to the detriment of the prudent and sound management of the institution'. Appropriate measures may be imposed, including the suspension of voting rights,[62] or penalties for the management. Another point of attention relates to the granting of a remuneration by the significant shareholders beyond the ratio for variable remuneration as agreed: the competent authority will have to be informed and the information passed to the EBA.[63]

2.4.2.1.3. The Corporate Governance Codes

Among the factors influencing company conduct and possibly also a company's ability to comply with financial regulation, one should mention the corporate

[57] See the criteria mentioned in Art 23 CRD IV.

[58] Art 26(2) CRD IV.

[59] Arts 7 and 14(1)CRD IV. Their names have to be communicated to the authorities; see Art 26 CRD IV.

[60] See for an application: Case C-219/17 *Berlusconi*.

[61] Art 14 CRD IV.

[62] Art 66(1)(f) CRD IV, suspension of voting rights.

[63] Art 94(1)(g) CRD IV, measures relation to the variable elements of remuneration.

governance codes applicable to all listed companies. Endorsement of the code is mandated in many states' company legislation, although on a technically non-binding basis.[64] Some provisions of the code may directly affect banks, eg on independence or on ethical directors rules, on the evaluation of directors, or on their compensation.[65] The company will report on the implementation of the code in its annual report, allowing its shareholders (as well as future investors) to evaluate the way the board has implemented the governance principles. In most states, there is no official mechanism overseeing the adequate implementation of the code although prudential authorities may base their observations on statements in the code.

Deficient governance is sometimes exposed in the press as a factor for assessing the board's behaviour and will influence the valuation of the shares of the company. This has recently been quite common for boards being criticised for their attitude towards climate change, racial discrimination, or more generally towards lack of sustainability.[66] These reports will motivate board members to undertake a stronger follow-up on the code's provisions, and academic writing may also contribute to more awareness of the standards of governance in certain jurisdictions. Some corporate governance provisions have a tendency to migrate to hard (ie binding) law: remuneration and gender issues are well known in this respect.

2.4.2.1.4. Anti-Money Laundering and Terrorist Financing (AMLTF)

The EU has undertaken substantial regulatory action to combat money laundering (ML) and terrorist financing (TF), as banks are often confronted with ML transactions of which the illegal origin is unknown to them.[67] Due to an increasing number of violations and the damaging visibility of several of these, often involving the most important financial institutions, this subject has attracted considerable attention: see Commission Report on the assessment of recent alleged money laundering cases involving EU credit institutions, 24 July 2019 Com (2019) 372. Deficiencies identifying ML will be considered a weakness in the board's monitoring function, may damage its reputation and relationship with other banks, and

[64] The corporate governance codes have been declared mandatory in company law, but companies have flexibility in applying the code, invoking the 'comply or explain' provision in the codes, and stating the reasons. For the list of Corporate Governance Codes, see ecgi.global/content/codes.

[65] See EBRD, 'Corporate Governance for Banks', available at ebrd.com/what-we-do/sectors/legal-reform/corporate-governance/banks.html; BIS, 'Corporate governance principles for banks' (8 July 2015); EBA Final Guidelines on Internal Governance (EBA-GL-2017-11) 26 September 2017; cf ECB, 'Decision-making', referring to legally binding decisions, available at www.bankingsupervision.europa.eu/organisation/decision-making/html/index.en.html.

[66] See: C van der Elst, 'The Belgian Struggle for Corporate Governance Improvements' ECGI – Law Working Paper No 114/2008 (June 2019), available at papers.ssrn.com/sol3/papers.cfm?abstract_id=1261448. Its implementation is verified by the FSMA, the securities markets authority. Some provisions of the code may directly affect banks: eg the French AFEP-Medef Code of listed. Companies, mentioning inter alia independence of directors, ethical rules, evaluation of directors or their compensation.

[67] See for an overview: 'Commission steps up fight against money laundering and terrorist financing' (7 May 2020) Q&A, available at ec.europa.eu/commission/presscorner/detail/en/qanda_20,_821.

in some cases may even lead to complicity with these illegal practices. Therefore, many banks have developed a special function for tracing ML. Cumulatively, banking supervisors and public prosecutors have become very active in investigating these abuses. Also at the EU level, much attention has recently been paid to the coordination of the national regimes and for Europe-wide actions combatting ML. Although banking supervisors and banks have a direct interest in identifying these cases,[68] the follow-up is in the hands of specialised judicial bodies and of the public prosecutors. As some striking weaknesses appeared in the last decade, an overhaul was launched by the Commission, leading to a substantial shift in organisation. The Commission has tabled an 'Action Plan for a comprehensive Union policy on preventing money laundering and terrorist financing', announcing that it will pursue more organisational centralisation and coordination, to be delegated to the Anti-Money Laundering Authority (AMLA).[69] The draft Regulation was published on 20 July 2021.[70]

2.5. Implementation of EU Banking Law – Adapting National Law to EU Law

As explained above, EU banking law has to be implemented in the Member States, so that their laws correspond to the provisions of the EU law. Changes in the national law may be necessary, whether by adapting the national law to the directives, or by introducing rules or techniques which allow the EU regulations to be fully implemented by the NCAs.The Commission is the main authority in monitoring the application of EU law, and has published several annual reports describing the progress made and the weaknesses remaining in this process.[71] It has analysed in depth the application of the four main directives, and published a report on recovery and resolution.[72] But NCAs and ESAs, and other parties, may still claim that national law does not conform to EU legislation, in which case the ECJ may impose a binding interpretation, to be applied to all parties.

[68] D Starkman, 'Belgium's biggest banks propose system to share suspected money laundering information' (ICIJ, 17 November 2020), available at icij.org/investigations/fincen-files/belgiums-biggest-banks-propose-system-to-share-suspected-money-laundering-information.

[69] Communication from the Commission, 'Action Plan for a Comprehensive EU policy on Preventing Money Laundering and Terrorist Financing' (7 May 2020), available at ec.europa.eu/finance/docs/law/200507-anti-money-laundering-terrorism-financing-action-plan_en.pdf; with special attention to EU-level supervision.

[70] Commission proposal, 20 July 2021 Com (2021) 421. See also ch 10 of this volume, S Allegrezza.

[71] See: 'Monitoring the Application of European Union Law, 2019 Annual Report', available at ec.europa.eu/info/sites/default/files/file_import/report-2019-annual-report-monitoring-application-eu-law_en.pdf.

[72] 'Report on on the application and review of Directive 2014/59/EU (Bank Recovery and Resolution Directive) and Regulation 806/2014 (Single Resolution Mechanism Regulation)' (30 April 2019), available at ec.europa.eu/info/sites/default/files/business_economy_euro/banking_and_finance/documents/190430-report-bank-recovery-resolution_en.pdf.

In the case of continuing refusal to transpose a directive, applied after voluntary dialogues have failed, the ESA, after having issued a recommendation to the NCA, will apply to the Commission for a formal opinion requiring the NCA to comply with Union law. If the NCA does not comply, the ESA may adopt an individual decision addressed to the financial institution requiring the necessary action.[73] The ultimate enforcement mechanism to be used by the Commission is its recourse to the Union court. Moreover, the Commission may impose fines for late or imperfect transposition of directives.[74] The regulations may originate from different sources, such as the European Commission, the Council and Parliament or ESAs. As a means of enforcement, in case of failure to act by an ESA, the case may be submitted to the Court of Justice and the ESA can be required to take the necessary measures to comply with the Court's judgment.[75] Ensuring the implementation of European law is the result of supervisory action. The supervisory authorities will require and monitor the way the entities subject to their supervision are implementing different EU regulatory provisions. These may have been translated into national law or are directly applicable being contained in formal EU 'regulations', or in non-regulatory instruments which are voluntarily adopted by the firms under supervision.

2.6. The EU-Wide Implementation of EU Public Financial Supervision

2.6.1. The Overall Structure of the EU Banking Supervisory System

Supervision of financial institutions is organised in two layers. In the Member States, supervisory bodies oversee supervision on banking, insurance, and securities markets and transactions. Their action is coordinated at the EU level within the ESAs, which have special programmes for the harmonisation and coordination of the supervisory action, towards building a common supervisory culture and an integrated financial market.[76] These efforts include actions at the EU level for ensuring application of the financial regulation all over the Union – what implies

[73] Arts 17(8) and 43(5) EBA Regulation.

[74] See Commission, 'The Single Market Scoreboard', with inter alia data about the infringements, available at ec.europa.eu/internal_market/scoreboard/_archives/2014/02/index_en.htm; for later years; see: Commission, 'The Single market scoreboard 2020, Member States need to do more to ensure the good functioning of the EU Single Market' (3 July 2020). For ESMA: 'Public Statement: European common enforcement priorities for 2020 annual financial reports' ESMA32-63-1041 (28 October 2020).

[75] Art 61 EBA Regulation. See also ch 3 in this volume.

[76] See ESMA, 'Supervisory Convergence; also: EBA Report on Convergence of Supervisory practices in 2020' EBA/REP, 2021/09 (12 May 2021), referring to EBA's 2021 Convergence plan, and specific fields as SREP, supervisory colleges, policy work, and the two Union-wide Strategic Supervisory Priorities (Art 29(a) EBA Regulation).

disciplinary action for breaches of Union law[77] or mediation instruments for solving conflicts between the national supervisors.[78] In the banking field, the EBA has made extensive efforts to develop a common framework. The 'EBA regulation and institutional framework',[79] lays down the institutional structure, its supervisory framework, and mandate and rules for daily operation.[80] Pursuant to the EBA's foundational plans, it published an interactive 'Single Rulebook' with the long-term aim of creating a unified regulatory framework. The Single Rulebook deals with a wide range of subjects, covering a large part of effective banking supervision, and contains numerous guidelines addressed to the national supervisors with a view of the coordination of their supervisory action, and their governance arrangements with a perspective of supervisory convergence.[81] The individual ESAs takes into account and benefits from the expertise developed by the other ESAs for supervisory actions, allowing easier coordination between them. Representatives of the Commission and the other ESAs take part in their board meetings. The allocation of the supervisory powers to national competent authorities has led to the introduction of the comparable supervisory structures within each of the Member States, applying generally comparable rules, although with some local differences. The resulting situation with at least 27 players may seem quite complex and, in some respects, confusing. Several ideas have been launched to improve the present system especially by centralisation of supervision, but generally this has not been well received by the Member States, which prefer to limit EU-wide involvement to their participation in the governance of the ESAs. A limited – but increasing – number of direct supervisory tasks has been centralised at ESMA: supervision or rating agencies of trade repositories, data reporting service providers. In the money laundering field the Commission proposes to create a single supervisor (Commission report 24 July 2019).

The introduction of the SSM by Council Regulation has started a development toward remodeling banking supervision not only at the EU level, but also in each of the Member States.

With respect to the Member States part of the Euro area in addition to Bulgaria and Croatia,[82] the SSMs applies: it creates two regimes of banking supervision,

[77] See Art 17 on Breach of European law, or Arts 19 and 20 on Settlement of disagreements between competent authorities in the same sector but belong to different Member States, or across sectors. A common board of appeal for the three ESAs will hear cases submitted by natural or legal persons, or NCAs against decisions of an ESA.

[78] Arts 19 and 20 EBA Regulation.

[79] See eba.europa.eu/about-us/legal-framework/eba-regulation-and-institutional-framework.

[80] EBA Regulation and institutional framework: eba.europa.eu/about-us/legal-framework/eba-regulation-and-institutional-framework.

[81] See EBA, *The Single Rulebook*, available at eba.europa.eu/regulation-and-policy/single-rulebook, Supervisory reporting. Also: eba.europa.eu/regulation-and-policy. Among the recent Guidelines: 'Guidelines on outsourcing arrangements' (25 February 2019); 'Guidelines on cooperation agreements between deposit guarantee schemes'; 'Guidelines on methods for calculating contributions to Deposit Guarantee schemes' (23 March 2021). 'EBA consults on new Guidelines on cooperation and information exchange in the area of anti-money laundering and countering the financing of terrorism' (27 May 2021).

[82] Bulgaria and Croatia joined the SSM by requesting the establishment of close cooperation between the ECB and their NCA, membership expected in 2023.

one for LSIs and one for SIs. In both regimes the ultimate authority will be exercised by the ECB, acting with the assistance of the NCAs: for the LSIs, banking supervision will in essence remain national, the supervisory action being exercised by the NCAs, while for the SI, it will become European, under the direct action of the ECB, with assistance from the NCAs. Between these two regimes, many bridges have been introduced, creating a largely SSM. The organisation of banking supervision under the new structure – ie under the SSM and SRM – has introduced a system of far-reaching harmonisation in the fields of prudential supervision and (recovery and) resolution. Principles applicable to all institutions have been formulated, and although based on European principles, are applied by national supervisory institutions. A mix of EU legal provisions and national practices has been the outcome, leading to a balance between often different practices, but constituting the fundamental components of the EU banking supervisory system, as implemented in all 27 Member States. This balance is further complemented by declaring the full supervisory system applicable to the SIs, under the direct supervision of the ECB – with the assistance of the NCA – while a more differentiated system is applicable to the LSIs.

These regimes are complemented by a third regime: this is the regime of national banking supervision applied to the banks in the non-euro states, which are part of the EU, but do not belong to the SSM which is reserved for the euro states under the final responsibility of the ECB. Close cooperation agreements with the authorities of these states outline the relationship with the SSM.[83] The regulations adopted by the Commission and other regulatory instruments adopted by the EBA will still be applicable.

2.6.2. Decentralised European Banking Supervision: The LSI Regime

In each of the Member States, NCAs exercise financial supervision. In some cases, the same body also supervises insurance and securities activities. This results in 27 individual bodies, but in some states, the same body is in charge of two, or all three, business lines. Each body applies its financial laws in its own jurisdiction, but as these have been harmonised pursuant to the EU directives, and are complemented by the directly applicable EU regulations, the outcome is a high level of harmonised regulation, and the resulting supervisory system leads to a substantial degree of convergence. For the LSI, the implementation of the financial regulation is the primary task of the NCAs. The tools for exercising this function are formulated in their national legislation, as complemented by the instruments derived from the EU directives and regulations, and by the EU bodies, ie the ECB and the SRB.[84] The NCAs' action is coordinated and supervised at the European level by the

[83] See Art 7 SSM Regulation. An agreement between the ECB and the NCA of the candidate member will have to intervene.

[84] CDR IV, CRR and SSM; also by the SRB.

three ESAs, overseeing respectively banking, securities and insurance.[85] With the aim of ensuring greater convergence and integration of the markets, the present system is governed by a convergent regulatory apparatus and controlled by efficient enforcement of the common rules. The ESAs have been created to enhance the cooperation and coordination of the national supervisory authorities, promote supervisory convergence, and exchange experiences in their specific supervisory fields. In its Interactive Single Rulebook, the EBA has assembled the different legislative and regulatory instruments relating to its supervisory activity.[86] Its action focuses on the coordination of the supervisory activities of the NCAs, but not on exercising individual supervisory activities, which are reserved to the NCAs.

The ESAs have the regulatory competences to develop draft standards to be submitted to the Commission, develop common supervisory practices between the national supervisory authorities and assess supervisory oversight with respect to the supervisory activity of the NCAs. Thus, the ESAs have developed special programmes dealing with the guidelines for coordination of the application of their respective regulatory bodies of rules and building a common supervisory culture.[87] This harmonisation includes coordination and disciplinary action for divergent interpretations of regulations or of Union law,[88] extending to mediation between conflicting views of national supervisors.[89]

ESAs develop common standards with respect to the activity in their field of oversight of the NCAs: these are adopted by the Commission and formally issued as regulations. To implement their role as effective supervisors of the way the NCAs implement their tasks in their respective markets, the ESAs have developed different tools, some of which are preparatory, other implementing, assessment, or remediation tools.[90] Peer reviews are powerful instruments identifying the differences between the national supervisory systems and regulations, and may be the first steps for further improvements.

2.6.3. Centralised Banking Supervision: The ECB Supervises the Significant Institutions

In the 19 Member States in which the euro is the primary currency, ie the Eurozone, supervision is exercised within the framework of the SSM.[91] Their monetary

[85] These are EBA, ESMA and EIOPA.

[86] See EBA, Interactive Single Rulebook.

[87] See ESMA, 'Supervisory Convergence, strategic priority for 2016–2020', available at https://www.esma.europa.eu/system/files_force/library/2015/11/2015-935_esma_strategic_orientation_2016-2020.pdf.

[88] See Art 17 EBA regulation on Breach of Union law, or Arts 19 and 20 EBA Regulation on Settlement of disagreements between competent authorities in the same sector but belong to different member states, or across sectors. A common board of appeal for the three ESA will hear cases submitted by natural or legal persons, or NCAs against decisions of an ESA.

[89] See Art 19 EBA Regulation, Supervisory convergence: see esma.europa.eu/convergence/supervisory-convergence.

[90] EBA has developed a peer review programme with a view of supervisory convergence, including best practices. It follows a uniform methodology to ensure consistency: EBA, 'Decision of 28 April 2020, adopting a methodology for the conduct of peer reviews' EBA/DC/2020/327. ESMA undertakes

authority is the Eurosystem, composed of the ECB and the national central banks of the euro area states. The Eurosystem's primary objective is to safeguard financial stability and promote European financial integration. The ECB has been recognised as the sole supervisor for the banking system. The supervision of the largest banking groups is directly exercised by the ECB, with assistance from the NCAs, while the NCAs exercise the core supervisory functions for the LSIs.

With respect to the SIs, the ECB exercises the direct supervision on the largest banking groups, as defined in the regulation, mainly on the basis of a quantitative criterion – the total balance sheet being the most significant.[92] With respect to the granting and withdrawal of banking licences, and also the assessment of the acquisition of qualifying holdings,[93] decisions will be adopted by the NCA and ratified by the ECB.[94]

ESAs develop common regulatory or technical standards with respect to the activity in their field of oversight of the NCAs: these are adopted by the Commission and formally issued as regulations. To implement their role as effective supervisors of the way the NCAs implement their tasks in their respective markets, the ESAs have developed different tools, some of which are preparatory, other implementing, assessment or remediation tools.[95] Peer reviews are powerful instruments identifying the differences between the national supervisory systems and regulations, and may be the first steps for further improvements. The three ESAs function on more or less identical patterns, using largely the same instruments, in some cases even developing common regulations.

The continuous supervision of the SIs is exercised by the ECB on an independent basis,[96] according to the Framework Regulation[97] and imposing the application

an annual peer review on the activities of the NCA as objective assessment and comparability require these to be conducted according to a well-established methodology. Reports are published on specific topics, eg, its 'Fast track peer review on the application of the Guidelines on the enforcement of financial information by BaFin and FREP in the context of Wirecard' (3 November 2020); ESMA42-111-5349; 'Annual Peer review of CCP Supervision' (8 April 2021).

[91] Created by the SSM Regulation. Banking supervision is a core part of the ECB's functions.

[92] See for the legal basis Art 6(4) SSM Regulation, containing a list of almost all components of regular banking supervision.

[93] See Art 14 SSM Regulation, according to which the application for authorisation will first be submitted the NCAs of the future location of the bank, its draft decision to be adopted by the ECB. Withdrawal will follow the inverse order; the ECB will decide, following consultations by the NCA. For the acquisition of a 'qualifying holding', the acquisition will first be submitted to the NCA, which will assess the acquisition and submit its proposal to the ECB (Art 15 SSM Regulation). NCAs remain in charge of all supervisory tasks which were not transferred to the SSM, such as consumer protection or anti-money laundering. For an application, see the ECB Case C-219/17 *Berlusconi and Fininvest v Bank of Italy*, ECLI:EU:C:2018:1023, [160].

[94] See for the sequences of decision making: Art 14 SSM Regulation.

[95] EBA has developed a peer review programme following a uniform methodology: EBA, 'Decision of 28 April 2020' EBA/DC/2020. Reports are published on specific topics, eg its 'Fast track peer review on the application of the Guidelines on the enforcement of financial information by BaFin and FREP in the context of Wirecard' (3 November 2020).

[96] The accountability framework of the ECB is further articulated in the SSM Regulation, an Interinstitutional Agreement between the European Parliament and the ECB, and a Memorandum of Understanding (MoU) between the EU Council and the ECB.

[97] Regulation (EU) No 468/2014 of the European Central Bank of 16 April 2014 establishing the framework for cooperation within the Single Supervisory Mechanism between the European Central

of all relevant Union law, as this is composed, on the one hand, of directives – in which case the ECB will apply the national law transposing the directives – and, on the other, of the directly applicable regulations – including the Commission- or EBA-developed regulations. This system creates an equal playing field for both categories of institutions.[98] In its supervisory action, the ECB will be exclusively competent for the main supervisory tasks, as listed in the regulation: it will execute these tasks with the 'assistance' of the NCAs, who will be instructed accordingly by the ECB. The ECB will be considered the competent authority in the Member States in which it exercises the main supervisory tasks, as listed in the regulation, and including all the powers of the NCAs in supervisory or investigatory matters.[99] This results for the ECB in a position which – as far as the applicable regulations are concerned – is largely similar to the position of an NCA: it will apply to the SIs all relevant Union law, including the Commission regulations,[100] the recommendations and guidelines developed by the EBA, or by the Joint Committees of the ESAs.

The ECB exercises direct supervision on the SIs and, when appropriate, has the power to impose certain actions or sanctions. The ECB implements its supervisory mandate for the SI on the basic of the Framework Regulation.[101] Actual supervision will be implemented under the direction of the Supervisory Board, composed of chair and vice-chair and four representatives of the ECB[102] and one of each of the NCAs of each participating Member State.[103] The Supervisory Board exercises its function through its organisational departments and is carried out on the field by the joint supervisory teams (JST). These teams exercise the whole range of supervisory duties, as planned in the annual priorities and risk plans.[104] The ECB has released supervisory guides giving insight into its supervisory objectives and priorities. An important instrument is the Supervisory Review and Evaluation Process (SREP), dealing especially with the analysis of the risks of the individual banks. This scheme allows for effectiveness and convergence of interests between the ECB and the Member State. But it also expresses the fundamental principle of cooperation in good faith between the ECB and the NCAs[105] and supports the joint implementation of the SSM supervisory scheme.

Bank and national competent authorities and with national designated authorities (SSM Framework Regulation) (ECB/2014/17) [2014] OJ L 141/1.

[98] Art 4(3) SSM Regulation, applying all relevant Union law, national law transposing directives and the acts adopted pursuant to Arts 290–91 TFEU, including the technical standards developed by EBA.

[99] Art 4(1) SSM Regulation.

[100] Reference is made to Arts 290 and 291 TFEU.

[101] Art 6(7) SSM Regulation (EU) No 468/2014 containing the practical arrangements for organising the supervision: in this supervision the NCAs will be consulted.

[102] These are the chair and vice-chair and four representatives of the ECB, Art 26(1) SSM Regulation.

[103] See Art 26(1) SSM Regulation.

[104] The Supervisory Manual will be guiding the actions of the JST. See: SSM Supervisory Manual, available at www.bankingsupervision.europa.eu/ecb/pub/pdf/ssm.supervisorymanual201803.en.pdf; SSM Supervisory Manual; European banking supervision: functioning of the SSM and supervisory approach (March 2018).

[105] As stipulated in Art 6(3) of the SSM Regulation, where the NCAs have been declared responsible for 'assisting the ECB'. This feature of the SSM was clearly identified in Case C-450/17 P *Landeskreditbank*

With respect to the LSIs, supervision will be exercised by the NCAs, but under the general guidance of the ECB, which can issue guidelines, regulations and general instructions, or launch joint inspections by an NCA on an LSI when indicated in areas which are not covered by the SSM Regulation.[106] The ECB oversees their supervision to ensure their activities meet the published high supervisory standards. The NCAs will apply their national banking laws, as well as the applicable EU regulations and ECB standards. Differences in the supervised population explain the different ways this supervision is structured. NCAs remain in charge of all supervisory tasks which were not transferred to the SSM, such as consumer protection or anti-money laundering.

There has been some discussion whether these two levels of banking supervision under the general authority of the ECB have to be seen as different, mutually exclusive levels, one not being held to the rules applicable to the other. Both on the basis of the SSM Regulation[107] and the ECJ case law, the answer is negative: they form part of one single banking supervisory system, albeit with different modalities of exercising the supervisory function.[108] In accordance with the Framework Regulation, the NCAs will act in 'assistance' to the ECB for any of the core supervisory tasks and with respect to all credit institutions, in accordance with the ECB instructions.[109] Therefore, ECB has been declared responsible for the effective and consistent functioning of the entire SSM.[110]

2.7. Judicial Review of Decision-Making in Banking

The implementation of the EU banking rules finds its ultimate consecration in the decisions of the judiciary on the controversies relating to their application.[111] The resulting case law is central to the interpretation of the EU rules, especially in their conflict with national law and practices, and has in many respects contributed to developing the fundamental characteristics of the EU legal system, identifying some if its core notions. The critical factor is the legality test of its decisions in the context of the provisions of the Treaty and Treaty-based rules.

Baden-Württemberg – Förderbank v ECB, ECLI:EU:C:2019:372: 'The Regulation has conceived the SSM supervision as an integrated model, …. whereby the NCA intervene in an "assistance" mode, while recognizing the ultimate decision-making power of the ECB'. See: F Annunziata, 'European Banking Supervision in the Age of the ECB Landeskreditbank Baden-Wuerttemberg – Foerderbank v ECB' (2020) 21 *European Business Organization Law Review* 545.

[106] Art 6(6) SSM Regulation.

[107] See Art 4(1) SSM Regulation referring to 'the ECB … being exclusively competent …. for the – listed – tasks in relation to all credit institutions'. See Art 6(1) on the role of the NCAs as assistants to the ECB.

[108] As detailed in Art 6(5) SSM Regulation; see Case C-450/17 P *Landeskreditbank Baden-Württemberg – Förderbank v ECB*, ECLI:EU:C:2019:372, [119].

[109] Art 4(1) and 6(3) SSM Regulation.

[110] Art 6(1) SSM Regulation.

[111] See, extensively, ch 6 of this volume.

As far as judicial review of banking decisions is concerned, taking into account the characteristics of the supervisory system, three levels can be distinguished. The first is composed of the acts of banking institutions located in the non-euro Member States: they remain subject to the supervision by their national supervisors, applying their national laws, including the transposed directives and the directly applicable regulations. Decisions based on these legislative instruments would be subject to review based on EU law. To check the alleged illegality of their decision, or for resolving interpretation questions, litigation could be brought before the national courts, with possible review by the Union courts on the basis of alleged illegality or for interpretation questions by a prejudicial ruling. Appeal against national decisions will be submitted to the national courts of appeal, which may apply for review by the Union courts.

On the second level, banking institutions are subject to the SSM, and their legal regime has been embedded in the SSM framework, distinguishing the SIs and LSIs. While the former are mainly subject to the ECB's supervisory authority, judicial action will address the ECB decisions,[112] for which only the EU courts are competent. The LSIs are mainly supervised by the NCAs, and judicial action will address their decisions, with appeal before the Union courts for aspects relating to EU banking law.

On a third level, they could also start an action on the basis of illegality relating to decisions by other bodies (eg ESAs) – matters for which the Union courts are competent. If the case if brought before a national jurisdiction, the latter can invite the opinion of the European courts by way of a preliminary ruling, allowing them to adopt an opinion which will resist any doubt about its compatibility with EU law. With respect to decisions of NCAs or ESAs, the national decision will then be fully error-proof. The reverse position is not available: the European courts cannot submit the case for clarification of the legal regime under national law to a national court, by way of a 'reverse preliminary request', inviting the national jurisdiction, 'to obtain a position of a national court on the application of national law to the identified issue'. Judicial review in the field of banking is essentially the result of ECJ decisions, based on the EU banking regulatory system, including Union Treaties and the Charters of Fundamental Rights.[113] The list of cases in which the European courts have intervened is long, so they have become a substantive component of EU banking law. The judicial review of the rules and decisions applicable to the banking activity is a central feature to safeguard that the supervisory system and its applications conforms to the principles as laid down in the fundamental documents creating the Union's banking regulatory system, based on the ECB decisions which are formally binding.[114] In this multilayered system of supervision, the judicial review should be structured following some of the same principles.

[112] One should add the numerous cases against the SRB, separately or along with the ECB.

[113] See European Banking Institute, 'The Banking Union and Union Courts: overview of cases as at 1 September 2021'. This list has been produced by R Smits and F Della Negra.

[114] Art 288 TFEU: 'a regulation is binding in its entirety'.

2.7.1. Layers of Judicial Review

Decisions of national supervisory bodies, or complaints by individual parties may be submitted to national courts for final decisions. But parties may object on the basis of the incompatibility of that decision with EU law, in which case they will require the decision to be submitted to legality review, in accordance with Article 263 of the TFEU. This legality review addresses several shortcomings in EU acts: the Treaty mentions lack of competence, infringement of essential procedural requirements, infringement of the Treaties and of any rule relating to their application,[115] and misuse of powers.[116] This review can be requested by all EU bodies, where the main objective is to guarantee that all main EU bodies remain within the limits defined in EU law: this addresses the acts of the legislature, of the Commission and the Council, European Parliament and of the ECB. For acts of other EU bodies, offices or agencies, the mentioned grounds will suffice to bring the action for illegality, provided individual plaintiffs can show that these acts are intended to produce legal effect in relation to them, and are of direct and individual concern.[117] Although the standard for review is limited to the legal conformity of the decision with EU law, in some cases, a wider reasoning has been followed by the court, sometimes based on wider social or policy grounds.

Internal decisions by these bodies are not included in this review procedure, which is limited to acts which are 'intended to produce legal effects vis-a-vis third parties'. Therefore, recommendations and opinions are not included. The remedy extends to acts of 'bodies, offices and agencies'. The acts of lower ranged bodies are included under the condition of legal effect. Once an act has been declared illegal, it will be denied any consequences: it will be void. However, the court may decide to some effect of the act to be definitive.[118] In the same sense, the court has unlimited jurisdiction with regard to penalties imposed on the basis of regulations adopted by the Parliament and the Council, or by the Council.[119]

Claims can also be filed by any person – natural or legal – provided the criticised act is of direct and individual concern to that person and does not entail implementing measures, that means that the act is final.[120] Whether an act produces legal effects is determined by the court after a factual analysis of its content,[121] and

[115] Covering the rule of law, the general principles of law and of subsidiarity/proportionality. The standard of review is restricted to the legal conformity of the decision. The court may include a detailed analysis of the ECB's findings: see Case T-733/16 *Banque postale*, ECLI:EU:T:2018:477 in which the court annulled the ECB decision to refuse to several French banks the exemption from the leverage ratio for savings to be transferred to the CDC, stating at [114] that the ECB had not made a 'detailed examination of the characteristics of the regulated savings'.

[116] See Art 263 TFEU for the precise formulation.

[117] Art 263 TFEU last paragraph.

[118] Art 264 TFEU.

[119] Art 261 TFEU. Does this aim to more, or to less severity, or to better adapted sanctions?

[120] Art 263 TFEU: 'no implementing measures'.

[121] 'Affecting the applicant and his legal position by restricting his rights', Case C-60/81 *IBM v Commission*, ECLI:EU:C:1981:264.This would also be the case if the act is directly addressed to him/her and that he/she has a legal interest or advantage in having the act annulled.

would as a rule, not include voluntary instruments such as guidelines, guides, or recommendations.[122]

The decision whether a request for a preliminary ruling will be submitted to the court is in the hands of the Member State's judge and should depend on his ability to render a qualitative, a convincing decision.[123] Most of the time the judge will follow the suggestion of the claimant and allow a preliminary request to the court. The TFEU declares that a request will be mandatory in one case, ie if no further judicial remedy would be available under national law.[124] In many cases the preliminary ruling procedures serve to verify the court's opinion on matters to be decided by the national court or tribunal. The court's decision will be final: no further appeal is possible.

The Union courts have exclusive jurisdiction to review the legality of SSM acts. In some cases, an SSM act is double-layered, partly a national act, and partly of ECB origin. These are called the 'common procedures' in which the NCA and the ECB are involved, the clearest case being the act of the national authority, allowing a candidate bank for authorisation, but subject to the decision of the ECB as to its final authorisation under the SSM.[125] Most of the time the national decision will be seen as a mere preparatory act which is not binding on the ECB. It cannot be litigated before a national court: the court has to rely on the national act. In the Berlusconi case, the review of the ECB decision was considered to include the review of the defects of the preparatory acts which would affect the final ECB decision.[126]

Acts of the ECB can only be reviewed by the Union courts: only Union courts may review the legality of Union acts and their decisions will be binding: the court

[122] But see the opinion of Advocate General Bobek with respect to the assessment of non-binding EU acts, Case C-911/19, *Federation bancaire française v ACPR*, ECLI:EU:C:2021:599, [156]. For more details see further section 2.7.4.

[123] See for a different opinion: Case-561/19 *Consorzio Italian Management e Catania Multiservizi and Catania Multiservizi v Rete Ferroviaria Italiana SpA*, ECLI:EU:C:2021:291; Opinion of the Advocate General in the case C-561/19, ECLI:EU:C:2021:291: 'the Court should revisit its case-law (the CILFIT criteria) on the duty of national courts of last instance to request a preliminary ruling'. This opinion was contested by Advocate General Bobek, Case-561/19 *Consorzio Italian Management e Catania Multiservizi and Catania Multiservizi v Rete Ferroviaria Italiana SpA*, ECLI:EU:C:2021:291 putting into doubt the actual practice under Art 267(3) TFEU, allowing the last instance preliminary questions under three conditions: 'first, that the case raises a general issue of interpretation of EU law, which may, second, be reasonably interpreted in more than one possible way and, third, the way in which the EU law at issue is to be interpreted cannot be inferred from the existing case-law of the Court of Justice'. The argument that access to this remedy should be restricted as there are already too many requests for preliminary rulings should be dismissed: the judicial authorities should be the addressees of this demand.

[124] This position was criticised by Advocate General Bobek in Case C-911/19 *Federation bancaire française v ACPR*, ECLI:EU:C:2021:294. A professional association may challenge an illegality plea for guidelines for its members, even if these may not be of direct or individual concern to it. The subject of Guidelines on product oversight do not fall within the scope of the regulation establishing the EBA, and are therefore invalid.

[125] Arts 14 and 15 SSM Regulation; see also Art 90 SSM Regulation.

[126] See: Case C-219/17 *Berlusconi and Fininvest v Bank of Italy*, ECLI:EU:C:2018:1023, [160]. See for a more elaborate analysis of this case ch 6 of this volume.

will review the legality of acts of the ECB, but also of other Union bodies, offices and agencies, provided these are intended to produce legal effects vis-à-vis third parties. This would include the acts of the ESAs. A national court is not entitled to declare the EU rules invalid but may be requested by the claimant to submit to the Union court a request for a 'preliminary ruling'.[127] The scope of a preliminary ruling may include both the validity and the interpretation of the Union's institutions – bodies, offices or agencies – allowing for a relatively wide reading of the subject matter. This preliminary process is not limited to binding acts, but allows to clarify the legal status of the act to be analysed, and lead to a uniform interpretation. Preliminary rulings are instruments which are widely recognised as contributing to the legal integration in the Union,[128] although some criticise the process as giving priority to European over national law. In the banking field where integration is one of the leading priorities of the Union, the latter argument would not be very convincing.

In the national systems, judicial review allows verification of the conformity with the national regulatory provisions and conformity to the higher level of EU regulation and legal principles.[129] It should be carried out by a tribunal, with full jurisdiction, according to local law. This is in essence a legality check, but in some cases it includes conformity with the overall legal system, such as the Charter of Human Rights or the European Convention on Human Rights.

Acts by NCAs are reviewable before the national courts and tribunals. This rule applies to all NCA decisions, including those relating to the LSIs, and extends to the act of the NCAs implementing the guidelines of the ECB. Acts of an ESA may be submitted to its Board of Appeal, and further submitted to the ECJ for a legality check. CRD IV and the CRR state that acts adopted pursuant to these legal instruments are subject to a right of appeal, including an effective remedy and a fair trial.[130] The opinions of a tribunal should be binding, impartial and independent from the parties, it should have full jurisdiction, and have the right to decide both at law and in fact.[131] But it should not have the same expertise as the NCA against which appeal is taken (only marginal control), nor substitute its opinion to that of the NCA.

Except in the field of sanctions, the tribunal will not have the power to substitute its assessment to that of the author of the act. In cases dealing with serious

[127] Art 267 TFEU. The national courts have no jurisdiction to declare that community acts are invalid, but have to submit a preliminary question, if there is no judicial remedy at the national level. EU courts do not apply national law, but exclusively interpret EU law.

[128] See CJ Carrubba and L Murrah, *Legal integration and the Use of the Preliminary Ruling Process in the European Union, International Organization* (Cambridge, CUP, 2005).

[129] According to Art 19(1) TEU, effective legal protection has to be secured. A right of appeal has to be guaranteed by Art 64 CRD IV, or Art 72 CRR.

[130] On the basis of Art 47 CFR and Art 6(1) ECHR. See also Art 64 CRD IV. There are similar provisions in the BRRD.

[131] Which means that jurisdictions as a cour de cassation (in this case the French Supreme Court) would not meet this criterion, as they only decide on the legal elements and not the factual ones.

sanctions, the tribunal may assess the proportionality of the sanction, and amend it accordingly.[132]

2.7.2. Leading Judicial Decisions on Banking Supervision

It would be impossible to give an overview of all decisions of the European Court dealing with banking law. Only a few leading cases will be briefly analysed below.[133]

In a case in which the ECB withdrew the banking licence of a *Latvian bank*, the Latvian NCA ordered the liquidation and appointed a liquidator, who revoked all powers in the former bank. The shareholders objected. The ABoR considered the allegations to be unfounded. The court considered that while the bank could no longer continue its activity, and hence not distribute dividends to the shareholders, their right to participate in the company and receive dividends had not been affected by the withdrawal decision. The liquidation is not an implementation of the withdrawal decision as it is 'purely automatic and results from EU rules alone',[134] but was a separate decision adopted by the Latvian court. The General Court was wrong in taking account of the non-legal, economic effects of the withdrawal decision on the situation of the shareholders. The withdrawal did not legally affect the existence of the bank but was merely a financial consequence thereof. Therefore, the Court held their action to be inadmissible. From a company law of view, this decision may seem surprising: the withdrawal of the banking authorisation might not necessarily have put an end to the legal entity, but would have removed the purpose of the company. Further analysis under national company law might be useful.

Some banking groups are structured as groups of companies, subject to consolidated supervision. Others are composed of separate banks but have a common commercial presentation and are managed on a uniform basis. This formula has been used by several French banking groups and has been the subject of litigation at the Union level. The litigation in connection with the *Arkea* group has led to several decisions.

Article 10 of the CRR deals with the 'waiver for credit institutions permanently affiliated to a central body' where the conditions for the CRR grants national competent authorities the right to apply a more lenient regime to these

[132] On the basis of Art 6(1) ECHR; see the Engel-criteria in *Engel and others/Netherlands*, ECLI:CE:ECHR:1976:0608JUD000510071.

[133] See for an elaborate list: European Banking Institute, 'European cases and jurisprudence', available at ebi-europa.eu/publications/eu-cases-or-jurisprudence. See also n 11.

[134] Cases C-663-17 P, C 665/17 P and C 669/17 *ECB v Trasta*, ECLI:EU:C:2019:923.

'groups' by allowing a waiver of the requirements of Parts 2–8 of the CRR.[135] The fact that the central body does not have banking status does not limit the application of the related waiver, provided that the central body guarantees the liabilities of the affiliated entities, that solvency and liquidity of the group are monitored on a consolidated basis and that instructions can be given by the central body.[136]

In the *Arkea case*,[137] the discussion turned on the question whether Credit Mutuel had in place the necessary measures 'to ensure the liquidity and the solvency of each of the affiliated institutions and companies and of the network' which are sufficient to permit an obligation to transfer capital and liquidities within the group to ensure that the liabilities towards the creditors would be fulfilled. The case has been litigated both in France and at the ECJ level, and led to three court decisions. In the decision of 20 October 2019, a decisive opinion of the French Conseil d'état held that under applicable French law,[138] especially Art 511-31 of the French code monétaire et financier, the French legislature had entrusted to the Confédération Nationale du Crédit Mutuel (CNCM) – 'as a parent undertaking in the Union' – responsibility for collectively representing Credit Mutuel branches and companies, for ensuring that the network operates cohesively, and to identify the different types of collective liability or behaviour, inter alia, under the form of transfer capital and liquidity.[139] On that basis the Court concluded that the substantive conditions laid down in Article 10(1)(a) of the CRR were satisfied.

As an aside, this decision illustrates the need for the EU courts to have a precise view on the national law which is discussed in their decisions. In the *Arkea* case, the opinion of the court was considerably strengthened by the analysis made by the Conseil d'Etat in its opinion which predates the Arkea litigation. This council's opinion could be called an '*ex ante* reverse preliminary opinion'!

2.7.3. Preliminary Rulings

In principle, national courts often submit controversial matters relating to the interpretation of Union law to the Union court in the context of a preliminary ruling in which the Court is expected to deliver an authoritative opinion on the

[135] Dealing with own funds, capital requirements, large exposures, transferred credit risk, liquidity, disclosure, leverage. See Art 10(1) CRR.

[136] See Art 10(1) CRR.

[137] Case C-152/18 P *Crédit Mutuel Arkea v. ECB and European Commission*, ECLI:EU:C:2019:810; this is an appeal from Case T-712/15, ECLI:EU:T:2017:900.

[138] Décision of the Conseil d'État du 9 mars 2018, n° 399413; Interpretation according to Frech contract law.

[139] Case C-152/18 P *Crédit Mutuel Arkea v ECB and European Commission*, ECLI:EU:C:2019:810, [104]–[107].

application of EU law.[140] The ruling may extend to the validity of acts on the institutions, bodies, offices or agencies. It may also apply to non-binding acts. The national courts are free to decide to submit a preliminary question, but it might be indicated when the invalidity of the act is apparent, or if the court judges that the parties have convincing arguments for the invalidity. The request is freely introduced and formulated by the national court.

In the *Berlusconi* case,[141] a reference for a preliminary ruling had been introduced by Berlusconi and Fininvest with respect to the ECB decision as to whether Berlusconi could be authorised to acquire, as shareholder and as owner in Fininvest, a qualifying block of shares in another Italian bank, Mediolanum. Berlusconi had been found guilty of tax fraud, so the Banca d'Italia decided that he had to divest the existing participation up to 9.99 per cent. It also advised the ECB to refuse the authorisation for the acquisition.

The Italian Council of State, at the request of Berlusconi and Fininvest, decided that the authorisation procedure was composed of two steps: first, a national one which would be subject to judicial review at the national level; and second, an EU one decided by the ECB and reviewed by the EU courts. The Council applied for a preliminary ruling, essentially asking whether national courts are prevented from reviewing national decisions in a 'common procedure' for authorisation. The court denied that the national act could be reviewed separately, as the procedure established the exclusive decision-making power of the EU institution. National acts adopted in a common procedure have to be qualified as *preparatory* for the adoption of a final EU act by the ECB. In this case, a specific cooperation mechanism is introduced which results in the exclusive decision-making power of the EU institution. The EU court excluded the separate jurisdiction of national courts even in light of a compliance action undertaken at the national level. Otherwise, divergent assessments in the same procedure will not be avoided. Any other outcome might also have exposed the Court's review actions to disruptive, parallel national initiatives.[142]

2.7.4. Court Cases Dealing with Non-Binding Acts

Whether non-binding acts – often referred to as 'soft law' – qualify for legal review is controversial. Here, one refers to the guidelines, recommendations,[143]

[140] Art 267 TFEU. The ruling may extend to the validity of acts on the institutions, bodies, offices or agencies.

[141] Case C-219/17 *Berlusconi and Fininvest v Bank of Italy*, ECLI:EU:C:2018:1023, [160].

[142] See extensively on this topic, ch 6 in this volume.

[143] The Court has indicated that 'since recommendations cannot be regarded as having no legal effect, national courts are bound to take recommendations into consideration to decide disputes', Case C-322/88 *Salvatore Grimaldi*, ECLI:EU:C:1989:646. This disorderly status is likely to create confusion and leave blanks in its effectiveness.

instructions and Q&As, which constitute a form of 'soft harmonisation'.[144] The ECB issues guidelines and recommendations addressed to the NCAs and the financial institutions, which shall make every effort to comply, but the obligation is on an 'comply or explain' basis.[145] Its recommendations and opinions are non-binding. For different instruments or messages – such as guides,[146] letters,[147] presentations, supervisory expectations[148] – it will be difficult for the practitioner of banking law to distinguish which acts are binding and which are mere recommendations. Several cases have been rendered on this issue: among older cases, there was discussion on the standards for competition fines.[149] In 2002, in a judgment concerning internal measures adopted by the administration, the court held that although those measures may not be regarded as rules of law which the administration is always bound to observe, they nevertheless form rules of practice from which the administration may not depart in an individual case without giving reasons that are compatible with the principle of equal treatment.[150] To avoid confusion, the qualification of these instruments and the possibility of having them challenged in court should be clarified in the regulation or by the court, to avoid surprises in later judicial application. For example, recommendations and Opinions 'have no binding force' (Article 288 TFEU). The ESA guidelines and recommendations are binding, but on a best-efforts basis, and institutions will disclose whether they will comply.[151] The ECB Instructions and guidelines are binding for the NCAs to which they are addressed, while the EBA guidelines and the ECB recommendations are generally not binding.[152]

However, the reality is sometimes more complex, as illustrated in the following case. In 2016, the EBA adopted 'Guidelines on product oversight and governance arrangements for the retail banking products'. These guidelines fall into its consumer protection remit (Article 9 EBA Regulation), which include mortgages,

[144] See for an overview, R Bax and A Witte, 'The taxonomy of ECB instruments available for banking supervision' (June 2019), available at www.ecb.europa.eu/pub/economic-bulletin/articles/2019/html/ecb.ebart201906_02~3e2f0e4f63.en.html.

[145] Art 16(3) EBA Regulation implying moral sanction by way of disclosure and communication to the Parliament, Commission and Council.

[146] See ECB Supervisory Guides, available at www.bankingsupervision.europa.eu/legalframework/supervisorypolicy/html/supervisoryguides.en.html.

[147] 'Letters to banks', available at www.bankingsupervision.europa.eu/press/letterstobanks/html/index.en.html. 'Bank boards and supervisory expectations', speech by E McCaul (3 December 2020), available at bankingsupervision.europa.eu/press/speeches/date/2020/html/ssm.sp201203~4c2c39db9d.en.html.

[148] For the ECB's supervisory policy documents, see www.bankingsupervision.europa.eu/legalframework/supervisorypolicy/html/index.en.html; also EBA guidelines and recommendations.

[149] See Art 15 Council Regulation No 17 of 6 February 1962 implementing Art 81(1) of the Treaty establishing the European Community; See Case C-189/02 P *Dansk Rørindustri A/S*, ECLI:EU:C:2005:408.

[150] Case C-171/00 P *Liberos* v *Commission*, ECI:EU:C:2002:17, [35].

[151] See Art 16(2)–(3) EBA Regulation for the limits to the binding character. 'The competent authorities and financial institutions shall make every effort to comply' (Art 16(3) EBA Regulation). Parliament, Council and Commission will be informed about the ESA members who did not comply.

[152] R Bax and A Witte, 'The taxonomy of ECB instruments available for banking supervision' (June 20190, available at www.ecb.europa.eu/pub/economic-bulletin/articles/2019/html/ecb.ebart201906_02~3e2f0e4f63.en.html#toc3.

personal loans, deposits, payment accounts, payment services, and electronic money. These topics are further governed by different directives in which the protection remits have been formulated, although with different wording (eg 'disclosure', 'information', 'substantive requirements'). The Guidelines – in French called 'Orientations' – as developed by the EBA are addressed to the competent NCA. The French ACPR approved the Guidelines for matters of product oversight and for governance arrangements within its statutory mission, specifically for payment services and mortgage credit. The ACPR decision was contested by the French Banking Federation, which sued the French banking supervisor before the Conseil d'Etat, alleging that ACPR had transgressed its mandate, and therefore applying for a preliminary ruling from the European Court.[153] The Court first considered whether the EBA Guidelines could be declared illegal, which was not the case as they have no binding force. However, the Guidelines should be checked on their 'validity' as Union acts. This distinction between illegality and validity would mean that guidelines may not be enforceable before EU jurisdictions, but they still 'constitute legally valid instruments', if adopted on an appropriate legal basis. They constitute instructions by the EBA to ESAs with a view of 'exhorting financial institutions to alter their practices'. The court then proceeded to review the different directives in which product oversight and governance arrangements have been mentioned, especially referring to the tasks of the EBA for enhancing consumer protection. The EBA has competence to issue guidelines only to the extent provided in the EU legislation. The legal basis of this action is to be found in the provisions of the EBA regulation necessary for consistent and effective application of the referred directives. Product oversight and governance arrangements have to be integrated in the institutions' internal framework. Therefore, the court did not identify any factor affecting the validity of the guidelines.This decision of the court extends considerably the legal standing of guidelines and recommendations, while opening a widely defined scope of legal action to the EBA.

2.8. Non-Judicial Review of Supervisory Decisions

2.8.1. The Administrative Board of Review

Within the ECB, the ABoR is in charge of administrative review of decisions proposed to be adopted by the ECB, upon request of any person to which the decision is addressed or which is of direct and individual concern to him/her, but not by NCA*s*. The ABoR's opinion is not binding and remains unpublished.[154]

[153] Case C-911/19 *Fédération bancaire française v Autorité de contrôle prudentiel et de resolution*, ECLI:EU:C:2021:599.

[154] See the reference to ABoR's position on the supremacy of EU law over French law: in Joined Cases T-133/16 to T-136/16 *Crédit Agricole v. ECB*, ECLI:EU:T:2018:219, [220].

The ABoR is not a jurisdictional body, its decisions are not binding, and the procedure does not pre-empt the right to institute proceedings before the Court of Justice. As the review takes place prior to the Governing Council formally adopting the proposal submitted by the Supervisory Board, this review process is to be considered internal and preliminary.[155] The procedure before the ABoR has been laid down in an ECB decision,[156] providing for due process, absence of suspension of the procedure, and guarantees of confidentiality, and documents being only accessible to the parties. The ABoR will analyse the matter from procedural and substantive points of view.[157] If the review concludes that the case is admissible, its non-binding opinion will be addressed to the Supervisory Board, allowing it to prepare a new draft decision, taking into account the opinion of the ABoR, and submitting a new draft to the Governing Council. Unless the Governing Council objects, the new draft decision will be deemed adopted.

2.8.2. The Mediation Panel

The SSM Regulation[158] affirmed the strict separation of the ECB's monetary function from its supervisory and other tasks. This implies strict secrecy rules and organisational separation. The Governing Council also holds separate meetings and agendas dealing with one or the other subject. With respect to objections of the Governing Council to drafts decisions of the Supervisory Board, the regulation has introduced a mediation panel in charge of resolving differences of views between the NCAs with respect to an objection of the Governing Council. This panel aims to find a balance between the positions of the Governing Council and Supervisory Board, but its opinion is not binding on any of these parties. A new – compromise – decision may be submitted by the Supervisory Board to the Governing Council.

2.8.3. The ESA's Board of Appeal

The Board of Appeal is a joint body set up by the three ESAs for the financial services sector.[159] It will decide on the appeals introduced by any person, including

[155] Decisions of the Governing Council cannot be challenged before the ABoR. A fortiori, decisions of the Supervisory Board, being preliminary cannot be appealed, but if the latter agrees, it may change the proposed decision.

[156] Decision of the European Central Bank of 14 April 2014 concerning the establishment of the Administrative Board of Review and its Operating Rules (ECB/2014/16), available at www.ecb.europa.eu/ecb/legal/pdf/en_dec_2014_16_f_sign. pdf.

[157] Meaning that the margin of discretion is left to the ECB to decide on the 'opportunity to take those decisions' (Recital 64, SSM Regulation). A similar approach is followed in Art 13 SSM Regulation, dealing with decisions involving on-site inspections, where the national judiciary intervenes.

[158] Art 25(5) SSM Regulation.

[159] Art 58 ESA Regulation; Joint Board of Appeal, eba.europa.eu/about-us/organisation/joint-board-of-appeal.

NCAs, against a decision of the relevant ESA in matter of conflicts between the ESAs,[160] or any other decision of the ESA in relation to any of the fundamental directives and regulations applicable in the banking field, provided the decision is directly addressed to that person or is of direct and individual concern to him/her.[161] Its decision may be reviewed by the Union courts.[162]

2.9. Other Contributions to the Implementation of Financial Regulation

Formal decision-making – however important – is not the only factor contributing to the implementation of financial regulations in the EU. The process is more complex as it includes several forms of informal – 'non-legal' – influence on banking practice, including in subsequent stages, as a consequence of judicial decisions, in the administrative practice and in diverse legal developments. Although no systematic analysis has been undertaken, it is quite likely that the supervisory authorities – as well as the largest banks in Europe – follow these developments with due attention and will adapt their policies and decisions to the published case law, or at least are inspired by the lessons to be drawn from it. However, not all participants are equally diligent: the number of fines imposed – on Member States and major banks[163] – indicates that a more systemic risk approach could usefully be developed, eg under the leadership of the banking associations, rendering their members more sensitive to these sometimes transformational developments. The same could be said about certain recent lending abuses or AML cases which are causing considerable damage.[164]

Rather than exposing themselves to legal risks, banks and other financial firms should not only adapt to the lessons to be drawn, not only from judicial decisions, but also from the forward-looking opinions of the Advocates General. More directly relevant information can readily be drawn from the various opinions and statements, published by the supervisory authorities. The statements published by the Supervisory Board of the ECB, but also by the ESAs and the national supervisors, reflect positions or sensitivities indicating the direction to which future decisions and developments might point in later formal decisions. This is especially the case for new subjects such as the green agenda and cryptocurrencies.

[160] These are the cases of Breach of Union law, Emergency matters, or Settlement of disagreements between competent authorities in cross-border situations, mentioned in Arts 17, 18 and 19.

[161] Art 60 EBA Regulation.

[162] In accordance with Art 263 TFEU.

[163] Referring here to the fines imposed for late or imperfect transposition of Directives.

[164] See the cases of *Wirecard* (S Beiter et al, 'Consequences of Wirecard Scandal: New requiremnets for corporate governance and audit for German Listed Companies' Gibson Dunn (7 June 2021)) and *Greensill* (E Nelson, J Ewing and L Alderman, 'The Swift Collapse of a Company Built on Debt' *New York Times* (28 March 2021)).

However, although non-binding, some of these statements carry a certain authority, as a warning or indicating a safer line of action. They may be seen as incentives for better market practices by market participants, or at least as a defence in case of later supervisory action.

2.10. The Impact of Market Practices on Regulatory Implementation

As well as financial regulation, several other factors determine the reaction of bank leaders to the outside world. The first relates to the messages the regulatory system conveys to the regulated world, projecting its views on future developments of the regulatory and supervisory system. The second consists of the messages the markets generate or receive with respect to the bank's activity. The reactions of the media, credit-rating agencies, social networks and the political world all play a role in modelling the banking system of the future. Technological innovations are among the most visible changes, backed up by complex innovations. In terms of implementation, several of these impulses lead to changes in the business model, to regulatory changes all leading to adaptations to the internal functioning of the banks. Changes in the relationship with clients – becoming increasingly virtual, leading to new communication methods; stricter safety measures; systems for payments or for the transmission of securities orders, resulting in more cross-border and worldwide business – have already had visible effects on the banks' physical infrastructure, location and employment policies. The impact on the bank's behaviour and organisation is undoubtedly significant and likely to become even more transformative. As was visible in the London markets, the need for physical meetings is triggering a debate on the usefulness of having extensive space for in-person meetings. Location policies may be the next on the agenda.

The enforcement drivers in these cases will be innovation and market pressure, ie the willingness of the investors to take advantage of new products and techniques, notwithstanding some negative information. Banking regulation and especially supervision, including recovery and resolution, may play a decisive role. The supervisory authorities will be critical factors in meeting the challenges of the new financial world.

2.11. Conclusion

The financial system, especially but not exclusively the banking system, is organised on the basis of a very elaborate scheme of regulation, aiming at maintaining the overall confidence in its correct functioning and its solvency. The function of the supervisors is also to build and maintain this confidence in individual financial institutions, but also generally in the financial economy as whole. The regulatory system – in both its macro and micro aspects – pursues this confidence objective by maintaining the financial stability of individual banks, and of the financial system as a whole. Due to the many changes in the financial system, these tasks are likely to become increasingly sophisticated, complex and demanding. The supervisory system will be confronted by new, often quite different challenges, with new varieties of addressees as a consequence of the increasing changeover to an increasingly virtual financial system. The present regulatory system will need to adapt decisively to this new world. Implementation of the new system should be the result of cooperative efforts between the financial system and the supervisory world, so that the technical and commercial outcomes satisfy the objectives of both parties. In this new environment, enforcement will remain a key supervisory tool, although part of it may become increasingly automated, as is already the case in some parts of the system.

The future will be challenging and demanding, but for those willing to fully engage, it will be really bright.

3

Some Thoughts on the *Ratio*, Creation and Enforcement of EU Financial Services Regulation in Private Law

KARL-PHILIPP WOJCIK

3.1. Introduction

By now it is understood that the European Union's (EU) response to the global financial crisis which started in 2007 led to a great expansion of the EU's *acquis* in the field of financial services regulation. Various financial areas which had not been regulated by the EU, such as the activities of credit rating agencies,[1] are now subject to EU financial services rules. Other areas of already existing EU financial services regulation have been quantitatively and qualitatively enhanced, often on the basis of global regulatory consensus, such as banking supervision[2] and market regulation.[3] At the same time, the institutional landscape of financial services supervision in the EU has dramatically changed. In some areas, the EU has been entrusted with direct supervisory powers over financial services actors.[4]

[1] Regulation (EC) No 1060/2009 of the European Parliament and of the Council of 16 September 2009 on credit rating agencies [2009] OJ L 302/1.

[2] See for instance Regulation (EU) No 575/2013 of the European Parliament and of the Council of 26 June 2013 on prudential requirements for credit institutions and investment firms and amending Regulation (EU) No 648/2012 [2013] OJ L 176/1 and Directive 2013/36/EU of the European Parliament and of the Council of 26 June 2013 on access to the activity of credit institutions and the prudential supervision of credit institutions and investment firms, amending Directive 2002/87/EC and repealing Directives 2006/48/EC and 2006/49/EC [2013] OJ L 176/338.

[3] See Directive 2014/65/EU of the European Parliament and of the Council of 15 May 2014 on markets in financial instruments and amending Directive 2002/92/EC and Directive 2011/61/EU (MiFiD II) [2014] OJ L 173/349 and Regulation (EU) No 600/2014 of the European Parliament and of the Council of 15 May 2014 on markets in financial instruments and amending Regulation (EU) No 648/2012 [2014] OJ L 173/84.

[4] The Banking Union with the ECB supervising credit institutions within the SSM and the SRB being in charge of their resolution in the SRM is a case in point. See C Zilioli and K-P Wojcik, 'European Banking Union: a giant step towards European integration and a challenge for judicial review', in C Zilioli and K-P Wojcik (eds), *Judicial Review in the European Banking Union* (Edward Elgar, 2021) 1.01 ff.

This expansion of the EU law *acquis* in the field of financial services has had a profound impact on the relationship between the EU-level and the national legal systems.[5] Whilst both systems are closely intertwined, the proliferation of one of these 'legs' necessarily leads to a recalibration between both levels towards a new equilibrium. This recalibration can be viewed as a dynamic process involving a multitude of legal aspects, to varying extents. In any case, the new relationship between EU law and national law, both in their institutional and substantive dimensions, merits a closer legal analysis.

In particular, this chapter intends to explore and assess that recalibration with a view on the interaction between EU financial services rules and private law as well as the enforcement of EU financial services law. That perspective adds another layer to an already complex relationship of vertical interaction between EU law and national legal systems since it needs to deal with the relationship between private and administrative law. While I understand private law as the body of law, irrespective of who its originators are, which regulates the horizontal level relationship between legal subjects, the way in which I understand administrative law in this context is determined by administrative law as the body of rules governing relationships which involve or are linked to the exercise of public powers, often (but not necessarily) including elements of subordination and hence verticality. Nevertheless, as we shall see, the lines between private and administrative law as described are not impermeable. On the contrary, particularly when looking from the angle of enforcement of financial services rules we can observe that they are often closely intertwined, sometimes mutually reinforcing or even dependent on each other.

3.2. The Creation of EU Financial Services Regulation and the Attempt to Categorise its Interaction with Private Law

Although it may not always be obvious, financial services regulation and private law are not separate realms of law, but closely connected – if not interdependent. In fact, financial services regulation understood as a system of at least partially binding, state-originated rules of an abstract and general nature often only becomes relevant after economic activities between private actors have become a 'rule-worthy' phenomenon. There exists a plethora of examples in this respect. I limit myself to mentioning banking and cryptocurrencies. Banking in the sense of taking deposits from the public and lending them out is an ancient economic activity, reflected in many private law rules which aim to facilitate such exchanges. Nevertheless, proper regulation in the modern sense of this fundamental financial service only became more prevalent around the turn of

[5] M Haentjens, 'Private law in Banking Union litigation', in C Zilioli and K-P Wojcik (eds), *Judicial Review in the European Banking Union* (Edward Elgar, 2021) 5.01.

the twentieth century.[6] Recently, the emergence of distributed ledger technology and its use for financial services transactions has led to new financial services regulation in reaction to this phenomenon. These examples illustrate the typical sequence of events: first there is a new economic activity (often due to the progress of science or technology or because of the emergence of new economic needs) between individuals based on private autonomy and private law relations, then more sophisticated (financial services) regulation is developed to harness this phenomenon.

3.2.1. Objectives of EU Financial Services Regulation

This sequence of events can be explained by the typical objectives of general and financial services regulation in particular.

One of the most fundamental functions of regulation is the limitation of the abuse of powers by private individuals and therefore the protection of the weaker party in an economic transaction. In financial services regulation this translates, for instance, into the protection of those who have less information ('information asymmetry'), those who are less acquainted with the workings of complex financial products, or those with fewer economic resources who require a specific service.

Another fundamental objective of financial services regulation, in particular, is the prevention of externalities. Certain economic activities may cause harm which is not borne by the parties to the transaction and which is therefore not taken into account by them, meaning the transaction is not properly priced. Financial stability is a case in point: while a certain transaction may make perfect sense for the private parties involved, from a public policy perspective it may endanger the working of the system as a whole.

Finally, financial services regulation does not only seek to limit private economic transactions; on the contrary, it intends to make the free exercise of these private transactions possible by creating a stable and secure legal framework (the 'enabling function'). A good example of this is the creation of the so called 'EU passport', allowing the cross-border exercise of certain regulated activities in the EU with only one (regulatory) licence. Without this legal framework in place, the cross-border exercise of certain economic freedoms would be much more difficult and sometimes even impossible.

3.2.2. Principles of EU Financial Services Regulation and its Creation

Before expanding on the typical categories in which EU financial services law impacts private law, it seems useful to briefly touch upon the EU's approach to financial services regulation and how it is created.

[6] The European Economic Community as a predecessor of the EU started regulating banking only in the 1970s.

The EU's regulatory activity in the field of financial services indeed follows closely the three fundamental goals described in paragraph 3.2.1. However, looking back to the beginnings of the EU's regulatory activity in this area, which began in earnest in the 1970s, one outstanding characteristic of the EU's regulatory approach to financial services is its emphasis on the 'enabling function' of its regulatory approach. The EU's financial services regulation serves in particular to create a European Financial Area as part of the internal market in which the fundamental freedoms – in particular the freedom to provide services, the freedom of establishment and the free movement of capital and payments – can be exercised without barriers. In this way, the EU pursues its various goals enshrined in Article 3 TEU, among which the economic and monetary union with the euro as its common currency, which has become increasingly important in the last decade.

In addition to the specificities of the regulatory goals pursued as summarised above, the EU legislator's approach when regulating financial services in the EU rests on three basic principles: (i) decentralised supervision of market participants by Member States authorities; (ii) mutual recognition of authorisations granted (more commonly known in the financial service sector as 'passporting'); and (iii) the use of EU directives as the preponderant legislative instrument to harmonise national laws.[7]

Nevertheless, as I have shown elsewhere, since the global financial crisis, these three principles have undergone an erosion in the field of EU financial services regulation.[8] The principle of decentralised supervision of market participants by Member States authorities is being replaced by centralised supervision by EU authorities. A case in point is the Banking Union with the conferral of specific tasks of banking supervision on the European Central Bank (ECB) (single supervisory mechanism; SSM) and of bank resolution tasks on the single resolution board (SRB) as part of the single resolution mechanism (SRM).[9] In parallel, there is a proliferation visible in the use of EU regulations instead of using EU directives. As a consequence of the conferral of specific tasks of banking supervision to the EU level, the EU passport is often no longer based on the principle of mutual recognition, but, where issued by an EU authority, on the principle of the EU-wide scope of that decision. This erosion of the fundamental regulatory principles in the area of financial services is beyond the scope of this chapter. I will simply refer to my other papers on this matter, where I argue that causes for this development are the perceived weakness of EU directives as legislative

[7] K-P Wojcik in H von der Groeben, J Schwarze and A Hatje (eds), *Europäisches Unionsrecht, Art. 63 TFEU* (CH Beck, 2015) para 88 ff.

[8] See, eg,Wojcik (ibid) para 88; K-P Wojcik and M Krauze, 'The use of EU regulations to establish qualitative requirements in the fields of banking supervision and resolution and their impact on civil law and corporate relationships' in BPM Joosen, M Lamandini and TH Tröger, *Capital and Liquidity Requirements for European Banks* (Oxford, OUP, forthcoming 2022).

[9] See also the recent proposal by the European Commission to establish a new Authority for Anti-Money Laundering and Countering the Financing of Terrorism (AMLA) in charge of applying and enforcing AML rules, COM(2021) 421 final.

instruments as well as the increased centralisation of supervisory powers with EU authorities.[10]

The point of this observation is that the erosion of these basic principles has important consequences when it comes to the interaction of EU financial services regulation with civil law and corporate relationships, both with regard to the applicable law as well as the enforcement of rights and questions of jurisdiction and procedure. One of them is that parties to relationships governed by civil or corporate law will not only have to respect and comply with their obligations stemming predominantly from national civil codes and national corporate law; they will also have to know and to comply with obligations stemming from EU law, in particular from decisions by EU authorities or from directly applicable EU regulations.

This increase in complexity for individuals as well as the compounding of possible interactions with national legal systems has been further exacerbated by a proliferation of different legal sources at EU level over the last 20 years. However, since the global financial crisis, the entry into force of the Lisbon Treaty and the creation of three supervisory authorities as part of a new European System of Financial Supervision (ESFS) following the so-called de Larosière Report of 25 February 2009[11] with the European Banking Authority (EBA) based in Paris, the European Supervisory Authority for Insurance and Company Pensions (EIOPA) based in Frankfurt and the European Securities and Markets Authority (ESMA) based in Paris, this proliferation has sped up considerably. This is also due to the legislative and non-legislative process specific to the EU financial services area. In fact, as of 2001 a special four-level process in accordance with the Lamfalussy Report[12] was applied in the EU financial services regulation field. With the entry of the Lisbon Treaty in 2009 a modified Lamfalussy II procedure applies: it consists of a 'Level 1' text adopted by Council or European Parliament according to the ordinary legislative procedure (Art 289 TFEU) containing at least the essential political decisions. Non-legislative acts in the form of Commission Delegated Acts (Art 290 TFEU) or Implementing Acts by Commission or Council (Art 291 TFEU) are considered 'Level 2' acts which build on the 'Level 1' texts. Some of these Delegated or Implementing Acts are prepared, within their specific field of competence, by one of the three ESAs according to specific rules laid down in their founding regulations and called Regulatory Technical Standards (RTS) or Implementing Technical Standards (ITS) respectively. The term 'Level 3 texts' commonly refers to a variety of regulatory acts by the ESAs or by other EU authorities in charge of direct supervisory powers (such as the ECB or the SRB). Among those Level 3 texts one may find recommendations, opinions, guidelines and other acts, all of which are binding to varying degrees.

[10] See for example K-P Wojcik, 'Bankenunion, Brexit und EU-Aufsicht über die Finanzmärkte' (22 January 2018) 5.

[11] See ec.europa.eu/internal_market/finances/docs/de_larosiere_report_de.pdf.

[12] The final report by the Committee of Wise Men establishing CESR, available at www.esma.europa.eu/sites/default/files/library/2015/11/lamfalussy_report.pdf.

The above illustrates the dynamic development of EU financial services regulation in recent years and its increasing complexity, which stems from an increased Europeanisation of financial services regulation and the proliferation of EU regulatory actors and EU legal sources in this field.

3.2.3. Ways in which EU Financial Services Regulation may Impact Private Law

Against the background described above, I will now categorise typical methods in which EU financial services regulation may impact private law. These categories cannot be considered to be exhaustive or complete, and further research is necessary to fully map out such influences. Nevertheless, I consider it feasible to identify the following categories.

3.2.3.1. Category 1

EU financial services regulation may directly harmonise national civil laws. In such a case, EU financial law impacts civil laws directly, either by effectively creating an EU body of civil law through the use of EU regulations or by imposing an obligation on Member States to create or adjust national civil laws according to the objectives set out in EU directives. For example, the Winding Up Directive 2001/24/EC harmonises in the EU the rules on the applicable law and on jurisdiction for reorganisation measures vis-à-vis credit institutions.[13] Other examples are the Financial Collateral[14] and the Settlement Finality Directives[15] which concern the consequences of insolvency on specific financial transactions or the provision of collateral. Article 109 BRRD[16] partially harmonises the hierarchy of claims against credit institutions. The Solvency II Directive[17] harmonises pre- and intra-contractual information requirements in case of insurance contracts and the remedies for breaches.

[13] Directive 2001/24/EC of the European Parliament and of the Council of 4 April 2001 on the reorganisation and winding up of credit institutions [2001] OJ L 125/15.

[14] Directive 2002/47/EC of the European Parliament and of the Council of 6 June 2002 on financial collateral arrangements [2002] OJ L 168/43.

[15] Directive 98/26/EC of the European Parliament and of the Council of 19 May 1998 on settlement finality in payment and securities settlement systems [1998] OJ L 166/45.

[16] Directive 2014/59/EU of the European Parliament and of the Council of 15 May 2014 establishing a framework for the recovery and resolution of credit institutions and investment firms and amending Council Directive 82/891/EEC, and Directives 2001/24/EC, 2002/47/EC, 2004/25/EC, 2005/56/EC, 2007/36/EC, 2011/35/EU, 2012/30/EU and 2013/36/EU, and Regulations (EU) No 1093/2010 and (EU) No 648/2012, of the European Parliament and of the Council [2014] OJ L 173/190.

[17] Directive 2009/138/EC of the European Parliament and of the Council of 25 November 2009 on the taking-up and pursuit of the business of Insurance and Reinsurance (Solvency II) [2009] OJ L 335/1.

As a sub-type within this category one can distinguish provisions of EU financial services regulation which grant individual (often compensation) rights to legal persons or individuals vis-à-vis other market participants (horizontally) or vis-à-vis the state and its emanations (vertically). One example for such – still rather rare – vertical compensation right can be found in Article 35a of the CRA Regulation, which is the legal basis for civil liability claims by investors and issuers against credit-rating agencies.[18] Another example is the compensation claim by investors against the Single Resolution Fund in case of a breach of the 'no creditor worse off' principle in Article 76 SRM Regulation.[19]

3.2.3.2. Category 2

EU financial services regulation may set a framework with which private parties need to comply in addition to national civil laws when carrying out private law transactions. Examples of cases falling into this category are abundant. One can think about minimum initial capital requirements for financial institutions: if national corporate laws require less than the minimum initial capital requirement of €5 million mandatory for being granted a banking licence (see Article 12 CRD IV), then – indirectly – the need for a banking licence will transform the national corporate law requirement into the higher one set by EU banking supervision law. Other examples are the 'fit and proper' requirements for bank directors, which effectively limit the free choice by shareholders of the persons managing their undertaking,[20] or dividend payout restrictions.

I would also consider rules on capital requirements or on minimum requirement for eligible liabilities (MREL) and own funds as part of this category. In order to comply with prudential ratios, financial institutions may need to model certain financial instruments in a way that these meet the capital eligibility criteria. The impact of such rules not only stems from the substance, but also from the direct applicability and horizontal effects of EU regulations by virtue of Article 288 TFEU.[21]

[18] The Commission has recently proposed similar rules regarding the liability of issuers of crypto-assets, of asset-referenced tokens and of e-money tokens: see for instance Arts 14, 22 and 47 of the proposed Regulation of the European Parliament and of the Council on Markets in Crypto-assets, and amending Directive (EU) 2019/1937, COM/2020/593 final.

[19] Regulation (EU) No 806/2014 of the European Parliament and of the Council of 15 July 2014 establishing uniform rules and a uniform procedure for the resolution of credit institutions and certain investment firms in the framework of a Single Resolution Mechanism and a Single Resolution Fund and amending Regulation (EU) No 1093/2010 [2014] OJ L 225/1.

[20] Art 91 CRD IV.

[21] For a detailed analysis of the direct and horizontal effects of EU regulations on civil and corporate law see K-P Wojcik and M Krauze, 'The use of EU regulations to establish qualitative requirements in the fields of banking supervision and resolution and their impact on civil law and corporate relationships' in BPM Joosen, M Lamandini and TH Tröger, *Capital and Liquidity Requirements for European Banks* (OUP, forthcoming 2022).

3.2.3.3. *Category 3*

A third category of possible impacts by EU financial services law on private and corporate law relationships concerns outright interventions by the law or by supervisory authorities into private law governed relationships or rights. Such interventions can take the form of self-executive prohibitions of certain financial services activities or the empowerment of supervisory authorities to issue such prohibitions. Examples of these situations can be found in Arts 12–14 of the Short Selling Regulation.[22] These provisions prohibit individuals to enter into certain types of uncovered short sales outside the stringent conditions set out therein. Another example can be found in MiFiR Articles 40 and 42, which grant ESMA and national competent authorities powers to temporarily restrict or prohibit the marketing, distribution or sale of certain financial products.[23] Interventions can also take the form of transforming legal positions governed by private law. A good example is the far reaching bail-in powers of the SRB and the national resolution authorities by which shares and liabilities can be cancelled, written down or converted.[24]

3.3. Enforcement

Against the background of these categorisations and considerations, I will now turn to the question of enforcement of EU financial services rules related to private law matters. I will show that there is a rather complete and intertwined system of ensuring the respect and application of EU financial services rules.

From the outset, I will highlight a distinction between two methods of enforcement. The first – and more traditional, and thus more common – method of enforcement consists of ensuring compliance with financial services rules in vertical relations or relations of subordination. I will discuss this first. The second, which is linked to the private law nature of various EU financial services rules, consists of ensuring compliance in relations of horizontal nature. I will discuss this mode of 'private enforcement' in paragraph 3.4.3.

3.3.1. Enforcement of EU Financial Services Rules through Administrative Authorities

It is commonplace that the administrative enforcement of EU financial services regulation is a fundamental task carried out by national authorities or by European

[22] Regulation (EU) No 236/2012 of the European Parliament and of the Council of 14 March 2012 on short selling and certain aspects of credit default swaps [2012] OJ L 86/1.

[23] See regarding specific interventions, such as Contracts for Difference, www.esma.europa.eu/policy-activities/mifid-ii-and-investor-protection/product-intervention.

[24] Art 27 SRM Regulation.

bodies, such as the ECB, SRB or ESMA. By the term 'administrative enforcement' I understand the actions of public authorities to ensure compliance with the applicable financial services law by those persons or entities which are subject to these laws. This is the classic enforcement situation in the vertical model. Supervisors will have a diverse toolbox of various administrative measures at hand to ensure compliance with the rulebook.

To take an example from the field of banking supervision: Article 64 onwards of the CRD IV explicitly set out that banking supervisors need to be endowed with 'all supervisory powers to intervene in the activity of institutions … that are necessary for the exercise of their functions'. This includes, without prejudice to criminal sanctions, the power to impose administrative penalties and other administrative measures for the breach of financial services law requirements. Likewise, demonstrating my broad concept of vertical enforcement, in many cases authorisations or licences are required before a regulated activity can be taken up or before the financial entity may take certain measures (such as dividend payouts).

Returning to the categories of interactions between EU financial services regulation and national private law as developed in paragraph 3.2, I would emphasise the importance of administrative acts taken in the form of 'authorisations' for the second category. The need to apply for an authorisation is *the* way by which, for instance, minimum initial capital requirements for financial institutions which go beyond the minimum requirement set by national corporate law will be enforced.

It is obvious that administrative decisions are the principal avenue by which supervisory authorities interfere with private law-governed relationships or rights, which forms the third category of possible impacts by EU financial services law on private and corporate law relationships. As previously stated, an example of this type of interference can be seen in product-marketing prohibitions and short-selling bans by ESMA or national authorities. However, these examples illustrate the limits of the traditional enforcement model at the edge of public and private law.

As an example of a short selling ban is the one ordered by the German financial supervisor (BaFin) on 18 February 2019.[25] It was based on Article 20 of the Short Selling Regulation and it prohibited temporarily 'establishing a net short position as well as increasing an existing net short position with reference to the shares of … Wirecard AG (DE0007472060)'. I am not entering into the thorny and politically much-debated questions regarding the legality or the expediency of that short-selling ban. I would rather highlight the controversy in German legal doctrine as regards the civil law effect of that short-selling ban. Some authors argue that under German law, an administrative act of public law such as the short-selling ban would *ipso iure* trigger the nullity of any short-selling contract or consider the short-selling ban as a legal obstacle to performance of the contract (which could

[25] See www.bafin.de/SharedDocs/Veroeffentlichungen/EN/Aufsichtsrecht/Verfuegung/vf_190218_leerverkaufsmassnahme_en.html.

lead to the payment of damages).[26] Others deny such an immediate impact on the contract.[27] This example illustrates that in situations in which the administrative authority employs the classic enforcement model when interfering into private law governed relationships – ie issues administrative decisions ordering or prohibiting a specific behaviour – the effects of a public law act on the civil law positions is not immediately certain and that, in order to give full effect to the administrative law measure, public and civil law need to coordinate.

3.3.2. Enforcement of EU Financial Services Rules in the Vertical Relationship between the EU and Member States

In paragraph 3.3.2 I described the most common form of enforcement of EU financial services regulation. It takes place in a relationship of subordination between public authorities and individual persons or entities subject to EU financial services rules.

Another type of enforcement takes place in the relationship between the EU and Member States. It is linked to the former type of enforcement in that it forms part of the 'vertical mode' of enforcement described in paragraph 3.3. Its main objective, though, is to tackle, in the relationship between the EU and Member States, the absence of national financial services rules to be enforced and the wrong transposition or the wrong enforcement of EU financial services rules in the national legal order.

The case of absence or wrong enforcement of EU financial services regulation by national authorities is, in real terms, rare, and negligible for our purpose. Suffice to say that any such absence or wrong enforcement of EU financial services rules by national authorities can be considered a failure of the respective Member State to fulfil an EU law obligation. In such a situation, the Commission (or exceptionally another Member State)[28] can launch an infringement procedure (Article 258 TFEU) which would result in a final judgment by the Court of Justice to be complied with by the Member State. A specific feature for EU financial services regulation is the power of the European Supervisory Authorities (ie EBA, ESMA and EIOPA) to initiate specific 'breach of Union law' procedures in case a national authority has not applied EU financial services acts or where it has applied them wrongly.[29]

[26] D Zetzsche and M Lehmann, '§ 53 WpHG Überwachung von Leerverkäufen; Verordnungsermächtigung' in E Schwark and D Zimmer, *Kapitalmarktrechts-Kommentar* (CH Beck, 2020) para 29.

[27] F Schäfer, '§ 21 Leerverkäufe und Geschäfte in bestimmten Kreditderivaten' in H-D Assmann, RA Schütze and P Buck-Heeb, *Handbuch des Kapitalanlagerechts* (CH Beck, 2020) para 23.

[28] See Art 259 TFEU.

[29] Art 17 of the ESA Regulations. See also the recent judgment by the ECJ in Case C-501/18, *BT v Bulgarska Narodna Banka*, ECLI:EU:C:2021:249, on the validity of an EBA recommendation in the context of 'breach of Union law' procedures under Art 17 EBA Regulation.

Much more common – unfortunately – are cases in which EU directives containing EU financial services provisions have not or have not accurately been transposed into national law, despite a Member State's obligation to do so (Article 288 TFEU). This situation is problematic in various aspects. For cross-border business providers a lack of transposition of EU directives on financial services creates legal uncertainty because of lack of uniformity and can hence impede the functioning of the internal market for financial services. From an enforcement perspective, the lack of transposition simply leads to a lack of national financial services rules which could be enforced by national supervisory authorities; wrong transposition allows, by way of contrast, for enforcement, albeit in a way that deviates from what the European legislator has agreed.

To tackle these deficiencies, the EU Treaty grants the Commission the power to initiate infringement proceedings against the relevant Member State, according to Article 258 TFEU. Apart from condemning a Member State to transpose the relevant EU directive, the Court of Justice has, in addition, in a series of very recent judgments which also include EU financial services rules, condemned a number of Member States not only to transpose the relevant EU directives, but also to pay a lump sum under Article 260(3) TFEU.[30] In this way, the Court of Justice increases the pressure on Member States to behave in a Treaty-compliant manner.

One example in which infringement proceedings were necessary in order to force a Member State to transpose a piece of EU financial services law of crucial importance for private law relationships is the 2021 judgment by the Court of Justice in C-628/18 *Commission v Slovenia*. This infringement case is in itself an enforcement action by the EU against a Member State and it serves to create rules at national level which can then be enforced by the national supervisory authorities vis-à-vis individuals or businesses.

3.3.3. Enforcement of EU Financial Services Rules in Horizontal Relationships between Private Parties

Finally, I will discuss enforcement of EU financial services rules in horizontal relationships, ie between private individuals or legal persons.

At first sight, 'private enforcement' or enforcement in private law-governed horizontal relationships seem to be an oxymoron. In fact, private law disputes are characterised by horizontal relationsh when one party, on the basis of a private right, requests another party to do something (by either acting or making a payment), to abstain from doing something or to tolerate the action or inaction of the requesting party. However, upon closer inspection EU law does not take issue with the way in which EU regulation is enforced as long as – to use simple

[30] Case C-543/17 *Commission v Belgium*, ECLI:EU:C:2019:573; Case C-549/18 *Commission* v *Romania (Anti-money laundering)*, ECLI:EU:C:2020:563; C-550/18 *Commission* v *Ireland (Anti-money laundering)*, ECLI:EU:C:2020:564.

terms – the effect of EU regulation is ensured. From the perspective of EU law 'private enforcement' is not to be regarded as an oxymoron but, together with public enforcement, rather as the flipside of the same coin. The 'neutrality' of EU law in this respect is nowadays clearly enshrined in a number of principles consolidated by ECJ case law.

In this respect, the ECJ developed early on in its existence the 'principle of procedural autonomy' according to which, and in the absence of Union law on the subject, it is up to the domestic legal order of each Member State to designate the courts having jurisdiction and to lay down the detailed rules governing legal proceedings designed to safeguard the rights which individuals derive from Union law.[31] The principle of procedural autonomy is grounded in the principle of sincere cooperation as laid down in Article 4(3) TEU. It can be traced back also to the right to an effective judicial protection as enshrined in Article 47 of the EU Charter of Fundamental Rights. Member States' autonomy is, however, tempered by the principles of equivalence and of effectiveness. These 'twin principles' require that the conditions laid down by the national laws to that effect are not less favourable than those applicable to similar proceedings based on a breach of national law (principle of equivalence) and are not so adjusted as to make it impossible or excessively difficult in practice to obtain reparation (principle of effectiveness).[32]

Where does this take us in respect of horizontal enforcement of EU financial services law?

My first example concerns the breach of pre-contractual information requirements and the consumer's right to cancel his/her insurance contract within a stipulated period of time from the moment when he/she was informed that the contract had been concluded. That cancellation right was laid down in Article 15 of the Second Life Assurance Directive[33] and has been interpreted by the Court of Justice in case C-209/12 *Walter Endress*.[34] The private law dispute at the origin of the preliminary reference concerned Mr Endress and the insurer Allianz. In 1998, Mr Endress had concluded a life assurance contract with Allianz. In 2007, almost 10 years later, Mr Endress gave notice to Allianz of the termination of the

[31] Case C-33/76 *Rewe*, ECLI:EU:C:1976:188, [5].

[32] Case C-501/18 *BT v Bulgarska Narodna Banka*, ECLI:EU:C:2021:249, [116].

[33] Council Directive 90/619/EEC of 8 November 1990 on the coordination of laws, regulations and administrative provisions relating to direct life assurance, laying down provisions to facilitate the effective exercise of freedom to provide services and amending Directive 79/267/EEC [1990] OJ L 330/50, as amended by Council Directive 92/96/EEC of 10 November 1992 on the coordination of laws, regulations and administrative provisions relating to direct life assurance and amending Directives 79/267/EEC and 90/619/EEC (third life assurance directive) [1992] OJ L 360/1), read in conjunction with Art 31(1) of the third life assurance directive. The second and third life assurance directives were repealed and replaced by Directive 2002/83/EC of the European Parliament and of the Council of 5 November 2002 concerning life assurance [2002] OJ L 345/1, which was then itself repealed and replaced, with effect from 1 November 2012, by Directive 2009/138/EC of the European Parliament and of the Council of 25 November 2009 on the taking-up and pursuit of the business of Insurance and Reinsurance (Solvency II) [2009] OJ L 335/1).

[34] Case C-209/12 *Endress*, ECLI:EU:C:2013:864. The ECJ recently ruled on a number of follow-up cases in joined Cases C-355/18 to C-357/18 and C-479/18 *Rust-Hackner and Others*, ECLI:EU:C:2019:1123.

contract, claiming back the amount of his annual premia already paid (which was higher than the repurchase value of the life assurance contract). Civil courts in Germany handled this issue as a classic civil law dispute. Allianz objected to Mr Endress's action on the basis of the German law transposing Article 15 of the Second Life Assurance. That law stipulated that the policyholder's right to cancel expired one year after payment of the first premium, irrespective of whether pre-contractual information had been granted to the prospective policyholder. The Court of Justice in its preliminary ruling declared that a rule under which a right of cancellation lapses one year at the latest after payment of the first premium, where the policyholder has not been informed about the right of cancellation, as incompatible with the Second Life Assurance Directive. The civil law dispute had exposed Germany's incorrect transposition of an essential element of EU financial services regulation, ie the harmonisation of contractual cancellation rights for the conclusion of life assurance contracts.

In the face of such a legal situation, EU law provides for three possible avenues to nevertheless enforce rights stemming from EU (financial services) law in civil law disputes. The first remedy is the obligation incumbent on national authorities and national judges to interpret the whole body of domestic law, as far as possible, in the light of the wording and the purpose of the relevant directive in order to achieve the result sought by the directive and consequently to comply with Article 288 TFEU. That obligation to interpret national law in a manner consistent with EU law is inherent in the system of the TFEU, since it permits national courts, for matters within their jurisdiction, to ensure the full effectiveness of EU law when determining the disputes before them.[35] However, the principle of interpreting national law in conformity with EU law has certain limits. Thus, the obligation for a national court to refer to EU law when interpreting and applying the relevant rules of domestic law is limited by general principles of law and cannot serve as the basis for an interpretation of national law *contra legem*.[36]

Where the principle of interpreting national law in conformity with EU law cannot remedy the lack of correct transposition of the EU Directive, the individual may directly invoke the provision of a directive where that provision is unconditional and sufficiently precise.[37] However, there is a complication in disputes between opposing two private parties, because, in accordance with the Court's settled case law, a directive, even if sufficiently clear, precise and unconditional, cannot of itself impose obligations on an individual and cannot therefore be relied upon as such against an individual.[38] Accordingly, even a clear, precise

[35] See, inter alia, joined Cases C-397/01 to C-403/01, *Pfeiffer and Others*, ECLI:EU:C:2004:584, [114]; Case C-306/12 *Welter*, ECLI:EU:C:2013:650, [29].

[36] See judgments in Case C-268/06 *Impact*, ECLI:EU:C:2008:223, [100]; Case C-282/10 *Dominguez*, ECLI:EU:C:2012:33, para 25; and Case C-176/12 *Association de médiation sociale*, ECLI:EU:C:2013:491, [39].

[37] Case C-122/15 *Smith*, ECLI:EU:C:2016:391, [56].

[38] Case C-152/84, *Marshall*, ECLI:EU:C:1986:84, [48]; Case C-91/92 *Faccini Dori*, ECLI:EU:C:1994:292, [20]; Cases C-397/01 to C-403/01 *Pfeiffer and Others*, ECLI:EU:C:2004:584, [108]; Case C-441/14 *DI*, ECLI:EU:C:2016:278, [30].

and unconditional provision of a directive seeking to confer rights on or impose obligations on individuals cannot of itself apply in a dispute exclusively between private persons.[39]

As a consequence, the third remedy available to the private party adversely affected by the incompatibility of national law with EU law is the possibility to request compensation from the Member State for any loss sustained. That party would hence have to rely on the case law stemming from the judgment of 19 November 1991, *Francovich and Others*.[40] According to this case, individuals who have suffered damage have a right to compensation if three conditions are met, namely (i) that the rule of Union law infringed is intended to confer rights on them; (ii) that the infringement of that rule is sufficiently serious; and (iii) that there is a direct causal link between that infringement and the damage suffered by those individuals.[41]

Coming back to the civil dispute between Mr Endress and Allianz which gave rise to the ECJ's preliminary ruling in case C-209/12, the German Bundesgerichtshof was able to interpret the national law in a manner consistent with the requirements stemming from Article 15 of the Second Life Assurance Directive and ruled that Mr Endress was entitled by law to exercise a right of cancellation allowing him to claim in principle the full amount of premia paid.[42] We can conclude that, on the basis of principles developed by the European case law, Mr Endress was in a position to enforce EU financial services law in his contractual dispute against the insurance company.

I highligh the example of Mr Endress because the litigation initiated by him illustrates the 'traditional' and still prevailing way in which private individuals can contribute to enforcement of EU financial services rules.

I will now turn to a more recent phenomenon of private enforcement. We can observe that sometimes EU financial services regulation itself grants individuals an explicit legal right to request compensation from other individuals or legal persons. One such example is Article 35a of the CRA Regulation, according to which an investor or issuer may claim damages from a credit-rating agency where that agency has committed, intentionally or with gross negligence, an infringement listed in Annex III to the CRA Regulation, and where the damage was caused due to that infringement.[43] I have described this type of rule as a subtype of 'Category 1' provision above. If we look at the infringements listed in Annex III to the CRA Regulation and which are the one of the *fait générateurs* for the civil liability, we note that these infringements relate to regulatory requirements which

[39] Case C-122/15 *Smith*, ECLI:EU:C:2016:391, [43].

[40] Joined Cases C-6/90 and C-9/90 *Franchovic and Others*, ECLI:EU:C:1991:428.

[41] Case C-501/18, *BT v Bulgarska Narodna Banka*, ECLI:EU:C:2021:249, [113]; Case C-571/16 *Kantarev*, ECLI:EU:C:2018:807, [92], [94].

[42] Bundesgerichtshof, judgment of 7 May 2014, case IV ZR 76/11, available at juris.bundesgerichtshof.de/cgi-bin/rechtsprechung/document.py?Gericht=bgh&Art=en&nr=67786&pos=0&anz=1.

[43] See for a detailed analysis of Art 35a CRA: K-P Wojcik, 'Zivilrechtliche Haftung von Ratingagenturen nach europäischem Recht' (2013) *Juristische Wochenschrift* 2385 ff.

will normally be supervised and enforced by ESMA as the supervisory authority for credit-rating agencies. By basing the compensation claim directly on the compliance with these purely regulatory requirements – such as avoidance of conflicts of interest, disclosure requirements, etc – incumbent on the credit-rating agency, the EU legislator has created a dual track regarding public enforcement and private enforcement, effectively increasing the pressure on credit-rating agencies to comply with the regulatory requirements. The private plaintiff in such proceedings does not only pursue their own financial compensation interest, but also acts in the public interest.

In my view, Article 35a CRA Regulation can be read as an analogous application of the Court of Justice's case law which was developed in the area of competition law in *Courage*[44] and *Manfredi*.[45] In these cases, the Court of Justice held that any individual can claim compensation for the harm suffered where there is a causal relationship between that harm and an agreement or practice prohibited under Article 101 TFEU.[46] The *ratio* of these judgments can be found in Article 35a CRA Regulation, since one could also argue that the full effectiveness of the various regulatory requirements would be at risk if it were not open to an individual to claim damages for loss caused to him/her by an infringement of these regulatory requirements by the credit-rating agency.

Notably, Article 35a CRA Regulation presents one of the few cases in which EU law itself provides for the civil liability claim.[47] Normally, it will be in line with the aforementioned principle of procedural autonomy, for the domestic legal system of each Member State to designate the courts and tribunals having jurisdiction and to lay down the detailed procedural rules governing actions for safeguarding rights which individuals derive directly from Union law, provided that such rules are not less favourable than those governing similar domestic actions (principle of equivalence) and that they do not render practically impossible or excessively difficult the exercise of rights conferred by Union law (principle of effectiveness).[48]

Taking the Court's case law on private enforcement seriously, I would tend to think that infringements by financial entities against provisions of the *acquis* of EU financial services law which has so much increased in quantity and detail in recent years should be able to form the basis for civil liability claims against those individuals or entities who are obliged to comply with EU financial services regulation. We could, for instance, imagine compensation claims by a bank against its

[44] Case C-453/99 *Courage*, ECLI:EU:C:2001:465.

[45] Joined Cases C-295/04 to C-298/04 *Manfredi*, ECLI:EU:C:2006:461.

[46] Case C-453/99, *Courage*, ECLI:EU:C:2001:465, [26]; Joined Cases C-295/04 to C-298/04 *Manfredi*, ECLI:EU:C:2006:461, [60] ff.

[47] M Haentjens, 'Private Law in Banking Union Litigation' in C Zilioli and K-P Wojcik (eds), *Judicial Review in the European Banking Union* (Edward Elgar Publishing, 2021) para 5.11, calls it an 'extreme example'. However, it is to be noted that the Commission has recently proposed similar rules regarding the liability of issuers of crypto-assets, of asset-referenced tokens and of e-money tokens; see for instance Arts 14, 22 and 47 of the proposed Regulation of the European Parliament and of the Council on Markets in Crypto-assets, and amending Directive (EU) 2019/1937, COM/2020/593 final.

[48] Joined Cases C-295/04 to C-298/04 *Manfredi*, ECLI:EU:C:2006:461, [62].

directors for damages incurred (eg pecuniary penalties) due to the directors not having complied with corporate governance requirements under EU or national financial services law. Obviously, such situation will need to be examined carefully on a case-by-case basis, in particular with regard to causality between damage and regulatory infringement. In addition, the domestic rules governing actions for safeguarding rights, which individuals derive directly from Union law, will not be uniform from country to country. Nevertheless and despite all the practical difficulties, private enforcement of EU financial services rules through compensation claims between private individuals is here to stay.

3.4. Conclusion

The proliferation of EU financial services law as a result of the global financial crisis has led to a need of recalibration between the EU level and domestic legal systems. In particular, this chapter finds that EU financial services rules and domestic private law interact in more and new ways and offers an attempt of categorisation. The proliferation of EU financial services law puts the enforcement of that extended body of law in the limelight. The analysis shows that enforcement of EU financial services law in its vertical dimension can rely on an established and proven system of principles developed and refined in many other EU policy areas. A new and growing part of the picture will be filled, however, by private enforcement remedies. On the one hand, EU law itself provides for new (but overall rare) provisions in this respect; on the other hand, it can be expected that general principles of EU law will lead to an increase in private enforcement as a complementary element to ensure regulatory compliance in a dual-track mode.

4

Enforcement of Qualitative Capital Requirements for Banks

BART JOOSEN

4.1. Introduction

In this chapter, I build on the views set out by Karl-Philipp Wojcik in chapter three with a focus on the so-called qualitative capital requirements for EU credit institutions (hereinafter: banks) as ensuing from European Regulation (EU) No 575/2013 (CRR).[1] In his chapter, Wojcik draws attention to the influence of (European) financial law on private law relationships, and addresses, among other things, the enforcement of EU financial services rules in horizontal relationships between private parties. In order to ensure the effect of European law, he argues that horizontal relationships between two private parties can also be affected, for example because terms agreed between the parties are set aside if and when they are incompatible with provisions of European financial law. The very appealing example he gave of the European Court of Justice's (ECJ) ruling on *Endress*[2] shows how, in a civil dispute between two private parties, enforcement of European law can lead to the far reaching consequence that agreed contract terms (even if they

[1] Regulation (EU) 575/2013 of the European Parliament and of the Council of 26 June 2013 on prudential requirements for credit institutions and investment firms and amending Regulation (EU) 648/2012 [2013] OJ *EU* L 176/1 as amended by Commission Delegated Regulation (EU) 2015/62 of 10 October 2014 [2015] OJ *EU* L 11/37; Regulation (EU) 2016/1014 of the European Parliament and of the Council of 8 June 2016 [2016] OJ *EU* L 171/153; Commission Delegated Regulation (EU) 2017/2188 of 11 August 2017 [2017] OJ *EU* L 310/1; Regulation (EU) 2017/2395 of the European Parliament and of the Council of 12 December 2017 [2017] OJ *EU* L 345/27; Regulation (EU) 2017/2401 of the European Parliament and of the Council of 12 December 2017 [2017] OJ *EU* L 347/1; Commission Delegated Regulation (EU) 2018/405 of 21 November 2017 [2017] OJ *EU* L 74/3; Regulation (EU) 2019/630 of the European Parliament and of the Council of 17 April 2019 [2019] OJ *EU* L 111/4; Regulation (EU) 2019/876 of the European Parliament and of the Council of 20 May 2019 [2019] OJ *EU* L 150/1; Regulation (EU) 2019/2033 of the European Parliament and of the Council of 27 November 2019 [2019] OJ *EU* L 314/1; Regulation (EU) 2020/873 of the European Parliament and of the Council of 24 June 2020 [2020] OJ *EU* L 204/4; Regulation (EU) 2021/558 of the European Parliament and of the Council of 31 March 2021 [2021] OJ *EU* L 116/25; and Commission Implementing Regulation (EU) 2021/1043 of 24 June 2021 [2021] OJ *EU* L 225/52.

[2] Case C-209/12 *Walter Endress v Allianz Lebensversicherungs AG*, ECLI:EU:C:2013:864.

were compatible with the applicable national public law provisions), must be applied in a different way, or even disregarded altogether when they conflict with the applicable European directive provisions.

In his contribution, Eddy Wymeersch raises attention to the manner of enforcing the rules of European financial law and elaborates on the traditional enforcement tools, such as the imposing of administrative sanctions, the issue of public warnings and the withdrawal of the authorisation of banks altogether. In my view another instrument must be added to the toolkit for supervisors aiming at enforcing the applicable rules for financial institutions. This concerns cases where the competent authorities are more likely to apply informal tools, by alerting supervised companies to their compliance obligations without applying formal enforcement. In such a course of affairs parties come to a discussion (whether or not in a coercive atmosphere) about the perceived shortcomings, or a possible future development with regard to correct compliance with applicable regulations. This can also take place in the context of the (numerous) procedures that banks have to follow in order to obtain prior approval from the competent authorities to initiate a particular transaction, activity or process. In this chapter, I will examine a number of those (approval) procedures in the context of qualitative capital requirements. Although no fundamental, empirical research has been conducted into this topic, such enforcement can be a very effective way to encourage financial companies to comply with the rules, and concrete and effective results can be achieved.

In this chapter I will reflect on the qualitative capital requirements for banks, ie the rules arising from the European CRR regulation and the important Delegated Regulation Own Funds (also referred to as: RTS on Own Funds).[3] Here I intend to examine the way in which the relevant rules of qualitative capital requirements in fact influence the private law relationship between the bank and its financiers. The way in which these rules are applied will also be examined, often on the basis of a system of informal and discrete influence by the competent supervisory authorities, and by its very nature this could also lead to the harmonisation of those private law relationships between other banks in the EU and their financiers.

'Quantitative capital requirements' concern the amount of regulatory capital to be held, for example to meet applicable ratios (eg in Article 92 (1)CRR, eight per cent of own funds are to be held). But the concept of qualitative capital requirements may require further explanation. The relevant rules refer to the criteria that the corporate law or contractual relationship between a bank issuing capital instruments and the buyer and holder of those capital instruments must satisfy.

[3] Commission Delegated Regulation (EU) 241/2014 of 7 January 2014 supplementing Regulation (EU) 575/2013 of the European Parliament and of the Council with regard to regulatory technical standards for Own Funds requirements for institutions [2014] OJ *EU* L 74/8 as amended by Commission Delegated Regulation (EU) 2015/488 of 4 September 2014 [2015] OJ *EU* L 78/1; Commission Delegated Regulation (EU) 2015/850 of 30 January 2015 [2015] OJ *EU* L 135/1; Commission Delegated Regulation (EU) 2015/923 of 11 March 2015, [2015] OJ *EU* L 150/1; and Commission Delegated Regulation (EU) 2020/2176 of 12 November 2020 [2020] OJ *EU* L 433/27.

For example, one such criterion is that a buyer of a capital instrument must ensure that it is fully paid up so that the bank can make immediate and unrestricted use of the capital so obtained. The 'quality' of regulatory capital increases as a result of the application of that criterion, because it ensures that a bank can actually count on the availability of the capital, and does not, for example, have to first turn to the shareholder or (other type of) financier to request payment, whereas a bank may require having the capital at its disposal immediately when the need arises. If the terms of a capital instrument permit its purchaser to pay up later, it will not be able to meet the qualitative capital requirements.

4.2. Horizontal Effect of European Regulations

In 2015,[4] I mapped out the new qualitative requirements for the regulatory capital of banks, as they arise from the rules of CRR, in particular from Article 26 ff CRR for the so-called Common Equity Tier 1 instruments (CET1), Article 51 ff CRR for Additional Tier 1 capital instruments (AT1) and Article 61 ff CRR for Tier 2 capital instruments. In that contribution I sought to answer whether the use of a European regulation for the relevant requirements has a direct effect on the contractual and corporate law rules that apply between the bank and its financiers such as that may arise, for example, from the companies' articles of association. For example, to what extent would a clause in the terms and conditions of a CET1 instrument, in which shareholders are entitled to a preferential distribution, be invalid because it violates the provisions of Article 26(1)(h)(i) CRR?

If that direct application and direct binding effect were indeed to arise from the relevant rules, then virtual statutory European contract law or European company law would have been created, which in my opinion would be too far-reaching a consequence to be linked to this legal construction. But it is evident that with the introduction of the qualitative capital requirements, in addition to other arrangements for capital adequacy supervision at the level of a European regulation, the European legislator has had a strong desire to develop a uniform set of rules that applies equally within the EU and should be enforced in a uniform way.

This idea is also implied in the recent addition of the rules for the so-called definition of 'eligible liabilities' in Article 72a ff CRR.[5] To define what is an eligible

[4] BPM Joosen, 'Regulatory capital requirements and bail in mechanisms' in M Haentjens and B Wessels, *Research Handbook on Crisis Management in the Banking Sector* (Edward Elgar Publishing, 2015) 175–235.

[5] Introduced as a result of the implementation of the so-called Banking Package, in this particular case the provisions are introduced with the adoption of Regulation (EU) 2019/876 of the European Parliament and of the Council of 20 May 2019 amending Regulation (EU) 575/2013 as regards the leverage ratio, the net stable funding ratio, requirements for own funds and eligible liabilities, counterparty credit risk, market risk, exposures to central counterparties, exposures to collective investment undertakings, large exposures, reporting and disclosure requirements, and Regulation (EU) 648/2012 (CRR2).

liability in the context of the minimum own funds requirements and eligible liabilities (MREL), the regulations of Article 72a ff CRR apply to all banks within the EU. The important consequences of this choice by the legislator must not be underestimated. By including the definition of eligible liabilities in the CRR, the European legislator shows a very explicit ambition to influence the legal relationships based mainly on civil law across the Member States of the EU.

This influence relates in particular to the complex issue of creditor ranking in a possible insolvency situation, and the extent to which a bail-in applied by the resolution authority affects certain debt obligations of the bank. Article 72a ff CRR provide important rules for this, which should, among other things, promote that certain creditors in the EU are exempted from bail-in in a uniform manner; in other words, the CRR rules in question will protect categories of creditors. This is where the European legislator draws boundaries when it comes to enforcing rules that apply to banks.

It will be clear that for all creditors not specified in the lists of these provisions that define the eligibility of liabilities for a bail-in, there is a strong influence under their 'civil law' position. A creditor of a bank, who is not exempt from the definition of eligible liability, and may thus be subjected to the bail-in measure taken by the resolution authority, may face the consequence that its claim either be converted into an own fund instrument[6] or that its claim be written off. Such a creditor will have to endure the influence on its civil law relationship, including its property right(s), with the bank. It will only be able to rely on the legal remedies provided for in the relevant legal provisions, which are limited by their nature to a possible action for compensation. The intervention in the property right has then already taken place, and an *ex post* assessment is made to determine whether the intervention in its property right (which is based on a rule of public law) was justified.

In my opinion, there is an obvious influence on the horizontal civil law relationships between the bank and its financiers through the qualitative capital requirements and the regulations regarding the definition of eligible liabilities. The legislator intends that these civil law relationships are shaped in a certain way to ensure that banks, while drafting the contractual conditions and applying corporate law provisions, regulate those relationships in such a way that the bank complies with its public law compliance obligations. If the bank does not comply, it is in violation of those rules, and enforcement action can be taken. How this enforcement takes place is discussed later in this chapter.

[6] Throughout this chapter I will refer to the expressions 'own funds' and 'own funds instruments' as defined in CRR. 'Own funds' means in accordance with Art 4(1)(118) CRR, 'the sum of Tier 1 capital and Tier 2 capital'. And in accordance with Art 4(1)(119), CRR 'own funds instruments' means 'capital instruments issued by the institution that qualify as Common Equity Tier 1, Additional Tier 1 or Tier 2 instruments'. In common parlance, the 'regulatory capital' of a bank refers to the 'own funds' within the meaning of CRR.

4.3. *Ex Ante* Vetting of Conformity of CET1 Instruments with the CRR Rules

The legal relationship between a bank's financiers and the bank itself is pre-eminently governed by the applicable civil law rules. In the case of CET1 instruments that mainly consist of the issued and fully paid-in share capital of the bank, the main rights and obligations of the shareholders or members will generally arise from the applicable statutory corporate law rules and the articles of association of the company concerned. Furthermore, the rights and obligations will be coloured by the resolutions of the competent bodies of the company. In addition, there may be contractual arrangements between the shareholders themselves, or between the shareholders and the company. The legal basis can therefore consist of various statutory, corporate law and contractual grounds.

Under the relevant CRR arrangements, a bank will have to submit an intention to issue CET capital instruments for approval by the competent authority prior to the issuance. The relevant text of Article 26(3) CRR says: 'Institutions shall classify issuances of capital instruments as Common Equity Tier 1 instruments only after permission is granted by the competent authorities'. This choice of words leaves room to request permission after the issuance, but in practice such permission is often sought prior to the issue of new CET1 instruments.[7] No such prior approval arrangement existed in European banking law before the entry into force of CRR. This can rightly be called an innovation of enforcing banking rules. This form of enforcing the rules fits in with the above-mentioned method of (informally) influencing the way in which the relevant rules are enforced by supervisors, without necessarily requiring a court decision. This judicial intervention could arise if the regulator makes an unwelcome decision with regard to a submitted request for permission under Article 26(3) of the CRR. I will not discuss such a possible consequence of the application of this regulation. However, in Section 4.8 I will look at the opposite case, namely where a bank has failed to obtain the prior approval of the competent supervisory authority (in this case the ECB), and has nonetheless issued capital instruments that the bank wished to qualify for the CET1 portion of the bank's capital. This led, as we shall see, to strict enforcement by the ECB.

It is evident that if a bank intends to issue CET1 instruments and opts, on the basis of Article 26(3) CRR, to address the supervisory authority with a request for permission to include the to-be-issued instrument in the CET1 volume, the instruments then have simply not yet been issued, so there will be no legal relationship with shareholders at that time. Due to the relevant procedure, however, the competent supervisor can exercise significant influence in advance on a legal

[7] See in this regard the recent judgment of the ECJ of Case C 456/20 P to C 458/20 P *Crédit Agricole SA and others/ECB*, ECLI:EU:C:2021:502 in the appeal of which the issue of correct application of Art 26(3) CRR was part of the legal debate, and which issue led to the imposition of an administrative fine by the ECB amounting to approximately €5 million in total. This case is discussed in more detail in section 4.8.

relationship to be created, and the supervisor can have concrete involvement in the design of the terms and conditions of the instruments to be issued. If the regulator is of the opinion that proposed terms and conditions of those instruments do not conform to the requirements of Article 28 ff CRR, then permission to classify as a CET1 instrument is simply withheld. The bank will then have to make an adjustment before issuing the instruments concerned. If the bank makes the issuance without prior approval, the consequence is simple: whilst under the applicable corporate law rules, the capital instruments may be perfectly valid, the issued capital instruments will not qualify as CET1 capital, and the bank therefore risks that it will not meet the capital requirements. The bank in question will not be willing to accept such a consequence, since meeting the capital requirements is an essential foundation for its 'licence to operate'. Therefore, there is no option to follow a different angle. In this way, the relevant *ex ante* procedure for newly issued capital instruments is a robust way to enforce the relevant requirements of Article 28 ff CRR.

This method of informal enforcement also has limits in its nature, ie the competent supervisor does not in all cases have an *ex ante* influence on the establishment of horizontal private law relationships. Firstly, after the introduction of the new text of Article 26(3) CRR on the basis of the CRR2 amendments, an element of proportionality has been introduced with regard to the relevant approval process. If a bank wishes to issue new CET1 instruments whose terms and conditions[8] are the same as those of CET1 instruments issued in the past and approved by the regulator, there will be no need to request permission for the new instruments issued or to be issued. The bank is then free to issue this new CET1 instrument without requesting permission to include in the CET1 volume. The competent supervisory authority should only be notified of that fact.

Secondly, for AT1 and Tier 2, no comparable procedures exist as provided for CET1 instruments in Article 26(3) of the CRR. In other words, banks are not obliged to submit the terms and conditions drawn up by the bank to the competent supervisor prior to the issuance of an AT1 and Tier 2 capital instrument, and to have these conditions approved. One might well question the rationale of this distinction. After all, CET1 instruments, in view of the company law regulations that usually apply to the relationship between shareholders and the company, leave much less leeway for the company to make arrangements that deviate from corporate law. For AT1 and Tier 2 instruments, however, this is substantially different, because they concern contractual relationships under private law between the bank's financiers and the bank itself. In other words, the principle of freedom of contract provides scope for including clauses in the conditions that may conflict with the provisions for AT1 instruments such as those arising from Articles 51 ff CRR and for Tier 2 instruments as they arise from Articles 62 ff CRR.

Also, in view of this contractual flexibility, it could be expected that an *ex ante* review of the contract terms prior to issuance would be required than having

[8] The text of Art 26(3) CRR refers to 'the provisions governing those subsequent issuance'.

this for CET1 instruments only. For that reason, in a number of jurisdictions, including the Netherlands, shortly after the introduction of the CRR, such a prior review by supervisors was indeed introduced for AT1 and Tier 2 instruments on the basis of provisions of national law.[9] However, given the weak basis for this in the CRR (which, after all, has no provisions on this matter), such mandatory pre-assessments have been abolished in the Netherlands,[10] and the Dutch Central Bank instead offers an informal review process that market participants can follow to confirm that the applicable contractual terms indeed meet the criteria and requirements of CRR.

Banks will be happy to follow such an informal review, because there must be certainty that the regulatory capital instruments to be issued can indeed be classified as own funds, and that the bank will therefore be able to meet the capital requirements. As will be highlighted in the next section, a similar informal *ex ante* review process is offered by the ECB in respect of significant institutions subject to the direct supervision of the ECB under the Single Supervisory Mechanism (SSM).

4.4. ECB Guidance on the Review of the Qualification of Capital Instruments as AT1 and Tier 2 Instruments

In 2016, as part of its duties and powers in relation to the SSM, the ECB launched a Guidance Note on an *ex ante* review process for AT1 and Tier 2 capital instruments.[11] This is a good example of a practice in banking supervision, where 'informal influence' by a supervisor actually has an effect on the correct compliance with the relevant regulations. The ECB frames this process as a recommended procedure for significant institutions (SIs) as defined in Article 2(16) of Regulation (EU) 468/2014 (the SSM Framework Regulation). The ECB noted in 2016:

> The ECB recommends that entities follow this Guidance with respect to capital instruments issued after its date of publication. However, Section III.2 of the Guidance applies to all capital instruments irrespective of their date of issuance. Entities are responsible for ensuring that their capital instruments comply with all the relevant provisions of the CRR and the RTS on Own Funds, irrespective of the ex post review carried out by the ECB.[12]

[9] This was the case in the Netherlands pursuant to the Dutch Central Bank Regulation on specific provisions CRD IV and CRR, 9 December 2013, *Dutch Governmental Gazette* 2013, 35423. Not much is known in which Member States such *ex ante* approval procedures for AT1 or Tier 2 instruments exist(ed). The ECB's Guidance Note of 6 June 2016, 'Public Guidance on the review of the qualification of capital instruments as Additional Tier 1 and Tier 2 instruments', contains the following passage on this subject, which suggests at the very least that at the time (in 2016) such *ex ante* procedures existed in more Member States of the Eurozone. The ECB notes: 'This guidance is without prejudice to any requirements in respect of the recognition of AT1 or T2 instruments under applicable national law. If national law requires pre-approval, the ECB is competent to grant such pre-approval to the entities.'

[10] In the Netherlands this abolition occurred in 2015 by deleting the relevant provisions in the Regulation of 2013.

[11] See above, section 4.3.

[12] Guidance Note (n 9) 2.

This Guidance Note confirms on the one hand that institutions are free to issue AT1 or Tier 2 instruments without prior approval by the ECB. However, once the instruments have been launched on the market, the relevant bank must ensure that all relevant documentation is submitted to the ECB, which assumes that the ECB will conduct a full review of the relevant instrument and whether the bank is justified in including the issued instrument in the volume of eligible own funds items. The ECB also states in the Guidance Note that it encourages (informal) consultation with the ECB prior to issuance on the design of the instrument and the way in which this will be incorporated into the total of own funds instruments issued or to be issued. The ECB notes:

> Without prejudice to the ex post assessment, an informal dialogue on the specific features of a capital instrument is encouraged between an entity's representatives and the relevant JST[13] before issuance, in particular when the instrument to be issued has new or complex features.
>
> This informal dialogue does not represent an approval (either explicit or implicit) of any instruments, or confirmation of their eligibility as an AT1 or T2 instrument. Entities are responsible for ensuring that their capital instruments comply with all the relevant provisions of the CRR and the RTS on Own Funds.[14]

These *ex ante* informal consultation processes between an individual bank and the ECB naturally take place within the confidential environment of the individual supervisory relationship. The outcome of the discussions on the qualification of an AT1 or Tier 2 instrument that the bank in question intends to issue as eligible own funds of the bank is not public. The ECB also has no (anonymised) public list or publication of concrete agreements or concrete insights reached in the context of such informal discussions. Therefore, this informal review process is unlikely to have a harmonising effect. The applicable competition rules will also limit banks to consult with each other about the fruit of their discussions with the ECB.

It would, certainly in view of the consequences for the ultimate relationship of the bank with its lenders (the qualitative requirements for capital lead in many cases to a certain definition of the applicable contractual rights and obligations), distort competition if banks were to engage in such coordination. On the other hand, the result of the consultations will become public at some point due to the mandatory publication of certain documentation in the context of the issuance of the capital instruments, such as the prospectus to be published. However, joint coordination or consultation on such topics will, in my opinion, be subject to the aforementioned competition law restrictions.

As I will show below, a different method has been applied in Europe to achieve a certain degree of standardisation, and therefore harmonised application of the qualitative capital requirements, which, apart from the formation of law through

[13] Joint Supervisory Team, the individuals responsible for the supervisory routines in respect of significant institutions in the conduct of the tasks and responsibilities of the ECB in the SSM.

[14] Guidance Note (n 9) 4. The reference to the 'RTS on Own Funds' is to the Delegated Regulation Own Funds as referred to in n 3.

dispute settlement on enforcement matters by the courts, also offers an interesting perspective on the influence this has on the formation of harmonised contractual private law relationships between banks and their financiers.

In this section I will consider the influence that the informal review process that the ECB offers can have on such private law relationships. As discussed above, if a bank chooses to submit the AT1 or Tier 2 instruments to be issued by the bank, based on the draft documentation prepared for those instruments, there will be no question of a possible impact on the terms of those instruments on their purchasers. The instruments have not yet been issued at that time, and the bank is not yet in a relationship with the holders of the debt instruments. If the discussion with the ECB leads to the bank being required to make adjustments to the conditions, then from that perspective there will be no change in existing conditions; the conditions will be aligned to the requirements of the CRR according to the insights that the ECB gives to the bank.

However, the effect of this on the ultimate relationship between the bank and its financiers cannot be completely ignored. After all, strong ECB intervention during this *ex ante* process, in which, as it were, negotiations between the bank and the ECB about the permissible limits of the contractual arrangements to be ultimately applied take place, will lead to conditions being imposed upon the buyers of those instruments that may deviate from the bank's original wishes and policy, which must be adjusted as a result of the ECB's intervention. It is, of course, taboo for a bank to inform the markets for such instruments in advance of the intended issuance and the conditions under which it could take place. A bank would not be wise to start a book-building process before the ECB has had its say, as this could create bottlenecks in the sphere of expectations.

This is an interesting force field. Banks that intend to issue such capital instruments will of course want to gain insight into market conditions, they will review other issued instruments of (competing) banks and benchmark them against their own situation, and there will undoubtedly be confidential consultations with the parties that will arrange the new issue, if the bank engages such arrangers. On the other hand, there is the role of the ECB, which is involved at a certain stage in the design of the issuance of the instruments. The ECB will insist on doing this on the basis of concrete draft documentation, otherwise it will not be able to conduct a real review. See also the list of documentation described in the Guidance Note that banks must submit to the ECB after an issuance of AT1 and Tier 2 instruments has taken place, which undoubtedly has a reflex effect on the establishment of an *ex ante* file that is submitted to the ECB.[15] The inclusion of consultations with the ECB in connection with an *ex ante* review will therefore often take place in context of a lengthy preparation process prior to the actual launch of the issuance of such instruments on the public capital markets (if this form of issue is chosen).

[15] Guidance Note (n 9) 3.

The bank will therefore have to play chess on two boards. On the one hand, the bank will discuss the concrete details of the conditions with its arrangers, and on the other hand, the bank will want to obtain the ECB's view on the conformity of the instruments to be issued with the long series of requirements of CRR. In that context, a bank will seek to convince the ECB of existing and customary market practices and the conditions applied by (competing) banks.

To what extent do market practices play a role in achieving a balanced and level playing field? To what extent should the ECB take such factors into account in its evaluation? An informal review procedure such as that proposed by the ECB in the Guidance Note naturally takes place outside the framework of an administrative decision-making process, and the ECB is not bound by the rules of administrative law in that respect.[16] No principles of proper decision-making are required to be taken into account. For example, the ECB will not be obliged to observe the principle of equality in its considerations, eg by considering similar instruments placed on the market in its assessment.

I state with emphasis that there is a vulnerable balance in the SSM, especially when it comes to the possible deviations that can arise in the financial markets, where different supervisors can develop different insights about the conformity with CRR of certain contractual arrangements in respect of AT1 or Tier 2 instruments. Suppose that the ECB finds it incompatible with a CRR provision that a certain contractual condition is included in an AT1 instrument, while an NCA in a Member State takes the view in a comparable *ex ante* assessment of AT1 or Tier 2 instruments (to be issued by a less significant bank for instance) that this contractual provision complies with the CRR requirements. To what extent can the bank seeking consultations with the ECB rely on that comparison?

The ECB will, of course, follow its own reading of the CRR, and that view will mean that, if the bank were to include certain contractual terms that the ECB deems incompatible with CRR, it would be pointed out that it is potentially not acting in accordance with the legal provisions, the ultimate consequence being that the bank may not be able to meet its capital requirements. When that debate takes place with the supervisor, it is most likely that the bank will yield to accept the ECB's view here, notwithstanding the possible market differences of such financing instruments.

[16] In the ECB 'SSM Supervisory Manual – European banking supervision: functioning of the SSM and supervisory approach' (March 2018) 91–92 the process of the *ex post* evaluation of the AT1 and Tier 2 instruments is clearly framed in a decision-making process involving all the relevant bodies of the SSM. But the Manual does not provide further insight as to the *modus operandi* for the *ex ante* vetting of these instruments, should a bank take such a step. See www.bankingsupervision.europa.eu/ecb/pub/pdf/ssm.supervisorymanual201803.en.pdf. The stance that must be taken here is that any involvement of the ECB when asked to discuss in an *ex ante* review the compatibility of a to-be-issued AT1 or Tier 2 instrument, is to be considered a so-called 'operational act' of the ECB. These operational acts are framed on p 20 of the ECB SSM Supervisory Manual as follows: 'An operational act does not form part of the formal decision-making process. It does not have a required legal form and comprises non-binding and non-enforceable supervisory expectations, statements and other acts'.

It can be questioned whether it is desirable that such informal review processes and exchanges take place between the legal subject and the public authority. Also, should such informal decisions not be better formalised so that they are framed in an ECB decision-making process, which entails all the guarantees of legal protection? It is for this area of informal influence by regulators that I drew attention hereabove, and of which it can generally be stated that there is a vacuum with regard to the enforcement of law (and its possible review by the courts).

On the one hand, there is great value in these critical questions. On the other hand, pragmatism must also play an important role. Banks seek assurance that future actions (namely the issuance of the AT1 or Tier 2 instruments) will conform to the rules of CRR, and that assurance is necessary due to the fundamental nature of the legal requirements to be adhered to for the bank's existence. After all, a conflict over the capital requirements can have far-reaching consequences for the bank concerned.

My concern, as explained above, lies in the possible different interpretations that can arise in informal review processes within the framework of the SSM. Deviating views from the ECB do not necessarily have to be followed by the NCAs that organise comparable informal review processes. There is no regulation or procedure within the SSM, at least not according to Regulation (EU) No 1024/2013 (the SSM Regulation) or the SSM Framework Regulation, whereby the ECB can play a coordinating role in this area. After all, there are simply no rules for informal, non-binding and unenforceable guidance from the ECB on the one hand and the NCAs on the other. In my opinion, this is a vulnerability in the whole of the governance arrangements within the SSM, and a good example (of many that can be given) that the design of the SSM procedures and the roles of the ECB and the NCAs has been exposed to vulnerabilities and imperfections, especially where it comes to standardising policies and the interpretation of legal provisions such as the important regulations for qualitative capital requirements in the CRR. Below I will discuss further the procedures and rules that the European legislator has introduced in this area, which are aimed at harmonisation and unambiguous interpretation and application of the relevant legal provisions.

4.5. EBA Involvement in the Assessment of CET1 Instruments

As has been discussed above, great importance is attributed in the EU to the correct and full compliance with the qualitative capital requirements for CET1 instruments. With regard to newly issued capital instruments, banks must obtain permission from the competent supervisor to include the issued (or to be issued) capital instruments in the CET1 bucket. With regard to new issuances of instruments of the same type and with the same properties already approved in the past, banks are subject to a strict notification obligation, whereby they will be obliged to inform the competent supervisory authority of such new issue with the submission of extensive documentation. Some of the legal issues concerning capital instruments issued to purchasers that are not conforming to the qualitative capital requirements will be discussed in section 4.8 of this chapter, where I will discuss in more detail a number of legal cases in which this subject matter has been made subject to court decisions.

A number of further safeguards have been created in EU instruments in this area, which are aimed in particular at creating a harmonised set of applications of the relevant rules, and giving a strong role to the European Banking Authority (EBA) in reviewing possible interpretation issues and to promote supervisory convergence.

Article 26(3) CRR determines that: 'On the basis of information collected from competent authorities, EBA shall establish, maintain and publish a list of all forms of capital instruments in each Member State that qualify as Common Equity Tier 1 instruments'. The latest version of that list was published in December 2019, including one instrument that was nominated by the relevant NCA to the EBA for inclusion.[17]

What is the significance of this published list and the procedure in which EBA plays the role of coordinator of information collection on capital instruments that qualify as CET1 capital? When studying the list, one can immediately appreciate major differences in the approach taken by the different NCAs. NCAs from some Member States such as Austria, Italy and Germany have considered providing a comprehensive listing of all capital instruments that qualify as CET1 instruments with extensive references to the company law provisions of the relevant Member State. Other NCAs, such as the Netherlands, have only provided a limited statement of the available corporate law instruments that qualify as CET1 instruments.

In any event, the list of CET1 instruments acts as an important starting point for determining the structure of the CET1 capital of banks in the EU; it therefore has a harmonising effect both in terms of the application of capital adequacy rules and of the mandatory disclosure of key figures of banks with regard to the so-called key prudential ratios.[18]

The usefulness of the disclosed list is such that the public and anyone with an interest in understanding the soundness of the European banking sector can trust that published capital adequacy ratios are based on a closed system of recognition

[17] See 'EBA updates list of CET1 instruments' press release (19 December 2019), available at eba.europa.eu/eba-updates-list-cet1-instruments and the updated Excel file attached to that press release. The additional CET1 instrument included in this list concerned a class of non-voting ordinary shares in accordance with Latvian law.

[18] Based on Part 8 CRR and for which the templates are determined in Commission Implementing Regulation (EU) 2021/637 of 15 March 2021 laying down implementing technical standards with regard to public disclosures by institutions of the information referred to in Titles II and III of Part Eight of Regulation (EU) 575/2013 of the European Parliament and of the Council and repealing Commission Implementing Regulation (EU) 1423/2013; Commission Delegated Regulation (EU) 2015/1555; Commission Implementing Regulation (EU) 2016/200; and Commission Delegated Regulation (EU) 2017/2295 [2021] 136/1.

of capital instruments. Banks will therefore not be able to include alternatives in their volume of CET1 capital outside of the CET1 instruments that have been made public; in other words, this constitutes a system aimed at generating confidence in the robustness of bank capital in the European banking system.

Furthermore, a mandatory consultation by the competent authorities must be organised in the event they wish to grant permission for new forms of capital instruments that will be eligible to be classified as CET1 instrument. EBA is authorised to give advice as to whether such permission may be granted. The relevant provision of Article 26(3) CRR determines:

> Competent authorities shall consult EBA before granting permission for new forms of capital instruments to be classified as Common Equity Tier 1 instruments. Competent authorities shall have due regard to EBA's opinion and, where they decide to deviate from it, shall write to EBA within three months from the date of receipt of EBA's opinion setting out the rationale for deviating from the relevant opinion.

Based on the information delivered by the NCAs and the ECB, EBA assesses the compliance of CET1 instruments with the rules of Article 28 ff CRR and the RTS on Own Funds, although for the latter rules with regard to the definition of the qualitative requirements of capital, only some of the criteria of Article 28 CRR (with regard to ordinary company forms) are regulated in the form of a further regulatory technical standard.[19]

Pursuant to Article 80 of the CRR, the EBA has also been instructed to conduct a frequent review of own funds instruments issued in the EU and also, since the introduction of the Banking Package, instruments issued as liabilities eligible for resolution purposes.[20] These monitoring reports map out which bottlenecks exist in practice with regard to the qualitative capital requirements. Monitoring is aimed at ensuring that these qualitative capital requirements are applied in a consistent and effective manner throughout the EU. In section 4.7 I discuss the interesting results of the recent monitoring report on AT1 capital instruments in this area.

As a result, the EBA has been given an important role in enforcing the various qualitative rules for CET1 capital instruments. By their very nature, these regulations have a significant influence on the private law relationships between banks and their financiers, without there being an *ex post* enforcement by means of legal dispute settlement by the courts.

[19] It concerns the subject matters of multiple distributions constituting a disproportionate drag on own funds as determined in Art 7a Delegated Regulation Own Funds, preferential distributions regarding preferential rights to payments of distributions as determined in Art 7b Delegated Regulation Own Funds, preferential distributions regarding the order of distribution payments as determined in Art 7d Delegated Regulation Own Funds, indirect funding of capital instruments for the purposes of Art 28(1)(b) CRR as determined in Art 8 Delegated Regulation Own Funds and applicable forms and nature of indirect funding of capital instruments for the purposes of Art 28(1)(b) CRR as determined in Art 9 Delegated Regulation Own Funds.

[20] On 22 July 2019 EBA published the 'Report on the Monitoring of CET1 Instruments Issued by EU Institutions – Second Update' and on 29 October 2020, the 'Report on the Monitoring of TLAC-/MREL eligible liabilities instruments of European Union Institutions' EBA/REP/2020/27; both available at eba.europa.eu.

It is a powerful example of how, in terms of qualitative requirements for banks' capital, a public law framework has been created that has major implications for the creation of these relationships, setting limits on the freedom of banks to determine the conditions for their own financing through equity instruments.

It is true that it would be going too far, as I argued in section 4.2, as to assume that a statutory European contract law or company law has been created in this way, but it should be clear that the relevant regulations do have a major influence on those contractual or corporate relationships.

4.6. Public Law Impediments Affecting Private Law Relationships

We saw above that the regulations for qualitative capital requirements can be of great significance for the design of the private law relationships between banks and their financiers, and that this also involves a set of rules in which enforcement takes place outside the sphere of dispute settlement. I will discuss strict enforcement of qualitative capital requirements in section 4.8 in relation to the recent ECJ case of *Crédit Agricole/ECB*. But first, I will discuss another example of how the enforcement of these rules can influence private law relationships. This may concern cases in which the bank has to navigate between the cliffs of maintaining a sufficiently solid regulatory capital on the one hand and keeping the financiers (read shareholders) satisfied on the other.

As a hypothetical example, suppose a bank wants to expand its equity capital to strengthen the bank's CET1 ratio. The bank is listed on the stock exchange and its ordinary voting shares are traded. Assuming those shares fully complied and met the requirements of Articles 28 ff CRR and those of the RTS on Own Funds. The bank finds a private equity house willing to make a capital injection by means of the issuance of ordinary shares without voting rights; in other words, a second class of shares will be issued in addition to the exchange-traded voting shares. Therefore, pursuant to Article 28(3) of the CRR, the bank must request permission in advance from the competent authority before the shares can be issued to the private equity financier. The shares are included in the EBA list and the competent authority gives the necessary permission. The non-voting shares are privately placed with the private equity house, after the shareholders' meeting has approved the passing of the pre-emptive right of the existing shareholders, thereby accepting dilution.

The private equity house has accepted the bank's condition that the shares would not be entitled to vote in the expectation that a reasonable return will be achieved on the shares. Over the years, however, partly on the basis of the application of the rules on capital adequacy (for example, the rules on the maximum distributable amounts of Article 141 ff Directive (EU) 2013/36 (CRD IV)), the bank has paid almost no dividend to the shareholders, ie neither to the shareholders with voting shares nor to the venture capital house that holds the non-voting shares. The private equity house is dissatisfied and wants the bank to buy back the non-voting shares and enters into discussions with the bank's management and appeals to the fact that it is unreasonable that the private equity house, without being able to have any influence in the shareholders' meeting, is nevertheless 'trapped' and should therefore be bought out.

Article 28(1)(g) CRR provides for the following criterium for qualitative capital requirements:

> [T]he provisions governing the instruments do not indicate expressly or implicitly that the principal amount of the instruments would or might be reduced or repaid other than in the liquidation of the institution, and the institution does not otherwise provide such an indication prior to or at issuance of the instruments, except in the case of instruments referred to in Article 27 where the refusal by the institution to redeem such instruments is prohibited under applicable national law.

In the example above, the assumption is that the shares placed with the private equity house are approved and placed on the EBA list and, moreover, permission has been given in advance by the competent authority. It can therefore be assumed that the bank has not made any express or implicit commitment to the venture capital house as referred to in Article 28(1)(g) CRR (not even by means of side letters or other agreements, for example in a shareholders' agreement), otherwise the permission would not have been granted.

Article 28(1)(g) CRR in any event precludes the bank from being able to make concrete agreements in advance about the circumstances in which the bank will proceed with the future repurchase of the shares to be placed. These agreements may not follow expressly from the contractual terms or other arrangements, nor may they be implied. The recently introduced anti-abuse provision of Article 79a CRR precludes concrete stipulations from being agreed in this regard 'alongside' the explicit contractual provisions (eg in the Subscription Agreement to be concluded).[21] The financier will therefore not be able to rely on legally enforceable optional conditions, for example by exercising a put option.

In such cases, after a shareholder calls on management to come to a repurchase arrangement, the bank will have to proceed with great caution. Pursuant to Article 77 ff CRR, for such a purchase, the explicit approval of the competent authority will have to be requested in advance. I have presented the example in such a way that it may be very difficult for the bank in question to obtain the necessary approval from the supervisor, since the example assumes that the bank does

[21] The anti-abuse provision of Art 79a CRR is introduced on the occasion of CRR2, which reads as follows: 'Institutions shall have regard to the substantial features of instruments and not only their legal form when assessing compliance with the requirements laid down in Part Two. The assessment of the substantial features of an instrument shall take into account all arrangements related to the instruments, even where those are not explicitly set out in the terms and conditions of the instruments themselves, for the purpose of determining that the combined economic effects of such arrangements are compliant with the objective of the relevant provisions.'

not comfortably comply with the capital requirements. The bank is also listed, and the bank will therefore have to manoeuvre carefully from the perspective of the market abuse prohibition schemes, if it engages in confidential discussions with the private equity house, especially if it is surrounded by the great uncertainty about obtaining the necessary permission under Article 77 ff CRR.

In any event, the qualitative capital requirements for banks prevent the bank's management from discussions with this shareholder in an unrestricted way. Reference should be made here to the provision of Article 28(1) RTS on Own Funds which provides: '1. Redemptions, reductions and repurchases of own funds instruments shall not be announced to holders of the instruments before the institution has obtained the prior approval of the competent authority'. The private law relationship between the bank and its lender is therefore strictly linked to the public law restrictions arising from the approval process with regard to the repurchase or redemption of issued instruments. In fact, the bank management must tell the shareholder: 'I am not allowed to consult with you about the chances of a redemption of your shares, because the rules of banking supervision prohibit that'.

The bank and financiers aiming to be bought out of the capital of the company will at most be able to conduct some exploratory talks, in which the shareholder makes its wishes known, but the management can in no way make concrete commitments in this regard or create expectations that the mandatory approval procedure to be followed will be successfully completed. At most, the bank's management can promise to achieve the best results, but it cannot go much further. One can imagine that in practice this very subtle limit of admissibility of the granting of commitments is not always taken into account.

This example of the rules of qualitative capital requirements to be applied makes it clear that there is no question of a set of 'hard and fast rules' and that there is a twilight zone in which parties must act very cautiously. Their private law relationships are strongly influenced by the rules of public law, and the freedom to enter into contractual and enforceable agreements with each other in this area is significantly restricted.

The complex area of qualitative capital requirements has also led to some unusual cases, which I will cover in section 4.8. Before doing so, I will address another specific aspect regarding the application of informal influence in the context of the application and enforcement of qualitative capital requirements, vis-à-vis the special role given to the EBA with regard to the evaluation of AT1 and Tier 2 capital instruments.

4.7. EBA June 2021 Report on the Monitoring of AT1 Instruments of EU Institutions

In section 4.5, I discussed the rules of Article 80 CRR, which gave the EBA extensive powers to evaluate, by means of published monitoring reports, the own funds capital instruments and eligible liabilities instruments issued in the EU. In this section, I highlight the recent fourth EBA report on the monitoring of AT1 capital instruments (the 'June 2021 EBA AT1 Report').[22] In my opinion, it is a good example of the extent to which such EBA monitoring exercises also lead to a concrete influence on the contractual relationships between banks and the holders of such AT1 instruments.[23]

AT1 instruments are also referred to as 'hybrid instruments', as they are generally designed as debt capital instruments based on a contractual set of conditions. Those conditions must be very precise, and Article 51 ff CRR provide the criteria for this.[24] An interesting chapter in the June 2021 EBA AT1 Report concerns the development in practice to issue AT1 instruments that must also meet environmental, social and governance (ESG) criteria. The EBA is very critical of this combination and provides a number of guidelines to avoid that such an AT1 capital instrument, which is promoted as an instrument that serves ESG objectives, has internally contradictory (contractual) characteristics.

As already highlighted in EBA's previous reports on AT1 monitoring, EBA performs this monitoring by examining the relevant contractual terms and conditions that apply to AT1 instruments issued in the market. This examination led EBA to express views on the desirability or undesirability of drafting certain contractual terms, and to provide guidance on how certain terms could clash with the qualitative conditions applicable to this type of regulatory capital instrument. This could be considered an involvement or influence of a public law organisation with the horizontal private law relations between contracting parties.[25] Based on the EU rules following from the CRR, EBA's monitoring processes by their very nature place limits on the freedom of contracting parties to organise their relationships as they would prefer.

This preventive and *ex ante* influence, the reader will object, does not lead to the annulment of certain existing contractual terms, or to the reversal of conditions

[22] EBA 'Report on the Monitoring of Additional Tier 1 (AT1) Instruments of European Union (EU) Institutions – Update' EBA/REP/2021/19 (24 June 2021), available at eba.europa.eu.

[23] EBA fulfils this role based on input from the NCAs (and ECB) of new developments in the markets, and new instruments issued. Art 80 CRR requires competent authorities to provide such input. That provision reads: 'competent authorities shall, without delay and upon request by the EBA, forward all information to EBA that the EBA considers relevant concerning new capital instruments or new types of liabilities issued in order to enable EBA to monitor the quality of own funds and eligible liabilities instruments issued by institutions across the Union'.

[24] However, EBA indicates in the monitoring report that some of the recommendations in the monitoring of AT1 instruments will apply equally to Tier 2 instruments that are required to meet the criteria in Art 62 ff CRR. In that respect, EBA therefore notes that comparable contractual provisions in the contract documentation of Tier 2 instruments should also be assessed against EBA's findings for AT1 instruments.

[25] This ignores the fact that EBA in fact exerts an even greater influence on how the contractual relationship between parties entering into an AT1 transaction should be shaped. I refer to the report 'EBA standardised templates for Additional Tier 1 (AT1) instruments – Final' (2016). In that document, EBA even goes so far as to provide concrete contractual clauses for shaping the relationship between the bank and the holder of the AT1 instrument.

already agreed. But the big stick for the supervisors who have to assess the capital adequacy of banks on the basis of the EBA monitoring is obvious: if parties agree certain arrangements that appear to be contrary to the EBA's views in the monitoring report, the qualification of the AT1 instrument in question will be withheld, and the bank could be faced with a sudden breach of capital requirements. Such a conclusion would be unacceptable to the bank concerned, as the continuity of the bank could be jeopardised.

From that perspective, I believe that this EBA monitoring process has a strong influence on the shaping of contractual relationships in the horizontal private law relationship between banks and their financiers.

EBA itself, however, formulates the meaning of the recommendations in the monitoring report in a cautious manner. It states:

> The EBA has focused its work primarily on the assessment of selected AT1 issuances. The terms and conditions of these selected issuances are assessed against the regulatory provisions in order to identify provisions that the EBA would recommend and, in contrast, recommend avoiding.
>
> …
>
> In addition, the best practices mentioned in this report aim to shape market practices and should therefore pre-empt market practice (unless there is a material impossibility of applying the best practice demonstrated by the institution concerned).
>
> This review makes no claims to be fully comprehensive, but highlights areas where the EBA believes it necessary to revise the wording of certain existing clauses for future issuances or where the EBA would recommend avoiding in the future the use of some clauses currently under consideration.[26]

Below I give a few examples of the contractual arrangements that have been tested by the EBA in this area.

Under Article 52(1)(e) of the CRR, banks may not guarantee or otherwise act in such a way as to strengthen the 'seniority of the claim'. This somewhat difficult-to-read criterion gives rise to much debate in practice. In its monitoring report, EBA gives the example of a case in which the issuer, for example, makes a contractual commitment that in the event that the bank itself is subject to a legal restructuring as a result of a legal merger or legal split, the bank must promote the transfer or takeover of already issued capital instruments by another group entity, and may not include any clauses in the contract documentation that have the effect of providing security that the 'new debtor' will meet its obligations (eg the obligation to pay interest). Such a guarantee must lead to new, subordinate obligations of the guarantor, according to EBA, which furthermore states that 'there is no guarantee on the cancelled coupons, so that flexibility of payments is kept at any time, and the guarantee is specific enough and its scope is restricted to a change affecting the issuer'.[27]

[26] EBA AT1 Report (June 2021), paras 11, 13 and 14.
[27] ibid, para 32.

In view of this interpretation, the following customary clause in bond terms and conditions would not be permissible to be included in the terms and conditions of an AT1 instrument that needs to qualify as regulatory capital:

> The Trustee may, without the consent of the Bondholders agree with the Issuer to the substitution in place of the Issuer (or any previous substitute or substitutes under this Condition) as the principal debtor under the Bonds and the Trust Deed of any Subsidiary of the Issuer subject to (a) the Bonds being unconditionally and irrevocably guaranteed by the Issuer. [...]

Such a clause will attract the objections that it is too broadly formulated, that the guarantee does not lead to a subordinated obligation of the issuer, and that there is no clear possibility of the guarantor to suspend interest payments or to make other arrangements with regard to those interest payments. It provides a clear example of how, in practice, certain criteria of Article 51 ff CRR lead to the need to agree on different terms and conditions than for a 'regular' bond.

One of the important issues surrounding issued AT1 (and Tier 2) instruments concerns the bank's ability to make an (early) repayment or other means to terminate the exposure of the bondholders to the bank. In principle, AT1 instruments are perpetual; in other words, they may not have an expiry date. Tier 2 instruments must have a minimum maturity of five years. In practice, however, there will be a need to be able to recall the instruments in question (in other words, to take them off the market) if certain circumstances arise. For example, as discussed in the case of Lloyds TSB's capital instruments in section 4.8, a change in regulation or a change in policy on the part of the competent regulator can be such a trigger for the repurchase or redemption of instruments already issued. Under certain circumstances, exercising a regulatory call is then allowed.

However, in normal circumstances (ie outside the cases of permitted regulatory calls, tax calls, etc), an institution may not include in the terms and conditions in advance that there will be (an expectation as to) repurchase or early redemption. In any case, these clauses must respect that such repurchase or redemption may not take place in any event in the first five years after issuance.[28] Furthermore, the terms and conditions should clarify that the repurchase or redemption may only take place after prior approval by the competent supervisor on the basis of the rules set out in Article 77 ff CRR. This conditionality is an important part of the terms and conditions of the relevant regulatory capital instruments. Making the required approval procedures sufficiently explicit in the contractual terms and conditions is intended to provide investors with clarity from the outset as to what they can expect in this regard.[29]

[28] For AT1 instruments this is explicitly regulated in Art 52(1)(i) of the CRR.

[29] In the markets, such issues lead to much discussion. Recently, for example, there was discussion around an outstanding AT1 instrument of Banco Santander concerning the expectations that the markets might have regarding the exercise of a call by the bank to revoke the instruments placed. The bank chose not to do so and accepted that in the (extended) period that the instruments were outstanding on the markets, a higher interest rate had to be paid to the investors. This policy of the bank

There are many cases and practical issues to discuss in this area, and also a great deal of guidance from the EBA in the Q&A routine regarding the relevant CRR provisions. Below is a quote from one of the questions submitted to EBA regarding the way in which EBA dealt with the matter:[30]

> The EBA has received a Q&A asking if a subsidiary of an institution could purchase AT1 or Tier 2 instruments issued by this institution before five years from the date of issuance of the instrument. As indicated in the answer, one has to recall the eligibility criterion stipulated by Articles 52(1)(b) and 63(b) of the CRR, disqualifying instruments from being eligible as AT1 or Tier 2 in cases where those instruments are purchased by the institution or its subsidiaries, regardless of the nature and situation of the subsidiary. Therefore, the purchase by a subsidiary would qualify as a repurchase and would require prior permission by the competent authority. Within the first five years from the date of issuance, such permission would only be possible under the specific conditions of Article 78(4) of the CRR.[31]

This example is used to indicate that, in the context of the execution of certain transactions, the qualitative capital requirements mean that, before they can be carried out, these transactions are subject to certain strict requirements. In other words, parties do not have complete freedom to agree on these transactions among themselves, as they have to follow certain procedures and (as indicated above) have to obtain prior approval. The approval of the competent authority itself, is subject to a 'bound' decision, and in the present case the rules of Article 78(4) CRR draw clear limits to the power of the supervisory authority to grant the approval. In other words, the freedom of the contracting parties is curtailed, and so is the discretion of the supervisory authority itself. These considerations are framed in the strict circumstances described in CRR under which a decision to approve may be taken.

I conclude this section with a word on the interesting addition by the EBA in the June 2021 EBA AT1 Report on the design of regulatory capital instruments that the issuer also intends to use to meet ESG objectives. In particular, in the current era, these must be instruments that qualify as a 'social bond' or a 'green bond', in other words, financing raised by the bank with the aim of relaying certain social or climate objectives. EBA is quite critical of this new phenomenon, pointing out the possible conflicts of such transactions with the requirements for regulatory capital instruments.

EBA notes:

> ESG bonds are issued by entities that seek to have positive environmental, social and governance characteristics, the proceeds of which are meant to be invested in

deviated somewhat from the usual practice whereby an 'interest step up' usually leads to the repurchase or redemption of the relevant bond. See on this: 'The Spanish imposition: Santander's non-call sets precedent in AT1 bond market', available at www.fidelityinternational.com/editorial/blog (14 February 2019).

[30] Q&A 2017_3587 raised by the French Autorité de contrôle prudentiel et de résolution and the EBA response submitted as final on 27 April 2018.

[31] EBA AT1 Report (June 2021), para 54.

> ESG assets. These bonds are usually marketed as green bonds or social bonds, commonly follow green or social impact standards, and are certified by an independent verifier following the climate bond standard and certification scheme.[32]

EBA discusses in detail the bottlenecks it sees in labelling certain regulatory capital instruments as 'social' or 'green', while they should also comply with the qualitative capital requirements. In short, EBA sees bottlenecks in the consequences of incorrect use of the funding raised and the implications of such incorrect use. If, when a bond is issued, it is stipulated that the proceeds will be invested in certain assets to serve a 'social' or 'green' purpose, and if it is subsequently established that this cannot be achieved, a situation could arise in which the bank is either forced to make an early repayment, or even worse, there could be an explicit clause in the conditions that in that case an 'event of default' would occur, which should lead to acceleration of the payment obligations and termination of the issued instrument. EBA goes into great detail about the various issues it sees in that area. The EBA report has analysed this issue in detail, thus:

> Several articles in the CRR (including Article 52(1)(g), Article 52(1)(j), Article 63(h), Article 63(j), Article 63(l), Article 72b(2)(g), Article 72b(2)(j) and Article 72b(2)(h)) aim to ensure that own funds and eligible liabilities instruments do not include any incentive to redeem the bonds or give rights to the note holders to accelerate future payments, in the case of AT1 on a perpetual basis and in the case of Tier 2 and eligible liabilities prior to the stated maturity subject to certain specific conditions. Furthermore, in order to preserve capacity for loss absorption, Article 52(1)(l)(ii), Article 63(m) and Article 72b(2)(m) of the CRR ensure that the level of interest or dividends payments, as applicable, due on the instruments does not change due to the creditworthiness of the issuer at any time. This principle should always be upheld regardless of whether the bonds are labelled Green or ESG or not.[33]

This shows the sensitivities surrounding the design of regulatory capital instruments, as well as the major impact it has on the mutual contractual relationships between the bank and its financiers. In fact, in the relevant passages of the Report, it can be read that the EBA does not yet see any merit in combining the two objectives of issuing qualifying regulatory capital and serving ESG purposes.

4.8. Two Legal Cases Concerning Qualitative Capital Requirements

Above I referred to the sparse case law that has been developed on issues of qualitative capital requirements. In this section I will discuss two cases that deal with this matter. One of the cases took place in the UK, and is interesting because it deals with the complex issue of capital instruments issued and traded in the

[32] ibid, para 144.
[33] ibid, para 175.

public capital markets, for which impediments in respect of the compliance with qualitative capital requirements arose. The other, more recent, case involving a significant institution under the supervision of the ECB holds great significance for the manner in which the relevant qualitative capital requirements are enforced.

4.8.1. *LBG Capital No 1 Plc* and *LBG Capital No 2 Plc v BNY Mellon Corporate Trustee Services Limited*

I will first discuss the judgment of the UK Court of Appeal concerning (1) LBG Capital No 1 Plc (2) LBG Capital No 2 Plc (appellants, hereinafter: the 'issuers') and BNY Mellon Corporate Trustee Services Limited (respondent, hereinafter: the 'trustee').[34] This ruling of the Court of Appeal provides an interesting insight into the tension between applicable contractual relationships between a bank and the holders of bonds issued by the bank, and the interference that takes place of public law rules on those contractual relationships.

The issuers were two special-purpose companies in the Lloyds Banking Group (LBG) that issued in 2009 contingent convertible securities (enhanced capital notes; ECNs) worth about £8 billion. In 2015 ECNs were still outstanding with a worth of approximately £3.3 billion carrying a high coupon (averaging 10.338 per cent). The CRR regulations led to a tightening of those qualitative capital requirements compared to the applicable law under Directive 2006/48/EC[35] in the time that the dispute arose, which is the subject matter of the court case. The introduction of CRR and the tightening of the qualitative capital requirements prompted the LBG to reconsider the usefulness of the ECNs issued in 2009 for the purpose of meeting the capital adequacy obligations of the bank. Although the ECNs as such qualified as lower tier 2 capital instruments at the time of issue and under the applicable regime of Directive 2006/48/EC, a bottleneck arose under the new rules of CRR with regard to the ECNs and their qualification as usable regulatory capital.

In March 2013, on the eve of the introduction of the CRR rules, the Prudential Regulation Authority of the Bank of England (PRA) required LBG to make a significant increase in its regulatory capital to ensure that LBG could meet the new capital requirements. Further (macroprudential) analyses by the Bank of England and other relevant authorities during 2013 indicated a structural shortfall in the capital requirements of the English banking sector, including LBG. Significant pressure was placed on UK banks to strengthen capital.

At the end of 2013, it was announced by the UK authorities that with effect from 1 January 2014 (the day of application of the CRR), the 'old' capital definitions of the English regulations based on Directive 2006/48/EC would no longer be used. Amongst other things – and I am taking a very sharp turn here – this resulted in

[34] United Kingdom Court of Appeal (Civil Division) of 10 December 2015, [2015] EWCA Civ 1257.

[35] Directive 2006/48/EC of the European Parliament and of the Council of 14 June 2006 relating to the taking up and pursuit of the business of credit institutions (recast) [2016] OJ *EU* L 177/1.

the mandatory trigger moment for conversion of contingent convertible securities into (qualifying) share capital if CET1 capital would fall below 5.125 per cent. However, the authorities in England determined that in new issues that trigger percentage should be set at seven per cent, considerably higher than the percentage resulting from the minimum capital requirements regime of Article 52 CRR.

The LBG ECNs had a lower 'trigger percentage' (ie five per cent). LBG sought to remedy this by making a public offer in April 2014 to exchange the outstanding ECNs for qualifying AT1 instruments. This public offer was partly successful, as bondholders accepted the exchange offer for approximately £5 billion of ECNs. However, over £3 billion of ECNs remained outstanding. After having obtained the approval of the PRA on the basis of Articles 77–78 CRR for redemption of the ECNs prior to maturity, the issuers wished to redeem the outstanding ECNs on the basis of the occurrence (and the continuing) of a capital disqualification event as defined in Condition 19 of the terms and conditions of the ECNs. This capital disqualification event had been drafted as follows:

> 'Capital Disqualification Event' is deemed to have occurred (1) if at any time LBG or, where LTSB is a or the Guarantor, LTSB is required under Regulatory Capital Requirements to have regulatory capital, the ECNs would no longer be eligible to qualify in whole or in part (save where such non-qualification is only as a result of any applicable limitation on the amount of such capital) for inclusion in the Lower Tier 2 Capital of LBG or, as the case may be, LTSB on a consolidated basis; or (2) if as a result of any changes to the Regulatory Capital Requirements or any change in the interpretation or application thereof by the FSA, the ECNs shall cease to be taken into account in whole or in part (save where this is only as a result of any applicable limitation on the amount that may be so taken into account) for the purposes of any "stress test" applied by the FSA in respect of the Consolidated Core Tier 1 Ratio.

The issuers believed that the capital disqualification event was applicable, which, in short, gave the issuers the power to affect an early redemption of the ECNs. The trustee, acting as agent for the bondholders, took the view that such early redemption was not appropriate because the contractual condition permitting the bank to call an early redemption of the ECNs had not been met. Initially, the High Court of Justice ([2015] EWHC 1560 (Ch)) held that the trustee was correct to raise the defence that application of the capital disqualification event was not at issue, in part because the court argued that the ECNs would still be counted towards LBG's regulatory capital.

In short, the trigger for conversion would no longer be valid, not only under the rules of CRR, but also as a result of the UK authorities' own policy rules, because the trigger included in the ECNs ignored the point in time when capital enhancement was considered desirable. In other words, the ECNs would, as a result of their technical operation, never be able to make a significant contribution to strengthening the LBG's capital.

The judges were notable for their extensive refined explanations and complex considerations in this case. On appeal, the Court of Appeal reversed the High Court's decision and concluded that the capital disqualification event should have been applied and that redemption of the bonds was indeed in order. The interpretation of the contractual wording was particularly important; in sum, the capital disqualification event did not stand the test of time, because due to the radical changes in the rules for qualitative capital requirements, it appeared that the wording of this contractual clause was no longer correctly geared to the new situation in the stricter capital adequacy regime. What also played a special role here, in my view, was the role of the UK competent supervisor and the policy rules adopted at the time for UK banks, which imposed a stricter requirement for capital adequacy than those resulting from the CRR rules. The courts interpreted the consequences of this tightened policy, and therefore great influence was also attributed to these policy rules of the authorities.

4.8.2. *Crédit Agricole and Affiliates v ECB*

Crédit Agricole and affiliates v ECB was a recent ECJ ruling on appeal of an entirely different order, in which the legal sustainability of a sanction imposed by the ECB in the form of an administrative fine for non-compliance with the (procedures relating to the review of) qualitative capital requirements were litigated. The ECJ's judgment of 16 June 2021 in Joined Cases C-456/20 P and C-458/20 P addressed an important issue in the context of the ECB's powers under the SSM.[36] It concerned the application of Article 26(3) CRR (discussed in detail in section 4.3) and involved the *ex ante* vetting of conformity of CET1 instruments with the CRR rules. The case facts and proceedings were as follows.

By their appeals, Crédit Agricole SA and its affiliates sought the annulment of the judgments of the General Court of the EU of 8 July 2020.[37] The General Court dismissed the action brought by Crédit Agricole and its affiliates seeking annulment of the ECB decisions of 16 July 2018.[38] The ECB had thereby imposed administrative pecuniary sanctions of €4,300,000, €300,000 and €200,000 respectively for the persistent breach of the own funds requirements of Article 26(3) CRR.[39]

Crédit Agricole and its affiliates were blamed for, at least negligently, including, without the prior consent of the competent authority (ie the ECB) capital which resulted from three issues of ordinary shares into their CET1 capital buffer. In this respect, the ECB dismissed Crédit Agricole's and its affiliates' argument that these ordinary shares had been included in the list published by the EBA pursuant to Article 26(3) CRR. The ECB essentially considered an instrument's inclusion on the list did not exempt a credit institution from the obligation to obtain the prior consent of the competent obtain the competent authority's prior approval under Article 26(3) CRR.

[36] Cases C-456/20 P to C458/20 P *Crédit Agricole v ECB*, ECLI:EU:C:2021:502.

[37] It concerns Cases T-576/18 *Crédit Agricole v ECB*, EU:T:2020:304; T-577/18, EU:T:2020:305 (not published); and T-578/18, EU:T:2020:306 (not published).

[38] See ECB/SSM/2018-FRCAG-75; ECB/SSM/2018-FRCAG-76 and ECB/SSM/2018-FRCAG-77.

[39] The power to impose this administrative sanction is regulated in Art 18(1) SSM Regulation.

The appeals were partly dismissed by the ECJ as manifestly inadmissible and partly as manifestly unfounded. In my opinion, the appeal has hardly discussed the substance of the case, and mainly concerns complaints by Crédit Agricole and its affiliates about the handling of the case on appeal by the General Court of the EU. One point of interest in this case, however, is the contention of Crédit Agricole and its affiliates that, by finding that the ECB had committed an infringement in relation to the second quarter of 2016, the General Court committed an error of law consisting in a breach of the principle of retroactive application of the more lenient penal law, which is enshrined in Article 49(1) of the Charter of Fundamental Rights of the European Union, Article 49(2) of the Charter of Fundamental Rights of the European Union and the case law of the ECJ and the European Court of Human Rights (ECHR), by refusing to apply Article 26(3) of Regulation 575/2013, as amended, to the case of the applicant. This new provision in fact constitutes a less severe penal law, since it provides that, under certain conditions, successive issues of the same form as issues already authorised are no longer subject to prior authorisation, but only to notification is required.

This touches on the amendment to Article 26 CRR as discussed in section 4.3 above, which means, in short, that if a bank wants to issue certain CET1 instruments, which have already been reviewed by the competent authority in the past, and it is established that the new instruments to be issued have 'the same terms and conditions' as the already approved instruments, then there is only a duty of notification to the competent authorities. Crédit Agricole became stuck in the chronology of events by admitting in its earlier defences that the consent with respect to the 'third issue' was obtained only after the placement of the CET1 capital, so that, according to the Court, it cannot hide behind the argument that the consent given for the first two issues of CET1 instruments count as consent within the meaning of the new regime of Article 26(3) CRR. However, the point itself does give raise questions from the perspective of the interpretation of the negligence criterion against which any imposition of a sanction should be tested. In my view, this concerns the following.

As indicated above, the qualitative capital requirements for banks are a matter of many subtleties, potential pitfalls and, to put it mildly, an extremely complex set of rules. It seems to me that, particularly in respect of CET1 instruments, the new rules of Article 26(3) CRR have led to a significant relaxation of the need for each issue of such capital instruments to be reviewed in advance by the competent authority. However, as stated above, the rules of common, national company law and any contractual arrangements in respect of CET1 instruments should not be the main source of dispute as to whether such CET1 instruments comply with the qualitative capital requirements. To put it bluntly, ordinary shares in the capital of companies, the share premium accounted for on them and any (recognised) profit reserves are governed by more or less unchangeable rules. And CET1 instruments issued by banks will always be very similar for that reason.

How different is this for AT1 instruments and Tier 2 instruments? There is a much greater risk that such instruments, making use of the freedom of contract that applies between the bank and the buyers of the relevant bonds, may entail conflicts with the applicable CRR rules. I explained above that banks are not required to submit new issues of AT1 and Tier 2 instruments to the regulator for approval in advance. What is the interpretation of the principle of negligence, if a bank decides not to make use of the possibility for informal review of newly issued instruments provided by the regulators (see above)? Although banks are not obliged to organise this *ex ante* assessment for AT1 and Tier 2 instruments, can they be reproached legally if they fail to do so, issue an AT1 or Tier 2 instrument which is subsequently found by the competent supervisory authority not to comply with the qualitative capital requirements, and the supervisory authority (therefore) establishes that the bank has (culpably) breached the capital requirements?

In my opinion, *Crédit Agricole and affiliates v ECB* shows that the enforcement of the rules on qualitative capital requirements is an extremely important matter for supervisors. The case has led to the imposition of serious fines and a high-profile dispute between the ECB and the supervised bank. After all, there can be no other conclusion than the bank's management is being accused of negligence in complying with fundamental rules of banking supervision.

Therefore, despite all the efforts of the EBA in publishing guidance and actively handling Q&As, I believe that a clearer procedural arrangement for the pre-assessment of, in particular, AT1 and Tier 2 instruments is needed to avoid banks falling into traps and being accused of violating capital adequacy rules.

4.9. Concluding Remarks

In this chapter I examined some aspects of the qualitative capital requirements. I found that these public law regulations in CRR and in the RTS on Own Funds are not 'contract law' or 'company law' per se, but they do have a far-reaching influence on the private law relationships between banks and their capital providers. At the very least, it can be established that the qualitative capital requirements set limits on the contractual freedoms of the parties, but also strongly influence the way in which the private law agreements are implemented and performed, if they do not impose binding rules. Is it then too much to say that in this area there is at least a hybrid system in which contract law and company law are framed by the public law regulations regarding bank capital?

In the complex system of 'informal influence' by the competent authorities, EBA has an important role to play in Europe. Through the various monitoring powers of this authority, the aim is to ensure uniform application of the qualitative capital requirements and also to closely observe the principle of supervisory convergence. While the organisation of conditions between banks and their financiers for CET1, AT1 and Tier 2 instruments issued by banks is primarily a matter of the application of the national (company and contract) law of the Member States concerned, EBA must ensure that the application of that national law does not lead to the diminishment of the quality of regulatory capital in the EU through the application of local exceptions, local special rules of contract or company law and similar variables. In order to provide insight into EBA's far-reaching role in this area, I discussed the mandatory contributions of national competent authorities to the maintenance of the CET1 list and, in addition, the extensive guidance that EBA has developed over the years in the context of monitoring AT1 and Tier 2 instruments.[40]

In the EU, as in the other countries participating in the Basel Committee, strict enforcement of the quality of CET1 capital has been the main focus since 2013. This has led to the establishment of the monitoring system mentioned above. In my opinion, insufficient attention has been paid to the possible impairment of the quality of AT1 and Tier 2 instruments issued by banks. The procedures for monitoring the quality of such capital instruments are much more non-committal than for CET1 capital. In my opinion, there is reason, not least to provide certainty for participants in the capital markets and investors in banks, to change this. AT1 and Tier2 instruments should also be subject to mandatory *ex ante* assessment in order to ensure that the issuance of such instruments does not depend too heavily on the design of the terms and conditions by the issuing bank in negotiations with the future financiers.

There is not a great deal of case law on qualitative capital requirements; I have only been able to address a few rulings that are relevant to this issue. I concluded that the purpose of monitoring the core capital of banks means that: (1) there is strict enforcement if a bank does not comply with the rules in this area; and (2) when it comes to determining the applicable contractual terms, there appears to be a wide margin of appreciation for courts, at least under English law, to interpret contractual terms in such a way that banks remain within the boundaries drawn by the law when it comes to compliance with the qualitative capital requirements, even if this would lead to a different application of what the parties had agreed. This is where the contractual freedom of the parties gives way to the strict application of the qualitative capital requirements.

[40] Other powers of the EBA concern the monitoring of CET1 instruments itself, but also since CRR2 the monitoring of the issued instruments that are required to comply with rules of the 'eligible liabilities' within the meaning of the European resolution framework and, lastly, the work on the (permitted) grandfathering of legacy instruments issued prior to the adoption of CRR. For work of EBA in this respect, see 'EBA Report on the Monitoring of CET1 Instruments issued by EU Institutions' (23 May 2017); 'EBA Report on the Monitoring of TLAC-/MREL eligible liabilities instruments of European Union Institutions' EBA/REP/2020/27 (29 October 2020); and 'Opinion of the European Banking Authority on the Prudential Treatment of Legacy Instruments' EBA/Op/2020/17 (21 October 2020).

5

Administrative Enforcement of European Financial Regulation

SASKIA NUIJTEN

5.1. Preface

Until the 1980s financial supervisory law was a relatively small part of legislation in the EU. It has developed since then and is at present a large and complex set of regulations based mainly upon European directives. These European rules have been implemented on a national level, and supervision and enforcement are mainly carried out by the national supervisors.

This European legislative base is now changing, and two developments are having a major impact on the enforcement of financial law. The first development is that the number of regulations is rapidly growing at the expense of the directives. Consequently, the substantive provisions of financial law no longer need to be implemented and are therefore identical in all Member States. However, this is often not the case for the procedural and formal provisions and therefore the enforcement powers. With regard to enforcement, the regulation often still bears a strong resemblance to the directive. For example, the PRIIPS Regulation,[1] Chapter V concerns administrative penalties and other measures. Although all substantive rules apply without implementation, Chapter V orders Member States:

> [T]o lay down rules establishing appropriate administrative sanctions and measures applicable to situations which constitute an infringement of this Regulation and shall take all necessary measures to ensure that they are implemented. Those sanctions and measures shall be effective, proportionate and dissuasive. Member States may decide not to lay down rules for administrative sanctions as referred to in the first subparagraph for infringements which are subject to criminal sanctions under their national law.[2]

[1] PRIIPs Regulation (Regulation (EU) No 1286/2014 of the European Parliament and of the Council of 26 November 2014 on key information documents for packaged retail and insurance-based investment products (PRIIPs) [2014] OJ L 352/1).

[2] Article 22(1) PRIIPs Regulation.

Article 24 PRIIPs does not prescribe specific enforcement measures to either a national or a European supervisor. In contrast, this chapter summarises only the minimum standards that must be met by the national legislation for enforcement. Thus, the substantive provisions are the same in all Member States, but the differences in enforcement practice still lead to major differences in the regulatory framework between Member States.

A second development in financial law relates to the European supervisory authorities (ESAs). Three ESAs have been established: the European Banking Authority (EBA),[3] the European Securities and Markets Authority (ESMA)[4] and the European Insurance and Occupational Pensions Authority (EIOPA)[5] and, based on the de Larosière Report,[6] were given two tasks:

(1) '[T]o contribute to the establishment of high-quality common regulatory and supervisory standards and practices, in particular by providing opinions to the Union institutions and by developing guidelines, recommendations, and draft regulatory and implementing technical standards'[7] or involvement in Level 2 and 3 legislation, which is – in the Lamfalussy process – not the framework legislation in directives and regulations but the guidelines, recommendations, technical standards, Q&As based on these frameworks.
(2) '[T]o contribute to the consistent application of legally binding Union acts, in particular by contributing to a common supervisory culture, ensuring consistent, efficient and effective application of the acts, preventing regulatory arbitrage, mediating and settling disagreements between competent authorities, ensuring effective and consistent supervision of financial institutions, ensuring a coherent functioning of colleges of supervisors and taking actions, inter alia, in emergency situations',[8] 'or contributing to a uniform practice of supervision of financial firms and markets by the national supervisory authorities.

Although the primacy of enforcement thus continues to be vested in the national supervisory authorities, a development has subsequently started in which

[3] Regulation (EU) No 1093/2010 of the European Parliament and of the Council of 24 November 2010 establishing a European Supervisory Authority (European Banking Authority), amending Decision No 716/2009/EC and repealing Commission Decision 2009/78/EC [2010] OJ L 331/12.

[4] Regulation (EU) No 1095/2010 of the European Parliament and of the Council of 24 November 2010 establishing a European Supervisory Authority (European Securities and Markets Authority), amending Decision No 716/2009/EC and repealing Commission Decision 2009/77/EC [2010] OJ L 331/84.

[5] Regulation (EU) No 1094/2010 of the European Parliament and of the Council of 24 November 2010 establishing a European Supervisory Authority (European Insurance and Occupational Pensions Authority), amending Decision No 716/2009/EC and repealing Commission Decision 2009/79/EC [2010] OJ L 331/48.

[6] 'Final Report of the Committee of Wise Men on the Regulation of European Securities Markets' (15 February 2001), available at www.esma.europa.eu/sites/default/files/library/2015/11/lamfalussy_report.pdf.

[7] See eg Art 8(1)(a) Regulation (EU) No 1093/2010.

[8] See eg Art 8(1)(b) Regulation (EU) No 1093/2010.

supervision and enforcement are also vested more in European financial supervisors. ESMA has already been given direct supervisory powers in two areas: supervision of credit-rating agencies and trade repositories.[9] As of 1 January 2022 ESMA is also directly supervises certain data-reporting services providers and benchmark administrators.[10] This was the outcome of a process that started with a proposal by the European Commission to transfer even more direct supervisory authorities to ESMA and the other ESAs.[11] For banking supervision, there are also direct European supervisory powers although these were not attributed to EBA but to the European Central Bank (ECB). The ECB in particular is a supervisor with many powers under the Single Supervisory Mechanism (SSM). An important new development is the proposal to establish a European supervisor for anti-money laundering and combating the financing of terrorism (AML/CFT) supervision.[12] The powers in the area of AML are currently predominantly national. This development means that new rules for enforcement need to be developed and attributed in specific regulations.

This chapter does not primarily address legal protection against enforcement,[13] but the kind of procedural and formal rules that apply in case of enforcement of financial law in different scenarios: the general rule of fair decision-making and impartiality; the (online) provision of information on existing procedures; the management of procedures and procedural rights; time limits for concluding procedures; the rules for gathering information, inspections and investigating; the duty to cooperate and the privilege against self-incrimination; the use of witnesses and experts; access to the file; the right to be heard and consultation of interested parties; the duties to specify the decision, give reasons and indicate available remedies; language requirements; rules on electronic communication and legal representation; notification of decisions and correction of obvious inaccuracies in a decision; rectification and withdrawal, etc. These are the rules and guarantees relevant for every administrative decision with direct effects for a specific person, and therefore legal certainty requires these rules to be clear. Clear and codified

[9] See for a description: www.esma.europa.eu/supervision/supervision.

[10] Arts 4 and 5 Regulation (EU) 2019/2175 of the European Parliament and of the Council of 18 December 2019 amending Regulation (EU) No 1093/2010 establishing a European Supervisory Authority (European Banking Authority), Regulation (EU) No 1094/2010 establishing a European Supervisory Authority (European Insurance and Occupational Pensions Authority), Regulation (EU) No 1095/2010 establishing a European Supervisory Authority (European Securities and Markets Authority), Regulation (EU) No 600/2014 on markets in financial instruments, Regulation (EU) 2016/1011 on indices used as benchmarks in financial instruments and financial contracts or to measure the performance of investment funds, and Regulation (EU) 2015/847 on information accompanying transfers of funds [2019], OJ L 334/1.

[11] Communication of the European Commission 'Reinforcing integrated supervision to strengthen Capital Markets Union and financial integration in a changing environment' COM (2017) 542 final. See CM Grundmann van de Krol, 'ESMA als toezichthouder: enkele verschillen vergeleken met de AFM' (2020) *Ondernemingsrecht* 112.

[12] See ch 10 in this volume.

[13] For an extensive overview of legal protection in banking supervision see L Wissink, *Effective Legal Protection in Banking Supervision* (European Law Publishing, 2021), and ch 6 in this volume.

rules on these subjects will give legal certainty and contribute to the accessibility, transparency and predictability of European legislation and therefore also to the legitimacy of and trust in European institutions. These are all objectives that need to be met if we decide to enlarge the role and powers of European institutions and supervisors.

In addressing this kind of procedural and formal rules, this chapter raises the question of whether European administrative law is sufficiently well developed for the enforcement practice that has emerged, and will emerge, based on the two developments described above. After describing different enforcement scenarios (section 5.2), an overview is provided of the general rules and guarantees governing enforcement by European supervisory authorities based on European or national powers (section 5.3). In paragraph 5.4 I discuss the cooperation between Member States in case of enforcement by national supervisory authorities. section 5.5 leads to the conclusion that it is necessary to pay more attention to enforcement of European legislation and to constitute a general legal framework for enforcement.

5.2. Scenarios

European financial supervisory authorities cooperate with national supervisory authorities in the use of their direct supervisory powers as well as with regard to other subjects of financial regulation. This cooperation may take different forms with regard to enforcement. In some cases the European supervisor has the authority to enforce and uses the European enforcement authorities itself. For example, the ECB can impose administrative fines on European banks for certain violations since 2014. On its website, the ECB has currently published 14 administrative fines it has imposed in the period 2017–19.[14] On the same webpage, the ECB shows another possibility: enforcement measures may be imposed by national supervisory authorities at the ECB's request. In most cases, however, the national supervisory authority is the only authority with direct enforcement powers. Based on the current directives and regulations these are the following scenarios:

- a national supervisory authority enforces a European regulation after implementation in national law;
- a national supervisory authority enforces a European directive;
- a European supervisory authority (ESA) enforces a European directive with specific European powers;
- an ESA enforces a European directive with national powers;
- an ESA orders a national supervisory authority to enforce a European directive or regulation.

[14] See www.bankingsupervision.europa.eu/banking/sanctions/html/index.en.html.

When supervising and investigating before enforcement measures are imposed, the European and national supervisory authority sometimes work together in a way that makes it difficult to make the distinction above. This ambiguity does not exist in formal enforcement, since it is always clear from the enforcement decision which authority has made the decision.

With the increasing role for the European supervisory authorities and the increasing power for direct enforcement, the question arises to which requirements this European enforcement is bound. This is therefore the first topic to be discussed below.

Since a large part of the enforcement is still carried out by national supervisory authorities, the second topic of this chapter is international cooperation between national supervisors in enforcement. After all, an important reason for the increasing European integration of regulations is that financial services often do not stop at national borders. It is precisely this transnational nature, for example, that is the reason an ESA for AML is now proposed. Therefore it is of great importance that international coordination and cooperation in enforcement is ensured, for supervised entities as well as for the purposes of the legislation.

5.3. Rules and Guarantees for Enforcement by European Supervisory Authority

5.3.1. Good Administration and Charter

With European law traditionally containing primarily substantive standards that are to be applied at the national level by national authorities, little attention was paid initially to the procedural standards and enforcement on a European level. Consequently, the focus was on the so-called 'Rewe' principles[15] of equivalence and effectiveness, both relating to the exercise of European law in Member States. Furthermore, the principle of loyal cooperation is important for enforcement, which, according to case law of the ECJ, means that a Member State is under an obligation to initiate criminal or disciplinary proceedings for infringement of European law, should such infringement occur in its jurisdiction. However, neither of these principles relate to enforcement by an ESA.

For enforcement by European institutions[16] some guidelines have been introduced by case law and these has been implemented in Article 41 of the Charter:[17]

> 1. Every person has the right to have his or her affairs handled impartially, fairly and within a reasonable time by the institutions, bodies, offices and agencies of the Union.

[15] Case C-33/76 *Rewe*, ECLI:EU:C:1976:188.

[16] From Case C-277/11 *M*, ECLI:EU:C:2012:744 it is clear that the safeguards of Art 41 of the Charter are also applicable to Member States under certain circumstances when acting within the scope of EU law.

[17] Charter of Fundamental Rights of the European Union.

2. This right includes:
   a) the right of every person to be heard, before any individual measure which would affect him or her adversely is taken;
   b) the right of every person to have access to his or her file, while respecting the legitimate interests of confidentiality and of professional and business secrecy;
   c) the obligation of the administration to give reasons for its decisions.
3. Every person has the right to have the Union make good any damage caused by its institutions or by its servants in the performance of their duties, in accordance with the general principles common to the laws of the Member States.
4. Every person may write to the institutions of the Union in one of the languages of the Treaties and must have an answer in the same language.

Some of these rights resemble national principles of good administration; some even go beyond the national rights. Table 5.1 below provides a comparison between the Charter, the General administrative law act (*Algemene wet bestuursrecht* (Awb)) and the Financial Supervision Act (*Wet op het financieel Toezicht* (Wft)).

Charter	**Right**	**Awb/Wft**	**Right**	**Comparison**
41(1)	Handled impartially and fairly	2:4 Awb	Handled impartially and without prejudice	Similar
41(1)	Within reasonable time	4:13 Awb	Within reasonable time	Similar
41(2)	Right to be heard	4:8 Awb	Right to be heard if requirements are met for all interested parties	Dutch right is more limited
41(2)	Access to file	5:49 Wft 7:4 Awb 8:39 Awb	Only access to file in objection, appeal or in case of an administrative fine	Dutch right is more limited
41(2)	Give reasons	3:46 Awb	Each decision must be reasoned	Similar
41(3)	Right to damages	1:25d Wft	Only right to damages if intentional or gross fault	Dutch right is more limited
41(4)	All languages of Treaties	2:6 Awb	Dutch	Similar

These rights become relevant when an ESA makes a decision or imposes an enforcement measure. This means the ECB for example needs always to give reasons for its decisions although assessment of this requirement is depending on the circumstances of the case, in particular the content of the measure in question, the nature of the reasons given and the interest which the addressees of the measure, or other parties to whom it is of direct and individual concern may have in obtaining explanations.[18] In 2020 the General Court of the European Union annulled three decisions from the ECB imposing administrative fines on the basis that inadequate reasons were given for those decisions.[19] In those cases the ECB was entitled to impose administrative fines of up to 10 per cent of the total annual turnover of the group to which the supervised company in question belonged. The General Court concluded that the ECB enjoys a wide discretion to determine the amount of the administrative fine, and that therefore, respect for the rights, which include the right of the interested party to receive a sufficient statement of reasons for the decision at issue, is of even more fundamental importance.

Other rights as codified in the Charter may also be relevant in case of administrative enforcement. Article 16 Charter provides the freedom to conduct a business. This right is limited by licensing requirements, but may even be further limited by enforcement measures since the ECB has the power to restrict or limit the business, operations or network of institutions, or to request the divestment of activities that pose excessive risks to the soundness of an institution.[20] Article 17 Charter concerns the right to property, a right that is limited, for example, in the case of an administrative fine imposed by the ECB. Title V Charter provides rights with regard to justice: the right to an effective remedy and to a fair trial, the presumption of innocence and right of defence, principles of legality and proportionality of criminal offences and penalties, and the right not to be tried or punished twice in criminal proceedings for the same criminal offence. Article 52 Charter provides a link to the rights of the European Convention for the Protection of Human Rights and Fundamental Freedoms. The rights codified in the Charter may have an impact on administrative enforcement, either punitive enforcement measures like administrative fines or recovery enforcement measures aimed at recovery, eg an order to restrict the business operations. However, none of these human rights provides a uniform set of enforcement measures to be used by supervisors. Furthermore none provides procedural guarantees designed specifically for administrative enforcement, although the rights relevant for criminal punishment will often also apply to administrative fines.[21]

5.3.2. Specific Regulation

Since there are no general rules for the powers of administrative enforcement by an ESA, the relevant regulation must determine the scope and limits.

[18] Case C-450/1 *Landeskreditbank Baden-Württemberg*, ECLI:EU:C:2019:372, [87].

[19] Case T-576/18 *Crédit Agricole*, ECLI:EU:T:2020:304; Case T-577/18 *Crédit Agricole*, ECLI:EU:T:2020:305; Case T-578/18 *Crédit Agricole*, ECLI:EU:T:2020:306.

[20] Art 16(2)(e) SSM Regulation (Council Regulation (EU) No 1024/2013 of 15 October 2013 conferring specific tasks on the European Central Bank concerning policies relating to the prudential supervision of credit institutions [2013] OJ L 287/63).

[21] But not always; see eg ECtHR 8 June 1976 *Engel and others/Netherlands*, ECLI:CE:ECHR:1976:0608JUD000510071; ECtHR 21 Febuary 1984 *Öztürk*, ECLI:NL:XX:1984:AC954; ECtHR 25 Augustus 1987 *Lutz*, ECLI:NL:XX:1987:AC9955.

5.3.2.1. ECB

For the ECB this is the SSM Regulation and SSM Framework Regulation.[22] Articles 16 and 18 SSM Regulation confers upon the ECB the following powers:

- to require institutions to hold own funds in excess of the applicable capital requirements;
- to require the reinforcement of the arrangements, processes, mechanisms and strategies;
- to require institutions to present a plan to restore compliance with supervisory requirements;
- to require institutions to apply a specific provisioning policy or treatment of assets in terms of own funds requirements;
- to restrict or limit the business, operations or network of institutions or to request the divestment of activities that pose excessive risks to the soundness of an institution;
- to require the reduction of the risk inherent in the activities, products and systems of institutions;
- to require institutions to limit variable remuneration as a percentage of net revenues when it is inconsistent with the maintenance of a sound capital base;
- to require institutions to use net profits to strengthen own funds;
- to restrict or prohibit distributions by the institution to shareholders, members or holders of Additional Tier 1 instruments where the prohibition does not constitute an event of default of the institution;
- to impose additional or more frequent reporting requirements, including reporting on capital and liquidity positions;
- to impose specific liquidity requirements, including restrictions on maturity mismatches between assets and liabilities;
- to require additional disclosures;
- to remove at any time members from the management body of credit institutions who do not fulfil the relevant requirements;
- to impose administrative fines of up to twice the amount of the profits gained or losses avoided because of the breach where those can be determined, or up to 10 per cent of the total annual turnover and to publish the penalty;
- to impose periodic penalty payments.

The SSM Regulation and the SSM Framework Regulation provide a number of procedural safeguards for acts and decisions of the ECB as listed above.

[22] SSM Framework Regulation (Regulation (EU) 468/2014 of the European Central Bank of 16 April 2014 establishing the framework for cooperation within the Single Supervisory Mechanism between the European Central Bank and national competent authorities and with national designated authorities ('SSM Framework Regulation') [2014] OJ L 141/1.

These safeguards are offered to the applicant and the addressee of an ECB decision. Third parties do not enjoy these safeguards. The safeguards are mainly a duplication of the rights from the Charter discussed above. The SSM Framework Regulation grants the right to be heard (Article 31), access to the ECB's file, with the exception of confidential information and the business secrets of others (Article 32) and imposes the obligation to give reasons to supervisory decisions (Article 33). Furthermore, a party may be represented in a supervisory procedure (Article 27 SSM Framework Regulation) and reports of alleged infringements are treated as confidential (Article 37 Framework Regulation).

For administrative pecuniary sanctions and fines, an additional safeguard has been created by the mandatory establishment of an independent investigation unit (Article 123 SSM Framework Regulation). The ECB must refer a case – inter alia – to this unit if there is suspicion that a major supervised entity is violating an ECB regulation or decision. The unit investigates and prepares a proposal for a full draft decision for the Governing Council, together with an investigation file.

5.3.2.2. ESMA

ESMA also has the authority to impose certain enforcement measures, but to analyse these powers and their safeguards, we have to investigate the specific relevant European regulations. For example, on 23 March 2021 ESMA imposed five fines to Moody's[23] for violation of Regulation 1060/2009.[24] Based on this Regulation ESMA has several powers such as the withdrawal of the registration of the credit-rating agency, imposing a temporary prohibition from issuing credit ratings, but also the imposition of administrative fines and periodic penalty payments. The procedural safeguards for the imposition of administrative fines and periodic penalty payments based on this Regulation are adopted in a delegated act: Commission Delegated Regulation (EU) No 946/2012.[25] These include again the right to be heard and access to the file and use of documents, but also limitation periods for the imposition of penalties.

Since there are no general rules regarding enforcement and/or general administrative European law, the enforcement powers are always necessarily based on specific provisions for each Regulation. This means it is important to carefully check the safeguard and other procedural rules since they may differ and the changes may be significant. This also means that case law with regard to a

[23] See www.esma.europa.eu/supervision/enforcement/enforcement-actions

[24] Regulation (EC) 1060/2009 of the European Parliament and of the Council of 16 September 2009 on credit rating agencies [2009] OJ L 302/1 as amended by Regulation (EU) No 513/2011 of the European Parliament and of the Council of 11 May 2011 [2011] OJ L 145/30.

[25] Commission Delegated Regulation (EU) No 946/2012 of 12 July 2012 supplementing Regulation (EC) No 1060/2009 of the European Parliament and of the Council with regard to rules of procedure on fines imposed to credit rating agencies by the European Securities and Markets Authority, including rules on the right of defence and temporal provisions [2012] OJ L 282/23.

specific Regulation may, but does not need to, be relevant for enforcement based on another Regulation.

5.3.3. Regulation on EU Administrative Procedures

On 15 January 2013 the European Parliament adopted a resolution with recommendations to the Commission to draft a law of administrative procedure of the EU.[26] The Parliament considered that citizens are increasingly directly confronted with the Union's administration, but that the existing rules and principles on good administration are scattered across a wide variety of sources: primary law; the case law of the Court of Justice of the European Union; secondary legislation; soft law; and unilateral commitments by Union's institutions. Since rules on good administration promote transparency and accountability and since a core set of principles of good administration is widely accepted among Member States, the Parliament requested the Commission to submit a proposal for a regulation on European Law of Administrative Procedure based on the proposal it had drafted. The resolution was adopted by an overwhelming majority (572 in favour, 16 against, 12 abstentions) but the Parliament's request was not followed up by a Commission proposal. The Commission did not heed the request because it argued that such general rules are too rigid and would seriously slow down the decision-making process.[27]

In response, the Parliament itself drafted a proposal for a regulation in 2016: a regulation for an open, efficient and independent EU administration.[28] Parliament invited the Commission to consider the proposal for a regulation and called on it to include a legislative proposal in its work programme for the year 2017. The European Commission replied in November 2016, however, that it was 'not convinced that the benefits of using a legislative instrument that would codify administrative law would outweigh the costs'.[29] Therefore, the Parliament carried out a public consultation and an impact assessment.

The key findings of the public consultation were that most respondents supported additional measures at EU level to simplify EU administrative rules and procedures and to enhance measures to enforce the public's right to good administration. The findings were published in 2018.[30] The impact assessment was also

[26] European Parliament resolution of 15 January 2013 with recommendations to the Commission on a Law of Administrative Procedure of the European Union (2012/2024(INL)) [2015] OJ C 440/17.

[27] Commissie Europeanisering algemeen bestuursrecht, *Europa en het algemeen bestuursrecht, Burger en bestuur in de gemeenschappelijke rechtsorde* (Boom Juridisch, 2021) 47.

[28] A regulation for an open, efficient and independent European Union administration, European Parliament resolution of 9 June 2016 for an open, efficient and independent European Union administration (2016/2610(RSP)) [2018] OJ C 86/126.

[29] 'Possible action at EU level for an open, efficient and independent EU administration', Impact Assessment, 5, available at europarl.europa.eu/RegData/etudes/STUD/2018/621841/EPRS_STU(2018)621841_EN.pdf.

[30] See europarl.europa.eu/cmsdata/150700/consultation-eu-law-summary-report.pdf.

published in 2018.[31] In the impact assessment, three options were discussed and compared: Option zero is not changing anything; Option 1 is to make the European Ombudsman Code binding; and Option 2 is to adopt the European Parliament's proposed regulatory framework. The conclusion in the impact assessment was that

> the introduction of a set of harmonised rules on administrative procedure would contribute positively to good governance in the EU and lead to enhanced levels of protection, in particular with respect to the right to good administration and to the enhanced openness, efficiency and independence of EU institutions, agencies and bodies, in line with Article 298 TFEU. The preferred option (Option 2), which corresponds to the proposal tabled by the European Parliament in 2016, would also improve the compatibility of EU administrative law with the rules on administrative procedure adopted by most Member States. It would also prepare the EU administration to make the most of the upcoming digital transformation in the administration. This option could also become the first important step to introducing more ambitious options in the future, such as a fully fledged Administrative Procedure Act, also covering rulemaking. This option was not fully considered in this report because it was not thought to be feasible in the near future; in any case it is subject to the adoption of a comprehensive set of rules on administrative procedure.

To date, however, the Commission has not proposed a regulation as suggested by Parliament. This questions the need for such a regulation to accompany the developments described above. Although it is difficult to assess the possible consequences of a regulation that was not adopted or even proposed, the Annual Report of the European Ombudsman[32] shows that the majority of complaints lodged concern the European Commission (210 complaints, or 56.8 per cent) and at least 67 per cent of the complaints concern subjects that may (partially) be addressed in such a regulation: transparency and accountability (97, or 25 per cent); respect for fundamental rights (59, or 10 per cent); proper use of discretion (67, or 17 per cent); and respect for procedural rights (59, or 15 per cent).[33] (See Figures 5.1 and 5.2.)

Although it is not clear what was the subject of the behaviour complained about, and probably only a small number of these complaints relate to enforcement, still this overview does suggest that clear procedural rules and guarantees would help. For example, most complaints are about transparency and accountability including access to information and documents. As described above, this is one of the topics that could and should be subject to general rules for administrative decision-making. Furthermore, 17 per cent of the complaints is about proper use of discretion including in infringement procedures, and 15 per cent about respect for procedural rights. These are the main topics for such general rules as described in the introduction.

Based on this overview, we have to ask whether the enforcement of financial law can be increasingly entrusted to the European level without binding and

[31] See Impact Assessment (n 29).

[32] Note that at time of writing, the 'Ombudsman' is Emily O'Reilly, so *Ombudsvrouw* or the more neutral 'Ombudsperson' would be linguistically more correct.

[33] European Ombudsman, 'Annual Report 2020' 33–34.

Figure 5.1 Institutions investigated by the European Ombudsman in 2020

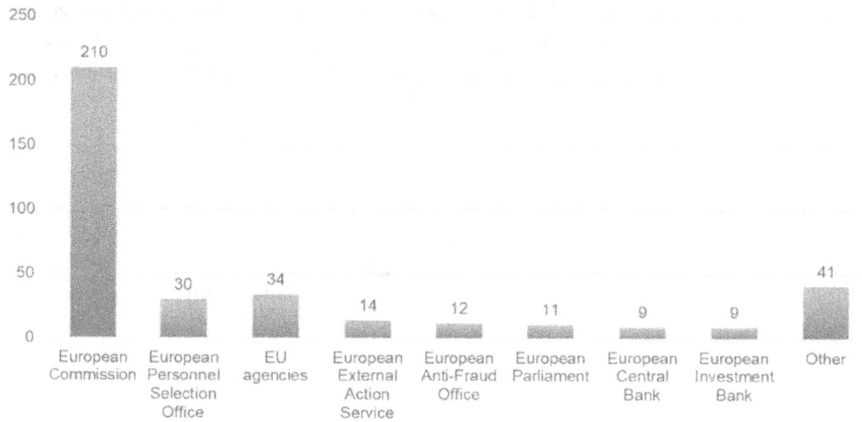

Source: Annual Report 2020 of the European Ombudsman.

Figure 5.2 Behaviours investigated by the European Ombudsman closed in 2020

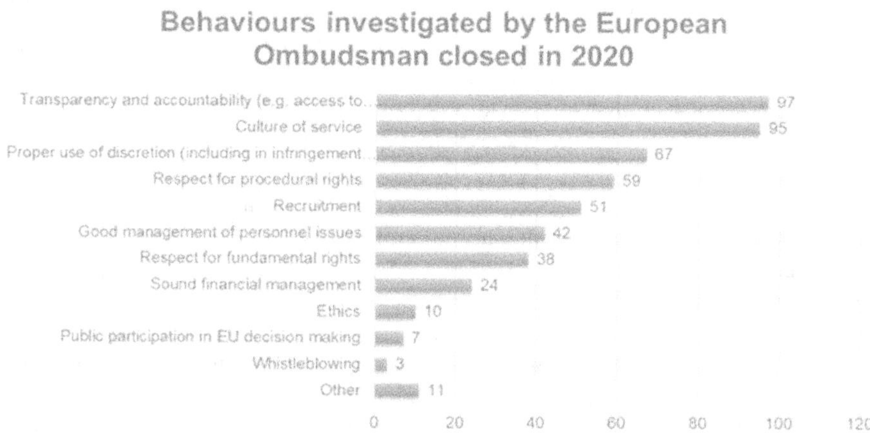

Source: Annual Report 2020 of the European Ombudsman.

clear procedural rules. At that level, there appears to be a serious need for general provisions on procedures and safeguards for the actions and decisions of EU administrative bodies, including European supervisors.

Despite all the efforts of the European Parliament and the large majority that voted in favour of its proposals, such a regulation has not been adopted or even proposed. The European Commission never stated that such a regulation would need adjustment of the Treaty or that there are other legal impediments for the regulation as drafted by the European Parliament. The main objection of the European Commission was that it was not convinced that the benefits of legislation to codify administrative law would outweigh the costs, but this objection has been countered by the impact assessment, which showed that adopting such a regulation (Option 2 of the impact assessment) would be the preferred option, since it would lead to clear advantages in terms of cost savings for the public, as well as the accessibility, transparency, legal certainty and predictability, as well as the legitimacy of, and trust in, EU institutions. The fact that there still is no Commission proposal raises the even more fundamental question of whether a system in which the democratically elected body has no right of initiative is suitable for directly interfering with the rights and powers of citizens and taking enforcement action itself. I will leave this question unanswered, but I believe that further Europeanisation of financial law enforcement, including the creation of a European AML supervisor, or of any other kind of administrative enforcement, should not take place without having this discussion.

If the European Commission continues to oppose a regulation with general administrative rules for all European authorities, alternative general administrative rules could be proposed at least for the financial ESAs. For the ECB there already are some general rules with regard to the imposition of sanctions (ie administrative fines and periodic penalty payments).[34] Maybe these rules could be extended to the other enforcement decisions, as listed above, and to other European financial supervisory authorities.

5.3.4. ReNEUAL Model Rules

Next to the proposals by the European Parliament, the Research Network on EU Administrative Law (ReNEUAL) presented Model Rules on Administrative Procedures in September 2014. The objective of the ReNEUAL Model Rules was to determine how the constitutional values of the Union can best be translated into rules on administrative procedure for non-legislative implementation of EU law and policies:[35]

> Well-designed rules for implementation of EU law and policies could improve the quality of the EU's legal system. They have the potential to add to the compliance with general principles of EU law, to help simplify the legal system, enhance legal certainty and fill gaps in the legal system.[36]

According to ReNEUAL, rules on administrative procedures need to be designed to maximise equally the twin objectives of public law: to ensure that the instruments in question foster the effective discharge of public duties and, at the same time, that the rights of individuals are protected. The Model Rules serve to protect

[34] Council Regulation (EC) 2532/98 of 23 November 1998 concerning the powers of the European Central Bank to impose sanctions [1998] OJ L 318.

[35] Model Rules, Executive summary of the introduction, 2, available at reneual.eu/projects-and-publications/reneual-1-0#:~:text=The%20ReNEUAL%20Model%20Rules%202014,general%20principles%20of%20EU%20law.

[36] ibid.

principles such as legality, legal certainty, proportionality of public action and the protection of legitimate expectations.[37] All these principles also play an important role in enforcement decisions, although they are not, or at least not always and not all, part of the specific regulations.

Both the proposal of the European Parliament and the ReNEUAL Model Rules do not present rules for the legislative procedure[38] although it was anticipated that this could be the subject of new rules after adopting the rules for decision-making in specific cases, ie for single-case decision-making or the application of the general rules to a specific case. The Model Rules consist of six books: after general provisions in Book I, Book II concerns rule-making, Book III single case decision-making, Book IV contracts, Book V mutual assistance between the EU and the Member States' authorities, and Book VI information management. For enforcement Books III and V are the most relevant.

Enforcement decisions are single-case decisions by definition. Enforcement decisions have no specific rules in the Model Rules but may be the subject of a future addition to the Model Rules.[39] The Model Rules do give rules for inspections,[40] some of which even go beyond the framework presented in the Dutch Awb. For example the Model Rules also relate to 'investigation by request'[41] as opposed to an information request with a duty to cooperate (investigation by mandatory decision).[42] Although in the case of investigation by request there is no duty to answer the questions if possible, the Model Rules prescribe that it is not allowed to provide misleading or incorrect information. The Model Rules also provide a right to be heard and a right of access to one's file. The right of access to the file arises even before the enforcement decision is taken. In Dutch administrative law such a right only exists in case of a draft decision to impose an administrative fine (*bestuurlijke boete*).

Article 14 of Book III concerns the privilege against self-incrimination and the legal professional privilege.[43] If these privileges are violated in the course of information-gathering, the information must not be used as evidence in procedures by public authorities provided this violation of procedural rights could have had an impact on the content of the decision. Although the Awb does not provide a similar rule, the same principles were formulated in recent Dutch case law.[44]

[37] Model Rules, Background and mission of the ReNEUAL project: EU administrative procedures and constitutional principles, 4.

[38] The rule-making procedures by the EU authorities acting in an executive capacity, ie those that remain outside the formal legislative procedures provided for in the EU, are part of the Model Rules (see Book II).

[39] Commissie Europeanisering algemeen bestuursrecht, *Europa en het algemeen bestuursrecht* (2021) 157 ff.

[40] Model Rules, Book III, Arts 5, 11, 12, 13, 16 and 17.

[41] ibid, Art 11.

[42] ibid, Art 12.

[43] ibid, Art 14. See on the privilege against self-incrimination also ch 8 in this volume.

[44] Hoge Raad (Dutch Supreme Court) 12 July 2013, ECLI:NL:HR:2013:BZ3640 and eg College van Beroep voor het bedrijfsleven (Board of Appeals for business) 10 January 2018, ECLI:NL:CBB:2018:3.

The Model Rules and the proposal from Parliament both provide important general provisions that need to be guaranteed if the powers of European authorities that directly impact specific persons, such as enforcement measures, increase. Without such general provisions, these guarantees may only be indirectly derived from the specific regulations and general provisions in the Charter and Treaties and therefore will be left to the CJEU to uphold. However, this outcome undermines the transparency and accessibility of legal safeguards and the rights and principles on which they are based.

The Model Rules do not provide an overview of possible enforcement decisions, as the Awb does. The Awb provides general rules for three kinds of enforcement decisions: the administrative fine; the periodic penalty order (*last onder dwangsom*); and the administrative order (*last onder bestuursdwang*). Other enforcement measures for the financial sector have a general basis in the Wft. If in a specific act the authority to impose one of these enforcement decisions is delegated to a specific supervisory authority, the Awb or the Wft determines the relevant rules of good administration, procedure and legal protection. Adding a chapter with such general rules for specific enforcement decisions may attribute to the objectives of the Model Rules.

5.3.5. Enforcement Based on National Law

The ECB is not limited to enforcement powers attributed directly to the ECB in regulations, but may also use national enforcement powers based on European directives and regulations.[45] The question is if the ECB, or any other ESA that may be granted the same powers in the future, is bound by all relevant national legislation in such a case.[46]

As explained above, the Dutch legislator decided to centralise the procedural rules and guarantees for enforcement decision to the extent possible in the Awb. The administrative fine, the periodic penalty payment and the administrative order are therefore regulated in the Awb. The Wft provides additional provisions, for example on the maximum height of an administrative fine and the consequences of recidive. Other enforcement measures, such as the instruction, the appointment of a trustee, withdrawal of a licence or the imposition of conditions and restrictions on a licence, and the professional ban, are all regulated in the Wft, although the general principles for decision-making in the Awb continue to apply.

Not all of these provisions in the Awb and Wft regarding enforcement are directly based on implemented European directives. For example, based on Article 5:51 Awb the administrative authority needs to decide if it will impose an administrative fine within 13 weeks after the mandatory report on the violation

[45] Art 9 SSM Regulation (n 20).

[46] See SMC Nuijten, 'Rechtsbescherming bij toezicht onder het SSM' (2014) 11 *Tijdschrift voor Financieel Recht* 470.

was drafted. Since this provision is not part of the implementation of a (prudential supervision) directive, it could be argued that the ECB is not bound by the provision. It is also clear from the Awb that it does not apply to the ECB if the ECB uses enforcement measures based on the Wft since the administrative law legal protection is only available if a decision is taken by either: (a) an organ of a legal entity established under public law, such as the council or the municipal executive; or (b) any other person or body vested with public authority.[47] The ECB is established under public law. The ECB was established on 1 June 1998 and is referred to as an EU institution in Article 13(1) of the Treaty on European Union (TEU). Under Article 282(3) of the Treaty on the Functioning of the European Union (TFEU), the ECB has legal personality. Nonetheless, the ECB is not an administrative body as referred to under (a) or (b0 above, because this was expressly not the intention of the Dutch legislator. The Explanatory Memorandum to the Awb[48] states:

> For the sake of completeness, it is noted here that the scope of the Awb does not extend – and cannot extend – to bodies that have been established by or pursuant to a treaty and are vested with public authority that they exercise (also) within the Netherlands (in particular the bodies of the European Communities that take decisions by virtue of Community law that are directly applicable here). After all, the hierarchical relationship between supranational and national law precludes the Dutch legislature from laying down rules for the exercise of powers by bodies established by international regulations.

Thus, when exercising European law powers directly attributed to the ECB, the ECB will not be subject to Dutch administrative law. However, as explained above, the European legislation does not provide general administrative rules for European supervisory authorities.

5.4. Enforcement by National Supervisory Authorities and Cooperation between Member States

When the national supervisory authority takes enforcement measures, national powers are usually used, although sometimes powers to national administrative bodies are granted at European level. If national powers are used, national conditions and safeguards must also be met.[49] Case law[50] shows that a national administrative body that uses European powers is also bound by the general Dutch requirements and guarantees because in that case 'the requirement of a statutory basis (as meant in Article 1:3 Awb, red.) has been met, since a regulation is just as directly binding within the national legal order as a national statutory provision'.

[47] Art 1:3 Awb.
[48] *Kamerstukken II* 1988–89, 21 221, 3, 29.
[49] See Nuijten, 'Rechtsbescherming bij toezicht onder het SSM' (2014) 471.
[50] College van Beroep voor het bedrijfsleven (Board of Appeals for business) 28 August 2008, AB 2008, 344; *Kamerstukken II* 1993–94, 23 700, 3, 41.

However, these general Dutch requirements and guarantees are not based on European legislation and therefore there may be important differences between Member States. Even if the legislative framework would be the same in all Member States, differences in supervisory practice may still lead to relevant differences between Member States.

In order to limit possible differences as much as possible, various instruments have been used at European level. First of all, in directives and regulation provisions are included concerning the minimum level of enforcement that should be possible at the Member State level. For example, Article 22 of the PRIIPs Regulation,[51] cited above, stipulates that Member States have to lay down rules establishing appropriate administrative sanctions and measures applicable to situations which constitute an infringement of the PRIIPs Regulation unless they choose criminal enforcement. Those sanctions and measures have to be effective, proportionate and dissuasive. The PRIIPs Regulation also provides a series of enforcement powers that have to be attributed to the national competent authorities, such as specific orders, a public warning and administrative fines.[52] Furthermore, the Regulation prescribes that the maximum administrative fines should at least be up to €5 million, or twice the amount of the profits gained or losses avoided in the case of a legal entity, and at least up to €700,000 or twice the amount of the profits gained or losses avoided in the case of a natural person. Another example is CRD IV.[53] In Article 67 CRD IV, the Member States are ordered to ensure administrative measures include at least a public statement, an order to cease and desist, a temporary ban on functions for a member of the management body, and pecuniary penalties up to 10 per cent of the total annual net turnover or twice the amount of the profits gained or losses avoided. Based on these provisions there is some harmonisation or convergence between Member States in possible enforcement measures.

Secondly, most European directives and regulations relating to financial law, order competent authorities to cooperate closely and to coordinate their action. See for example Article 79 MiFID II[54] or Article 22(2) PRIIPs Regulation. Article 157 CRD IV states the following:

> The competent authorities of the Member States concerned shall collaborate closely in order to supervise the activities of institutions operating, in particular through a branch, in one or more Member States other than that in which their head offices are situated. They shall supply one another with all information concerning the management and ownership of such institutions that is likely to facilitate their supervision and

[51] PRIIPs Regulation (n 1).

[52] Art 24 PRIIPs Regulation (n 1).

[53] Directive 2013/36/EU of the European Parliament and of the Council of 26 June 2013 on access to the activity of credit institutions and the prudential supervision of credit institutions and investment firms, amending Directive 2002/87/EC and repealing Directives 2006/48/EC and 2006/49/EC [2013] OJ L 176/338.

[54] Directive 2014/65/EU of the European Parliament and the Council of 15 May 2014 on markets in financial instruments and amending Directive 2002/92/EC and Directive 2011/61/EU [2014] OJ L 173/349.

> the examination of the conditions for their authorisation, and all information likely to facilitate the monitoring of such institutions, in particular with regard to liquidity, solvency, deposit guarantees, the limiting of large exposures, administrative and accounting procedures and internal control mechanisms.

In the Netherlands these cooperation requirements with regard to enforcement have been implemented in Articles 1:58–1:59a Wft.[55] Most of the requirements relate to the notification of other relevant supervisory authorities. There are no provisions for international cooperation in enforcement procedures to the effect that, for example, an administrative fine imposed by a national supervisory authority may be recovered in another Member State. These rules are referred to as 'mutual assistance' and are one of the subjects of the ReNEUAL Model Rules. These are important since national supervisory authorities are bound by the principle of territory.[56] According to this principle, an authority is only competent to act on the territory of its own state. For any extraterritorial supervisory enforcement, transnational cooperation is essential (mutual administrative assistance). Since financial supervision is in many cases supervision of activities taking place in more than one Member State, it is important to have clear rules not only about notifications and sharing information but also about the international cooperation in enforcement procedures. This is especially true, since in practice it appears that it is not always clear which national supervisory authority may use its enforcement powers.[57]

Thirdly, the European authority may order a national authority to use enforcement measures. Article 17 of the ESA Regulations,[58] for instance, stipulates that upon request of the European Parliament, the Council, the Commission or the relevant stakeholder group, or on its own initiative, the ESAs may investigate an alleged breach or non-application of Union law and give a recommendation to the competent national authority to take the actions necessary to comply with Union law. If the recommendation is not complied with, the Commission may issue a formal opinion. If the formal opinion is not complied with, the ESAs may adopt an individual decision addressed to a financial institution requiring the necessary action to comply with its obligations under Union law, including the cessation of any practice. This infringement procedure should be seen as an extension of the 'supervision role', which aims to ensure that the national supervisory authorities monitor compliance by financial market participants with Union legislation. In other words, this procedure aims to ensure a level playing field by trying

[55] Also in other acts like the *Wet toezicht accountsorganisaties* (Act Oversight Accountant organisations).

[56] See P Boswijk, OJDML Jansen and RJGM Widdershoven, 'Transnationale samenwerking tussen toezichthouders in Europa' (WODC, 2008).

[57] See eg Rechtbank Rotterdam (Court of First Instance Rotterdam) 20 December 2018, ECLI:NL:RBROT:2018:10909.

[58] See Art 17 of Regulation (EU) No 1093/2010 (n 3), Regulation (EU) No 1095/2010 (n 4) and Regulation (EU) No 1094/2010 (n 5).

to ensure that Union legislation is applied and enforced in the same way in all Member States.

It appears that the Article 17 procedure has been applied by EBA on only a few occasions.[59] Requests to initiate this procedure have usually been rejected.[60] However, recently this power was used with regard to AML/CFT enforcement. The Commission and European Parliament requested EBA to start an Article 17 procedure to enforce compliance with AML-CFT provisions by Denmark in the context of the Danske Bank scandal,[61] and EBA launched an Article 17 procedure. Furthermore EBA issued a recommendation to the Maltese authorities on compliance with AML/CFT legislation based on an investigation into developments at Pilatus Bank Ltd.[62]

Finally, Article 18(5) SSM Regulation also provides the ECB with the power to require national supervisory authorities to take enforcement action if this is deemed necessary for the purpose of carrying out the tasks conferred to the ECB by this Regulation. The penalties applied by national supervisory authorities need to be effective, proportionate and dissuasive.

5.5. Equality

Title III Charter concerns equality, and Article 20 provides that everyone is equal before the law. Article 21 Charter prohibits discrimination. Based on these principles, the existing framework for administrative enforcement, as described above, raises some questions that need to be addressed.

If a European administrative body takes enforcement measures, it should apply its powers in the same way in similar cases.[63] Based on the above it is clear that this is not always possible. In many cases, the ECB will have to use national powers to enforce compliance with European directives, and those national powers may differ between Member States. The only way to prevent this kind of inequality would be if European regulation provides enforcement powers or a detailed description of the enforcement powers that need to be implemented.

[59] See the report of the first evaluation of the ESA Regulations (COM(2014)509) of 8 August 2014: the ESAs did not give recommendations or take binding decisions based on Arts 17–19 ESA Regulations.

[60] Case T-660/14 *SV Capital v EBA*, ECLI:EU:T:2015:608.

[61] Requests of the Commission of 21 September 2018 to EBA (Ref Ares(2018)4866024 and letter EBA to Commission of 18 February 2019 (EBA-2019-D-2288).

[62] Requests of the Commission of 23 October 2017 (see recommendation 11 July 2018, EBA/REC/2018/02).

[63] It could be argued that this principle only applies to recovery measures, such as a periodic penalty payment, and not to administrative fines since these are punitive sanctions. Whether or not a punitive sanction is imposed is not only determined by the existence of a violation, but also by the principle of proportionality and the principle of opportunity. Therefore in similar circumstances the supervisor should take similar recovery measures, but may take a different approach with regard to punitive sanctions. This margin of discretion in punitive sanctions is limited by the prohibition of arbitrariness.

If enforcement powers have been attributed to a national supervisory authority as well as an ESA, there will also be inequality. Under Dutch law, for instance, the Awb applies to the actions and decisions of the Dutch supervisory authorities but not to the actions and decision of the European supervisory authorities. This also may lead to inexplicable differences within the same Member State: if the Dutch supervisory authority decides to impose an administrative sanction, it is bound by national legal deadlines, conditions and rules for legal protection that do not apply to the ESA. For example, an administrative fine imposed by the Dutch authority may be reduced by a judge if the authority did not decide whether or not to impose an administrative fine within 13 weeks after the fine report has been drawn up.[64] The European supervisor is not bound by such a deadline if it imposes a fine using its own European supervisory powers for the same violation.

If enforcement powers have been attributed to national supervisory authorities only, there may be differences between Member States. These may be caused by differences in the legal powers, but also by differences in policies and practice between Member States.

None of these differences is beneficial to the transparency and effectiveness of the enforcement of European financial law.

5.6. Conclusion

Enforcement is the least developed part of European (financial) law for the following reasons:

- Even if European substantive rules are directly binding because they are laid down in a regulation, the regulation usually does not provide uniform, directly applicable enforcement measures. The regulation usually only contains a legislative assignment to the Member States with, at most, a few minimum criteria that have to be met in such legislation.
- There are no European rules on mutual assistance applicable to all enforcement measures based on European legislation and binding for all Member States.

As a consequence, there are differences in enforcement practices between Member States, which may hinder cooperation. These differences undermine the efficiency and effectiveness of European rules, but may also undermine legal protection and may infringe the principle of equality. The only way to prevent differences in enforcement practice, is (1) to centralise the rules of enforcement as well as (2) to centralise or harmonise the enforcement power. The rules of enforcement (1) may be centralised by creating a European legal framework for enforcement measures and by attributing enforcement powers in regulations. However, to prevent differences in enforcement practices, there should also be centralisation

[64] Art 5:51 Awb.

or harmonisation of powers (2), because even if all Member State supervisors have the same powers to impose administrative enforcement measures, one supervisor may prefer administrative fines, another supervisor may prefer reparatory sanctions and a third may prefer informal discussions and measures.

Although this may seem to lead to the conclusion that a European supervisor is the preferred option, at this moment there are critical flaws that need to be addressed before the powers of European supervisors are to be increased. When centralising enforcement, it is also vital to provide rules on the expected behaviour of European authorities and guarantees against the actions of European authorities. Standardisation of enforcement measures could contribute to this, as could standardisation of the applicable procedural and other rules. However, standardising the existing procedural rules will not suffice: it has become clear in this chapter, after discussing the applicable principles, that a more comprehensive legal framework of rules on EU administrative law is needed.

The proposal of the European Parliament and the ReNEUAL Model Rules are a good start in this respect. But as long as this development is blocked by the European Commission, the desirability of a more far-reaching Europeanisation of enforcement powers themselves must be questioned.

6

The EU Courts as *Juges de Droit National* in the Single Supervisory Mechanism?

JOUKE TEGELAAR

6.1. Preface

In the last decade, EU financial regulation and supervision has increasingly and with an unprecedented speed become an area of 'integrated administration'. In an integrated administration, national authorities and Union authorities cooperate so closely in the implementation of EU law that it is often difficult to distinguish between their respective responsibilities and competences.[1] Traditionally, financial supervision has been left to the Member States. Yet, today, the increasing europeanisation of financial supervision has resulted in a system in which EU and national supervisory authorities closely cooperate. Most notably, the centralisation of eurozone banking supervision at the European Central Bank (ECB) in the Single Supervisory Mechanism (SSM), and the establishment of the European Supervisory Authorities (ESAs) and their expanding powers, have contributed to an ever-closer integration.

The ever-closer integration between EU and national financial supervision contrasts with the EU system of judicial protection and judicial review.[2] Whereas financial supervision in the EU may often be considered a shared responsibility between the EU and the Member States, the system of judicial protection assumes a clear distinction between Member State powers on the one hand and EU powers on the other. This paradox and the challenges it may pose for judicial protection are not unique for financial supervision, as they are inherent to all areas in

[1] S Prechal and RJGM Widdershoven, 'Inleiding' in S Prechal and RJGM Widdershoven (eds), *Inleiding tot het Europees bestuursrecht* (Ars Aequi Libri, 2017) 26 ff.

[2] More generally on the issue of an integrated administration and a dualistic judicial system, see, inter alia, AH Türk, 'Judicial review of integrated administration in the EU' in HCH Hofmann and AH Türk, *Legal Challenges in EU Administrative Law. Towards an Integrated Administration* (Edward Elgar, 2009) 218–56 and M Eliantonio, 'Judicial Review in an Integrated Administration: the Case of "Composite Procedures"' (2015) 7 *Review of European Administrative Law* 65.

which the EU and national levels cooperate in the application and implementation of EU law. Yet, especially the revolutionary set-up of the SSM, including the strong centralisation of prudential banking supervision at the ECB and the ECB's competence to apply national law, has raised new questions and evoked crucial developments in the General Court's and Court of Justice's case law.[3]

An integrated administration is inherently multi-jurisdictional.[4] Both national law and European law govern actions taken within it. The basic principle is: Union law governs the actions of EU authorities[5] and both Union law and national law govern actions by national authorities. The multi-jurisdictional nature may pose challenges for judicial protection. One of these challenges is judicial review of composite procedures, a specific type of integrated administration, and the role of national law in judicial review. Landmark judgment *Berlusconi and Fininvest v Bank of Italy* sheds new light on this issue.[6] In this judgment, the Court introduced the principle of a 'single judicial review' for composite procedures in which an EU authority has the 'exclusive decision-making power'.[7] According to this principle, the EU Courts have exclusive jurisdiction to review such composite procedures, including any national preparatory acts. The Court stressed in *Berlusconi and Fininvest v Bank of Italy* that national courts are thus precluded from exercising jurisdiction over such national acts.

An important issue that remained unanswered in *Berlusconi* concerns the role of national law in the EU Courts' 'single judicial review'. Should the EU Courts be considered *juges de droit national* in SSM composite procedures? This chapter addresses this question with the following four sub-questions, specifically for the SSM:

- Are the EU Courts competent to apply national law?
- How should the EU Courts determine the content of national law?
- Are the EU Courts competent to review the lawfulness of a national financial supervisory authority or national competent authority (NCA)?
- How should the EU Courts' jurisdiction over national preparatory acts be interpreted?

As it will be concluded that the jurisdictional limits will lead to a national law 'blind spot', the follow-up question is posed whether this should be remedied.

[3] The General Court and the Court of Justice, both constituent courts of the Court of Justice of the European Union, will hereinafter together be referred to as the 'EU Courts'. The Court of Justice will be referred to as the 'Court'.

[4] For this designation see eg HCH Hofmann, 'Multi-Jurisdictional Composite Procedures. The Backbone of the EU's Single Regulatory Space', Université du Luxembourg Legal Working Paper Series 003 (2019).

[5] The term 'EU authorities' refers to the EU bodies, encompassing both the EU institutions (as listed in Art 13 Treaty on European Union (TEU)), including the ECB, and the EU agencies, such as the ESAs and the Single Resolution Board (SRB).

[6] Case C-219/17 *Berlusconi and Fininvest v Bank of Italy*, ECLI:EU:C:2018:1023.

[7] ibid, [49].

The structure of this chapter is as follows. First, the concept of a composite procedure will be introduced and the role of national law in such procedures, focusing on the SSM. Then, the Court's doctrine on the division of jurisdiction in composite procedures is discussed with an analysis of the *Borelli* and *Berlusconi* judgments that constitute the fundaments of the Court's doctrine. Finally, by addressing the four sub-questions and the follow-up question, this chapter intends to reflect on the role of national law and of the EU Courts as *juges de droit national* in SSM composite procedures.

6.2. Composite Procedures and National Law

6.2.1. General

Composite procedures constitute a specific type of integrated administration.[8] The concept of a composite procedure is not legally defined and the term has not as yet been used by the EU Courts.[9] In legal scholarship, however, several definitions have been formulated.[10] Generally, a composite procedure refers to a procedure in which both national authorities and EU authorities are involved in the decision-making, and which culminates in a national act or an EU act. The SSM comprises composite procedures, but they also exist, inter alia, in the fields of European structural funds, the protection of geographical indications and designations of origin and the authorisation of genetically modified organisms.[11] The method of cooperation in a composite procedure differs per policy area.[12] It may consist of a mere information exchange, while in other procedures the cooperation involves both national and EU decision-making.[13]

Due to the involvement of both national and EU authorities, a composite procedure is inherently multi-jurisdictional.[14] In a composite procedure, both national

[8] More extensively on the concept of composite procedures in EU law, see, inter alia, O Jansen and B Schöndorf-Haubold (eds), *The European Composite Administration* (Intersentia, 2011); Eliantonio, 'Judicial Review in an Integrated Administration' (2015); HC Röhl, 'Procedures in the European Composite Administration' in J Barnes (ed), *Transforming Administrative Procedure* (Global Law Press, 2008) 75–96.

[9] Although in *Berlusconi*, the Court quotes the term 'composite procedure' (*procedimento cd. composto*) as used by the Italian Consiglio di Stato, see Case C-219/17 *Berlusconi and Fininvest v Bank of Italy*, ECLI:EU:C:2018:1023, [38]. Yet, the term 'composite procedure' had a central position in AG Campos Sánchez-Bordona's Opinion in *Berlusconi*, see Opinion AG Campos Sánchez-Bordona in Case C-219/17 *Berlusconi and Fininvest v Bank of Italy*, ECLI:EU:C:2018:502.

[10] For definitions of a composite procedure, see, among others, Eliantonio (n 3) and Hofmann, 'Multi-Jurisdictional Composite Procedures' (2019) 2.

[11] cf Opinion AG Campos Sánchez-Bordona in Case C-219/17 *Berlusconi and Fininvest v Bank of Italy*, ECLI:EU:C:2018:502, [3].

[12] HCH Hofmann, 'Composite decision making procedures in EU administrative law', in HCH Hofmann and AH Türk, *Legal Challenges in EU Administrative Law. Towards an Integrated Administration*, (Edward Elgar, 2009) 138.

[13] M Eliantonio (n 3) 71.

[14] Hofmann (n 5).

law and Union law are applied. Nevertheless, a composite procedure concludes either with a national act or an EU act. Depending on the administrative level adopting the final act, a distinction can be made between top-down procedures and bottom-up procedures.[15] A top-down procedure starts at European level and concludes with a national act. In a bottom-up procedure, the situation is the other way around: it starts at national level and culminates in a final EU act. This contribution focuses on bottom-up procedures in the SSM.

6.2.2. Composite Procedures in the SSM

6.2.2.1. Cooperation between the ECB and National Competent Authorities

The SSM institutional framework involving close cooperation between the ECB and the NCAs qualifies as an integrated administration. The ECB has the 'exclusive competence' for prudential banking supervision[16] and the ECB alone is 'responsible for the effective and consistent functioning of the SSM'.[17] Yet, the SSM provides for various decentralisation mechanisms which 'redistribute' part of the ECB's supervisory competences to the NCAs.[18] Most importantly, the NCAs are responsible for directly supervising the less significant banks. In that capacity, the NCAs take independent supervisory decisions directly vis-à-vis supervised credit institutions. In addition to their direct supervisory tasks, the NCAs have an ongoing role in assisting with the implementation and execution of ECB decisions, for example by implementing ECB instructions. Thus, although the ECB has been conferred the exclusive competence for prudential banking supervision, the exercise of supervision is effectively shared between the ECB and the NCAs.

In view of the SSM's objective of achieving uniformity in prudential banking supervision,[19] relying on decentralisation may be seen as a necessary evil. Uniformity and coherence may best be achieved by a truly single

[15] For this distinction, see, among others, G della Cananea, 'The European Union's Mixed Administrative Proceedings' (2004) 68 *Law & Contemporary Problems* 199.

[16] Art 4(1) SSM Regulation (Council Regulation (EU) No 1024/2013 of 15 October 2013 conferring specific tasks on the European Central Bank concerning policies relating to the prudential supervision of credit institutions [2013] OJ L 287/63).

[17] Art 6(2) SSM Regulation.

[18] In *Landeskreditbank Baden-Württemberg – Förderbank v ECB* the General Court interpreted the division of supervisory competences between the ECB and the NCAs as 'allowing the exclusive competences delegated to the ECB to be implemented within a decentralised framework, rather than having a distribution of competences between the ECB and the national authorities'; see Case T-122/15 *Landeskreditbank Baden-Württemberg – Förderbank v ECB*, ECLI:EU:T:2017:337, [54].

[19] Recital 12 SSM Regulation: 'As a first step towards a banking union, a single supervisory mechanism should ensure that the Union's policy relating to the prudential supervision of credit institutions is implemented in a coherent and effective manner, that the single rulebook for financial services is applied in the same manner to credit institutions in all Member States concerned, and that those credit institutions are subject to supervision of the highest quality, unfettered by other, non-prudential considerations'.

supervisory authority. But although on paper a complete centralisation of prudential supervision at the ECB may seem the best solution for achieving these goals, several elements point in a different direction. One of the reasons for retaining a role for the national authorities, for instance, is that it would be practically impossible to confer upon the ECB on a standalone basis supervision of 6,000 eurozone banks.[20] Another pragmatic reason is that by decentralising certain supervisory tasks, the SSM will not rely exclusively on the ECB's limited resources, but also on those of the Member States.[21] In addition, the 'single rulebook' for a significant part still is national in nature, most notably consisting of national law implementing CRD IV. The regulatory differences that result from national implementation require involvement of the NCAs, that are experts in respect of their own, national regulatory framework.[22]

The SSM composite procedures clearly reflect the NCAs' assisting role and their national regulatory expertise. The SSM comprises several bottom-up procedures, starting at an NCA and culminating in an ECB act.[23] In some procedures, the relevant NCA merely functions as an intermediary for information to the ECB, for instance by serving as a front desk for a credit institution's notification concerning its intention to extend its activities directly or via a branch to another Member State ('EU passport').[24] In other procedures, the NCAs play a more substantive role in the decision-making process. These procedures include granting and withdrawing a banking licence,[25] the assessment of acquisitions of qualifying holdings[26] and the fit and proper assessments for significant credit institutions.[27]

[20] TH Tröger, 'The Single Supervisory Mechanism – Panacea or Quack Banking Regulation?' (2024) 15 *European Business Organization Law Review* 466; N Moloney, 'European Banking Union: assessing its risks and resilience' (2014) 51 *CMLR* 1609, 1645.

[21] G Ferrarini and L Chiarella, 'Common Banking Supervision in the Eurozone: Strengths and Weaknesses', ECGI Law Working Paper No 223/2013; C Enoch et al, 'Securing a Safer Financial System for Europe' in C Enoch et al (eds), 'From Fragmentation to Financial Integration in Europe' Report International Monetary Fund (2013) 19.

[22] See also recital 37 SSM Regulation: 'National supervisors have important and long-established expertise in the supervision of credit institutions within their territory and their economic, organisational and cultural specificities. They have established a large body of dedicated and highly qualified staff for those purposes'.

[23] For an overview, see the table in R D'Ambrosio, 'The Involvement of the NCAs in the ECB's Supervisory Proceedings' in RD Ambrosio (ed), *Law and Practice of the Banking Union and its governing Institutions (Cases and Materials)* (Quaderni di Ricerca Guiridica, 2012) 177–79.

[24] Arts 11 and 12 SSM Framework Regulation (Regulation (EU) No 468/2014 of the European Central Bank of 16 April 2014 establishing the framework for cooperation within the Single Supervisory Mechanism between the European Central Bank and national competent authorities and with national designated authorities (ECB/2014/17) [2014] OJ L 141/1) when the host Member State is a participating Member State and Art 17 SSM Framework Regulation when the host Member State is a non-participating Member State.

[25] Art 14(1)–(4) SSM Regulation, elaborated in Arts 73–79 SSM Framework Regulation (authorisations); Art 14(5)–(6) SSM Regulation, elaborated in Arts 80–84 SSM Framework Regulation (withdrawal of authorisation).

[26] Art 15 SSM Regulation, elaborated in Arts 85–87 SSM Framework Regulation.

[27] Art 93 SSM Framework Regulation. This provision does not state that the NCAs are responsible for preparing the ECB's assessment, but the NCAs' preparatory role is explicitly mentioned in ECB, 'Draft guide to fit and proper assessments' (November 2016) para 2.1.

6.2.2.2. *Procedure for the Assessment of a Qualifying Holding*

The procedure for the assessment of acquisitions of qualifying holdings was the subject of *Berlusconi and Fininvest v Bank of Italy*. In brief, the procedure for this assessment is as follows. A person intending to acquire a qualifying holding in a credit institution sends a notification to the NCA of the Member State in which the target credit institution has its registered office.[28] The NCA prepares a draft decision which is sent to the ECB. The ECB subsequently decides on whether or not to oppose the acquisition. The ECB's decision is taken on the basis of its own assessment of the proposed acquisition, as well as on the NCA draft decision.

Both the relevant NCA and the ECB thus have a decision-making role in the procedure. The requirements for acquiring a qualifying holding are laid down in CRD IV and are implemented in national law. The ECB as well as the NCAs must apply national law.[29] More specifically, Article 4(3) SSM Regulation obliges the ECB to apply national law where necessary: a novelty in EU law.[30] Consequently, the ECB does not employ a one-size-fits-all requirements framework but, due to the different national implementations of the CRD IV requirements, potentially it may have to apply as many different frameworks as there are participating Member States. Yet, national laws are likely to only differ on specific issues, as the requirements are effectively harmonised by the ESAs Joint Guidelines for the prudential assessment of acquisitions of qualifying holdings. These guidelines qualify as soft law, but are de facto binding as financial supervisory authorities must integrate these guidelines in their supervision.[31]

Thus, within the SSM, both the relevant NCA and the ECB apply (substantive) national law laying down the requirements for acquiring a qualifying holding. In addition, as the EU lacks a harmonised and codified European administrative law framework,[32] general national (administrative) law governs the national preparatory acts pursuant to the EU principle of national procedural autonomy.

6.3. Division of Jurisdiction in Composite Procedures

6.3.1. The Court's Doctrine on the Division of Jurisdiction: A Two-Track Approach

The division of jurisdiction between the national courts and the EU Courts in the judicial review of composite procedures is a complicated issue. The Court has

[28] For the full procedure, see Art 15 SSM Regulation, elaborated in Arts 85–88 SSM Framework Regulation.

[29] K Lackhoff, *Single Supervisory Mechanism. A Practitioner's Guide* (CH Beck-Hart-Nomos, 2017) 173.

[30] A Witte, 'The Application of National Banking Supervision Law by the ECB: Three Parallel Modes of Executing EU Law?' (2014) 21 *Maastricht Journal of European and Comparative Law* 105.

[31] VPG de Serière and BCG Jennen, 'De betekenis van 'soft law' in de financiële toezichtwetgeving' (2017) 143 *Ondernemingsrecht* 805.

[32] See ch 5 in this volume.

developed a doctrine for the division of jurisdiction, which will be discussed in more detail below. The doctrine's groundwork was laid with *Borelli* in 1992 and, for the present, is concluded with *Berlusconi*.

The Court's doctrine entails a mutually exclusive two-track approach.[33] Notwithstanding the inherent combination of a national and EU act in a composite procedure, this approach designates only one competent judicial level, viz either EU or national. In short, and as elaborated upon in the next section, the EU judicial level has jurisdiction where the EU authority has the 'exclusive decision-making power' in the composite procedure and the national judicial level where the national act was binding on the EU authority and therefore dictated the outcome of the EU act. Due to the traditionally strict separation of competences between the national courts and the EU Courts, each judicial level in principle only has jurisdiction with regard to those acts that are adopted by the authorities that belong to their respective legal orders. National courts' jurisdiction is confined to reviewing national acts[34] and EU Courts' jurisdiction to reviewing EU acts. *Berlusconi*, however, brought changes to this strict separation of competences.

6.3.2. The First Track: *Borelli*

The *Borelli* judgment is still relevant for the Court's doctrine on the division of jurisdiction in composite procedures.[35] *Borelli* concerned a composite procedure for funding from a European structural fund, in which the European Commission adopted a final decision following an 'opinion' from the competent national authorities which could be favourable or unfavourable. Borelli, an Italian company, wished to obtain funding from the fund. Borelli's application was rejected by the Commission upon an unfavourable opinion of the Italian authorities. The outcome of this rejection was dictated by the unfavourable opinion of the Italian authorities. Pursuant to the applicable legislation, a favourable opinion was a necessary prerequisite for funding. Borelli wished to challenge the opinion at the national court. The national court, however, denied jurisdiction, as it qualified the national opinion as an unreviewable preparatory decision. Borelli then started an action for annulment against the Commission decision at the Court. Borelli argued that the unlawfulness of the national opinion must lead to the Commission decision's invalidity and that otherwise it would be deprived from judicial redress, due to the Italian court's denial of jurisdiction.[36] Borelli reasoned that the Commission decision 'encapsulates all the decisions of the institutions and bodies involved in

[33] F Brito Bastos, 'Judicial review of composite administrative procedures in the Single Supervisory Mechanism: *Berlusconi*' (2019) 56 *Common Market Law Review* 1355, 1368–69.

[34] See Case C-314/85 *Foto-Frost*, ECLI:EU:C:1987:452.

[35] F Brito Bastos, 'The *Borelli* Doctrine Revisited: Three Issues of Coherence in a Landmark Ruling for EU Administrative Justice' (2015) 8 *Review of European Administrative Law* 269, 276; P Craig, *EU Administrative Law* (OUP, 2018), 330–31. See, eg, Case C-269/99 *Carl Kühne and Others*, ECLI:EU:C:2001:659, Case C-64/05 P *Sweden v Commission*, ECLI:EU:C:2007:802 and Case C-219/17 *Berlusconi and Fininvest v Bank of Italy*, ECLI:EU:C:2018:102.

[36] Case C-97/91 *Borelli*, ECLI:EU:C:1992:491, [7].

the procedure'.[37] In this line of reasoning, national errors led to 'contamination' or 'derivative illegality' of the Commission decision.[38] The Court rejected Borelli's argument.

The Court firstly stressed that in the context of an action for annulment under Article 263 Treaty on the Functioning of the European Union (TFEU), the Court does not have jurisdiction to rule on the lawfulness of a national act.[39] The Court went on to consider that

> that position cannot be altered by the fact that the measure in question forms part of a Community decision-making procedure, since it clearly follows from the division of powers in the field in question between the national authorities and the Community institutions that the measure adopted by the national authority is binding on the Community decision-taking authority and therefore determines the terms of the Community decision to be adopted.[40]

In this case, the national unfavourable opinion was binding on the Commission and determined the outcome of its decision. It followed from the applicable legislation that an unfavourable opinion led to rejection of the application.[41] As a result, the Commission could, according to the Court, 'neither follow the procedure for the examination of the project in accordance with the rules laid down in that regulation nor *a fortiori* review the lawfulness of the opinion thus issued'.[42] The Court continued that therefore 'any irregularity that might affect the opinion cannot affect the validity of the decision by which the Commission refused the aid applied for'.[43] The Court thus ruled that any errors made by the Italian authorities could not affect the validity of the Commission decision.

The decisive criterion for both the Court's denial of jurisdiction and the rejection of derivative illegality was that the national act was binding on the Commission and thus determined the outcome of the procedure. In this case, the national opinion was unfavourable, dictating the outcome of the Commission decision. In the view of the Court, the Commission had been deprived of any decision-making room or discretion. Had the Italian authorities issued a positive opinion, the Commission would have been able to independently assess the funding application and would therefore have had discretion. In that scenario, the Court would probably have assumed jurisdiction to review the Commission decision.

With a denial of jurisdiction by both the Italian court and the EU Court, Borelli would find itself in a judicial protection vacuum. To remedy this vacuum,

[37] Report for the ECJ Hearing 3 December 1992, Case C-97/91 *Borelli*, ECLI:EU:C:1992:491, I-6318.

[38] The terms 'contamination' and 'derivative illegality' are used by Brito Bastos, see F Brito Bastos, 'Derivative Illegality in European Composite Administrative Procedures' (2018) 55 *Common Market Law Review* 101.

[39] Case C-97/91 *Borelli*, ECLI:EU:C:1992:491, [9].

[40] ibid, [10].

[41] The relevant provision, Art 13(3) Regulation 355/77, read: 'In order to receive aid from the Fund, a project must have been approved by the Member State on the territory of which it is to be carried out'.

[42] Case C-97/91 *Borelli*, ECLI:EU:C:1992:491, [11].

[43] ibid, [12].

the Court called upon the national courts for judicial protection, referring to the principle of effective judicial protection.[44] The Court considered that

> it is for the national courts, where appropriate after obtaining a preliminary ruling from the Court, to rule on the lawfulness of the national measure at issue on the same terms on which they review any definitive measure adopted by the same national authority which is capable of adversely affecting third parties and, consequently, to regard an action brought for that purpose as admissible even if the domestic rules of procedure do not provide for this in such a case.[45]

The Court thus required national courts to assume jurisdiction, even if national law would not allow for judicial review.[46]

Two principles may be distilled from *Borelli*: one relating to the division of jurisdiction in composite procedures, the other one to the issue to what extent errors in national decision-making can lead to invalidity of the subsequent EU act, viz to 'derivative illegality'.[47] The first principle entails that in a composite procedure in which a national act dictates the outcome of an EU act and therefore leaves no discretion for the EU institution, national courts are obliged to review that national act under the same conditions as those applicable to national final decisions adversely affecting third parties. Pursuant to the second principle, in a composite procedure where a national act dictates the outcome of an EU act and thus leaves no discretion for the EU institution, errors at national level will not affect the validity of the EU act.

6.3.3. The Second Track: *Berlusconi*

The *Berlusconi* judgment is a mirror image of *Borelli*.[48] *Berlusconi* constitutes, for the time being, the final piece of the Court's doctrine on the division of jurisdiction in composite procedures. Similarly to *Borelli*, the composite procedure in *Berlusconi* was concluded with an EU act, more specifically an ECB decision opposing to the acquisition of a qualifying holding. Yet, unlike in *Borelli*, the Court did assume jurisdiction. It assumed exclusive jurisdiction over both the ECB act and any national preparatory acts. The Court stressed that due to its exclusive jurisdiction, national courts are precluded from reviewing national preparatory acts. Before the Court discussed the specific composite procedure in *Berlusconi*, the Court took the opportunity to introduce a new puzzle piece to its doctrine:

> 43. Any involvement of the national authorities in the course of the procedure leading to the adoption of such acts cannot affect their classification as EU acts where the acts

[44] ibid, [14]–[15].

[45] ibid, [13].

[46] For a critical consideration from the point of view of national procedural autonomy, see H Nehl, 'Legal Protection in the Field of EU Funds' (2011) 10 *European State Aid Law Quarterly* 629, 650.

[47] See Brito Bastos (fn 35) 273 ff.

[48] Brito Bastos, 'Judicial review of composite administrative procedures' (2019) 1370–75.

> of the national authorities constitute a stage of a procedure in which an EU institution exercises, alone, the final decision-making power without being bound by the preparatory acts or the proposals of the national authorities (see, to that effect, judgment of 18 December 2007, Sweden v Commission, C-64/05 P, EU:C:2007:802, paragraphs 93 and 94).
>
> 44. In such a situation, where EU law does not aim to establish a division between two powers – one national and the other of the European Union – with separate purposes, but, on the contrary, lays down that an EU institution is to have an exclusive decision-making power, it falls to the EU Courts, by virtue of their exclusive jurisdiction to review the legality of EU acts on the basis of Article 263 TFEU (see, by analogy, judgment of 22 October 1987, Foto-Frost, 314/85, EU:C:1987:452, paragraph 17), to rule on the legality of the final decision adopted by the EU institution at issue and to examine, in order to ensure effective judicial protection of the persons concerned, any defects vitiating the preparatory acts or the proposals of the national authorities that would be such as to affect the validity of that final decision.

In the paragraphs cited above, the Court described a situation where the national preparatory acts are not binding on the EU authority and where the latter has 'exclusive decision-making power'. This situation is the opposite of *Borelli*, where the Commission was constrained by the unfavourable national opinion resulting in the Commission having no discretion. However, in the situation outlined above, involving a non-binding national preparatory act and an 'exclusive decision-making power' for the EU authority, the Court did assume jurisdiction to rule on the legality of the EU act. And, most notably, the Court stressed that it also has exclusive jurisdiction 'to examine … any defects vitiating the preparatory acts or the proposals of the national authorities that would be such as to affect the validity of that final decision'. The Court's jurisdiction over national preparatory acts was prompted by the principle of effective judicial protection. By centralising jurisdiction over composite procedures, the Court confirmed the 2007 *Sweden v Commission* judgment and clarified that the principle that was formulated in that judgment, which was tailored to the specific decision-making procedure for the disclosure of documents, is general in scope and applies to all composite procedures in which the national act is not binding and the EU authority has the exclusive decision-making power.[49] The *Berlusconi* judgment has been confirmed in *ICCREA*, which involved a Single Resolution Board (SRB) decision on the calculation of *ex ante* contributions to the Single Resolution Fund (SRF).[50]

Yet, the Court not only confirmed *Sweden v Commission*, but went a step further. For the first time, the Court explicitly stated that its exclusive jurisdiction over national preparatory acts implies that national courts do not have jurisdiction over such national acts.[51] The principle of sincere cooperation is the guiding principle for precluding national courts from reviewing national preparatory acts.

[49] Case C-64/05 P *Sweden v Commission*, ECLI:EU:C:2007:802.
[50] Case C-414/18 *ICCREA Banca*, ECLI:EU:C:2019:1036.
[51] Case C-219/17 *Berlusconi and Fininvest v Bank of Italy*, ECLI:EU:C:2018:1023, [47].

Accepting parallel national jurisdiction would, according to the Court, entail the risk of 'divergent assessments in one and the same procedure'.[52] In addition, a 'single judicial review' is necessary for the effectiveness of the composite procedure,[53] which could be hampered if national preparatory acts were eligible for judicial review at national courts before the ECB has adopted the final decision. After the Court set out the scope of its exclusive jurisdiction, the Court confirmed that the *Borelli* judgment still applies. National courts have jurisdiction to rule on non-binding national acts in composite procedures in which the EU institution has 'only a limited or no discretion'.[54]

After the foundations for the division of jurisdiction had been laid down by the Court, the Court zoomed in on the SSM procedure for the assessment of the acquisition of qualifying holdings. The Court was brief: the NCA's draft decision is not binding on the ECB and the ECB 'alone has the decision-making power'.[55] The SSM procedure for the assessment of the acquisition of qualifying holdings therefore qualifies as the type of composite procedure described by the Court in paragraphs 43–44 and falls in its entirety under the exclusive jurisdiction of the Court under Article 263 TFEU. The EU Courts' jurisdiction thus extends to both the ECB final decision and any national preparatory acts.

6.4. The EU Courts as *Juges de Droit National* in the SSM?

6.4.1. Jurisdictional Limits

While *Berlusconi* supplements and further clarifies the Court's doctrine on the division of jurisdiction in composite procedures, it raises a new, pressing question: how will the EU Courts deal with their exclusive jurisdiction over national acts? May the EU Courts be regarded as *juges de droit national*? The national courts' qualification as *juges de droit commun* is generally accepted.[56] National courts are even considered to be the 'ordinary courts' of EU law where it concerns the application, interpretation and enforcement of EU law.[57] Yet, due to the limited competence of national courts to declare EU acts invalid, the designation as ordinary courts is less appropriate where the invalidity of an EU act is raised before the national courts.[58] The EU Courts applying, interpreting and enforcing national law is less evident. In addition, it may be questioned whether the EU Courts' jurisdiction over national

[52] ibid, [50].
[53] ibid, [49].
[54] ibid, [45], with reference to Case C-97/91 *Borelli*, ECLI:EU:C:1992:491, [9]–[10].
[55] ibid, [53]–[56].
[56] For this qualification see, for example, K Lenaerts, 'The Rule of Law and the Coherence of the Judicial System of the European Union' (2007) 44 *Common Market Law Review* 1625, 1645.
[57] Opinion AG Jacobs in Case C-50/00 P *Unión de Pequeños Agricultores v Council*, ECLI:EU:C:2002:197, [41].
[58] ibid.

acts qualifies as assessing the validity of a national act. Should the EU Courts be regarded as *juges de droit national* in the SSM? This question will be addressed on the basis of four sub-questions, focusing on the procedure for the assessment of the acquisition of qualifying holdings.

The first and most fundamental sub-question is whether the EU Courts are competent to apply national law. As stated above, both national and EU law are applied in the procedure for the assessment of the acquisition of qualifying holdings. The ECB also applies national law, required by Article 4(3) SSM Regulation. National law is therefore not only the NCAs' *lex materiae*, but also the ECB's. Does the ECB's competence to apply national law lead to the EU Courts' competence to apply national law? The constitutional limits to the EU Courts' jurisdiction cast doubts. Article 263 TFEU has not been written for such a situation and it is questionable whether an infringement of national law constitutes 'infringement of the Treaties or of any rule of law relating to their application' as ground of appeal.[59] Yet, since this ground of appeal includes secondary Union law and the SSM Regulation obliges the ECB to apply national law, this, in my view, may be regarded an indication that the EU Courts are competent to use national law as defined Article 4(3) SSM Regulation as a yardstick for reviewing ECB acts.[60] It furthermore appears from the SSM case *Caisse régionale de crédit agricole mutuel Alpes Provence v ECB* that the General Court agrees with that view, as it held:

> Article 4(3) of Regulation No 1024/2013 necessarily requires the Court to assesses [sic] the legality of the contested [ECB, JTT] decisions in the light of both Article 13(1) of Directive 2013/36 and the second paragraph of Article L. 511-13 of the CMF [French monetary and financial code, JTT].[61]

It consequently assessed the ECB decision against French national law and extensively discussed the interpretation of the national provisions at issue, referring, inter alia, to the case law of the French Conseil d'État.[62] In *Crédit mutuel Arkéa v ECB*, the General Court also assessed ECB actions against national law.[63] From the appeal case it follows that the Court of Justice does not seem to have any problems with assessing ECB acts against national law either.[64] The Court examined the pleas in detail on the basis of French national law and French case law.[65]

[59] In this regard, see E Gagliardi and L Wissink, 'Ensuring effective judicial protection in case of ECB decisions based on national law' (2020) 1 *Review of European Administrative Law* 47–48.

[60] See also Gagliardi and Wissink (ibid) 55. cf Brito Bastos, 'Derivative Illegality in European Composite Administrative Procedures' (2018) 85. For a further discussion of different forms of references in EU law to national law, see M Prek and S Lefèvre, 'The EU Courts as "National" Courts: National Law in the EU Judicial Process' (2017) 54 *Common Market Law Review* 369, 378–83.

[61] Joined Cases T-133/16 to T-136/16, *Caisse régionale de crédit agricole mutuel Alpes Provence v ECB*, ECLI:EU:T:2018:219, [49].

[62] Joined Cases T-133/16 to T-136/16, *Caisse régionale de crédit agricole mutuel Alpes Provence v ECB*, ECLI:EU:T:2018:219, [48]–[50].

[63] Case T-712/15 *Crédit mutuel Arkéa v ECB*, ECLI: EU:T:2017:900.

[64] Gagliardi and Wissink, 'Ensuring effective judicial protection' (2020) 47–48. See Joined Cases C-152/18 P and C-153/18 P *Crédit mutuel Arkéa v ECB*, ECLI:EU:C:2019:810.

[65] Joined Cases C-152/18 P and C-153/18 P *Crédit mutuel Arkéa v ECB*, ECLI:EU:C:2019:810 [99]–[108].

From the above, it may thus be assumed that the EU Courts' jurisdiction is aligned with the ECB competence to apply national law under Article 4(3) SSM Regulation. The scope of national law as referred to in Article 4(3) SSM Regulation is however limited, thus constraining the EU Courts' jurisdiction. It is argued, for instance, that the ECB is not required to apply general national procedural law and national principles of good governance.[66] Neither is the ECB competent to apply national law in the area of AML/CFT (anti-money laundering/countering the financing of terrorism), as AML/CFT has remained within the remit of the national authorities.[67] Notwithstanding these limits to the ECB's competence to apply national law, NCAs in principle are subject to a larger spectrum of national law, also when acting within the framework of the SSM. This follows from the principle of national procedural autonomy. Consequently, for instance when enforcing EU financial regulation, and in that context prepare a draft decision for the ECB, NCAs need to apply not only national law that implements EU banking law, but also any general rules on financial supervision and national administrative law, including national principles of good administration. The scope of national law applied in an SSM composite procedure thus is broader than the definition of national law in Article 4(3) SSM Regulation. The follow-up question is therefore whether the EU Courts are competent to assess national acts against the full scope of national law. Although Article 4(3) SSM Regulation may be considered to provide for the EU Courts' jurisdiction to assess legality of ECB acts in light of national law as defined in that provision, connections for assuming jurisdiction to apply national law outside of the scope of Article 4(3) SSM Regulation are lacking. It therefore must be concluded that the EU Courts do not have jurisdiction to assess whether the relevant NCA acted in compliance with the full scope of national law.[68]

As it may be assumed that the EU Courts have jurisdiction to assess ECB acts in light of national law, the second sub-question emerges: how should the EU Courts determine the content of national law? An important circumstance is that in such a situation national law fulfils the function of law and not of fact.[69] National law and EU law together constitute the ECB's *lex materiae*. The classification as fact or law is of importance for the question who bears primary responsibility for determining the content of national law: the parties if it qualifies as fact and the EU Courts if it qualifies as law.[70] If the EU Courts have to assess ECB acts against national law, the responsibility for its interpretation should therefore lie primarily

[66] Lackhoff, *Single Supervisory Mechanism* (2017) 108.

[67] Recital 28 SSM Regulation. On the lack of ECB competence in assessing a credit institution's compliance with the AML/CFT provisions in the procedure for withdrawing a banking licence, see Joined Cases T-351/18 and T-584/18 *Ukrselhosprom PCF and Versobank v ECB*, ECLI:EU:T:2021:669 [184] ff.

[68] For a similar view, see F Brito Bastos, 'An Administrative Crack in the EU's Rule of Law: Composite Decision-making and Nonjusticiable National Law' (2020) 16 *European Constitutional Law Review* 63, 74–75.

[69] Prek and Lefèvre, 'The EU Courts as "National" Courts' (2017) 379, 381. Similarly, Gagliardi and Wissink (n 58) 49.

[70] Prek and Lefèvre (ibid) 388–91.

with the EU Courts and not with the parties. That responsibility is not without difficulties, as the interpretation of national law is primarily a task for the national courts. The EU Courts therefore have repeatedly held that for the interpretation of national law they rely on 'the interpretation given to them by national courts', also when assessing ECB acts in light of national law.[71] The General Court added in *Crédit mutuel Arkéa v ECB* that in the absence of a national court judgment, interpretation is a matter of the General Court itself.[72] But how then should the EU Courts establish the content of national law, the interpretation of which primarily is a task of the national courts? Gagliardi and Wissink advocate the involvement of national (administrative) courts and formulate some practical recommendations that should lead to better informed EU Courts and aim to safeguard the uniformity of national law.[73] One of the recommendations is to create a 'dialogue' by requesting the national court on the basis of Article 24(2) Statute of the Court of Justice of the European Union[74] to inform the EU Courts on the interpretation of national law.[75] This may serve as an alternative to a fully fledged reverse preliminary ruling procedure.

The third sub-question relates to the interpretation of the Court's exclusive jurisdiction over national acts and its effects: are the EU Courts competent to review the lawfulness of an NCA act? Short and simple: the Treaties do not confer upon the EU Courts such jurisdiction to review the lawfulness of national acts. Therefore, the Court stressed in *Borelli*: 'the Court has no jurisdiction to rule on the lawfulness of a measure adopted by a national authority'.[76] It thus cannot review an NCA act, let alone annul it. Logically therefore, the Court did not construe its competence in *Berlusconi* as a lawfulness review, but rather as a competence 'to examine … any defects vitiating the preparatory acts or the proposals of the national authorities that would be such as to affect the validity of that final decision'.[77]

Yet, shortly after *Berlusconi*, the Court for the first time did review and annul a national act in *Ilmārs Rimšēvičs and ECB v Republic of Latvia*, a case in the context of the European System of Central Banks (ESCB).[78] Due to the unique legal context of the case, the judgment may not be extended to judicial review of NCA acts

[71] Case T-712/15 *Crédit mutuel Arkéa v ECB*, ECLI:EU:T:2017:900, [132]; Joined Cases T-133/16 to T-136/16, *Caisse régionale de crédit agricole mutuel Alpes Provence v ECB*, ECLI:EU:T:2018:219, [84]. The General Court refers to Case C-490/04 *Commission v Slovakia*, ECLI:EU:C:2015:602, [81].

[72] Case T-712/15 *Crédit mutuel Arkéa v ECB*, ECLI:EU:T:2017:900, [132].

[73] Gagliardi and Wissink (n 58) 65–68.

[74] Art 24(2) Statute of the Court of Justice of the European Union reads: 'The Court may also require the Member States and institutions, bodies, offices and agencies not being parties to the case to supply all information which the Court considers necessary for the proceedings.'

[75] Gagliardi and Wissink (n 58) 66–67.

[76] Case C-97/91 *Borelli*, ECLI:EU:C:1992:491, [9].

[77] Case C-219/17 *Berlusconi and Fininvest v Bank of Italy*, ECLI:EU:C:2018:102, [44].

[78] Joined Cases C-202/18 and C-238/18 *Ilmārs Rimšēvičs and ECB v Republic of Latvia*, ECLI:EU:C:2019:139. Also on this judgment in the context of *Berlusconi*, see P Dermine and

within the SSM.[79] In *Ilmārs Rimšēvičs and ECB v Republic of Latvia*, the Latvian anti-corruption office adopted a decision temporarily suspending Mr Rimšēvičs, governor of the Central Bank of Latvia, from office. A unique remedy is codified in Article 14.2 ESCB Statute, providing that such national decisions 'may be referred directly to the Court of Justice by the Governor concerned or the Governing Council [of the ECB, JTT] on grounds of infringement of these Treaties or of any rule of law relating to their application'. The Court sought to interpret this remedy and its effects and investigated whether Article 14.2 ESCB Statute constitutes a remedy seeking a declaratory judgment that a Member State has failed to fulfill its obligations, which requires subsequent national measures to give effect to such a judgment, or an action for annulment, which would upon annulment result in immediate voidance of the national act. After an extensive analysis, AG Kokott in her Opinion concluded that the remedy must be interpreted as an action for declaration, taking due account of the separate legal spheres of the EU and the Member States and the serious interference of an annulment of a national act with the national legal order.[80] The Court, however, did not follow AG Kokott's line of reasoning. It held that Article 14.2 ESCB Statute amounts to an action for annulment and, while deviating from the general division of jurisdiction between the EU Courts and the national courts, provides for the Court's competence to review the lawfulness of a national act.[81] It supported the existence of this remedy by referring to the specific context of the ESCB: 'a novel legal construct in EU law which brings together national institutions, namely the national central banks, and an EU institution, namely the ECB, and causes them to cooperate closely with each other, and within which a different structure and a less marked distinction between the EU legal order and national legal orders prevails'.[82] By substituting 'national central banks' with 'national competent authorities', this clarification could have been about the SSM. Yet, despite the similarities, the exceptional legal context of this judgment, particularly the remedy codified in Article 14.2 ESCB Statute, written for a highly specific situation, cannot lead to the general conclusion that the Court has jurisdiction to review the lawfulness of NCA acts, or annul them. The judgment instead reinforces the Court's unwillingness to expand its jurisdiction by assuming competence to review the lawfulness of national acts, save where an explicit legal basis exists.

M Eliantonio, 'Case Note: CJEU (Grand Chamber), Judgment of 19 December 2018, C-219/17, Silvio Berlusconi and Finanziaria d'investimento Fininvest SpA (Fininvest) v Banca d'Italia and Instituto per la Vigilanza Sulle Assicurazioni (IVASS)' (2019) 12 *Review of European Administrative Law* 237, 246–49.

[79] See also V Di Bucci, 'Procedural and Judicial Implications of Composite Procedures in the Banking Union' in C Zilioli and K-P Wojcik (eds), *Judicial Review in the European Banking Union* (Edward Elgar, 2021) para 8.11 and Dermine and Eliantonio (ibid) 249.

[80] Opinion AG Kokott in Joined Cases C-202/18 and C-238/18 *Ilmārs Rimšēvičs and ECB v Republic of Latvia*, ECLI:EU:C:2018:1030, [52] ff.

[81] Joined Cases C-202/18 and C-238/18 *Ilmārs Rimšēvičs and ECB v Republic of Latvia*, ECLI:EU:C:2019:139, [64] ff.

[82] ibid, [69].

The EU Courts may thus not review the lawfulness of a national act. How then to interpret the EU Courts' jurisdiction to examine any defects vitiating the national act that would affect the validity of the final EU act? This is the fourth and last sub-question that will be addressed. Particularly indicative of how the EU Courts' jurisdiction should be interpreted is the direct link drawn by the Court between national defects and the validity of the final EU act. Hence, the purpose of examining national preparatory acts is establishing possible national defects and assessing whether these would invalidate the EU final act, viz assessing any contamination effects or derivative illegality. The Court in *Berlusconi* explicitly accepted derivative illegality in composite procedures in which an EU authority has the exclusive decision-making power. The Court simultaneously seems to narrow down the type of national defects that may lead to derivative illegality, as it refers to defects 'that would be such as to affect the validity of' the final EU decision. What defects would qualify as such? And can violations of national law by an NCA lead to the invalidity of the final ECB decision? Brito Bastos systematically explores the conditions under which the Court accepts derivative illegality.[83] On the basis of an analysis of case law, he concludes that derivative illegality is only accepted where national acts are vitiated on grounds of EU law.[84] He does, however, concede that the case law remains implicit on the existence of this prerequisite for derivative illegality.[85] Solely accepting derivative illegality where a national act is vitiated on grounds of EU law effectively excludes national law from judicial review.[86]

6.4.2. A Blind Spot to be Remedied? Conflicting Principles and Practical Solutions

The preliminary questions have been answered in *Berlusconi and Fininvest v Bank of Italy*. Yet the principal questions on validity of the final ECB decision, 'contamination effects' of errors originating at NCA level and EU Courts' jurisdiction to apply national law have remained unanswered in the General Courts' judgment in *Fininvest and Berlusconi v ECB*.[87] As must be inferred from the previous paragraphs, jurisdictional contraints prevent the EU Courts from applying national law. Specifically with respect to the SSM, therefore, national law that is not included in the definition of Article 4(3) SSM Regulation will remain outside of the scope of judicial review by the EU Courts. National law has become a blind spot. Should this blind spot be remedied by expanding the EU Courts' competence?

[83] Brito Bastos (n 38).
[84] ibid, 126–30.
[85] ibid 127.
[86] Brito Bastos, 'An Administrative Crack in the EU's Rule of Law' (2020) 78–79; Brito Bastos (n 38) 113.
[87] Case T-913/16 *Fininvest and Berlusconi v ECB*, ECLI:EU:T:2022:279. The plea alleging the illegality of the national preparatory acts was dismissed as inadmissible since it was submitted after the application was lodged.

Brito Bastos gives an extensive account of the intricacies of balancing the various principles involved in the issue of EU jurisdiction in reviewing national preparatory acts under national law.[88] Whilst the principles of rule of law and effective judicial protection would advocate in favour of such a competence, according to Brito Bastos, the absence of jurisdiction to apply national law and the principles of uniformity and autonomy of EU law bring about that the rule of law and effective judicial protection are necessarily to be compromised.[89] Brito Bastos is of the view that the uniform implementation of EU law and thus the EU principle of uniformity of EU law do not allow for the validity of the ECB final decision being dependent 'on the variations between the administrative laws of the Member States in which the preparatory acts were adopted'.[90] The EU principle of autonomy, he asserts, also precludes that the validity of an EU act is made dependent on national law.[91] Pursuant to this principle, the legality of EU acts may only be assessed against EU law.[92] Therefore, in his view, the EU Courts have no choice but to neglect national law in adjudicating composite procedures.

In 2000, Gaja advances a more pragmatic argument in his commentary on *Association Greenpeace France*[93] in favour of jurisdiction to apply national law, arguing that 'the Court should in principle be entitled to examine all the questions that are relevant for ascertaining the validity of the Community act – whether these questions relate to facts, EC law or national law'.[94] He argues that there is no reason for the Court not to do this where necessary for exercising its judicial functions and that is has the competence to do so.

Although I see the relevance of the EU principles of uniformity and autonomy of EU law, pushing for a single judicial review without national law, a less rigid interpretation and application of these principles in the SSM could be equally justifiable. By establishing an SSM heavily relying on preparatory work by NCAs that are subject to national law for ECB final decisions and by requiring the ECB to apply national law, the EU legislature explicitly acknowledges the crucial importance of national law for the SSM. Furthermore, the ECB competence to apply national law is challenging the principle of autonomy of EU law in and of itself. One could argue that consequently, within the SSM, the balance may be tipping in favour a principle of uniformity allowing for national diversity, and in favour of accepting dependence on national law, instead of autonomy, paving the way for incorporating national law in judicial review by the EU Courts.

If the EU Courts are not willing to expand their jurisdiction in judicial review of composite procedures to national law, this could be achieved via Treaty reform. This is currently highly unlikely to happen.[95] Practical solutions proposed in legal

[88] Brito Bastos (n 66) 63–90.

[89] ibid, 87–88.

[90] ibid, 76, see also 77, 85–86.

[91] ibid, 77.

[92] ibid, 77.

[93] Case C-6/99 *Association Greenpeace France* [2000], ECLI:EU:C:2000:148.

[94] G Gaja, 'Case C-6/99, Association Greenpeace France and Others v. Ministere de l'Agriculture et de la Peche and Others' (2000) 37 *Common Market Law Review* 1427, 1431.

[95] See also Brito Bastos (n 66) 88–89.

literature to mitigate the rule of law gap arising as a result of the unreviewability of national law include attributing errors originating at NCA level to the ECB via the principle of care, comprising of a duty to examine carefully, fairly and impartially all relevant factual and legal aspects of a case,[96] and elaborating the national phase of composite procedures in much greater detail in EU law.[97]

6.5. Concluding Remarks

Judicial review of composite procedures remains an area in motion. Although the *Berlusconi* judgment provided more clarity on the division of jurisdiction between national courts and EU Courts in composite procedures, the introduction of the principle of a 'single judicial review' raises new questions on the role of national law in judicial review by the EU Courts. Even though composite procedures are partly governed by national law, it was shown above that application of national law by the EU Courts is not self-evident. Yet, the SSM is unique, as national law finds its way to judicial review of ECB acts by the EU Courts through Article 4(3) SSM Regulation that requires the ECB to apply national law. The scope of national law that may be applied by the EU Courts is however constrained by the definition of national law in Article 4(3) SSM Regulation. It therefore is unlikely that NCA preparatory acts can be assessed against the full scope of national law. Moreover, it is clear from the Court's case law that derivative illegality of a final ECB act may only arise where an NCA act is vitiated on grounds of EU law. Violation of national law rules that do not have an EU equivalent cannot invalidate the subsequent ECB decision. Thus, even though the Court in *Berlusconi* assumed exclusive jurisdiction over NCA preparatory acts, the EU Courts' jurisdiction with regard to national law is limited. Furthermore, due to the EU principles of uniformity and autonomy of EU law it is not expected that the Court will expand its jurisdiction. It is however submitted that the SSM may call for a less rigid interpretation and application of the two principles, enabling the EU Courts' to include national law in judicial review of composite procedures. To learn how the EU Courts will deal with the delicate exercise of balancing partly conflicting principles we will have to continue to focus our attention on the EU Courts, which, after *Berlusconi*, are on the cusp of shaping their role as *juges de droit national*.

[96] As proposed by Demková, see S Demková, 'The Grand Chamber's Take on Composite Procedures under the Single Supervisory Mechanism. Comments on Judgment of 27 June 2018, C-219/17 Silvio Berlusconi v Finanziaria d'investimento Fininvest SpA (Fininvest) v Banca d'Italia and others, EU:C:2018:502' (2019) 12 *Review of European Administrative Law* 214 ff.

[97] As suggested by Brito Bastos, see Brito Bastos (n 66) 89.

7

Criminal Enforcement of EU Financial Standards

DAAN DOORENBOS

7.1. Introduction

Financial law is to a large extent European Union law. The standards are set by the European legislator in the form of regulations and directives. Where necessary, these EU standards are subsequently made suitable for application in the national legal system through the intervention of the national legislator. Enforcement of these standards is entrusted to the individual Member States. Financial criminal law is largely national law.

As an EU Member State, the Netherlands must ensure that its national enforcement system is well aligned with the European system of standards. Where criminal law is concerned, the principle of legality obviously sets certain minimum requirements that the legislator must meet and which the criminal courts will have to review. The European standard must be properly anchored in the national legal system and the interpretation of that standard must always be EU-compliant.

This chapter examines the way in which the criminal courts deal with the European dimension of the regulations they ought to apply, against the background of the way in which the legislator has shaped the criminalisation of offences. Many cases involve blanket criminal legislation, in which the Dutch legislator refers explicitly or implicitly to European standards. This can lead to a lack of clarity. There is also the question of how this technique of criminal law relates to the principle of legality and the *lex certa*. This issue is discussed in more detail, partly on the basis of a recent opinion of the ECtHR.

7.2. EU Dominates Financial Legislation – Also Financial Criminal Law?

Given the current state of financial law, national criminal law needs to ensure that EU rules are respected both in letter and spirit. At national level, the European origin of the standard that is enforced by criminal law will always have to be taken into account. That standard must be interpreted in accordance with its authentic wording, the system of the regulation or directive from which it derives and the scope which must be attributed to it. It will not be sufficient for the court to consult national legal sources.[1] As long as the European origin is conspicuous, because the national criminal provisions are directly linked to it or explicitly refer to it, it is obvious that the aspects just mentioned will be taken into account in the interpretation. However, if the European origin is less obvious after implementation in national legislation, there is a risk of interpretations that deviate from what the EU legislator intended. It is difficult to assess how real this risk is. It is a fact that the possibility of referring questions to the European Court of Justice (ECJ) for a preliminary ruling in Dutch criminal cases in the field of financial legislation is rarely used, despite this legislation being dominated by EU law.[2] This may indicate that the national criminal courts can usually resolve the legal questions quite easily, but it may also mean that case law is developing that is giving its own interpretation of the European rules. If no recourse to Luxembourg is made, it may only become apparent after some time that the national court has given an interpretation which is not in accordance with what the ECJ considers to be correct. This knowledge will then be too late for the defendant.

This can be illustrated by a specific example from the financial criminal law practice. In the Netherlands, two members of the management board and the chairman of the supervisory board of the listed company Content Beheer NV were prosecuted for awarding employee stock options at a time when they had inside information about a takeover bid. It follows from the *Georgakis* ruling of the ECJ that this award was not prohibited.[3] The scope of the prohibition on insider trading was described by the ECJ in *Georgakis* as ensuring the equality of the parties to a stock exchange transaction. The prohibition aims to prevent a contracting partner who possesses inside information, and therefore has an advantage over other investors, from benefiting from this to the detriment of other investors who do not possess this information.[4] As such, it was not considered insider trading when two parties who both possessed the same insider information traded with each other: neither one could benefit from an information discrepancy as there was none. Seen in that light, the prohibition was not at issue in the internal transactions between Content Beheer NV and its employees. After all, Content Beheer NV did not gain an advantage to the detriment of its counterparties – its own employees – as they were aware of the takeover bid and, insofar as the options

[1] See further on this subject: MJJP Luchtman and RJGM Widdershoven, 'Het Nederlandse strafrecht in de ban van het Unierecht' (2018) *Ars Aequi* 887.

[2] This is in line with the observation that Dutch criminal courts generally refer very few questions for a preliminary ruling. See about this, inter alia, JIMG Jahae and TOM Dieben, 'Prejudiciële vragen aan het HvJ EU: liever geen pottenkijkers?' (2015) *Strafblad* 30.

[3] Case C-391/04 *Georgakis*, *ECLI*:EU:C:2007:272.

[4] ibid, [38]–[39].

were granted to its own directors, there was no unequal information position either. The financial market and the investors in that market were not involved in these transactions between the issuing institution and its employees. The applicable EU standard therefore offered no basis for this criminal prosecution, but in 2006 the Hoge Raad (Dutch Supreme Court) nevertheless annulled the acquittal given by the Amsterdam Court of Appeal, citing the history of how the Dutch implementing legislation was created.[5] The interpretation of the national regulations, which contained exceptions to the prohibition clause but were not applicable according to the Hoge Raad, dominated the discussion in this criminal case at the time. The rationale of the prohibition clause itself – the intention that the European legislator attributed to it – was not sufficiently taken into account in the interpretation of the law by the Hoge Raad. The ruling in the *Content Beheer* case is therefore not in line with ECJ case law.

This last observation can of course be dismissed as hindsight, but could also be seen as an illustration of a certain tendency to settle or wanting to settle discussions about national legislation mainly on the basis of national legal sources, even when it concerns the implementation of European standards.[6] This tendency is sometimes also reinforced by the national legislator, where it provides European concepts with a more detailed explanation, or where it refers to earlier national parliamentary documents instead of the European source documents when amending legislation. However, that does carry the risk of an autonomous interpretation that differs to a greater or lesser extent from that advocated by the European institutions.[7]

This can also be illustrated by an example from the financial criminal law practice. Spreading false information about a listed institution can influence the price of the financial instruments it issues. Anyone who manipulates the price in this way while carrying out transactions that may benefit them is in the position of knowing something that other market participants do not know. This concerns not only the transactions planned and carried out by themselves, but also, and above all, the knowledge that false reports have been spread. Does this person have inside information? And if so, can the transactions they carry out be qualified as insider trading? This is and remains a fascinating legal question. In the Netherlands, the Hoge Raad (Dutch Supreme Court) ruled that the information position of a price manipulator did not constitute inside information.[8] This ruling was largely based on statements made by the Dutch Government during the drafting of the national

[5] Hoge Raad (Dutch Supreme Court) 4 April 2006, ECLI:NL:HR:AU4658 (*Content Beheer*).

[6] PJ Wattel, 'Nog vragen?' (2014) 719 *NJB* 893.

[7] JW Ouwerkerk and PAM Verrest, 'De struisvogel voorbij. Pleidooi voor een actieve participatie in de Europese rechtsontwikkeling inzake fundamentele rechten in de strafrechtspleging' (2021) 47 *Delikt en Delinkwent* 585. The authors conclude (at 599) that the Dutch legislator and the Supreme Court of the Netherlands are regularly ignoring the importance of EU law.

[8] Hoge Raad (Dutch Supreme Court) 6 February 2007, ECLI:NL:HR:2007:AY6713 (*Cardio Control*) and similarly Hoge Raad 2 July 2013, ECLI:NL:HR:2013:6.

implementation legislation. In Luxembourg, however, the ECJ decided that the information position of the price manipulator did constitute inside information.[9] In so doing, the ECJ made the nuanced observation that as long as the price manipulator does not conduct transactions with unknowing investors on the financial market, he does not benefit from his/her information position and therefore does not make use of his/her inside information. We see two substantially different approaches between the ECJ and the Hoge Raad, caused by the fact that the national court mainly follows the national legislative history, and the European judge gives his/her autonomous interpretation.[10]

It is plausible that such differences of interpretation in the field of market abuse have, in principle, been eliminated under the MAR regime.[11] Since 2016, practically all standards that must be enforced under criminal law have been laid down in European regulations. Subsequently, the role of the national legislator has been limited to incorporating these European standards into the criminal law system. The standards themselves already have direct effect in the national legal system and may not be transposed into national regulations. In other areas of financial law, however, the standardisation of regulations is less advanced. There are numerous European directives whose standards ultimately have to be 'achieved' by national criminal law, and it is therefore very important not to lose sight of the European dimension in specific criminal cases.

7.3. Criminalisation of Breaches of EU Standards

In order to keep an overview of the European origin of the standard, it is helpful when the national legislator explicitly refers to the relevant regulation or directive in the penalisation or description of the offence. This does not always happen, however. Considerable variation in this regard can be found in Dutch criminal legislation.

7.3.1. EU Regulations

The most obvious variant of direct criminalisation of the infringement of provisions of European regulations can be found, for example, in Article 1(2) Economic

[9] Case C-391/04 *Georgakis*, *ECLI*:EU:C:2007:272, [33]–[34].

[10] FGH Kristen in his notes to the ruling of the Hoge Raad (Dutch Supreme Court) in *NJ* 2008/467 about the difference in approach between the Hoge Raad and the ECJ.

[11] Differences in the language versions of the EU Regulation can of course still give rise to differences in interpretation in the various Member States. See about this, inter alia, JGH Altena, *Het legaliteitsbeginsel en de doorwerking van Europees recht in het Nederlandse materiële strafrecht* (dissertation, Leiden) (Wolters Kluwer, 2016) 147.

Offences Act (*Wet op de economische delicten*). This national provision directly links up with the specific provisions of a number of European regulations in the field of financial law, including the Market Abuse Directive, the Benchmark Regulation and the Prospectus Regulation.[12] The wording has been chosen such that rules implementing the aforementioned provisions of the European regulations – eg rules of delegated regulations of the Commission – also fall within the scope of the criminalisation. The wording states that 'breaches of the rules set out in or under Regulation (EU) No … the articles' are economic offences. The criminalisation therefore not only covers the explicitly mentioned Articles of the regulation, but also any rules that have been or will be adopted on the basis of those articles ('under').

What we have here is a form of blanket criminal legislation.[13] The Dutch legislator criminalises the breaches of EU regulations by a single reference, without it being possible to see what those regulations entail: to that end, one will have to consult the enumerated articles of the regulation. In addition, the Dutch legislator even criminalises the breaches of EU regulations that are yet to be enacted. Even the national legislator does not know in advance, of course, which regulations the Commission will adopt and how they will be formulated. However, the criminalisation is already in place, as a blank cheque or carte blanche to the delegated legislator.[14]

The latter is questionable. First, delegated regulations are even less visible than the basic standard of the regulation, which is also not visible in Article 1 Economic

[12] Market Abuse Regulation (Regulation (EU) No 596/2014 of the European Parliament and of the Council of 16 April 2014 on market abuse (market abuse regulation) and repealing Directive 2003/6/EC of the European Parliament and of the Council and Commission Directives 2003/124/EC, 2003/125/EC and 2004/72/EC [2014] OJ L 173/1); Regulation (EU) No 2016/1011 of the European Parliament and of the Council of 8 June 2016 on indices used as benchmarks in financial instruments and financial contracts or to measure the performance of investment funds and amending Directives 2008/48/EC and 2014/17/EU and Regulation (EU) No 596/2014 [2016] OJ L 171/1 and Regulation (EU) No 2017/1129 of the European Parliament and of the Council of 14 June 2017 on the prospectus to be published when securities are offered to the public or admitted to trading on a regulated market, and repealing Directive 2003/71/EC [2017] OJ L 168/12. See also on this model of criminalisation DR Doorenbos, 'De Verordening marktmisbruik in het economisch strafrecht' (2016) 12 *Tijdschrift voor Financieel Recht* 538.

[13] This term is not, or not yet, very common in the Netherlands. We usually speak of the setting of standards in multiple phases, which refers to the phenomenon that the criminalisation is fleshed out at various levels by different legislators. Broadly speaking, however, both expressions refer to the same phenomenon. The ECtHR's Advisory Opinion on 'the use of the 'blanket reference' or 'legislation by reference' technique, which will be discussed below, also uses a fairly general description. I did not consider it necessary to devise a more detailed definition for the purpose of this chapter.

[14] The Hoge Raad (Dutch Supreme Court) once issued a famous ruling on the *Blanketwet* (Framework Act) of 1818, which threatened punishment in advance against regulations that the King could issue. The Hoge Raad Court ruled that this did not grant the King a general and indefinite power, but that the criminal provision could only be in line with regulations that the King might issue under the law. See Hoge Raad 13 January 1879, W 4330: the Meerenberg ruling. This ruling is considered important from a constitutional law point of view because it restricted the King's legislative power. This is now laid down in article 89 of the Constitution. However, this *cause célèbre* in Dutch legal history also implies that a criminal provision which refers to another – as yet unknown – provision for the contents of the standard, is not in itself considered inadmissible (see section 7.4 below).

Offences Act (*Wet op de economische delicten*). In addition, the text of such delegated regulations may not be at all suitable to serve as a description of the offence, for example due to the use of very open formulations or concepts with a civil law orientation. The text of European legislation rarely describes offences as sharply as can be found in the Dutch Criminal Code (*Wetboek van Strafrecht*). This is the case for the core provisions and will not be substantially different for the delegated provisions. The Commission will also probably not take into account the fact that its implementing provisions will, if necessary, be 'automatically' provided with criminal sanctions in the Netherlands. The technique of criminalisation from the Economic Offences Act (*Wet op de economische delicten*) may have the charm of simplicity, but it lacks a great deal of nuance in this respect.[15]

An extreme example is the criminalisation in Article 1(3) Economic Offences Act (*Wet op de economische delicten*) of the breach of 'rules made under' Article 11 of the Market Abuse Regulation (EU) No 596/2014. This provision of the Market Abuse Regulation concerns market soundings, where potentially price-sensitive information is communicated to potential investors to gauge their interest in participating in a transaction. As a rule, communicating inside information to another person is prohibited under Article 10 Market Abuse Regulation, but Article 11 Market Abuse Regulation lays down conditions under which this can nevertheless be permitted. These conditions are regulated in an extensive and detailed manner. The Dutch criminalisation extends not only to the various paragraphs of Article 11 itself, but also to the regulatory and implementing technical standards developed by ESMA and adopted by the Commission.[16] These standards are laid down in the Delegated Regulation (EU) 2016/960 and in the Implementing Regulation (EU) 2016/959. The Dutch legislator has also added a final criminal law element to all the rules of conduct laid down in these supplementary regulations. And the same applies, remarkably, to the guidelines drawn up by ESMA, which should help potential investors to deal carefully with the information provided to them to avoid infringements of the Market Abuse Regulation. Those guidelines are also rules, established under Article 11 Market Abuse Regulation,[17] and therefore their infringement is also punishable as an economic offence.

I regard this example as rather extreme because it ultimately concerns an exception to the prohibition on unlawful disclosure of inside information. It is by no means self-evident that the person who fails to comply with any rule entailed in the exception should be independently punishable for that. Certainly not, since the preamble to the Market Abuse Regulation explicitly states that market participants who fail to comply with the rules when carrying out a market sounding are not

[15] See also DR Doorenbos, *Schets van het economisch strafrecht* (Wolters Kluwer, 2015) 22–25.

[16] ESMA and the Commission derive their authority to develop and adopt these implementing rules from Art 11(9)–(10) Market Abuse Regulation (n 12).

[17] Art 11(11) Market Abuse Regulation (n 12), the provision underlying the MAR Guidelines on Persons receiving market soundings (ESMA/2016/1477).

automatically deemed to have unlawfully disclosed inside information.[18] They will have to demonstrate, by other means, that they acted with due care or were acting in the normal exercise of their employment, profession or duties. In that case, they would still be acquitted as far as the prohibition of Article 10 Market Abuse Regulation is concerned, but as a result of the Dutch criminalisation, they could nevertheless be prosecuted in the Netherlands for infringing Article 11 Market Abuse Regulation, or the implementing regulations or guidelines based thereon.

7.3.2. EU Directives

7.3.2.1. Introduction

Where directives, rather than regulations, are concerned, European standards are generally first transposed into national regulations. This may lead to the introduction of new legal obligations and prohibitions, which are linked to the national criminal law system by Article 1 Economic Offences Act (*Wet op de economische delicten*). In addition, a directive may give rise to the amendment and supplementation of existing criminal provisions. It is also possible that the legislator is of the opinion that the directive does not need further implementation, because in its opinion national criminal legislation already sufficiently meets European requirements.

In most cases, it is no longer possible to deduce directly from the national regulation that it is based on a European directive, or that this national regulation must implement it. This is certainly the case if the regulation already existed before the European directive was drafted. Although the European dimension is evident from the legislative history and is usually mentioned in the preamble to the implementing instrument (a law, decree, or regulation), the link to the underlying directive will often disappear out of sight after the amendment is made, certainly where amendments to existing legislation are involved. Thus, there is a risk, at least in theory, that the interpretation of the national provision will build on national sources of law rather than on the new European rules. That risk will vary in practice depending on the visibility of the European dimension and the extent to which parties to the proceedings draw attention to it.

7.3.2.2. Implementation with Reference to the Source

In some cases, the implementation regulation still contains a reference to the underlying directive. In such cases, there is a direct relationship that will be explicitly addressed in criminal proceedings, because the provision of the directive referred to is an element of the offence on which the court must rule.

[18] Recital 35 Market Abuse Regulation (n 12).

For example, in a criminal case concerning an infringement of Article 8 Money Laundering and Terrorist Financing Prevention Act (*Wet ter voorkoming van witwassen en financieren van terrorisme*) – the failure to conduct an enhanced client screening – it will have to be determined whether the institution concerned took the risk factors referred to in Annex III to the Fourth Anti-Money Laundering Directive (Directive (EU) 2015/849) into account. In addition, the court will have to examine whether the institution's client was indeed resident or established in a state that was designated by the European Commission as presenting a higher risk of money laundering or terrorist financing under Article 9 Fourth Anti-Money Laundering Directive. It is the Dutch description of the offence that prompts the court to examine these points, by explicitly linking them to the underlying European directive.

By way of illustration, reference may also be made to Article 3:288a Financial Supervision Act (*Wet op het financieel toezicht*), a regulation that concerns the minimum capital requirements of an 'insurance guidelines group' (*verzekeringsrichtlijngroep*). This statutory provision is contained in Article 1(2) Economic Offences Act (*Wet op de economische delicten*). In Article 3:288a Financial Supervision Act, explicit reference is made to the European Solvency II Directive (2009/138/EC) and to the national implementation regulations relating to it. These are laid down in the Prudential Supervision of Financial Undertakings (Financial Supervision Act) Decree (*Besluit prudentieel toezicht financiële groepen Wft*), which contains numerous references to specific provisions of the directive. The regulations of the Solvency II Directive have thus been criminalised in the Netherlands by the link to Article 1(2) Economic Offences Act, the Financial Supervision Act and national implementation regulations. The latter even applies to the further rules that the national banking regulator DNB can still set, taking into account the delegated regulation that the Commission has adopted in addition to the Solvency II Directive.[19] Such DNB rules are also adopted 'under' Article 3:288a Financial Supervision Act and their infringement would therefore constitute an economic offence. This is remarkable, as DNB is ultimately an organisation structured under private law, but on this basis has the power to create new criminal provisions. It is again a rather far-reaching example of blanket criminal legislation.

7.3.2.3. *Implementation without Reference to the Source*

In most cases, there is no reference to the underlying directive and the European dimension is therefore less obvious. The European dimension is however embedded in the national provision that is central to the criminal case.

For example, Article 23b Money Laundering and Terrorist Financing Prevention Act contains a general obligation for anyone who offers custodial

[19] Article 4f Prudential Supervision of Financial Undertakings (Financial Supervision Act) Decree (*Besluit prudentieel toezicht financiële groepen Wft*), in which DNB is given the power to set rules regarding the mandatory supervisory reports of insurers and holding companies.

wallets in or from the Netherlands, in a professional or business capacity, to register with DNB. The same obligation applies to anyone who offers, in or from the Netherlands, professional or business services for the exchange of virtual currencies and fiduciary currencies. Whoever fails to comply with these obligations, breaches Article 23b Money Laundering and Terrorist Financing Prevention Act (*Wet ter voorkoming van witwassen en financieren van terrorisme*) and thus commits an economic offence under Article 1(2) Economic Offences Act (*Wet op de economische delicten*). Although the legislative text does not refer to it, the Fifth Anti-Money Laundering Directive (Directive (EU) 2018/843) will have to be consulted for interpretation of the terms 'custodial wallet', 'virtual currencies' and 'fiduciary currencies', respectively. These are core elements of the definition of the offence that will have to be interpreted in line with the Directive.

7.3.2.4. Interpretation in Line with the Directive and Questions Referred for a Preliminary Ruling

In principle, the European background should always be taken into account when interpreting a national description of an offence that originates from a directive or is intended to implement it. Whether this always happens is open to debate. The published case law contains relatively few criminal cases in which there is explicit discussion on the question as to where an interpretation in line with the directive should lead. This is in line with the earlier observation that referring questions for a preliminary ruling is highly unusual in criminal cases. If there is little discussion about the question of what the correct interpretation in line with the directive should be, there will rarely be any reason for a potentially time-consuming trip to Luxembourg. But, is it always clear what the European legislator intended, and did the Dutch legislator subsequently implement it perfectly in its implementing legislation? That would be wonderful, but I have my doubts.

For example, as a lawyer in the *Flexovit* insider trading case,[20] I would have liked the national court to have referred the case to the ECJ for a preliminary ruling on the required degree of influence on the share price that can reasonably be expected when disclosing information. Dutch law at the time required no more than 'influence' on the share price, whereas the European Directives required 'a significant influence' on the share price. The national Court had ruled that it was sufficient that the share price could be influenced 'to a not insignificant extent'. The question was whether an interpretation in line with the Directive should not have led to a more stringent requirement. I would think that a price movement that is 'not insignificant' cannot automatically be regarded as 'significant'. There is a linguistic difference: not only in Dutch, but especially if the language variations of the (old) European Market Abuse Directive are taken into account. Those other

[20] Hoge Raad (Dutch Supreme Court) 31 May 2005, ECLI:NL:HR:2005:AR8021 (*Flexovit insider trading*).

language versions also contained words that sounded stronger than 'not insignificant', such as '*erheblich*', '*significant*', '*de façon sensible*' and '*in modo sensibile*'. The Dutch Supreme Court, however, thought otherwise and therefore did not consider it necessary to refer questions for a preliminary ruling. I still regard this as a missed opportunity, even though it must be said that the debate about this part of the definition of inside information focuses today on the question of what 'the reasonable investor' would or would not do with the information. The question of the extent to which his/her actions will influence the price has gradually been relegated to the background.

Apart from this example, my general impression is that the criminal courts would rather avoid going to Luxembourg and prefer to cut the Gordian knot themselves. ECJ case law also allows for this, as long as the national court can reasonably argue that the issue is sufficiently clear: the doctrine of the *acte clair* or *acte éclairé*. In my opinion, however, questions of interpretation within financial legislation are often unclear, in the sense that the interpretation can reasonably be debated, while there is rarely any case law in which the answer has already been provided. The amount of regulatory legislation with European roots is now so large when compared to the number of court cases on it that an unprecedented concrete interpretation issue will be encountered relatively often. Moreover, financial legislation is highly dynamic and is constantly amended. And yet the national criminal courts almost always resolve these issues without consulting the ECJ.

The criminal courts rarely state explicitly that they are giving an interpretation in line with a Directive. Rather, the reader of the judgment will have to assume so. Moreover, the national provision in question will have to allow for an interpretation in line with Europe-based legislation, because that interpretation cannot go so far that it would result in an interpretation *contra legem*.[21] However, the cases in which such a situation is established and the court should disapply the national provision accordingly on the grounds of incompatibility with European law are extremely rare. As a result, the discussion on the correct interpretation of national rules that originate from or implement European standards is settled by the Dutch court in the vast majority of cases. This is where it starts, and where it usually ends.

7.4. Blanket Criminal Legislation

7.4.1. Introduction

As outlined above, the Dutch legislator often provides European financial law with extensive protection under criminal law. In doing so, a technique of criminal law

[21] Further on this subject: Luchtman and Widdershoven, 'Het Nederlandse strafrecht in de ban van het Unierecht' (2018) 888.

is used that often results in criminal liability in case of infringements of European standards and implementation rules, even without this being immediately evident. The European legislator will not always assume that its regulations must also function as a description of an offence, while offenders in the Netherlands will not always realise that the regulations they are dealing with fall within the scope of criminal law. Seen from a principle of legality point of view this is questionable.[22] Because of the *lex certa*-principle, every citizen must be able to know for what conduct he can be punished. In the case of blanket criminal legislation, the criminalisation refers to rules of conduct that have been or will be laid down elsewhere, often by a legislator other than the one who creates the criminalisation. It often requires a great deal of effort on the part of the person to whom the standard applies to find out which regulations apply to his/her behaviour and whether these have also been made punishable.[23] This is especially true if the basic standard originates from European legal sources, but the national legislator has incorporated it in implementing provisions which do not themselves refer to these legal sources.

7.4.2. Use and Admissibility

Recently, the ECtHR ruled in general terms on the question of whether the use of references in criminal legislation – in which the criminalisation refers to a provision that has been laid down elsewhere – is in itself compatible with Article 7 ECHR: the principle of legality.[24] The ECtHR answered that question in the affirmative: 'using the "blanket reference" or "legislation by reference" technique in criminalising acts or omissions is not in itself incompatible with the requirements of Article 7 of the Convention'. Note in this regard that this technique of criminal legislation is used by the vast majority of States that are party to the ECHR. Curiously, the ECtHR thinks that this is only different in the Netherlands and Malta. This must be based on a misunderstanding. As outlined above, the Dutch legislator uses this technique on a large scale: Dutch financial criminal law is almost entirely made up of blanket criminal legislation. The Economic Offences Act (*Wet op de economische delicten*) has been the textbook example for some 75 years of an Act in which there is virtually no behavioural standard, but in which there are references to

[22] The principle of legality is laid down in Art 7 ECHR, Art 49 EU Charter, article 16 Constitution and article 1 Dutch Criminal Code (*Wetboek van Strafrecht*).

[23] See in that context, inter alia, FGH Kristen, 'Het materieelrechtelijk legaliteitsbeginsel' in FGH Kristen, RMI Lamp, JMW Lindeman and WS de Zanger (eds), *Bijzonder strafrecht, Strafrechtelijke handhaving van sociaal-economisch en fiscaal recht in Nederland* (Boom Uitgevers, 2019) 428–35.

[24] See ECtHR (Grand Chamber), Advisory Opinion P16-2019-001 dated 29 May 2020, concerning the use of the 'blanket reference' or 'legislation by reference' technique in the definition of an offence and the standards of comparison between the criminal law in force at the time of the commission of the offence and the amended criminal law. The opinion was discussed by J Cnossen and JH Gerards in *EHRC Updates* (ECtHR 2020-0160) and by P Van Sasse van Ysselt in *NJCM Bulletin* 2020/4, 498–512.

other regulations on an unprecedented scale: regulations, directives, laws, orders in council, ministerial regulations, regulations set by administrative bodies, etc.[25]

Specifically, where European regulations are concerned, criminalisation at national level can hardly be realised by other means than through references. After all, it is not permitted to copy the text of the regulation in a national regulation.[26] A reference must therefore be made. Moreover, financial regulatory law forms part of an infinitely large complex of European and national economic law, of which it is difficult to imagine that the criminal legislator can control and keep up to date without using blanket criminal legislation.

7.4.3. Legal External Borders

Do borders still exist? Are there situations in which the offender must go unpunished because the criminalised standard in the web of regulations was too unclear or too far removed from its basis in terms of content? Probably. The ECtHR makes it clear that the legislator must observe the minimum requirements that have already been identified in earlier case law. In addition, the ECtHR gives the criminal legislator advice that it may take to heart to prevent infringement of Article 7 ECHR.[27] After the general opinion that the legislative technique of the reference in criminal law is not in itself incompatible with Article 7 ECHR, the ECJ considers:

> 72. However, in order to comply with Article 7 of the Convention a criminal law defining an offence by making use of the 'blanket reference' or 'legislation by reference' technique must fulfil the general 'quality of law' requirements, that is, it must be sufficiently precise, accessible and foreseeable in its application. Given that the referenced provision becomes part of the definition of the offence, both norms (the referencing and the referenced provision) taken together must enable the persons concerned to foresee, if need be with the help of appropriate legal advice, what conduct may make them criminally liable. In the Court's view, this follows from the general principles of its case-law regarding the requirements of the quality of law and is also supported by the comparative-law materials available to it …
>
> Furthermore, the Court considers that the most effective way of ensuring clarity and foreseeability is for the reference to be explicit, and for the referencing provision to set out the constituent elements of the offence. Moreover, the referenced provisions may not extend the scope of criminalisation as set out by the referencing provision. In any event, it is up to the court applying both the referencing provision and the referenced provision to assess whether criminal liability was foreseeable in the circumstances of the case.

[25] See also J Cnossen and JH Gerards (ibid) and by P Van Sasse van Ysselt in *NJCM Bulletin* 2020/4, para 16 ff.

[26] There is a prohibition on copying, according to Altena, *Het legaliteitsbeginsel en de doorwerking van Europees recht* (2016) 81.

[27] The ECtHR's Advisory Opinion is not in itself binding.

We can see that the Dutch legislator has so far pursued a different course than the ECtHR considers desirable. The references in Article 1 Economic Offences Act (*Wet op de economische delicten*) (the 'referencing provision') are extremely sparse. It merely refers to regulations that can be found elsewhere, without any additional text, let alone mentioning any element of the offence. This is contrary to the opinion and detracts from clarity and foreseeability. Moreover, we have seen that the provision to which reference is made (the 'referenced provision') often itself refers in a general sense to other provisions, which further compromises clarity and predictability. A statutory provision that refers to other rules to be laid down by or under an order in council does not make the reader much wiser and opens the door to even more implementing rules. Such implementing rules are by definition different from the 'referenced provision' referred to in Article 1 Economic Offences Act. In other words, anyone who infringes a provision of an order in council, a ministerial regulation or any other type of regulation referred to in the financial legislation – and this may also be a provision of a European directive – is infringing a provision to which Article 1 Economic Offences Act itself does not refer. This seems to be a situation that the ECtHR has failed to consider yet, and one that will probably not be considered positively.

The ECtHR also mentions a more substantive principle. The regulation referred to may not exceed the scope of the criminal provision referred to. This is a logical assumption. However, in the context of Article 1 Economic Offences Act, it cannot be applied to this provision itself (the 'referencing provision') because no substantive boundary is indicated there. As mentioned, Article 1 Economic Offences Act only refers to a provision that has been laid down elsewhere (the 'referenced provision') and it is only in that provision that the scope of the standard to be enforced by criminal law will be determined. In financial legislation, this is often done in such a way that the provision of the law (the 'referenced provision') mentions the subjects that will be regulated in more detail in implementing regulations in orders in council or ministerial regulations. In the end, it comes down to testing whether the delegated or subdelegated legislator has kept to these boundaries. If its implementing rules also relate to subjects that can no longer reasonably be included in the enumeration given in the law or in the decree, it can be argued that the rule in question is non-binding.[28]

Regarding the reconciliation between the 'referencing provision' and the 'referenced provision', it can regularly be observed in the context of Article 1 Economic Offences Act that the referring provision actually criminalises more than necessary, given the content of the provision referred to. The references in Article 1 Economic Offences Act are often quite coarse: they refer to whole Articles consisting of various parts (paragraphs) of which sometimes only a few parts actually

[28] See also BF Keulen, *Economisch strafrecht* (Guida Quint, 1995) 30 ff. and also JMW Lindeman, 'De zwakste schakel, Enkele gevolgen van het stelsel van gelede normstellingen' (2004) *Tijdschrift voor Onderneming en Strafrecht* 78.

contain rules of conduct. An example of this has already been given above. It is up to the legislator to conclude that he/she did not mean to include the other Articles or paragraphs in the scope of the criminalisation (the 'referencing provision'). For example, paragraphs in which a particular task is assigned to the financial regulator or paragraphs in which an exception is indicated in respect of a prohibition. As long as investigating officers and the Public Prosecution Service follow this benevolent reading, things will be fine, but it is nevertheless far from ideal.

7.4.4. Short-Circuiting between 'Referencing Provision' and 'Referenced Provision'

The emphasis on clarity and foreseeability, in combination with the advice given by the ECtHR, could prompt the Dutch criminal legislator to pay more attention to the use of the technique of criminalisation through the Economic Offences Act (*Wet op de economische delicten*).[29] Although legal practice has gained experience with this system for many decades and fundamental criticism of it is rare, the question is whether we do not sometimes deal with it too easily. I am thinking, for example, of the situation in which statutory provisions from the enumeration in Article 1 Economic Offences Act are inadvertently set aside if the legislator, when amending the underlying standards (the 'referenced provisions'), fails to amend the references (the 'referencing provisions'). This happens regularly. For, on the one hand, the legislative technique of referencing offers the legislator great ease of use, but, on the other hand, any amendment of a law or regulation to which Article 1 Economic Offences Act refers creates risks. If the legislator is negligent in amending the reference, this can cause a short circuit. The Economic Offences Act then still refers to statutory provisions that have already lapsed, while contravention of the new or amended statutory provisions is not criminalised. However, the Hoge Raad (Dutch Supreme Court) does not penalise such omissions by the legislator. Although at the time of the conduct the criminalisation may have been non-existent for some time, according to our highest court a conviction can still follow if it is assumed that the legislator made a mistake here.[30]

From a principle of legality point of view, this flexible attitude is by no means obvious. The assumption is that everyone should be able to read in the law at the time of their actions whether they are punishable. In a general sense, it seems to me to be an overstrained demand to expect citizens and businesses to assume that, in the absence of proper criminalisation, the legislator will still take action and

[29] cf JS Nan, *Het lex certa-beginsel* (dissertation, Tilburg) (Sdu Uitgevers, 2011) 255, who states as a requirement of sufficient clarity 'that as little use as possible should be made of setting standards in multiple phases.'

[30] See eg Hoge Raad (Dutch Supreme Court) 30 August 2005, ECLI:NL:HR:2005:AT7546 and Hoge Raad 19 September 2006, ECLI:NL:HR:2006:AV1141.

that they should adapt their behaviour to that expectation. The approach in which the court essentially grants retroactive effect to remedial legislation of which the defendant could not have been aware at the time of his/her actions, does not seem to me to be in accordance with the first sentence of Article 7(1) ECHR. In its recent opinion, the ECtHR has once again sharply outlined the limits and principles of blanket criminal legislation. Against the background of these considerations, the national case law that forgives 'manifest errors' by the legislator seems to be open to reconsideration. A stricter attitude towards the legislator does not seem unreasonable either. The technique of criminal legislation by reference offers the legislator many advantages and enables it to link large numbers of higher and lower regulations to the criminal sanctions system with a single reference. Citizens and businesses are subsequently often forced to go to great lengths to determine the scope of the criminalisation. The least they can expect from the legislator is that its references are carefully drafted and kept up to date. If negligence and inattention on the part of the legislator are not punished in practice, this will not promote the already dubious quality of blanket criminal legislation.

7.5. Awareness of Standards and Liability

In practice, defences against the application of criminal provisions that are perceived as too vague or complex are subsequently rarely accepted.[31] They tend to run up against the argument that persons or legal entities engaged in regulated activities on a professional or commercial basis should be properly aware of the applicable rules beforehand.[32] If they are unable to do so themselves, they should seek legal advice.[33]

It is doubtful whether this argument can be used to dismiss the *lex non certa* defence in all cases. In the very extensive and densely regulated field of financial-economic legislation, situations arise that are entirely new, even for the expert legal advisor, who cannot always offer the clarity sought by the natural or legal person concerned. If that person thinks that there is sufficient legal basis for carrying out his/her activities, while this later turns out to be different, the question arises which criminal charge is appropriate. Is it a case of conditional intent because he/she was in any case aware of the possibility that he/she would be breaking the law? Or is it conscious negligence, because awareness of the risks was accompanied by a reasoned expectation that the activities were more likely to be lawful? Or can there perhaps also be an error on a point of law because the person concerned can argue that he/she acted in excusable ignorance of the applicable

[31] Regarding this, see Altena (n 11) 147.

[32] See eg Hoge Raad (Dutch Supreme Court) 31 October 2000, ECLI:NL:HR:2000:AA7954 (*Krulsla*).

[33] See eg ECtHR 21 October 2013 *Del Río Prada v Spain* (App No 42750/09) in [79], in which the ECtHR refers to 'taking appropriate legal advice'.

criminal provision? Or is there, on the contrary, 'full intent' because in the sphere of Dutch financial criminal law the doctrine of 'neutral intent' applies, in which it does not matter in law whether the person concerned was aware that he/she was infringing a provision, as long as his/her actions were intentional? There is no complete unanimity in the Dutch legal sphere regarding these questions.

In case law, the strict line prevails in which defences about lack of knowledge of the applicable regulations are parried with reference to the duty of care of professionally acting parties and the doctrine of neutral intent. The consequence of this approach is that it is relatively easy to conclude that the perpetrator has committed a crime, because he ultimately acted intentionally, with his awareness of the standard playing no major role. The Hoge Raad (Dutch Supreme Court) usually goes along with this, although it is sometimes critical when it comes to substantiating the evidence of this intention: the court must, if necessary, give some substance and reasoning to this.

Meanwhile, especially in the literature, one can also find advocates of less strict approaches. For example, it has been argued that financial criminal law should allow for taking a reasonably defensible position with respect to the interpretation of complex standards.[34] If the incorrect interpretation followed by the person concerned was or is reasonably defensible according to objective criteria, there would be insufficient grounds for a criminal charge. In such a case, intent could no longer be proven and, moreover, there could be an absence of all guilt – the most general excuse.[35] The suspect should then be discharged from prosecution. This doctrine of the reasonably defensible position has been applied for decades in tax legislation, to prevent incorrect choices in tax returns from becoming too easily punishable. It can be argued that financial legislation is now no less dynamic, changeable, and complex than tax legislation. Therefore, financial law should also allow for such a correction of liability.

In addition, a more nuanced classification of offences in financial criminal law has been advocated.[36] In addition to intentional offences (serious offences) and non-intentional offences (minor offences), the legislator could introduce a category of culpable offences. This would make it possible, where appropriate, to do more justice to the degree of culpability of the accused.

Finally, it has been proposed to abandon or re-abandon the doctrine of neutral intent in the area of financial criminal law.[37] According to this proposal, acting intentionally on the part of the perpetrator would no longer be sufficient

[34] See inter alia DR Doorenbos, 'Specialisatie en rechtsvinding in het economisch strafrecht' (2010) 7 *Trema* 281.

[35] GJME de Bont, 'Het pleitbaar standpunt als bijzondere strafuitsluitingsgrond?' (2020) 4 *Strafblad* 219.

[36] RCP Haentjens, *De wederrechtelijkheid in het financiële strafrecht*, (Universiteit van Amsterdam, 2016) 18, 27–28.

[37] See DR Doorenbos, 'Opzet in de Wet op de economische delicten: beter boos dan kleurloos' (2021) *Ars Aequi* 253–57.

for assuming a criminal offence, but it would also have to be proven that the perpetrator was aware that his/her conduct was unlawful. If the latter cannot be proven, the perpetrator would be less severely liable: he could then only be punished for a minor offence and not for a serious offence.

7.6. Conclusion

Financial law is dominated by the EU, yet national criminal justice in this area does not always pay attention to this European dimension. This need not be a problem, as long as the criminal justice system leads to outcomes that can be deemed 'EU compliant'. If there is reason to doubt the correct interpretation of the standard, the criminal court should not, in my view, be reluctant to refer questions for a preliminary ruling.

Financial criminal law makes frequent use of blanket criminal legislation. This offers the legislator the advantages of simplicity and flexibility, while it is also unavoidable in the criminalisation of the directly effective provisions of EU regulations. However, blanket criminal legislation requires a great deal of effort on the part of the parties to which the standard applies, who are often forced to go to great lengths to find out exactly which rules regulate their activities and whether (and, if so, how) these actions are also subject to criminal sanctions. Where appropriate, the criminal court could show more understanding of this complexity for natural and legal persons subject to these laws, by being less strict in its assessment of the question of guilt. Furthermore, it does not appear to be overreaching to require the legislator not to bring the regulations within the scope of the criminal law unnecessarily broadly, and further to keep the reference accurately up to date. And criminal courts at their turn should play a role in this by keeping the legislator on its toes by punishing negligence where appropriate.

8

Full Cooperation versus the Right not to Incriminate Oneself: Oil and Water?

JOOST NAN*

8.1. Introduction

Financial law is governed by an impressive amount of European Union (EU) instruments. The enforcement thereof depends in part on the cooperation of (legal) entities in those branches. They are often obliged to inform and work with supervisory authorities. Breaches of, or non-compliance with, many rules constitute a criminal offence and/or are enforced by way of administrative sanctions and/or criminal penalties. In that way, the EU hopes to establish an effective enforcement regime to combat malversations on financial markets, money laundering, financing terrorism, etc. The EU, however, not only wants to establish financially fair level playing fields, but also wants to be an area where fundamental rights are respected, such as well-known criminal fair-trial rights (see for instance Articles 47 and 48 of the Charter of Fundamental Rights of the European Union; the 'Charter'). It concerns, inter alia, the right to remain silent and the right not to incriminate oneself (privilege against self-incrimination; *nemo tenetur*). These rights are also acknowledged by the European Court of Human Rights (ECtHR) through Article 6 of the European Convention on Human Rights (ECHR). They hold the same eminent place in both EU law and the case law of the ECtHR to ensure fair proceedings and to avoid miscarriages of justice. Not under all circumstances can cooperation be coerced or can non-compliance be penalised. Requiring all these (possibly) punitive sanctions for infractions of the financial EU instruments might have brought in a Trojan horse in regard to the enforcement-through-cooperation strategy. The question therefore rises whether the obligation to cooperate with the authorities, that (have to) have equally far-reaching supervisory powers in the field of financial law, will always be compatible with the right not to incriminate oneself if faced with a criminal charge.

* Special thanks is extended to Vincent Boer, former student assistant with the Criminal Law department.

To answer this question, I will first discuss the scope of the right not to incriminate oneself as included in Article 6 ECHR, for this is, in part, still somewhat unclear (section 8.2). I will then map the parallel right in EU law, where the interpretation by the EU legislator of the case law of the ECtHR will help to define the actual scope of the privilege (section 8.3). It is then appropriate to address the question whether legal persons can invoke the privilege against self-incrimination just as natural persons (section 8.4). After that I will discuss the field of EU instruments on money laundering, terrorist financing and on market abuse, focusing more specifically on the obligations to cooperate (section 8.5). This enables me to analyse the compatibility of both ends that the EU strives for (section 8.6). I will finish with some concluding remarks (section 8.7).

8.2. The Right not to Incriminate Oneself; Article 6 ECHR

8.2.1. Introduction

Much has been written on the right not to incriminate oneself.[1] This right has a solid basis in Europe and stems directly from EU law and the ECHR. In this chapter I want to work with the current idea of what this principle entails to see whether full cooperation in the enforcement of financial law can always be upheld in the case of (looming) proceedings of a criminal/punitive nature. In this section I will address Article 6 ECHR and the case law of the ECtHR on the right not to incriminate oneself.

8.2.2. Criminal Charge

Two points should be made. First, the privilege against self-incrimination can only be invoked in case of a criminal charge. The ECtHR restated in *Ibrahim* that a criminal charge exists

> from the moment that an individual is officially notified by the competent authority of an allegation that he has committed a criminal offence, or from the point at which his situation has been substantially affected by actions taken by the authorities as a result of a suspicion against him.[2]

[1] See for its history: RH Helmholz, 'Origins of the Privilege against Self-Incrimination: The Role of the European Ius Commune' (1990) 65 *New York University Law Review* 962.

[2] ECtHR 13 September 2016 *Ibrahim and others/United Kingdom*, ECLI:CE:ECHR:2016:0913JUD005054108, [249].

This means that one does not have to have the official status of accused or suspect to invoke the principle. It is enough to be materially subjected to scrutiny by the authorities.

Secondly, proceedings and sanctions that are nationally labelled 'administrative' could very well in fact be nevertheless criminal in nature, given the autonomous meaning of the terms 'criminal charge' and 'penalty'. When it comes to the question of whether certain proceedings are criminal in nature, the viewpoint of the ECtHR and the Court of Justice are aligned. For a very long time now, the ECtHR has used the so-called Engel criteria to determine whether a person's 'charge' is criminal and thus falls under the protection of the criminal limb of Article 6 ECHR.[3] The Court of Justice does exactly the same with the so-called *Bonda* criteria, referring to the *Engel* judgment.[4] They are often called the *Engel–Bonda* criteria. These three criteria can be further explained by using case law of the ECtHR and the Court of Justice. The first criterion is the legal classification of the offence under national law. This is only a starting point and of little weight. If by national law the offence is a criminal one, it automatically falls under the criminal limb of Article 6 ECHR and the EU criminal rights. If proceedings are, instead, nationally deemed to be of an administrative nature, one must look at the other two criteria.

The second criterion, which is more important, is the nature of the offence. According to Advocate General Pikamäe, this criterion seeks to grasp the true nature of the offence. If the purpose of the penalty involved is punitive, this is a strong indication that the charge is criminal in its autonomous meaning, regardless of its classification on the national level. Generally speaking, a reason to classify the penalty as criminal would be (and has been) where the penalty provided for by national law is directed towards the general public and not towards a clearly defined group of individuals; where the offence is established with the aim of punishment and deterrence instead of seeking only compensation for pecuniary damage; and where the national provision imposing a penalty safeguards a legal interest which is normally protected by criminal law.[5] In *Garlsson* the Court of Justice considered, for instance

> that a penalty with a punitive purpose is criminal in nature … and that the mere fact that it also pursues a deterrence purpose does not mean that it cannot be characterised as a criminal penalty (…) it is of the very nature of criminal penalties that they seek

[3] ECtHR 8 June 1976 *Engel and others/Netherlands*, ECLI:CE:ECHR:1976:0608JUD000510071, [82]–[83], as used by the Grand Chamber very recently in its judgment on 22 December 2020 *Jonsson and Hall/Iceland*, ECLI:CE:ECHR:2020:1222JUD006827314, [75].

[4] Case C-489/10 *Bonda*, ECLI:EU:C:2012:319, [37]. Repeated inter alia in Case C-617/10 *Fransson*, ECLI:EU:C:2013:105, [35] and Case C-537/16 *Garlsson*, ECLI:EU:C:2018:193, [28]. The *Engel* criteria were also previously used in Case C-45/08 *Spector Photo Group NV and Chris Van Raemdonck*, ECLI:EU:C:2009:806, [42].

[5] See both the Guide on Art 6(18) and the opinion of Advocate General Pikamäe in Case C-481/19 *DB*, ECLI:EU:C:2020:861, [56].

> both to punish and to deter unlawful conduct. By contrast, a measure which merely repairs the damage caused by the offence at issue is not criminal in nature.[6]

The third criterion, which is more an alternative to the second than a cumulative requirement (although they could be used in combination), is the nature and degree of severity of the penalty that the person concerned risks incurring. This means that the potential penalty, not the actual penalty, is decisive. A strong indication is whether the penalty could be equated to a criminal one (detention, a substantial fine, imprisonment in lieu of compliance, entrance into the criminal record, etc).[7] In *Garlsson* the Court of Justice explained

> that an administrative fine which can be of an amount up to 10 times greater than the proceeds or profit obtained from the market manipulation has a high degree of severity which is liable to support the view that that penalty is criminal in nature.[8]

8.2.3. Improper Compulsion

As my purpose is to discuss the right not to incriminate oneself anno 2022, the starting point should be the landmark case of *Ibrahim* (2016), in which the Grand Chamber gave the most recent important overarching general principles on the right not to incriminate oneself, with reference to its most important previous case law.[9] The ECtHR starts by emphasising that the right not to incriminate oneself

> is primarily concerned with respecting the will of an accused person to remain silent and presupposes that the prosecution in a criminal case seeks to prove their case without resort to evidence obtained through methods of coercion or oppression in defiance of the will of the accused.[10]

The right to remain silent and the right not to incriminate oneself are generally recognised international standards which lie at the heart of the notion of a fair procedure under Article 6 ECHR. Among others, they have to protect the accused against 'improper compulsion by the authorities', which in turn contributes to the avoidance of miscarriages of justice (and to the fulfilment of the aims of Article 6).[11] The reliability of coerced evidence is therefore an aspect in this

[6] Case C-537/16 *Garlsson*, ECLI:EU:C:2018:193, [34].

[7] See both the Guide on Art 6(19) and the previously mentioned opinion of Advocate General Pikamäe, [57].

[8] Case C-537/16 *Garlsson*, ECLI:EU:C:2018:193, [35]. Repeated in Case C-596/16 & C-597/16 *Di puma and Zecca*, ECLI:EU:C:2018:192, [38].

[9] ECtHR 13 September 2016 *Ibrahim and others v United Kingdom*, ECLI:CE:ECHR:2016:0913JUD005054108.

[10] With reference to ECtHR 17 December 1996 *Saunders v United Kingdom*, ECLI:CE:ECHR:1996:1217JUD001918791, [68]–[69]; ECtHR 11 July 2006 *Jalloh v Germany*, ECLI:CE:ECHR:2006:0711JUD005481000, [100] and [102]; and ECtHR 10 March 2009 *Bykov v Russia*, ECLI:CE:ECHR:2009:0310JUD000437802, [92].

[11] With reference to ECtHR 8 February 1996 *Murray v United Kingdom*, ECLI:CE:ECHR:1996:0208JUD001873191, [45]; ECtHR 11 July 2006 *Jalloh v Germany*, ECLI:CE:ECHR:2006:0711JUD005481000, [100];

matter.[12] The person involved must have ample opportunity to challenge the authenticity of the evidence and oppose its use.[13] Furthermore, an important general notion is that the privilege against self-incrimination does not, according to the ECtHR, protect against the making of an incriminating statement per se, but against the obtainment of evidence by coercion or oppression. It is also not confined to statements which are directly incriminating.[14] The ECtHR has ruled in *Ibrahim* that because of the nature of the privilege against self-incrimination and the right to silence, 'in principle there can be no justification for a failure to notify a suspect of these rights'.[15]

The core of the right is as follows according to the ECtHR: 'It is the existence of compulsion that gives rise to concerns as to whether the privilege against self-incrimination has been respected'. It is for this reason that the ECtHR 'must first consider the nature and degree of compulsion used to obtain the evidence'. The ECtHR deems it unacceptable, if the degree of compulsion that is applied 'destroys the very essence of the privilege against self-incrimination'. Not all compulsion is prohibited: 'What is crucial in this context is the use to which evidence obtained under compulsion is put in the course of the criminal trial'.[16] A very small fine in case of a refusal to cooperate, for instance, may sometimes be considered as not improper.[17] Refusing to cooperate must be, in my owns words, a realistic possibility.

It should be mentioned that the ECtHR takes other factors into account as well. A constant factor in assessing whether the privilege against self-incrimination has been respected, is the existence of any relevant safeguards in the procedure.

and ECtHR 10 March 2009 *Bykov v Russia*, ECLI:CE:ECHR:2009:0310JUD000437802, [92]. It is also mentioned in ECtHR 17 December 1996 *Saunders/United Kingdom*, ECLI:CE:ECHR:1996:1217JUD001918791, [68].

[12] See ECtHR 5 November 2002 *Allan v United Kingdom*, ECLI:CE:ECHR:2002:1105JUD004853999 and ECtHR 29 June 2007 *O'Halloran and Francis v United Kingdom*, ECLI:CE:ECHR:2007:0629JUD001580902, [59]–[60].

[13] ECtHR 13 September 2016 *Ibrahim and others v United Kingdom*, ECLI:CE:ECHR:2016:0913JUD005054108, [274] and previously ECtHR 10 March 2009 *Bykov v Russia*, ECLI:CE:ECHR:2009:0310JUD000437802 and ECtHR 21 September 2016 *Khan v Germany*, ECLI:CE:ECHR:2016:0921JUD003803012.

[14] ECtHR 13 September 2016 *Ibrahim and others v United Kingdom*, ECLI:CE:ECHR:2016:0913JUD005054108, [268]: 'Testimony obtained under compulsion which appears on its face to be of a non-incriminating nature, such as exculpatory remarks or mere information on questions of fact, may be deployed in criminal proceedings in support of the prosecution case, for example to contradict or cast doubt upon other statements of the accused or evidence given by him during the trial, or to otherwise undermine his credibility'. See also ECtHR 19 March 2015 *Corbet and others v France*, ECLI:CE:ECHR:2015:0319JUD000749411.

[15] ECtHR 13 September 2016 *Ibrahim and others v United Kingdom*, ECLI:CE:ECHR:2016:0913JUD005054108, [273].

[16] With reference to ECtHR 21 December 2000 *Heaney and McGuinness v Ireland*, ECLI:CE:ECHR:2000:1221JUD003472097, [54]–[55]; ECtHR 29 June 2007 *O'Halloran and Francis v United Kingdom*, ECLI:CE:ECHR:2007:0629JUD001580902, [55]; ECtHR 10 March 2009 *Bykov v Russia*, ECLI:CE:ECHR:2009:0310JUD000437802, [92]; and ECtHR 17 December 1996 *Saunders v United Kingdom*, ECLI:CE:ECHR:1996:1217JUD001918791, [71], respectively.

[17] cf ECtHR 5 November 2002 *Allan v United Kingdom*, ECLI:CE:ECHR:2002:1105JUD004853999.

Another factor is the use to which any material so obtained is put in the punitive proceedings against the compelled. If the results of the coercion are not used as evidence against the coerced, in principle no problem arises.[18] Also, even though the ECtHR stresses that the general requirements of fairness following from a right to a fair trial 'apply to all criminal proceedings, irrespective of the type of offence at issue', this does not mean that the weight of the public interest (in the investigation and punishment of the particular offence at issue) may not be taken into consideration when determining whether the proceedings as a whole have been fair, according to the ECtHR. As the Court has previously stated: 'Public-interest concerns cannot justify measures which extinguish the very essence of an applicant's defence rights, including the privilege against self-incrimination guaranteed by Article 6 of the Convention'.[19] It has long been the case that 'the public interest cannot be invoked to justify the use of answers compulsorily obtained in a non-judicial investigation to incriminate the accused during the trial proceedings'. For instance, the interests involved in fighting corporate fraud or terrorism has not persuaded the ECtHR.[20] But, in *Ibrahim*, the weight of the public interest in the investigation and punishment of the offence at issue was positioned as a general viewpoint to see whether the right to a fair trial was breached.[21]

According to the ECtHR, the right not to incriminate oneself is not absolute. It all depends on the degree of compulsion. When the applied compulsion in a particular case destroys the very essence of the privilege against self-incrimination, proceedings will normally have not been fair. This also means that direct compulsion is not disallowed in all circumstances. What is crucial for the ECtHR in order to appreciate the coercion is 'the use to which evidence obtained under compulsion is put in the course of the criminal trial'.[22] Proceedings can still be fair, if the compulsion did not have a relevant impact on the outcome of the criminal proceedings. This means that if someone is, for instance, obliged to speak, this will not automatically breach the right to remain silent and the privilege against self-incrimination, and thus the right to a fair trial. When it is clear that the coerced statement will not be, or is not, used in proceedings of a criminal nature, normally no problem arises. The same goes for information demanded by, for instance, tax authorities.[23]

To summarise the general framework in order to assess whether (the very essence of) the privilege against self-incrimination is violated, the ECtHR looks,

[18] It had to have an impact on the case to the applicant's detriment; see, inter alia, ECtHR 19 March 2015 *Corbet and others v France*, ECLI:CE:ECHR:2015:0319JUD000749411.

[19] ECtHR 10 March 2009 *Bykov v Russia*, ECLI:CE:ECHR:2009:0310JUD000437802, [93].

[20] ECtHR 17 December 1996 *Saunders v United Kingdom*, ECLI:CE:ECHR:1996:1217JUD001918791, [74] and ECtHR 21 December 2000 *Heaney and McGuinness v Ireland*, ECLI:CE:ECHR:2000:1221JUD003472097, [57].

[21] ECtHR 13 September 2016 *Ibrahim and others v United Kingdom*, ECLI:CE:ECHR:2016:0913JUD005054108, [274].

[22] ibid [269].

[23] ECtHR 16 June 2015 *Van Weerelt*, (in)admissibility decision 784/14.

in particular, at the nature and degree of compulsion used to obtain the evidence, the existence of any relevant safeguards in the procedure and the use to which any material so obtained is put.[24]

8.2.4. Consequence of a Violation

Penalising a person for not complying after being unlawfully coerced to cooperate would violate the privilege against self-incrimination. If, on the other hand, he/she does comply, the question is whether the results of the coerced cooperation can be used to penalise him/her. In determining whether the right to a fair trial is violated, the ECtHR looks at the proceedings as a whole. For this assessment the ECtHR has a set of 10 non-exhaustive factors that could be taken into account, when appropriate, to see whether the proceedings as a whole, were fair.[25] This would leave an opening to uphold a punitive sanction, when, all circumstances considered, the trial was fair even though the right not to incriminate oneself has been breached. This could be the case if the results of the coerced cooperation did not have a significant impact on the outcome.

8.2.5. Three Specific Situations

The ECtHR in *Ibrahim* identified at least three kinds of situation which give rise to concerns as to improper compulsion in breach of Article 6 ECHR. The first type of situation, which is the most relevant for this chapter, is 'where a suspect is obliged to testify under threat of sanctions and either testifies in consequence … or is

[24] Also, to some extent, the weight of the public interest in the investigation and punishment of the offence at issue can be taken into account. ECtHR 11 July 2006 *Jalloh v Germany*, ECLI:CE:ECHR:2006:0711JUD005481000, [101] and [117]. See also the Guide on Art 6 of the European Convention on Human Rights, August 2018, [183]–[186].

[25] ECtHR 13 September 2016 *Ibrahim and others v United Kingdom*, ECLI:CE:ECHR:2016:0913JUD005054108, [274]: '(a) Whether the applicant was particularly vulnerable, for example, by reason of his age or mental capacity. (b) The legal framework governing the pretrial proceedings and the admissibility of evidence at trial, and whether it was complied with; where an exclusionary rule applied, it is particularly unlikely that the proceedings as a whole would be considered unfair. (c) Whether the applicant had the opportunity to challenge the authenticity of the evidence and oppose its use. (d) The quality of the evidence and whether the circumstances in which it was obtained cast doubt on its reliability or accuracy, taking into account the degree and nature of any compulsion. (e) Where evidence was obtained unlawfully, the unlawfulness in question and, where it stems from a violation of another Convention Article, the nature of the violation found. (f) In the case of a statement, the nature of the statement and whether it was promptly retracted or modified. (g) The use to which the evidence was put and, in particular, whether the evidence formed an integral or significant part of the probative evidence upon which the conviction was based, and the strength of the other evidence in the case. (h) Whether the assessment of guilt was performed by professional judges or lay jurors, and in the case of the latter the content of any jury directions. (i) The weight of the public interest in the investigation and punishment of the particular offence in issue. (j) Other relevant procedural safeguards afforded by domestic law and practice'.

sanctioned for refusing to testify'.[26] An early and important case is *Saunders*.[27] Saunders had to testify on several occasions with regard to an investigation into misconduct during an (unlawful) share-support operation. These statements were subsequently used to his detriment in a criminal trial. The ECtHR ruled that the complexity of corporate fraud and the vital public interest in the investigation of such fraud (and the punishment of those responsible) could not justify this and concluded that the privilege was breached. The same was true for *Shannon*, whose obligation to attend an interview by financial investigators and to answer questions concerning matters for which he had been already charged, was contrary to the privilege against self-incrimination.[28] He was penalised for failing to show up. The ECtHR stated that the security context – the special problems of investigating crime in Northern Ireland – could not justify this obligation. The ECtHR also referred to the cases of *Heaney and McGuinness*, who had to give information on their movements and actions for a specific time in light of a (terrorist) explosion. Even against this background, the compulsion to give this information, 'destroyed the very essence of their privilege against self-incrimination and their right to remain silent'.[29] In this category it does not, however, appear to be a problem when the registered owner of a car has to give information on the driver of the car on a specific time with regard to a traffic violation and is penalised for not complying. Having to state such a simple fact is not incriminating, the ECtHR ruled in *Weh*. If the information that has to be given is only of a limited nature, this could be acceptable, given the special nature of the regulatory regime at issue (*O'Halloran and Francis*).[30]

The second and third situations the ECtHR mentions are less relevant for this chapter and will be addressed only briefly. The second is where physical or psychological pressure, which often comes in the form of a certain treatment which constitutes a breach of Article 3 ECHR (torture, or inhuman or degrading treatment or punishment) is applied to obtain real evidence or statements.[31] The case of *Jalloh* is infamous in this respect. Jalloh was suspected of drug charges and forced

[26] With reference to ECtHR 17 December 1996 *Saunders v United Kingdom*, ECLI:CE:ECHR:1996:1217JUD001918791 and ECtHR 14 October 2010 *Brusco v France*, ECLI:CE:ECHR:2010:1014JUD000146607. See also ECtHR 21 December 2000 *Heaney and McGuinness v Ireland*, ECLI:CE:ECHR:2000:1221JUD003472097 and ECtHR 8 April 2004 *Weh v Austria*, ECLI:CE:ECHR:2004:0408JUD003854497.

[27] ECtHR 17 December 1996 *Saunders v United Kingdom*, ECLI:CE:ECHR:1996:1217JUD001918791.

[28] ECtHR 4 October 2005 *Shannon v United Kingdom*, ECLI:CE:ECHR:2005:1004JUD000656303.

[29] ECtHR 21 December 2000 *Heaney and McGuinness v Ireland*, ECLI:CE:ECHR:2000:1221JUD003472097, [55].

[30] ECtHR 8 April 2004 *Weh v Austria*, ECLI:CE:ECHR:2004:0408JUD003854497 and ECtHR 29 June 2007 *O'Halloran and Francis v United Kingdom*, ECLI:CE:ECHR:2007:0629JUD001580902. As we have seen, however, the privilege against self-incrimination is not confined to statements which are directly incriminating. And making exceptions could turn into a slippery slope, according to M Redmayne, 'Rethinking the Privilege Against Self-Incrimination' (2007) 27 *Oxford Journal of Legal Studies* 228.

[31] With reference to ECtHR 11 July 2006 *Jalloh v Germany*, ECLI:CELECHR:2006:0711JUD005481000, ECtHR 12 May 2015 *Magee and others v United Kingdom*, ECLI:CE:ECHR:2015:0512JUD002628912 and ECtHR 1 June 2010 *Gäfgen v Germany*, ECLI:CE:ECHR:2010:0601JUD002297805.

to regurgitate drugs which he apparently had swallowed just before the police came to arrest him.[32] The use of the thus-acquired drugs as evidence in the criminal trial constituted a breach of the right not to incriminate oneself, given the grave ill-treatment, which the interest of justice could not counter.[33] The third situation is where the authorities use 'subterfuge' to elicit information that they were unable to obtain during questioning. For this situation the ECtHR refers to *Allan*.[34] Allan was the suspect in a fatal robbery and a police informant was placed in his jail cell, who was coached and instructed to 'push him [Allan] for what you can'. Although Allan remained silent during lengthy police interrogations (which were supposed to 'rattle' or 'unsettle' him), he allegedly subsequently admitted the crime to the police informant who insistently questioned him on it. Later, the statement by the informant proved to be the essential evidence for his conviction.[35] The ECtHR rejected this way of gathering evidence. Although not impossible, in the context of the enforcement of financial law the second and third type of situation will not likely occur.

8.2.6. A Broader Scope

Another type of situation is not explicitly addressed in *Ibrahim*, but is very important for the enforcement of financial law (which depends on the cooperation of the branch itself). It is of course the case law stemming from *Funke*, through *JB* to *Chambaz*.[36] In *Saunders* the ECtHR already stressed that the privilege against self-incrimination

> is primarily concerned … with respecting the will of an accused person to remain silent. As commonly understood in the legal systems of the Contracting Parties to the Convention and elsewhere, it does not extend to the use in criminal proceedings of material which may be obtained from the accused through the use of compulsory powers, but which has an existence independent of the will of the suspect such as, inter alia, documents acquired pursuant to a warrant and breath, blood and urine samples, and bodily tissue for the purpose of DNA testing.[37]

[32] ECtHR 11 July 2006 *Jalloh v Germany*, ECLI:CE:ECHR:2006:0711JUD005481000, [11]–[13].

[33] According to the ECtHR 11 July 2006 *Jalloh v Germany*, ECLI:CE:ECHR:2006:0711JUD005481000, [118], this 'interfered with his physical and mental integrity. The applicant had to be immobilised by four policemen, a tube was fed through his nose into his stomach and chemical substances were administered to him in order to force him to surrender up the evidence sought by means of a pathological reaction of his body. This treatment was found to be inhuman and degrading, and therefore to violate Article 3'.

[34] ECtHR 5 November 2002 *Allan v United Kingdom*, ECLI:CE:ECHR:2002:1105JUD004853999.

[35] Interestingly, the 'confession' was not on any of the taped recordings and was contested (at [16]).

[36] ECtHR 25 February 1993 *Funke v France*, ECLI:CE:ECHR:1993:0225JUD001082884, ECtHR 3 May 2001 *JB v Switzerland*, ECLI:CE:ECHR:2001:0503JUD003182796 and ECtHR 5 April 2012 *Chambaz v Switzerland*, ECLI:CE:ECHR:2012:0405JUD001166304.

[37] ECtHR 17 December 1996 *Saunders v United Kingdom*, ECLI:CE:ECHR:1996:1217JUD001918791, [69]. See also ECtHR 11 July 2006 *Jalloh v Germany*, ECLI:CE:ECHR:2006:0711JUD005481000, [113], quoted in ECtHR 29 June 2007 *O'Halloran and Francis v United Kingdom*, ECLI:CE:ECHR:2007:0629JUD001580902, [52].

It thus appeared to place testimony opposite to 'real evidence'. But already in *Funke*, which precedes *Saunders*, the right not to incriminate oneself could be invoked (and breached!) regarding the obligation to hand over documents in a customs inspection. Funke was compelled to disclose and later on fined for not handing over documents (bank statements), which the French customs 'believed must exist, although they were not certain of the fact', while being 'unable or unwilling to procure them by some other means'. The attempt to compel Funke himself to provide the evidence of offences he had allegedly committed, was not in conformity with Article 6 ECHR. The special features of customs law could not justify the infringement.[38] After *Funke* and *Saunders* came *JB*. He was subjected to tax fraud allegations and could also invoke the aforementioned right when having to submit documents on his finances.[39] By fining *JB* considerably for not submitting the documents, the Swiss authorities had breached Article 6 ECHR. The documents were not comparable with the materials mentioned in *Saunders* and appeared to the ECtHR to be very important for the Swiss authorities, for they had tried to obtain the documents eight times.[40] The *Chambaz* case is similar and confirms this broader scope of the privilege.[41] It does not appear that uncertainty of the actual existence of the documents played a role, as it seemed to do in *Funke*. Therefore, coerced cooperation other than by giving testimony (such as by submitting documents) could, depending on the circumstances, also fall within the scope of the privilege against self-incrimination.

This case law is, surprisingly, not mentioned at all by the Grand Chamber in *Ibrahim*, even though it gave rise to speculation on the exact scope of the right not to incriminate oneself.[42] This has made the privilege somewhat elusive. There is no need to try to place this kind of situation under one of the three explicitly mentioned by the ECtHR. The list given in *Ibrahim* is non-exhaustive, so it leaves open a *Funke*, *JB* and *Chambaz* (hereafter '*Funke* et al') type of situation with a broader meaning next to *Jalloh* (in *Funke* et al there was no physical or psychological pressure to speak of). In its broader sense, the privilege against self-incrimination also extends to cases 'in which coercion to hand over incriminatory

[38] ECtHR 25 February 1993 *Funke v France*, ECLI:CE:ECHR:1993:0225JUD001082884, [41]–[44].

[39] See ECtHR 3 May 2001 *JB v Switzerland*, ECLI:CE:ECHR:2001:0503JUD003182796, [66]. This even though it was 'not for the Court to speculate as to what the nature of such information would have been', JB 'could not exclude that, if it transpired from these documents that he had received additional income which had not been taxed, he might be charged with the offence of tax evasion'.

[40] ECtHR 3 May 2001 *JB v Switzerland*, ECLI:CE:ECHR:2001:0503JUD003182796, [68]–[69].

[41] ECtHR 5 April 2012 *Chambaz v Switzerland*, ECLI:CE:ECHR:2012:0405JUD001166304. From the press release of 5 April 2012, ECtHR 142 (2012): 'The Court observed that by fining Mr Chambaz for refusing to produce all the items requested, the authorities had put him under pressure to furnish documents which would have provided information on his income and assets for tax assessment purposes. By upholding the fines while an investigation was ongoing into alleged tax evasion concerning matters linked to those in respect of which the applicant had exercised his right to remain silent, the Swiss courts had obliged him to incriminate himself.'

[42] See, for instance, Redmayne, 'Rethinking the Privilege' (2007) 213 and S Lamberigts, 'The Directive on the Presumption of Innocence: A Missed Opportunity for Legal Persons?' (2016) 1 *Eucrim* 25, 38.

evidence was in issue'.[43] So the coerced disclosure of already existing materials can cause problems in this regard. When it involves (bodily) material that exists independently of the will of the accused, (a little bit) more coercion could be permitted than in the case of any sort of testimony. It should be noted that the ECtHR does acknowledge the interests of authorities of having persons inform them on a wide variety of topics, such as information to be able to have a functioning taxation system; even the use of coercive powers is not forbidden.[44]

The privilege against self-incrimination therefore goes further than the right to remain silent and entails protection against producing other evidence for the authorities. A clear link with the presumption of innocence can be established, and that link can be used to comprehend this broader meaning. The presumption of innocence ensures, namely, that the burden of proof is on the prosecution and that any doubt should benefit the accused.[45] It is thus up to the prosecution to make a case against the accused and adduce sufficient evidence, not the other way around. The burden of proof must not be shifted from the prosecution to the accused. The drawing of inferences on the accused's silence is only allowed when the situation clearly calls for an explanation by the accused.[46] Thus, obligating the defendant to adduce evidence himself or convicting him/her for the crime he/she is accused of solely or mainly on the basis of his/her refusal to cooperate, would make the right to silence and the privilege against self-incrimination null and void. The ECtHR held 'self-evident that it is incompatible with the immunities under consideration to base a conviction solely or mainly on the accused's silence or on a refusal to answer questions or to give evidence himself'.[47] This could help explain the case law in *Funke* et al, in which a broad approach was sought by the ECtHR. For those applicants were compelled to hand over the very evidence, ie documents, themselves, which the authorities apparently desperately needed to secure a conviction without being able to get these in any other way.

[43] ECtHR 29 June 2007 *O'Halloran and Francis v United Kingdom*, ECLI:CE:ECHR:2007:0629JUD001580902, [54]. See also ECtHR 11 July 2006 *Jalloh v Germany*, ECLI:CE:ECHR:2006:0711JUD005481000, [111].

[44] ECtHR 5 November 2002 *Allan v United Kingdom*, ECLI:CE:ECHR:2002:1105JUD004853999.

[45] ECtHR 6 December 1988 *Barberà v Spain*, ECLI:CE:ECHR:1988:1206JUD001059083, [77].

[46] ECtHR 8 February 1996 *Murray v United Kingdom*, ECLI:CE:ECHR:1996:0208JUD001873191, [54], ECtHR 20 March 2001 *Telfner v Austria*, ECLI:CE:ECHR:2001:0320JUD003350196, [15] and ECtHR 18 March 2010 *Krumpholz v Austria*, ECLI:CE:ECHR:2010:0318JUD001320105, [40].

[47] ECtHR 8 February 1996 *Murray v United Kingdom*, ECLI:CE:ECHR:1996:0208JUD001873191, [47], referred to in ECtHR 29 June 2007 *O'Halloran and Francis v United Kingdom*, ECLI:CE:ECHR:2007:0629JUD001580902, [46]. See also Art 7(5) of the Directive (EU) 2016/343 of the European Parliament and of the Council of 9 March 2016 on the strengthening of certain aspects of the presumption of innocence and of the right to be present at the trial in criminal proceedings [2016] OJ L 65/1. Recital 28 reads: 'The exercise of the right to remain silent or the right not to incriminate oneself should not be used against a suspect or accused person and should not, in itself, be considered to be evidence that the person concerned has committed the criminal offence concerned. This should be without prejudice to national rules concerning the assessment of evidence by courts or judges, provided that the rights of the defence are respected'.

8.2.7. Summary

To summarise, in *Ibrahim* the ECtHR reiterated its previous case law on the right not to incriminate oneself. The privilege can be invoked in case of a criminal charge in its autonomous meaning and is primarily concerned with the right to remain silent. The ECtHR referred to three specific situations in which improper compulsion gives rise to concern. The most important one for this chapter is when a suspect is obliged to testify under threat of sanctions and either testifies in consequence or is sanctioned for refusing to do so. But it did not mention another very important situation. A type of situation which the ECtHR has created itself by giving the principle a much broader scope than just the right to remain silence (other than *Jalloh*). This is remarkable and the importance of this other category cannot be emphasised enough, especially when answering the question whether it is allowed to compel (legal) persons to cooperate with supervising authorities that have punitive powers. Of course, in the end, it very much depends on the circumstances of each case and the way the evidence was gathered. What truly matters ultimately, are the following factors: the nature and the degree of the compulsion at hand; the potential procedural safeguards surrounding it; and the use against the will of the accused. When the coercion destroys the very essence of the right to remain silent and the privilege against self-incrimination, a trial is not fair.[48] In light of the cases of *Funke, J.B., Chambaz* and also *Jalloh*, it is also safe to conclude that the approach of the ECtHR is 'means-based', and not, at least not so much, 'material-based'.[49] Most relevant is the way the authorities obtained or tried to obtain the evidence, even if it concerns non-testimonial material as mentioned in *Saunders*.

8.3. The Right not to Incriminate Oneself; EU Law

8.3.1. Introduction

As stated in section 8.1, the privilege against self-incrimination is also recognised in several instruments of EU law. In this section, I will address these instruments, the link with Article 6 ECHR and the case law of the ECtHR.[50]

8.3.2. TEU and the Charter

The fundamental right not to incriminate oneself is acknowledged in EU law such as the Charter of Fundamental Rights of the European Union ('Charter'). Such

[48] The weight of the public interest in the investigation and punishment of the offence at issue is sometimes also taken into account, but this can hardly justify recourse to a grave injunction of the rights of the accused, extinguishing these rights.
[49] See, for instance, Redmayne (n 30) 215.
[50] See also G Lasagni, *Banking Supervision and Criminal Investigation* (Springer, 2019) para 6.3.5.

fundamental rights are given by the EU legislator, which functions independently from those stemming from the ECHR. However, both sets of fundamental rights are closely linked and normally have the same contents. This also goes for the privilege against self-incrimination.[51] According to Article 6(3) TEU, the fundamental rights of the ECHR 'constitute general principles of the Union's law'. In the Charter, the right to a fair trial is laid down in Article 47 and the presumption of innocence in Article 48. Article 47 of the Charter reads, inter alia: 'Everyone is entitled to a fair and public hearing within a reasonable time by an independent and impartial tribunal previously established by law'. Article 48(1) reads: 'Everyone who has been charged shall be presumed innocent until proved guilty according to law'.[52] They have, as far as we are concerned, the same meaning and scope as the corresponding ones in Article 6 ECHR.[53] This results not only from the EU law itself, more specifically Article 52(3) of the Charter and the Explanations relating to the Charter of Fundamental Rights.[54] The Court of Justice also ruled accordingly.[55]

The Charter can only be invoked against the organs of the EU and against Member States when they are implementing EU law.[56] For the enforcement of financial law this will normally be the case.[57]

8.3.3. Directive on the Strengthening of Certain Aspects of the Presumption of Innocence

The EU instrument in which the right to remain silent and the right not to incriminate oneself are explicitly recognised is the Directive on the strengthening of certain aspects of the presumption of innocence and of the right to be present at the trial in criminal proceedings.[58] The right to remain silent and the right not to incriminate oneself are important aspects of the presumption of innocence.[59]

[51] See in general M Caianiello, *Right to Remain Silent and not to Incriminate Oneself in the European Union System* (research paper for University of Bologna, 2021).

[52] See in general S Peers et al, *The EU charter of fundamental rights: a commentary* (Hart Publishing, 2014) 1197–349.

[53] The Charter rights could provide a more extensive protection, see Art 52(3) of the Charter. Consistency is strived for, see Case C-537/16 *Garlsson*, ECLI:EU:C:2018:193, [24]–[25].

[54] [2007] OJ L 303/1.

[55] Case C-481/19 *DB*, ECLI:EU:C:2021:84, [37] with further references.

[56] See Art 51(1): 'The provisions of this Charter are addressed to the institutions, bodies, offices and agencies of the Union with due regard for the principle of subsidiarity and to the Member States only when they are implementing Union law. They shall therefore respect the rights, observe the principles and promote the application thereof in accordance with their respective powers and respecting the limits of the powers of the Union as conferred on it in the Treaties.'

[57] See, for instance, on Art 50 of the Charter (*ne bis in idem*), Case C-596/16 and C-597/16 *Di puma and Zecca*, ECLI:EU:C:2018:192, [26].

[58] Directive (EU) 2016/343 of the European Parliament and the Council of 9 March 2016 on the strengthening of certain aspects of the presumption of innocence and of the right to be present at the trial in criminal proceedings [2016] OJ L 65/1. See Cras and Erbežnik, 'The Directive on the Presumption of Innocence' (2016). MLV López, 'The presumption of innocence in Directive 2016/343/EC of 9 March 2016' (2017) 18 *ERA Forum* 335.

[59] Recitals 24–25 Directive (EU) 2016/343.

Therefore, they are separately mentioned in this directive. Article 7 stipulates that suspects and accused persons should have the right to remain silent in relation to the criminal offence that they are suspected or accused of having committed (para 1) and that they should have the right not to incriminate themselves (para 2). It is recommended to the Member States that suspects are informed of these rights early on.[60]

From the recitals accompanying the Directive, it becomes clear that both the right to remain silent and the right not to incriminate oneself are to be interpreted in the same way as the ECtHR does.[61] They entail the right for suspects and accused persons not to be forced, when asked to make statements or answer questions, to produce evidence or documents, or to provide information which may lead to self-incrimination (recital 25). Or more generally, they 'imply that competent authorities should not compel suspects or accused persons to provide information if those persons do not wish to do so' (recital 27). Special attention should be drawn here to recital 29, which states that:

> The exercise of the right not to incriminate oneself should not prevent the competent authorities from gathering evidence which may be lawfully obtained from the suspect or accused person through the use of legal powers of compulsion and which has an existence independent of the will of the suspect or accused person, such as material acquired pursuant to a warrant, *material in respect of which there is a legal obligation of retention and production upon request*, breath, blood or urine samples and bodily tissue for the purpose of DNA testing [emphasis added, JSN].

Lasagni reasons there are two ways to read the Directive and the recitals on this point. The strict one would include only documents which do not yet exist at the moment of the request. The broader one is that the privilege also covers the production of already existing documents, whereby those for which a positive obligation of retention exists (eg accounting records) are to be excluded.[62] I would opt for the broader interpretation and suggest a slight variation, because I think the materials for which an obligation of retention and production exist are not to be excluded from coverage by the privilege against self-incrimination. The Directive and recitals could, and I think should, be read as follows. The EU legislator wanted to confirm that the competent authorities can gather this type of evidence themselves, even though the person involved is obligated to preserve and produce them. This would connect best with the case law of the ECtHR.

[60] See Recital 31 Directive (EU) 2016/343. See on this I Ņesterova and A Meikališa, 'The right to information about the right to silence as EU procedural guarantee in criminal proceedings and its impact on national legal systems', available at law.muni.cz/sborniky/dny_prava_2012/files/pravoEU/NesterovaIrena_MeikalisaArija.pdf. Suspects must be informed on the right to remain silent, due to Art 3(1)(5) Directive 2012/13/EU of the European parliament and the Council of 22 May 2012 on the right to information in criminal proceedings [2012] OJ L 142/1.

[61] Recitals 25–29 Directive (EU) 2016/343.

[62] Lasagni, *Banking Supervision* (2019) 252.

The scope of this Directive is limited in three important ways.[63] The first is that it only applies to natural persons. The reason for this is that the presumption of innocence for natural persons is not problematic (given the case law of the ECtHR), but for legal persons this is less clear, according to the EU legislator.[64] In a recital it is mentioned that the Court of Justice has ruled 'that the rights flowing from the presumption of innocence do not accrue to legal persons in the same way as they do to natural persons'. The EU legislator therefore found it 'premature' to extend these rights to legal persons, although the application to legal persons is not prevented by it.[65] The second limitation is that the Directive only applies to 'criminal proceedings' as interpreted by the Court of Justice. It does not

> apply to civil proceedings or to administrative proceedings, including where the latter can lead to sanctions, such as proceedings relating to competition, trade, financial services, road traffic, tax or tax surcharges, and investigations by administrative authorities in relation to such proceedings.[66]

It looks like that within this specific context; the *Bonda* criteria are decisive in determining whether the proceedings have to be considered as a criminal charge, but this is not entirely clear.[67] The third limitation of the Directive is that it only applies to the criminal proceedings, and not afterwards. Its protection starts

> from the moment when a person is suspected or accused of having committed a criminal offence, or an alleged criminal offence, and, therefore, even before that person is made aware by the competent authorities of a Member State, by official notification or otherwise, that [they are] a suspect or accused person.

But its protection ends as soon as 'the decision on the final determination of whether that person has committed the criminal offence concerned has become definitive'. The wider protection of Article 6(2) ECHR (presumption of innocence) for subsequent proceedings and actions is cut off.[68]

8.4. Intermezzo; Legal Persons

It follows from the previous section that the scope of the privilege against self-incrimination often also depends on the question whether the accused is a legal person. In EU law, legal persons do not receive the same protection as natural persons from the right to remain silent and not to incriminate themselves.[69]

[63] See Art 2 Directive (EU) 2016/343.
[64] See inter alia Lamberigts, 'The Directive on the Presumption of Innocence' (2016) 36–42.
[65] Recitals 13–14 Directive (EU) 2016/343.
[66] Recital 11 Directive (EU) 2016/343.
[67] See, for instance, Lasagni (n 50) 247.
[68] See for this much wider scope ECtHR 12 July 2013 *Allen v United Kingdom*, ECLI:CE:ECHR:2013:0712JUD002542409, [98].
[69] See on this SA Trainor, 'A Comparative Analysis of a Corporation's Right Against Self-Incrimination' (1994) 18 *Fordham International Law Journal* 2139.

The Directive on certain aspects of the presumption of innocence categorically excludes its scope to legal persons. Also, in competition law proceedings, legal persons ('undertakings') must provide information requested by the Commission, although they cannot be coerced to an admittance of guilt.[70] Article 6 ECHR might provide legal persons with equivalent protection as natural persons, however. There is no case law of the ECtHR in which the privilege was awarded explicitly to legal persons.[71] However, it appears that legal persons can also invoke the European Convention rights. As Van Kempen stated in 2010, this depends on the right involved. On the privilege against self-incrimination, he writes that

> as the Court applies all fair trial rights to individuals and legal persons, and, moreover, since it does so equally, it will most probably also apply the right to freedom from self-incrimination equally to natural and legal persons to the extent possible'.[72]

I agree with this opinion. The ECtHR's subsequent ruling in 2014 in *Grande Stevens and others*, a case that is very relevant for the enforcement of financial law, proves that criminal trial rights may be invoked by legal persons.[73] In that case, the legal persons that complained, together with the natural persons involved, were treated equally with regard to several criminal fair trial rights, such as the presumption of innocence (burden of proof), the right to a hearing by an independent and impartial tribunal (all Article 6 ECHR) and the *ne bis in idem* principle (Article 4 of Protocol No 7).[74] There is no indication this will be different for the privilege against self-incrimination. I am of the opinion that – in general – it is correct that legal persons may rely equally on fair trial rights, because when legal persons can be held criminally accountable just as natural persons (and sometimes be punished even more severe), they should also be able to enjoy the same defence rights.

[70] Case T-71/03 *Tokai Carbon*, ECLI:EU:T:2005:220; Case C-374/87 *Orkem*, ECLI:EU:C:1989:387 and Case T-122/98 *Mannesmannröhren-Werke AG*, ECLI:EU:T:2001:61. See also RA Shiner, 'Corporations and the Presumption of Innocence' (2014) 8 *Criminal Law and Philosophy* 485 and I van Bael, *Due process in EU Competition Proceedings* (Wolters Kluwer, 2011). See M Veenbrink, 'The Privilege Against Self-incrimination in EU Competition Law: A Deafening Silence?' (2015) 2 *Legal Issues of Economic Integration* 119, and Lamberigts (n 42) 40.

[71] Fair Trials, 'Joint position paper on the proposed directive on the strengthening of certain aspects of the presumption of innocence and of the right to be present at trial in criminal proceedings' (position paper from NGO, available on fairtrials.org) 8, fn 12.

[72] PHPHMC van Kempen, 'Human Rights and Criminal Justice Applied to Legal Persons. Protection and Liability of Private and Public Juristic Entities under ICCPR, ECHR, ACHR and AfChHPR' (2010) 14 *Electronic Journal of Comparative Law* 16. See also PHPHMC van Kempen, 'The Recognition of Legal Persons in International Human Rights Instruments: Protection Against and Through Criminal Justice?' in M Pieth and R Ivory (eds), *Corporate Criminal Liability. Emergence, Convergence, and Risk, Ius Gentium: Comparative Perspectives on Law and Justice 9* (Springer, 2011).

[73] ECtHR 4 March 2014 *Grande Stevens and others v Italy*, ECLI:CE:ECHR:2014:0304JUD001864010.

[74] See also ECtHR 23 July 2013 *Lay Lay Company Limited v Malta*, ECLI:CE:ECHR:2013:0723JUD003063311, with regard to access to a court. See further ch 9 in this volume regarding the *ne bis in idem* principle.

8.5. Full Cooperation with Regard to Money Laundering, Terrorist Financing and Market Abuse

8.5.1. Introduction

In this section I will discuss in broad strokes the EU instruments on money laundering, terrorist financing and market abuse. I will discuss the obligations to cooperate with the authorities and the wide range of administrative and/or criminal liability for several acts and omissions in these fields of financial law. This is because the obligations and the possibilities of sanctioning are intertwined, in the sense that the risk of punitive liability for breaches of the rules (surrounding) money laundering, terrorist financing or market abuse limits the scope of the obligation to cooperate with the competent authorities because of the privilege against self-incrimination (see further the analysis in section 8.6).

8.5.2. Money Laundering or Terrorist Financing

When it comes to money laundering and terrorist financing, the Directive on the prevention of the use of the financial system for the purposes of money laundering or terrorist financing (AML) has several (enhanced) customer due diligence obligations, as well as several reporting obligations for the obliged entities in the financial system (such as credit institutions, financial institutions, auditors, external accountants, tax advisors, notaries and other independent legal professionals).[75] Article 33 in particular formulates an obligation for Member States to require obliged entities, and, where applicable, their directors and employees, to 'cooperate fully' on the following. Obliged entities must on their own initiative promptly inform the Financial Intelligence Unit (FIU), including by filing a report, if it knows, suspects or has reasonable grounds to suspect that funds, regardless of the amount involved, are the proceeds of criminal activity or are related to terrorist financing. Further, they must promptly respond to requests by the FIU for additional information in such cases. Obliged entities must also promptly provide the FIU directly, at its request, with all necessary information. And obliged entities have (to have) the duty to report all suspicious transactions, including attempted transactions. Of course, the competent authorities (should) have the power

[75] Directive (EU) 2015/849 of the European Parliament and of the Council of 20 May 2015 on the prevention of the use of the financial system for the purposes of money laundering or terrorist financing, amending Regulation (EU) No 648/2012 of the European Parliament and of the Council, and repealing Directive 2005/60/EC of the European Parliament and of the Council and Commission Directive 2006/70/EC [2015] OJ L 141/73, as amended by Directive (EU) 2018/843 of the European Parliament and of the Council of 30 May 2018 (amending Directive (EU) 2015/849 on the prevention of the use of the financial system for the purposes of money laundering or terrorist financing, and amending Directives 2009/138/EC and 2013/36/EU) [2018] OJ L 156/43.

to monitor the compliance with the Directive effectively and to take the necessary measures to ensure this. Therefore, obliged entities are, inter alia, subject to adequate supervision, including on-site and off-site supervision.[76] The competent authorities should also be able to compel the obliged entities to produce any information that is relevant to monitoring compliance and performing checks.[77] When in the course of monitoring the competent authorities discover facts that could be related to money laundering or to terrorist financing, they are to promptly inform the FIU.[78] The reporting is to be encouraged by the Member States.[79] Further, obliged entities are, in general, to refrain from carrying out transactions which they know or suspect to be related to proceeds of criminal activity or to terrorist financing until they have completed the necessary actions.[80]

Non-compliance with the Directive, in general, leads to (punitive) liability, at least in case of breaches on the part of obliged entities that are serious, repeated, systematic, or a combination thereof.[81] The Directive calls for rules on administrative sanctions and measures, which ensure that the competent authorities 'may impose such sanctions and measures with respect to breaches of the national provisions transposing this Directive'. These administrative penalties and measures are not necessary if the infringements of the Directive are already subject to criminal sanctions. This means Member States are free to fill in the liability of the obliged entities as long as 'any resulting sanction or measure shall be effective, proportionate and dissuasive'. The liability has to be extended to the members of the management body and to other natural persons who under national law are responsible for the breach, in case the obligations that are breached apply to legal persons.[82] Legal persons can be held liable for the breaches committed for their benefit by any person, acting individually or as part of an organ of that legal person, and having a leading position within the legal person based on any of the following: power to represent the legal person; authority to take decisions on behalf of the legal person; or authority to exercise control within the legal person. It is important to know that the legal person should also be held liable if the lack of supervision or control by one of these persons has made it possible to commit one of the breaches for it by a person under its authority.[83] For failure to comply with the obligations to cooperate fully with regard to suspicious transaction reporting or to avoid carrying them out, the Directive calls for administrative sanctions and measures that include at least maximum administrative pecuniary sanctions of

[76] Obliged entities are, inter alia, credit and financial institutions, auditors, external accountants and tax advisors, according to Art 2(1) Directive (EU) 2015/849.

[77] See Art 48 Directive (EU) 2015/849.

[78] See ibid Art 36.

[79] See ibid Art 61.

[80] See ibid Art 35.

[81] See ibid Arts 58–62.

[82] See ibid Art 58 and Recital 59.

[83] See ibid Art 60.

at least twice the amount of the benefit derived from the breach where that benefit can be determined, or at least €1 million.[84]

Besides this more or less functional liability, there is the (Sixth) Directive on combating money laundering by criminal law itself.[85] In that Directive, minimum rules concerning the definition of criminal offences and sanctions in the area of money laundering are established.[86] As always, the penalties have to be effective, proportionate and dissuasive.[87] EU Member States have to make sure that legal persons can also be held liable for these offences.[88] The construction of liability for the legal person does not rule out liability for natural persons who are perpetrators, inciters or accessories in these offences.[89] For legal persons the penalties also have to be effective, proportionate and dissuasive.[90]

While normally, of course, obliged entities will not engage in conduct such as money laundering, it is surely not a far-fetched idea. In fact, fairly recently three major Dutch banks have been penalised for not only breaching the rules on the prevention of money laundering, but also conducting (culpable) money laundering itself.[91] These banks entered into an agreement with the public prosecutor's office. Several high-ranking (former) officers with the banks are now under criminal investigation for their role in the conduct of the banks. There have been similar money laundering and terrorism financing incidents concerning other European banks.[92]

There is also the Directive on combating terrorism.[93] For the purpose of this chapter, it is important to know that, inter alia, terrorist financing must constitute a crime.[94] The liability for legal persons is mandatory[95] and the penalties for

[84] See ibid Art 59. For credit or financial institutions this should be even higher. See further section 8.6.2.

[85] Directive (EU) 2018/1673 of the European Parliament and of the Council of 23 October 2018 on combating money laundering by criminal law [2018] OJ L 284/22.

[86] See Art 1 Directive (EU) 2018/1673. It does not, according to para (2), apply 'to money laundering as regards property derived from criminal offences affecting the Union's financial interests, which is subject to specific rules laid down in Directive (EU) 2017/1371'.

[87] See ibid Art 5.

[88] According to ibid Art 7, when 'committed for their benefit by any person, acting either individually or as part of an organ of the legal person and having a leading position within the legal person'.

[89] See ibid Art 7(3).

[90] See ibid Art 8.

[91] ING (prosecutionservice.nl/documents/publications/fp/hoge-transacties/feitenrelaas/statement-of-facts-ing); ABN AMRO (prosecutionservice.nl/documents/publications/fp/2021/04/statement-of-facts-and-conclusions-of-the-netherlands-public-prosecution-service); Rabobank (money.cnn.com/2018/02/08/news/rabobank-mexico-drug-money-laundering/index.html).

[92] See on the Swedbank: reuters.com/article/us-europe-moneylaundering-swedbank idUSKCN1R9155. On the Danske Bank: reuters.com/article/us-danske-bank-moneylaundering-idUSKCN1SD1P3.

[93] Directive (EU) 2017/541 of the European Parliament and of the Council of 15 March 2017 on combating terrorism and replacing Council Framework Decision 2002/475/JHA and amending Council Decision 2005/671/JHA [2017] OJ L 88/6.

[94] See ibid.

[95] It can be construed the same way as with the directive on money laundering, see ibid Art 17.

both natural and legal persons have to be effective, proportionate and dissuasive.[96] Although (hopefully) not as likely as with money laundering, it is not unthinkable that obliged entities such as credit or financial institutions for example, (intentionally) finance terrorism.

8.5.3. Market Abuse

The regulation on market abuse aims to establish market integrity for integrated, efficient and transparent financial markets.[97] Both market undertakings and all economic actors are obliged to contribute to this in cooperation with the competent authorities 'with a view to guaranteeing efficient supervision of compliance with the provisions in this Regulation'.[98] The competent authority therefore has to have the power, inter alia, not only to access any document and data in any form, and to receive or take a copy thereof, but also to require or demand information from any person, including those who are successively involved in the transmission of orders or conduct of the operations concerned, as well as their principals, and if necessary, to summon and question any such person with a view to obtain information.[99] Market operators and investment firms that operate a trading venue have, inter alia, the duty to detect and report potential market abuse.[100] Failure to comply with the investigative authorities is to be subject to criminal liability and/or 'appropriate administrative sanctions and other administrative measures'.[101] The same goes for the duty to report and the market abuse itself, which is, in short, insider dealing (including attempting, recommending or inciting this), unlawful disclosure of information and market manipulation (including attempting this).[102] Both natural persons and legal persons are subject to the rules of this regulation and liability is to be conferred on both of them, according to national law.[103] The regulation calls for administrative sanctions and other administrative measures in case of a failure to cooperate and for more (pecuniary) sanctions and measures for the market abuse itself. These administrative penalties and measures are not necessary if the infringements

[96] See ibid Arts 15 and 18 respectively.

[97] Market Abuse Regulation (Regulation (EU) No 596/2014 of the European Parliament and of the Council of 16 April 2014 on market abuse (market abuse regulation) and repealing Directive 2003/6/EC of the European Parliament and of the Council and Commission Directives 2003/124/EC, 2003/125/EC and 2004/72/EC [2014] OJ L 173/1).

[98] See ibid Recital 63.

[99] See ibid Art 23. In para (2) is it also stated that in relation to commodity derivatives, they have the power to request information from market participants on related spot markets according to standardised formats, obtain reports on transactions, and have direct access to traders' systems.

[100] See ibid Art 16.

[101] See ibid Art 3(1)(b).

[102] See ibid Arts 14 and 15 in connection with Art 30(1)(a).

[103] See ibid Recital 40.

of the regulation are already subject to criminal sanctions.[104] The Directive on market abuse separately calls for the criminalisation of insider trading, unlawful disclosure of inside information and market manipulation, at least in serious cases and when committed intentionally.[105]

8.5.4. Summary

The EU instruments on combatting money laundering and terrorist financing and on market abuse create several far-reaching obligations to cooperate with supervising authorities, as well as several acts or omissions in those fields that should constitute (punitive) liability. The question is whether and how this compares to the right not to incriminate oneself.

8.6. Analysis

8.6.1. Introduction

From the previous sections it became apparent that both the ECHR and EU law acknowledge the privilege against self-incrimination. In essence, in case of a (looming) criminal charge, one cannot be coerced to make a statement, hand over documents, etc by the authorities (see sections 8.2 and 8.3). This could contravene the obligations to cooperate fully with the (same) competent authorities with regard to the supervision (see section 8.5). Lasagni rightfully states that recognising the application of the privilege to banking supervision is

> especially critical, as it risks nullifying the very reporting mechanism employed by administrative independent authorities, that is the duty of supervised entities to report and provide the requested information, to their supervisors and the existence of forms of liability in case of non-compliance.[106]

In this section, I will therefore compare the (possible) influence of the privilege against self-incrimination in the field of these instruments on financial law.

[104] See ibid Art 30(1). See further section 8.6.3.

[105] Market Abuse Directive (Directive 2014/57/EU of the European Parliament and of the Council of 16 April 2014 on criminal sanctions for market abuse (market abuse directive) [2014] OJ L 173/179. Of course, market abuse such as insider trading is as old as the stock market itself. It would be naïve to think it does not occur on the European markets. See, for instance, W Aussenegg, R Jelic and R Ranzi, 'Corporate Insider Trading in Europe' (2018) 54 *Journal of International Financial Markets, Institutions & Money* 27.

[106] Lasagni (n 50) 246.

8.6.2. Is the Privilege against Self-Incrimination Applicable in the Field of Financial Law?

The first question is whether the right not to incriminate oneself is applicable in the field of the addressed financial instruments. Would certain infractions constitute a *criminal* charge? In case of money laundering and terrorist financing, several administrative penalties and measures are prescribed in the Directive for the customer due diligence obligations and the reporting obligations. They are:

(1) a public statement which identifies the natural or legal person and the nature of the breach;
(2) an order requiring the natural or legal person to cease the conduct and to desist from repetition of that conduct;
(3) where an obliged entity is subject to an authorisation, withdrawal or suspension of the authorisation;
(4) a temporary ban against any person discharging managerial responsibilities in an obliged entity, or any other natural person, held responsible for the breach, from exercising managerial functions in obliged entities; and
(5) maximum administrative pecuniary sanctions of at least twice the amount of the benefit derived from the breach where that benefit can be determined, or at least €1 million.[107]

Looking at the *Engel–Bonda* criteria, the first four sanctions might, in general, not be deemed criminal in nature, if infractions are not upheld by national criminal law. They do not appear to have a punitive aim and will not reach the needed degree of severity, nor can they be compared to a regular criminal sanction. But I would think the fifth and last mandatory, pecuniary sanction will probably make the administrative proceedings criminal in nature. Because the fine should amount to at least double the profit, it seems punitive in nature and/or can be equated to a criminal penalty (substantial fine). The actual fine is not decisive in this matter. Money laundering and terrorist financing constitute crimes, as we have seen, which makes subsequent proceedings for those infractions criminal by default (see the first *Engel–Bonda* criterion). In both administrative and criminal proceedings, the privilege against self-incrimination can be invoked.

As to market abuse, the regulation leaves it to the Member States to adopt administrative penalties and measures and/or criminal sanctions.[108] For the failure to cooperate, these sanctions are not further specified. AG Pikamäe is of the opinion that administrative penalties can be effective, proportionate and dissuasive, on the one hand, without being considered as a criminal charge due to not

[107] See Art 59(2) and Recital 59 Directive (EU) 2015/849 (n 75). For credit and financial institutions, the pecuniary sanctions should even be higher (see Art 59(3)).

[108] Again, see Art 30(1) Market Abuse Regulation (n 97). Only in the Market Abuse Directive (n 105) (at least) 'serious' market abuse should constitute a crime.

meeting the threshold of the (second and third) *Engel–Bonda* criteria mentioned in section 8.2.2.[109] It could be that non-cooperation does not constitute a punishable act of a criminal nature. As long as that is the case, the privilege against self-incrimination is not applicable. However, should the sanctions be qualified as criminal in nature, then it is.

In the case of actual market abuse, the regulation calls for specifically mentioned administrative penalties and measures, some of which according to Pikamäe 'are very likely to be of a criminal nature according to the *Bonda* criteria'.[110] Penalties that are proscribed which are most likely of a criminal nature are, inter alia, maximum administrative pecuniary sanctions of at least three times the amount of the profits gained or losses avoided because of the infringement, where those can be determined, and maximum administrative pecuniary sanctions (for natural persons up to €5 million and legal person up to €15 million or 15 per cent of the total annual turnover of the legal person according to the last available accounts approved by the management body). Measures that clearly do not appear to have a criminal nature would be an order requiring the person responsible for the infringement to cease the conduct and to desist from a repetition of that conduct, or a public warning which indicates the person responsible for the infringement and the nature of the infringement. The fact that certain measures are not criminal in nature does not matter, however, because the regulation calls for both the penalties and the measures in this regard, if criminal sanctions are not applicable. From the case law of the Court of Justice, it can be derived that administrative proceedings in the case of acts that constitute market abuse will also be considered criminal in nature because of the severe fines that could be and usually are applied (just as for the corresponding criminal offences).[111] The principle of the right against self-incrimination could then be invoked.

For the instruments on money laundering and terrorist financing and market abuse, the privilege may usually be invoked by the person who must cooperate but was or might have been somehow involved in the potentially illegal conduct under supervision. Those infractions would normally constitute a criminal charge.

8.6.3. Consequences of Applicability

From the previous sections the following can be deduced. To start, it is not forbidden to compel players in the field of financial law to inform the competent authorities and for the latter to request information by way of giving testimony, handing over documents or even filing a report. This means that the desired cooperation can, in principle, be demanded and coerced. As long as the sanctions for

[109] Opinion of AG Pikamäe in Case C-481/19 *DB*, ECLI:EU:C:2020:861, [73].
[110] ibid [75].
[111] See Case C-45/08 *Spector Photo Group NV and Chris Van Raemdonck*, and Case C-596/16 and C-597/16 *Di puma and Zecca*, ECLI:EU:C:2018:192.

non-compliance are not criminal in nature (such as a ban from holding a position in an obliged entity), or only very moderate (such as a very small maximum fine), there will be no breach of the privilege against self-incrimination in that respect. Cooperation can even be coerced when the person who receives these kinds of sanctions can be regarded as charged with, for instance, neglecting customer due diligence obligations, actual money laundering or insider trading. This is because the coercion does not involve a criminal charge with regard to the handling of the non-cooperation itself. As said, the privilege cannot be relied on in proceedings of a non-criminal nature. Or, in case of very light punitive sanctions, because refusing to cooperate is still a realistic option. For the field of market abuse the following can be said. As the sanctions for non-compliance are not further specified in the regulation on market abuse, it could be that the privilege against self-incrimination is not applicable or not breached when someone is coerced to cooperate. For the field of money laundering and terrorist financing, however, this will not be the case. The directive on money laundering and terrorist financing proscribes sanctions for non-compliance that are (partially) punitive in nature and considerable.

Two situations in particular will definitively be problematic in light of the foregoing. One problem arises according to the privilege, when refusing to cooperate could result in a (significant) sanction of a criminal nature if one already is or will be substantially affected (in light of the request or the investigation). In that situation (further) compliance cannot be coerced and especially having to make any sort of statement is out of the question.[112] Conversely, if it is clear that no criminal charge will (ever) arise from the mandatory cooperation (in other words, the results of the coercion will not be used in that, punitive, way), the *nemo tenetur* principle cannot be invoked successfully. The person involved could then be penalised for not cooperating with the supervisory authorities. There should, of course, be sufficient guarantees that the information provided will indeed not be used against him/her.

The other problem arises when coerced cooperation does lead to any sort of statement, the handing over of documents, etc by the coerced and this result is then used against him/her to adjudicate a sanction of a criminal nature. That would be the case when the result of the improper compulsion is used in proceedings concerning breaches of the instruments on money laundering, terrorist financing and market abuse. The applicable and proscribed (administrative) penalties and measures are at least partially criminal in nature and sometimes also constitute a criminal offence. The results of the coerced submission or production of information can therefore not always be used by the authorities to penalise the submitter.

Of both these problems I will give a concrete example in the next section. Another situation that might be highly debatable and need to be addressed is the following. Does the privilege of the right against self-incrimination also protect

[112] A good example of this besides *Saunders* is ECtHR 21 April 2009 *Marttinen v Finland*, ECLI:CE:ECHR:2009:0421JUD001923503, [67]–[76].

against the use of information obliged entities, undertakings etc must provide to the competent authorities *on their own initiative*, at a moment when they are not yet criminally charged, but when that information could lead to such a charge? The Hoge Raad (Dutch Supreme Court) answers that question as follows. The reporting duty remains, but any (written) statement given must be excluded from use as evidence.[113] On the basis of the case law of the ECtHR, I expect that the ECtHR will not extend the privilege beyond this Dutch interpretation. The privilege predominantly ensures the right to silence, so indeed a statement should be excluded from use as evidence (think of *Saunders*). But merely having to report (on) an 'incident' such as a suspicious transaction, could be reconciled with the privilege against self-incrimination. That would be the case as long as it can be seen as a regular disclosure obligation (compare *Allan* and *Van Weerelt*) or as giving a simple, neutral fact (*Weh*) or information of a limited nature – which could be acceptable given the special nature of the regulatory regime at issue (*O'Halloran and Francis*), at a moment where one is not subject to an investigation (compare and contrast *Funke*, *JB* and *Chambaz*).

I expect the Court of Justice to limit the privilege given the conservative reasoning in its case law in competition law proceedings. Extending the privilege to the latter situation would hinder taking punitive action against offenders of the financial instruments, possibly making these instruments less effective. However, this would make complying with reporting obligations less attractive for the obliged entities, market undertakings, etc, since informing the authorities adequately on their own initiative could make them subject to an (punitive) investigation. If, on the other hand, they would have the certainty that the provided information will not be used against them in a punitive way, this could lower their reluctance to comply and report on it. There is thus a downside to both a broad and a narrow interpretation of the privilege on this point.

8.6.4. Two Examples

The recent case of *DB* before the Court of Justice makes the influence of the privilege against self-incrimination abundantly clear.[114] That case concerns a failure to cooperate with an investigation on insider trading and unlawful disclosure of inside information. DB was sanctioned in administrative proceedings by the competent Italian administrative authority for these infractions with fines of €200,000 and €100,000. DB refused to answer questions put to him when he appeared at a hearing, held at a moment when, under Italian law, parallel *criminal* proceedings for the same conduct were possible. This refusal led to an ancillary

[113] Lastly, Hoge Raad (Dutch Supreme Court) 15 June 2021, ECLI:NL:HR:2021:849 on Regulation (EC) No 273/2004 of 11 February 2004 on drug precursors.

[114] Case C-481/19 *DB*, ECLI:EU:C:2021:84.

penalty of temporary loss of status for a period of 18 months and a confiscation of assets of equivalent value to the profit or the means employed to obtain it. When DB contested this in front of the Italian courts, questions were put to the Court of Justice regarding the privilege against self-incrimination. To avoid a collision between substantive obligations for persons under the jurisdiction of the EU and their procedural human rights, the Court of Justice had to rule that Article 30(1)(b) Market Abuse Regulation (and its predecessor, Article 14(3) Directive 2003/6/EC), read in the light of Articles 47 and 48 of the Charter:

> [M]ust be interpreted as allowing Member States not to penalise natural persons who, in an investigation carried out in respect of them by the competent authority under that directive or that regulation, refuse to provide that authority with answers that are capable of establishing their liability for an offence that is punishable by administrative sanctions of a criminal nature, or their criminal liability.

Through this ruling the Court of Justice upheld human rights, just as the obligation to cooperate and to penalise non-compliance (albeit regarding the latter not fully). Normally, any person involved will have to comply with requests for information made by the competent authorities (given they had the power to do so). A failure to do so can be penalised. However, if a person runs the risk of thus providing information that could be used against him/her in either administrative proceedings of a criminal nature or in criminal proceedings, non-compliance does not have to be, and even may not be, penalised.

It is also interesting to refer to a recent Dutch example of a situation that primarily concerned other material that was eventually handed over.[115] A bank was under investigation by the authorities for, inter alia, misleading advertisements on financial (investment) products. The return on investment on certain products as advertised, was said to be too high compared to the actual return. The bank was ordered by the authorities to calculate the actual return on investment and to comment on it. This information was then used to penalise the bank for the misleading advertisements. On appeal, the highest administrative court on this matter ruled that the right not to incriminate oneself was violated, and that the information the bank was forced to hand over could not be used in the proceedings. The court ruled that the coerced information could not be compared to bank statements or portfolio overviews (which already exist or flow from the bank's system), as the authorities argued, but that the bank had successfully pleaded that it had to create a new algorithm to generate the information. Therefore, the existence of the information was dependent on the will of the bank, which lead to the conclusion that the requested information fell under the privilege against self-incrimination.

This outcome seems right to me. Having to calculate the return on investment would – in terms of the ECtHR – essentially destroy the privilege against

[115] College van Beroep voor het bedrijfsleven (Board of Appeals for business) 5 July 2019, ECLI:NL:CBB:2019:177.

self-incrimination, especially because the bank would have to comment on it as well. From an EU point of view, the following can be said. From the Directive on the presumption of innocence can be derived that the obligation to adduce documents falls under the scope of the privilege, because this is something else than giving the authorities the right to obtain or acquire documents pursuant to a search warrant.[116] Also, having to comment on the calculations comes awfully close to admitting guilt, which even the European Commission is not allowed to expect in competition law cases. I do think, however, the court put too much weight on the question of whether the information existed (in)dependently of the will of the accused. The more basic obligation to supply the authorities with bank statements or portfolio overviews, is also problematic.[117] In any case, this example does show that subjects cannot be compelled to hand over just any information the authorities want, when exercising their supervisory powers. At least, the results of that coercion cannot automatically be used in proceedings of a criminal nature.

8.6.5. Legal Persons

As all Member States are bound by the Convention rights, legal persons are most likely able to invoke the privilege against self-incrimination in national proceedings via Article 6 ECHR, even if the EU instruments deny them access (notwithstanding Article 6(3) TEU). Therefore, it doesn't matter whether the Charter rights are available to legal persons or not, nor that the rights given by the Directive on the presumption of innocence are certainly not. The different approaches could, however, result in a divergence in the protection of legal persons having to cooperate, depending on whether either Luxembourg (less protection) or Strasbourg (full protection) has a say in it. It would be a divergence that both courts usually try to avoid.[118]

If legal persons cannot be acknowledged as holders of the right not to incriminate themselves, a problem still arises for natural persons who, indirectly, become the potential target of a criminal charge themselves via the criminal liability of the legal person. Since several financial instruments call for the punitive liability of natural persons surrounding the acts and omissions of legal persons (directors, employees, etc), they can invoke the privilege against self-incrimination quite unproblematically. And natural persons may also invoke this privilege in

[116] Again, see both Recital 29 Directive (EU) 2016/343 (n 47) and ECtHR 17 December 1996 *Saunders v United Kingdom*, ECLI:CE:ECHR:1996:1217JUD001918791, [62].

[117] Compare section 8.2.6 on the cases of *Funke* et al. and section 8.3.3 on the interpretation of the EU legislator.

[118] See on this topic J Callewaert, 'The Privilege against Self-Incrimination in European Law: An Illustration of the Impact of the Plurality of Courts and Legal Sources on the Protection of Fundamental Rights in Europe' (2004) 5 *ERA Forum* 488. See on the relationship between the ECtHR and EU law also, J Callewaert, 'The European Convention on Human Rights and European Union Law: A Long Way from Harmony' (2009) 6 *European Human Rights Law Review* 768.

case they themselves are (potentially) directly suspected of infractions of financial law instruments and risk punitive sanctions (see *DB*). This would put managers and the like in an awkward legal position. As natural persons they do not have to cooperate; as agents of the legal person, they potentially do on behalf of their employer. At least they surely have a motive to avoid that the legal person supplies information that is incriminating to them. The legal person may then also have, in return, a motive not to hand over (reliable) information and not to cooperate, to protect its agents. One way or the other, demanding full cooperation of the obliged entities might prove to be more difficult than expected when these obligations were drafted.

8.7. Concluding Remarks

As soon as a criminal charge or sanctions of a criminal nature come into play, mandatory (full) cooperation with the competent supervisory authorities becomes problematic. The results of coerced cooperation cannot always be used in proceedings of a criminal nature and refusal to cooperate cannot always be punished. The right not to incriminate oneself, especially in its broad scope, will prohibit this. This has been made clear in this chapter for the fields of (the prevention of the use of the financial system for the purposes of) money laundering and terrorist financing and market abuse. Through the applicable EU instruments, numerous criminal offences or administrative penalties with a criminal nature are to be in place in the Member States' jurisdictions. Because the enforcement of these instruments depends partially on the cooperation of players within those fields, problems could arise when coercing them to comply with their obligations. In that way, the instruments created their own enemy. I do not think, however, the ECtHR and the Court of Justice will object to the obligation of obliged entities, market operators and such to merely report (on) an incident on their own initiative.

Natural persons can invoke the privilege against self-incrimination under both EU law and Article 6 ECHR. For legal persons this is different. For the moment, it looks like they can only rely on the ECHR, when they want to refuse to cooperate (given that the privilege is indeed extended to them by the ECtHR, as generally presumed). Furthermore, at least all natural persons who run the risk of being charged for an infraction do not have to cooperate, regardless of the obligation of the legal person. When they become 'criminally' liable either through the connection with the legal person (for example, a director), or directly for their own actions, they are protected by the privilege. As we have seen from the examples in the previous section, this may cause problems in practice.

It will be interesting to see how the friction between a human right such as the privilege against self-incrimination on the one hand and well supervised fields of financial law on the other, develops. Especially the case of *DB* shows that full cooperation and the right not to incriminate oneself sometimes truly relate like water and oil.

9

The Enforcement Paradox of the *Ne Bis in Idem* Principle in EU Criminal Financial Law: Not what it Seems

RIJNHARD HAENTJENS

9.1. Introduction

An essential element vis-à-vis enforcement in general is the question of the *ne bis in idem* principle. In jurisdictions where the enforcement is based upon administrative and criminal law, there is a greater chance of concurrence before, parallel to or after criminal or administrative law enforcement.[1] The principle of *ne bis in idem* should solve this problem. In this chapter, I will give a brief analysis of the main problems of the jurisprudence of the European Court of Human Rights (ECtHR) concerning *ne bis in idem* (section 9.2) and the Court of Justice of the European Union (ECJ) (section 9.3), relating to financial law. In my concluding remarks, I will conclude that the *ne bis in idem* principle has a relatively limited function in the protection of suspected or convicted natural and legal persons in cases relating to financial law. Despite the difference between the jurisprudence of the ECJ with its focus on the financial interests of the EU and that of the ECtHR, I plead a harmonisation of the jurisprudence of both courts regarding the *ne bis in idem* principle (section 9.4).

European law and national legislations develop legal instruments aimed to protect the internal market, to prohibit money laundering, to protect the Union's financial interests and to combat fraud, etc. These instruments provide for several administrative measures and penal sanctions. For example, the Dutch legislation criminalises the infringements of anti-money laundering legislation with penal sanctions – such as fines and imprisonment – and at the same time irregularities are labelled as administrative offences and handled as such with measures and fines. This double-track enforcement design raises the question which enforcement

[1] For convenience, I will use *ne bis in idem* and *non bis in idem* indiscriminately.

system prevails in concrete cases. Regarding EU law, the first clue lies in Article 50 of the Charter of Fundamental Rights of the European Union (the 'Charter').[2] This article reads as follows: 'No one shall be tried or punished again in criminal proceedings for an offence for which he or she has already been finally acquitted or convicted within the Union in accordance with the law'. The explanation of the EU regarding this Article refers directly to Article 4 of Protocol No 7 to the ECHR ('Article 4 P7').[3] Article 4 P7(1) reads as follows:

> No one shall be liable to be tried or punished again in criminal proceedings under the jurisdiction of the same State for an offence for which he has already been finally acquitted or convicted in accordance with the law and penal procedure of that State.

The referral hereto within Article 50 of the Charter implies the implementation of the *non bis in idem* principle in EU law. The principle prohibiting cumulation refers to the cumulation of two penalties of the same kind – that is to say, criminal law penalties – but what about administrative penalties concerning the 'same' facts?[4] Further, the explanation underlines that in accordance with Article 50 the *non bis in idem* principle applies not only within the jurisdiction of one state, but also between the jurisdictions of several Member States. As such, every citizen within the territory of the Union has the right to invoke the protection from the Treaties and the EU Charter regardless of state borders. That corresponds to the *acquis* in Union law (Articles 54 and 58 of the Schengen Convention).[5] Limitations are only tolerated within the limitations as referred to in Article 52(3)–(4).

The ECHR does not contain an equivalent Article, but it has – fortunately – found a way to insert the *ne bis in idem* principle in Article 6 ECHR through interpretation. As previously stated, it is further enshrined in Article 4 P7 ECHR. Some Member States, however, like the Netherlands, did not ratify Protocol 7 to the Convention. The ECtHR finds a complaint under Article 4 P7 inadmissible, when a complaint concerns a state that has not ratified the protocol.[6] The Lisbon Treaties provide a good way out in such a situation. In the field of *ne bis in idem* we must differentiate between the *ne bis in idem* principle in the national law of the Member States and the international elaboration of the principle rule in the relevant treaties and jurisprudence of the ECJ and the ECtHR. This chapter focuses on the jurisprudence of the two courts on the European level. In fact, having in mind the intensive legislative activity of the EU in criminal matters, the ECJ had increasingly taken over the tasks of the ECtHR to protect the fundamental rights of EU

[2] See Consolidated versions of the Treaty on the European Union and the Treaty on the Functioning of the European Union [2012] OJ C-326/391 and the Explanations [2007] OJ C-303/02, see also Art 3(2) EAW.

[3] Explanations [2007] OJ C-303/31.

[4] For short, I refer to ch 8 in this volume.

[5] The explanation refers also to some case law of the ECJ and EU-Conventions as Art 7 of the Convention of the Protection of the European communities' Financial Interests.

[6] ECtHR 7 November 2000 *Blokker v the Netherlands*, ECLI:CE:ECHR:2000:1107DEC004528299.

citizens in civil and criminal law matters.[7] But is the jurisprudence of the ECJ more severe than that of the ECtHR? Before we answer this question, we must note that the ECJ has rejected the proposal of joining the ECHR.[8] This implies that at the moment we have two different regimes of interpretation concerning the reach of the *ne bis in idem* principle. Moreover, since the Lisbon Treaties the ECJ is more charged with answers on prejudicial questions. The national judges who asked the prejudicial question should decide finally in conformity with it. As a result, the ECJ is in a position to influence the proceeding(s) directly. The ECtHR, however, is only confronted with national *res judicatae*. This is not the place to elaborate in detail on the jurisprudence of both Courts. The focus lies on the problem of the *ne bis in idem* principle in financial cases.[9] In this chapter I will only draw main lines.[10] For example, I will leave aside the problems with enforcement of competition law by national authorities and/or the Commission.[11]

9.2. The ECtHR and the *Ne Bis in Idem* Principle[12]

9.2.1. General Remarks

Article 4 P7 consists of three paragraphs.[13] The first paragraph reads as follows:

> No one shall be liable to be tried or punished again in criminal proceedings under the jurisdiction of the same State for an offence for which he has already been finally acquitted or convicted in accordance with the law and penal procedure of the State.

All the relevant clauses regarding the *ne bis in idem* principle concern a comparable situation: the *same* (natural or sometimes legal) person perpetrates an unlawful conduct on the same place and same time, which is prosecuted or tried while there already have been punitive (criminal or administrative) proceedings. But the point is, does this follow the law?

To answer this question, three more specific questions arise: (1) should both the proceedings be considered as a 'criminal charge' within the meaning of Article 6 ECHR; (2) do both proceedings concern the same offence; and

[7] See A-J Kargopoulos, 'ECHR and the CJEU, Competing, overlapping, or Supplementary Competences?' (2015) 3 *EUCRIM* 96, available at eucrim.eu.eu/articles/echr-and-cjeu.

[8] Opinions of the Court Avis 2/13, ECLI:EU:C:2014:2454. To date, it seems new proposals are being prepared.

[9] Apart from that, the leading cases are tax cases.

[10] See RCP Haentjens and M Jurgens, 'De Conceptrichtlijn Marktmisbruik, de Conceptverordening Marktmisbruik en de harmonisatie van handhaving' in R Stijnen en M Jurgens, *Toepassing van Europees Recht* (Kluwer, 2012) 113–38.

[11] See eg Case C-857/19 *Slovak Telekom*, ECLI:EU:C:2021:139, [39]–[48].

[12] It seems practical to set out the structure, because the Protocol to the Convention is ratified by a great number of other European countries.

[13] See eg the Guide on Article 4 P7 (30 April 2021) by the Registry of the Court of Human Rights.

(3) is there an actual duplication of proceedings?[14] This last question, in turn, consists of at least two relevant, but separate sub-issues: (a) whether there were new proceedings; and if so (b) whether the first set of proceedings was concluded by a final decision. Complaints regarding duplication of proceedings involving more than one country has been inadmissible by the organs of the Convention. The ECtHR did refer to the EU jurisprudence to solve problems in this field. First in relation to the scope of Article 4 P7 it said

> it must be understood as prohibiting the prosecution or trial of a second 'offence' (*idem*) in so far it arises from identical fact or facts which are substantially the same … and the facts constitute a set of concrete factual circumstances involving the same defendant and are inextricably linked together in time and space, the existence of which must be demonstrated in order to secure an conviction or institute criminal proceedings,

after a previous acquittal or conviction had acquired the force of *res judicata*.[15]

Another question is when an offence or a sanction has to be considered as 'criminal' or 'penal'.[16] The answer lies in the *Engel* criteria concerning 'mixed offences'.[17] First, the classification under national law is the starting point for further thinking, but not preponderant. Secondly, is the offence criminal 'in nature' (for instance, what is the interest or purpose)? Thirdly, what is the nature and severity of the potential penalty? The *Öztürk* case mirrors this line of reasoning, stipulating that the ECtHR makes use of autonomous concepts.[18] It reiterated these criteria as decisive to answer the question in his leading judgment in *Zolotukhin v Russia*.[19] The Court has structured its jurisprudence strongly so far.

9.2.2. Right not to be Prosecuted or Tried Twice

Regarding Article 4 P7, the ECtHR stated 'that the Court is strongly affirmed that Article 4 P7 was not confined to the right not to be punished twice but that it extended to the right not to be prosecuted or tried twice'.[20] Article 4 P7 thus concerns two subsequent questions: first, whether the cases concern the same offence, and second, whether there is a duplication of proceedings. Concerning the question whether the issue concerns the same offence, the Court emphasised that

[14] There are also proceedings which appear to be two separate proceedings – criminal and administrative – but which are so closely interconnected they may be considered as one procedure. See eg ECtHR 15 November 2016 *A and B v Norway*, ECLI: CE:ECHR:2016: 1115JUD002413011, [29], [146], [147].

[15] ECtHR 10 February 2009 *Zolotukhin*, ECLI:CE:ECHR:2009:0210JUD001493903, [52], [53], [80]–[82], [84].

[16] ECtHR 8 June 1976, Series A, no 22, ECLI:CE:ECHR:1976:1123JUD000510071, [81]–[84]. Regarding the *Bonda-Engel* criteria, see ch 8 of this volume.

[17] Mixed offences are criminal and disciplinary offences.

[18] ECtHR 21 February 1984, ECtHR, Series A, vol 73, [80]–[82].

[19] ECtHR 10 February 2009 *Zolotukhin*, ECLI:CE:ECHR:2009:0210JUD001493903.

[20] ECtHR 15 November 2015 *A and B v Norway*, ECLI:CE:ECHR:2016:1115JUD002413011, [110].

the prosecution or trial of an offence mimicking a penal administrative proceeding is prohibited in so far as it rises from identical fact or facts which are substantially the same.[21]

The ECtHR has repeated these considerations, for example in the *case of A and B v Norway*.[22] The proceedings in these last cases concerned the same (*idem*) offences, but was there an actual duplication of proceedings (*bis*)? The applicants in this joined case were first accused and indicted by the prosecution. They had tax penalties imposed on them by the tax authorities, which both applicants accepted and paid. Later, they were criminally summoned and convicted. Referring to the chronology of the proceedings, the first applicant added that he had been prosecuted twice (*bis*) over a long period.[23] The ECtHR took the view that Article 4 P7 should be understood as prohibiting the prosecution or trial of an individual for a second 'offence' in so far as it arose from identical facts or facts which are 'substantially' the same (*idem*) as those underlying the first offence.[24] The ECtHR preferred a 'single' enforcement track, but a 'double' track is allowed only if: different proceedings pursue complementary purposes; the duality of the proceedings was a foreseeable consequence, both in law and in practice of the same impugned conduct (*idem*); the relevant sets of proceedings are conducted in such a manner as to avoid so far as possible any duplication in the collection as well as the assessment of the evidence; and, finally, as to prevent that the individual concerned is in the end made to bear an excessive burden, aimed to avoid disproportionate penalties.[25] As such, the Court concluded that in *A and B v Norway*, there was no violation of the *ne bis in idem* principle, because there wasn't the same offence in substance.[26] The Court found that there was a sufficient connection in substance and in time between the tax proceedings and the criminal proceedings to be regarded as forming an integrated legal response. In its view, the circumstance that the first set of proceedings (the tax proceedings) became 'final' before the criminal proceedings (second set), did not preclude the criminal proceedings. The ECtHR found that 'the conduct of dual proceedings, with the possibility of different cumulated penalties, was foreseeable for the applicant'.[27] Finally, the criminal proceedings and the administrative proceedings were conducted parallel and were interconnected (the establishment of facts made in one set was used in the other set) and, as regards the proportionality of the overall punishment, the sentence imposed in the criminal trial had taken into account the tax penalty'.[28]

[21] ECtHR 10 February 2009 *Zolotukhin*, ECLI:CE:ECHR:2009:0210JUD001493903, [78]–[83], esp [82].

[22] ECtHR 15 November 2015 *A and B v Norway*, ECLI:CE:ECHR:2016:1115JUD002413011, [107].

[23] ibid, [56]. In this long period the first applicant was exposed to an unreasonably heavy burden, both physically and psychologically, leading to a heart attack.

[24] ibid, [108].

[25] ibid, [132]–[134].

[26] ibid, [142], [143]. The criteria are taken from ECtHR 10 February 2009 *Zolotukhin*, ECLI:CE:ECHR:2009:0210JUD001493903, [82], with the focus on the 'substance' of the facts.

[27] ibid, [142].

[28] ibid, [146].

The ECtHR is satisfied that, 'whilst different sanctions were imposed (because of different reasons) by two different authorities in different proceedings, there was nevertheless a sufficiently close connection between them, both in substance and in time, to consider them as forming part of an integral scheme of sanctions under Norwegian law'.[29] Therefore, no indication was found that the first applicant suffered any disproportionate prejudice or injustice as a result of the impugned integrated legal response to the applicant.

This trend of the ECtHR showing respect to the *ne bis in idem* principle was corroborated in the case of *Johannesson v Iceland*.[30] The applicants alleged that they had been tried twice for the same offence through the imposition of tax surcharges (25 per cent) and a subsequent criminal trial for aggravated tax offences. They complained that in violation of Article 4 P7 the two sets of proceedings had been based on identical facts. Relying on the *Bonda–Engel* criteria, they submitted that the imposition of tax surcharges constituted sanctions which were criminal in nature and fell under the scope of Articles 6, 7 and Article 4 P7. The Court concluded that both sets of proceedings indeed concerned a criminal matter within the autonomous meaning of Article 4 P7.[31] Note, that the *idem* element of the *ne bis in idem* principle is present.[32] In *A and B v Norway*, the Court exemplified what should be taken into account when evaluating the connection in substance and in time between dual criminal and administrative proceedings.[33] The Court did refer to *A and B v Norway*[34] and inserted these considerations in *Johannesson v Iceland*.[35] Given the limited overlap in time and the largely independent collection and assessment of evidence, the Court did not find a sufficiently close connection in substance and in time between the tax proceedings and the (subsequent) criminal proceedings to be compatible with the *bis* criterion in Article 4 P7.[36]

9.2.3. Multiple Criminal Proceedings with No Final Decision

It should be noted that the *ne bis in idem* principle also prohibits cumulating criminal proceedings, which haven't been concluded by a 'final' decision. In *Grande Stevens and others vs Italy* the ECtHR found unanimously a violation of Article 4 P7.[37] The case concerned the applicants' appeal against the administrative

[29] ibid, [147].
[30] ECtHR 18 May 2017 *Johannesson and Others v Iceland*, ECLI:CE:ECHR:201718JUD0022000711.
[31] ibid, [44].
[32] ibid, [45]–[47].
[33] ECtHR 15 November 2015 *A and B v Norway*, ECLI:CE:ECHR:2016:1115JUD002413011, [146].
[34] ibid, [132]–[133].
[35] ECtHR 18 May 2017 *Johannesson and Others v Iceland*, ECLI:CE:ECHR:201718JUD0022000711, [49].
[36] ibid, [49]–[56].
[37] ECtHR 4 March 2014 *Grande Stevens and Others v Italy*, ECLI:CE:ECHR:2013:0304JUD001864010.

penalty imposed on them by the Italian Companies and Stock Exchange Commission ('Consob') and the criminal proceedings to which they were currently subject after having been accused of market manipulation in the context of a financial operation involving the car manufacturer Fiat.[38] On the basis of Article 4 P7 the applicants complained that criminal proceedings were started in respect of events for which they had already received an administrative penalty. The ECtHR founded that the administrative fines imposed on the applicants by the financial market regulator had to be considered as 'criminal' for the purposes of both Article 6 ECHR and Article 4 P7. Further, the sentences imposed by Consob, which were partly reduced by the court of appeal, had become final. Accordingly, the applicants ought to have been considered as having already been convicted by a final judgment. Despite that, new criminal proceedings, which in the meantime the Italian authorities had started against them, were maintained and resulted in judgments at first and second instance. Given the first administrative proceedings before the Consob and the next criminal proceedings for the same facts before the District Court of Turin concerning the same facts, the Court found this to be a violation of Article 4 P7. An interesting point of this case was an argument by the Italian Government that the case law of the ECJ does not consider the protection of the *ne bis in idem* rule as absolute, because the ECJ lets the Union's financial interests combating unlawful conduct on the financial markets prevail. The ECtHR rejects this argument. The ECtHR argued that the ECJ had stated that under the *ne bis in idem* principle, a state could only impose a double penalty (fiscal and criminal) in respect of the same facts, if the first penalty was not criminal in nature.

9.3. The ECJ and the *Ne Bis in Idem* Principle

In this context, the starting points are Articles 50 and 52(3) Charter.[39] Article 52(3) reads as follows:

> In so far as this Charter contains rights which correspond to rights guaranteed by the Convention for the protection of Human Rights and Fundamental Freedoms (ECHR), the meaning and scope of those rights shall be the same as those had laid down by the said Convention. This provision shall not prevent Union law providing more extensive protection.[40]

Further, Articles 54–58 of the Convention implementing the Schengen Agreement (CISA) are relevant for evaluating the scope of the rule of *ne bis in idem* in

[38] 'Consob' is the Italian Commission tasked, in particular, with protecting investors and ensuring the transparency and the development of the stock markets.

[39] Art 52(3) Charter of Fundamental Rights of the European Union, C-326/391, 26 October 2012. See further for a recent overview of the case law of the ECJ: 'Case law by the Court of Justice of the European Union on the principle of *ne bis in idem* in criminal matters' (Eurojust, April 2020).

[40] This paragraph will not discuss the autonomy of Union Law and of that of the ECJ ([2007] OJ C-303/33).

EU law.[41] A great number of cases focuses on tax matters, and the ECJ has found the opportunity to make clear its position. *First*, the ECJ faced up to the relation between the legal framework of the ECHR, Article 4 P7 and Article 3(2) of the European Arrest Warrant Framework Detention (EAW FD). In the preliminary ruling, *Åklagen v Åkerberg Fransson*, Åkerberg was first summoned to appear before the District Court on charges of serious offences. He was also prosecuted for failing to declare contributions. According to the indictment, the offences ('criminal charges') were serious. The decision imposing the penalties was based on the same acts of providing false information as those relied upon by the Public Prosecutor's Office in the criminal proceedings. The question raised whether the charges against Åkerberg must be dismissed on the ground that he had already been punished for the same acts in other proceedings, as the prohibition on being punished twice (*bis*) laid down in Article 4 P7 and Article 50 of the Charter would be infringed.

The ECJ considered its jurisdiction vis-à-vis other legal European frameworks. The ECJ's settled case law states, in essence, that the fundamental rights guaranteed in the legal order of the EU are applicable in all situations governed by EU law, but not outside such situations (para 19). EU law doesn't govern the relations between the ECHR and the legal systems of the Member States, nor does it determine the conclusions to be drawn by a national court in the event of conflict between the rights guaranteed by that Convention and a rule of national law (para 49).[42] ECJ states that the *ne bis in idem* principle laid down in Article 50 Charter doesn't preclude a Member State from imposing successively a tax penalty and a criminal penalty in so far as the first penalty is not criminal in nature, a matter of which is for the national court to decide (para 37).[43] The ECJ referred in this regard to the jurisprudence of the ECtHR (para 35).[44]

In *Bonda*, the ECJ reiterated the *Engel* criteria: the legal classification under national law is not decisive, but a starting point: the nature of the offence and the nature and severity of the penalty that the person concerned faces are more relevant. But it's up to the national judge to decide. In *Bonda* these criteria failed,

[41] The Schengen acquis [2000] OJ L 239/19. Art 54 reads as follows: 'A person whose trial has been finally disposed of in one Contracting Party may not be prosecuted in another Contracting Party for the same acts provided that, if a penalty has been imposed, it has enforced, is actually in the process of being enforced or can no longer be enforced under the laws of the sentencing Contracting Party'. Moreover, the principle is also included in international instruments on cooperation in criminal matters as ground for refusal. See for example the Council Framework Decision 2002/584 JHA on the European arrest warrant and the Framework Decision (EAW FD, Art 3(2)).

[42] Case C-617/10 *Åkerberg Fransson*, ECLI:EU:C:2013:105, [44] reads 'although as Article 63 TEU confirms, the fundamental rights recognised by the ECtHR constitute general principles of EU law and although Art 52(3) of the Charter provides that the rights contained in the Charter which correspond to rights guaranteed by the ECtHR are to have the same meaning and scope as those laid down by that Convention, the latter does not constitute, as long as the European Union has not acceded to it, a legal instrument which has been formally incorporated into EU law'.

[43] Case C-617/10 *Åkerberg Fransson*, ECLI:EU:C:2013:105.

[44] Case C-489/10 *Bonda*, ECLI:EU:C:2012:319, [37].

as the administrative measures weren't criminal 'in nature' and – as such – didn't apply.[45] In the *Menci* case, Menci was subject to administrative proceedings during which it was alleged that he had failed to pay in his capacity as proprietor of sole trading business within the time limit stipulated by law.[46] The administrative authorities ordered Menci to pay the tax and imposed him an administrative penalty (about €850,000). After the conclusion of the administrative proceedings, criminal proceedings were initiated regarding the same acts. The two proceedings were conducted independently and came respectively within the competence of the judicial and administrative authorities. The Italian District Court stated that in conformity with the administrative law the penalties relating to the tax offences are not enforceable, unless the criminal proceedings have concluded by dismissal of the case, acquittal or termination of the proceedings. However, this does not prevent a person from being subject to criminal proceeding after having had a final administrative penalty imposed on him/her.[47] The Italian judge wanted to know whether Article 50 Charter, interpreted in the light of Article 4 P7, precludes the possibility of conducting criminal proceedings concerning an act for which already a final administrative penalty had been imposed. The ECJ states that:

> According to the explanations relating to Article 52 of the Charter, paragraph 3 of that article is intended to ensure the necessary consistency between the Charter and the ECtHR, without thereby adversely affecting the autonomy of the Union law and that of the Court of Justice of the European Union.[48]

It should be noted that Member States are obliged to take all legislative and administrative measures appropriate for ensuring collection of all the value-added tax (VAT) due on their territory and for preventing fraud.[49]

Moreover, Article 325 TFEU obliges the Member States to counter illegal activities affecting the financial interests of the EU through effective deterrent measures, and in particular, obliges them to take the same measures to counter fraud effecting the financial interests of the EU as they take to counter fraud affecting their own interests.[50] The financial interests of the EU include, in particular, revenue arising from VAT.[51] The ECJ ruled as follows:

> Article 50 of the Charter must be interpreted as not precluding national legislation in accordance with which criminal proceedings may be brought against a person for

[45] ibid, [42]–[43].
[46] Case C-524/15 *Menci*, ECLI:EU:C:2018:197.
[47] ibid, [11]–[15].
[48] ibid, [23].
[49] ibid, [18].
[50] ibid, [19].
[51] See for the same reasoning Case C-617/10 *Åkerberg Fransson*, ECLI:EU:C:2013:105, [25]. EU revenue includes VAT: see the Council Decision of 26 May 2014 on the system of own resources of the European Union (2914/335/EU, Euratom, 7.6.2014, L 268/105), recently renewed Council Decision (EU, Euratom 2020/2053, 15.12.2020, L 424,1-10 (ORD) repealing Decision 2014/335/EU, Eurtom. See also Case C-42/17 *MAS and MB*, ECLI:EU:C:2017:936, [30]–[31].

> failing to pay VAT due within the time limits stipulated by law, although that person has already been subject, in relation to the same acts, to pay a final administrative penalty of criminal nature for the purposes of Article 50 of the Charter, on condition that that legislation (1) pursues an objective of general interest which is such as to justify such a duplication of proceedings and penalties, namely combating VAT offences, it being necessary for those proceedings and penalties to pursue additional objectives, (2) contains rules ensuring coordination which limits additional disadvantage from a duplication of proceedings for the persons concerned, and (3) provides for rules making it possible to ensure that the severity of all of the penalties imposed is limited to what is strictly necessary in relation to the seriousness of the offence concerned.[52]

It is for the national court to ensure all the circumstances in the main proceedings are taken into account, and that the actual disadvantage resulting for the person concerned from the application of the national legislation at issue that that legislation authorises isn't excessive in relation to the seriousness of the offence committed.[53] In light of Article 52(3) Charter, which permits a wider protection vis-à-vis the ECHR, these exceptions are permitted.

In the leading case *MAS and MB* the ECJ went a step further. The ECJ held that

> Article 325(1) and (2) must be interpreted as requiring the national court, in criminal proceedings for infringements relating to VAT, to disapply national provisions on limitation, forming part of national substantive law, which prevent the application of effective and deterrent criminal penalties in a significant number of cases of serious fraud affecting the financial interests of the EU'.

The same applies in those cases

> which lay down shorter limitation periods for cases of serious fraud affecting the EU interests or which affect the financial interests of the Member State concerned, unless that disapplication entails a breach of the principle that offences and penalties must be defined by law because of the lack of precision of the applicable law or because of the retroactive application of legislation imposing conditions of criminal liability stricter than those in force at the time the infringement was committed.[54]

Thus, serious fraud – according to the Italian criminal law – which affects (as a matter of course) the Union's financial interest, may put aside the *ne bis in idem* principle, including the time limitation rules. So, if the national criminal rule prevents the imposition of effective and dissuasive penalties in a significant number of cases of serious fraud affecting the financial interests of the EU or provides for longer limitation periods in respect of cases of fraud affecting the financial interests of the Member State concerned, it is for the national court to verify that. The ECJ gives precedence to the provisions of the Directives and particularly the PIF Directive, which is aimed at protecting the Union's financial interests, putting aside – if necessary – the national limitations rules and *ne bis in idem* principle.

[52] Case C-524/15 *Menci*, ECLI:EU:C:2018:197, [63].
[53] ibid, [64].
[54] Case C-42/17 *MAS and MB*, ECLI:EU:C:2017:936, [62], [64].

In this vein, the ECJ has given some preliminary rulings which underline the Court's way of reasoning in relation to the *ne bis in idem* principle. An example is *Garlsson Real Estate SA*.[55] In that case, the Stock Exchange Commission in Italy had imposed an administrative fine because of market manipulation (€10.2 million). The conduct of the suspect also caused criminal proceedings against them which led to their penal conviction a prison sentence of four years and six months. At appeal, this was reduced to three years. The appeal became the final verdict. The Italian court had doubts about the applying of the *ne bis in idem* principle because of links between the administrative and criminal penalties and given the judgment of the ECtHR in *Grande Stevens and others*.[56] It noted that the conduct *in casu* was the object of administrative proceedings, which were the same as that for which the criminal penalty was imposed on him. Moreover, the referring judge questioned whether the national court may directly apply EU principles in connection with the *ne bis in idem* principle on the basis of Article 50 Charter, interpreted in the light of Article 4 P7 (in conjunction with Article 52(3)). The ECJ judged that 'Article 50 Charter must be interpreted as precluding national legislation which permits the possibility of bringing administrative proceedings against a person in respect of unlawful conduct consisting in market manipulation for which the same person has already been finally convicted, in so far that conviction is, given the harm caused to the company by the offence committed, such as to punish that offence in an effective, proportionate, and dissuasive manner'. The administrative proceedings and sanctions at stake are of a criminal nature. Thus, in this case a duplication appears to be of the same administrative and criminal offences, and in so far a breach of the *ne bis idem* rule, which is only under special conditions permitted, see Article 52 Charter.[57] The *ne bis in idem* principle, guaranteed by Article 50 Charter, confers on individuals a right which is directly applicable in the context of a dispute such as that at issue in the main proceedings. Very precisely, the ECJ formulated his ordeal about the reach of Article 50. The national judge has to obey the Charter even if the protection goes further than the national law permits (Article 50(3)). The trend in the jurisprudence of the ECJ goes even further: not only in tax cases, but also in those relating to insider dealing and in unfair competition cases.

In *Enzo di Puma and Zecca v Consob* (Cases C-596/16 and C-537/16) the Italian judge asked for a preliminary ruling concerning Article 50 and Directive 2014/57/EU of the European Parliament and the Council of 16 April 2014 on criminal sanctions for market abuse. The question concerned the legality of the administrative fines imposed in relation to insider dealing. The Italian Court of Cassation did ask whether Article 50 Charter must be interpreted as meaning that, where a court has delivered a final judgment finding a defendant not to have committed the criminal

[55] Case C-596/16 *Enzo di Puma*, ECLI:EU:C:2018:192; Case C-537/16 *Antonio Zecca v Consob*, ECLI:EU:C:2018:193.

[56] ECtHR 4 March 2014 *Grande Stevens and Others v Italy*, ECLI:CE:ECHR:2013:0304JUD001864010.

[57] ibid, [42].

offence alleged, it precludes the initiation of further proceedings based on the same facts with a view to the imposition of penalties which, on account of their nature and severity, may be regarded as criminal penalties, without it being necessary, for the national court to make any further assessment.[58] The ECJ points out 'that the bringing of proceedings for an administrative fine of a criminal nature, based on the same facts, constitutes a limitation of the fundamental right guaranteed by Article 50 of the Charter, referring to the *Menci* and *Garlsson Real Estate* cases'.[59] The ECJ considers that the objective of protecting the integrity of financial markets and public confidence in financial instruments justify (Article 52(1) Charter) a duplication of proceedings and penalties of a criminal nature such as that provided for by the national legislation at issue in the main proceedings, where those proceedings and penalties have, for the purpose of achieving such an objective, additional complementary objectives covering, as the case may be, different aspects of the same unlawful conduct at issue.

In *Åkerberg Fransson* the criminal proceedings had been brought after the imposition of a tax penalty, but in that case the question raised 'whether proceedings for an administrative fine of criminal nature may be brought where a final criminal judgment of acquittal has concluded that the acts capable of constituting a violation of the insider dealing …, were not established'. The ECJ ruled:

> [T]he directive market abuse, read in the light of Article 50 must be interpreted as not precluding national legislation in accordance with which proceedings for an administrative fine of a criminal nature may not be brought following a final criminal judgment of acquittal ruling, that the acts capable constituting a violation of the legislation relating to insider dealing, on the basis of which those proceedings had also been initiated, were not established.[60]

In brief, where there exists a final criminal judgment of acquittal finding there is no offence, the act of bringing proceedings for an administrative fine of a criminal nature does not infringe the *ne bis in idem* rule.[61]

9.4. Concluding Remarks

First, two jurisdictions on the European level recognise the *ne bis in idem* principle as a fundamental right: the ECJ and the ECtHR. Both are trying to

[58] Case C-596/16 *Enzo di Puma*, ECLI:EU:C:2018:192; Case C-537/16 *Antonio Zecca v Consob*, ECLI:EU:C:2018:193.

[59] See for *Menci*: Case C-596/16 *Enzo di Puma*, ECLI:EU:C:2018:192; Case C-537/16 *Antonio Zecca v Consob*, ECLI:EU:C:2018:193, [39]–[40]. For *Garlsson Real Estate*: Case C-596/16 *Enzo di Puma*, ECLI:EU:C:2018:192; Case C-537/16 *Antonio Zecca v Consob*, ECLI:EU:C:2018:193, [41].

[60] Case C-596/16 *Enzo di Puma*, ECLI:EU:C:2018:192; Case C-537/16 *Antonio Zecca v Consob*, ECLI:EU:C:2018:193.

[61] Case C-596/16 *Enzo di Puma*, ECLI:EU:C:2018:192, [46]; Case C-537/16 *Antonio Zecca v Consob*, ECLI:EU:C:2018:193, [46].

enforce within their own competencies this principle. In this context there is right away the knotty problem of demarcation between the ECJ and the ECtHR. The ECJ has found an elegant solution in Article 52(3) Charter. It opens a mutual understanding, not a formal mutual incorporation.[62]

Second, the *ne bis in idem* principle in criminal matters is a fundamental right. Indeed, it prohibits duplications of prosecutions, proceedings and penalties of offences of a criminal nature (*Engel*, *Bonda* and more recent case law affirming these criteria) and a criminal offence for the same acts and against the same person (*Garlsson Real Estate SA*), either within the same Member State or in several Member States if the person has exercised his/her right to freedom of movement (*WS*).[63] But it does not seem to be an absolute right.

However, there is – in my modest opinion – a difference between the judgments of the ECJ and the ECtHR in the way they apply the *ne bis in idem* principle. The ECJ focuses on the impact of the offence(s) upon the financial interests of the EU, as PIF offences or VAT-carrousels. This might be explained by the background and the purposes of the EU. In case of a duplication of prosecution or conviction of a criminal offence and an administrative offence for the same fact(s), which may be considered as criminal offence following the autonomous interpretation of the ECtHR, the instrumental enforcement approach by the authorities prevails over the protection of the *ne bis in idem* principle, provided that the sanctions are deterrent, persuasive and effective. The jurisprudence of the ECtHR is much stricter. Interpreting the *ne bis in idem* principle and Article 4 P7 the ECtHR upheld the opinion that only in special circumstances the principle may be set aside (because, for example, there wasn't a duplication of convictions) and only when a number of conditions is fulfilled (*A and B v Norway*).

Note, both the ECJ and the ECtHR have a joined opinion about the proportionality of penalties which may be imposed. Cumulating penalties – if the principle is infringed and duplication of penalties is allowed – is only permitted in case of due observance of the overall proportionality, paying attention to the seriousness of the offences and personal circumstances of the perpetrator. The ECJ rules that the national judge must take account of the proportionality of the penalties, which may not be disproportionate in light of the specific circumstances.

Third, most ECJ case law concerns tax matters. Nevertheless, it is allowed to extend the jurisprudence of the ECJ and the ECtHR relating financial offences, aimed at upholding the EU financial infrastructure, to other areas of the EU's interest where criminal and administrative enforcement intersect.[64] In that case this question needs a fine understanding, mutual assistance, and trust between the administrative and penal authorities to answer the question: 'how shall we

[62] H Satzger, 'Application Problems relating to "Ne bis in Idem as Guaranteed under Art. 50 CFR/ Art. 54 CISA and Art 4 Prot. No.7 ECHR' (2020) 3 EUCRIM 213, available at doi.org/10.30709/ eurocrim-2020-018.

[63] Case C-505-/19 *WS*, ECLI:EU:C:2021:376 concerning Art 54 CISA and data protection.

[64] eg, infringements of EU Directives and Regulations on the protection of the environment, etc.

the competences divide in this case'? Only in that way does there exist a strong enforcement with an open eye to an 'effective, deterrent and dissuasive' penalty, regarding the proportionality thereof.

Fourth, a duplication of proceedings depends on the question which proceedings are handled first by the competent authorities. Duplication of criminal proceedings in case of the same offences by the same person, after administrative proceedings is not allowed if the administrative proceedings are criminal in nature and final (*Zolotukhin*). If the proceedings were criminal and ended with a judicial decision, the later starting of administrative proceedings is generally allowed, provided that the criminal proceedings were deterrent, dissuasive and effective.

Fifth, following the jurisprudence of the ECJ, the administrative enforcement authorities may sometimes breach the rules of prescriptions. ECJ jurisprudence allowed the infringement of the *ne bis in idem* principle in certain circumstances. That is not a very solid protection in cases with serious financial offences to get away from the investing, convicting and sentencing authority, even there is the protection of Article 49(3) Charter.[65] It is up to the judge to impose proportional and appropriate sanctions in relation to the severity of the unlawful offences and the financial capacity of the perpetrators. Yet there are some differences indeed: first of all, the *ne bis in idem* principle applies for every natural and legal person within the borders of the EU. But what if the natural person is convicted within the competence of the Member States which have signed the ECHR and the legal person is accused of the same fact(s) but has not yet been convicted, and is not established in one of the Member States? Is the legal person protected by the *ne bis idem* principle? The principle, based on Article 4 P7 ECHR, is only applicable within the national Member States which have signed the ECHR and the protocol.

In all, this leads to the conclusion that on a European level the legislature and jurisprudence of the ECJ and the ECtHR should pay more attention to protect the natural and legal persons of the EU in case of presumable violations of the *ne bis in idem* principle, particularly in cases of financial offences regarding the Union's financial interests. There is an urgent need to harmonise the jurisprudence of the ECtHR and the ECJ. In that way there is a paradox of the *ne bis in idem* principle in EU criminal and financial law. This principle is a fundamental right within the jurisdictions of the ECHR and the EU. It should protect natural and legal persons in those cases in which the principle is applicable, especially in cases in which criminal and administrative enforcement coincide. But in relation to the enforcement of financial offences (criminal and/or administrative) the ECJ and the ECtHR have developed exceptions to this principle, which are not always in favour of the prosecuted of convicted natural or legal persons. The enforcement of financial interests of Member States and of the EU apparently prevails over the *ne bis in idem* principle as such, although from the perspective of the principle, as a fundamental right, the opposite would be expected.

[65] Art 49(3) Charter tries to protect the 'criminal' offender against disproportionate penalties.

10

European Strategies against Money Laundering: A Critical Overview of Current and Future Enforcement

SILVIA ALLEGREZZA

10.1. Introduction – From Inactivity to Scandal-Driven Reforms

Recent years have seen several European banks involved in major money laundering scandals. The ABVL, Danske Bank,[1] ING,[2] Société Générale,[3] Deutsche Bank, ABN AMRO and Rabobank cases are only the top of the iceberg. Anti-money laundering and counter-terrorism financing (AML/CFT) are world priorities:[4]

[1] The ABLV, the now-defunct Estonian branch of the Danske Bank, has been accused of allowing a flow of some US $230 billion in suspect Russian funds. Aivar Rehe, the former chief of the Danske Bank Estonian branch, committed suicide in September 2019.

[2] In September 2018, ING Groep, the Netherlands' largest financial institution, stated it would pay Dutch authorities EUR 775 million, or USD 900 million, in a historic settlement.

[3] In 2018 French Société Générale stated it was expecting to pay a penalty of €1.1 billion, or US $1.27 billion, to a host of US federal and state investigative and regulatory authorities for breaching US sanctions. The bank had to negotiate a high-profile settlement for financial crime compliance failures.

[4] In January 2021 the United States passed the National Defense Authorization Act for Fiscal Year 2021 whose Title LXIII intends to 'improving anti-money laundering and countering the financing of terrorism communication, oversight, and processes underlying the need to work on the following sectors': Improved interagency coordination and consultation (Sec 6301).Subcommittee on Information Security and Confidentiality (Sec 6302). Establishment of Bank Secrecy Act Information Security Officers (Sec 6303). FinCEN analytical hub (Sec 6304). Assessment of Bank Secrecy Act no-action letters (Sec 6305). Cooperation with law enforcement (Sec 6306). Training for examiners on anti-money laundering and countering the financing of terrorism (Sec. 6307). Obtaining foreign bank records from banks with United States correspondent accounts (Sec. 6308). Additional damages for repeat Bank Secrecy Act violators (Sec 6309). Certain violators barred from serving on boards of United States financial institutions (Sec 6310). Department of Justice report on deferred and non-prosecution agreements (Sec 6311). Return of profits and bonuses (Sec 6312). Prohibition on concealment of the source of assets in monetary transactions (Sec 6313). Updating whistle-blower incentives and protection (Sec 6314). See: docs.house.gov/billsthisweek/20201207/CRPT-116hrpt617.pdf.

money laundering[5] concerns roughly three per cent of the global GDP and 1.3 per cent of the European Union (EU) GDP.[6] Major cases are transnational by nature as such and they require a comprehensive regulatory effort in which international,[7] regional and national actors should promote convergence of supervisory and enforcement practice.[8] As the alarming numbers published by the Financial Action Task Force (FATF) have shown, the flow of dirty money deeply affects every aspect of the global economy and is essential to the very existence of major criminal organisations.[9] Its pervasiveness and coexistence with crime, including tax evasion, has a direct and indirect impact on the citizens and foundations of modern democracies. The FATF summit held in Paris in June 2021 reignited the international debate, reaffirming the urgency of a coordinated action worldwide and highlighting new areas of intervention.[10]

What is the role of the EU in this global strategy?

10.1.1. The Role of the European Union

In recent years, the EU has adopted many normative steps to reinforce the existing legal framework, always confirming the choice of a double track in which prevention is mainly conferred to administrative law whereas repression should in principle be left to criminal law, both handled exclusively at national level.[11]

[5] On the history of money laundering and its structure, see RW Baker, 'The Scale of the Global Financial Structure Facilitating Money Laundering' in B Unger and D van der Linde (eds), *Research Handbook on Money Laundering* (Edward Elgar, 2013) 190, 191. On techniques of laundering, with a focus on some European countries, see F Teichmann, 'Recent trends in money laundering' 2020 (73) *Crime, Law and Social Change* 237.

[6] See the Special Report of the EU Court of Auditors of June 2021: 'L'UE et la euro contre le blanchiment de capitaux dans le secteur bancaire: des efforts fragmentés et une mise en œuvre insuffisante', available at eca.europa.eu/Lists/ECADocuments/SR21_13/SR_AML_FR.pdf. For criticism on how to assess the real volume, see KJ McCarthy, 'Why Do Some States Tolerate Money Laundering? On the Competition for Illegal Money' in B Unger and D van der Linde (eds), *Research Handbook on Money Laundering* (Edward Elgar Publishing, 2013) 127, 129.

[7] G Stessens, *Money Laundering: A New International Law Enforcement* (CUP, 2008) 15 ff; for a complete overview, see W Blair, R Brent and T Grant (eds), *Banks and Financial Crime. The International Law of Tainted Money*, 2nd edn (OUP, 2017) 3 ff.

[8] On the concept of 'global criminal law', see: A Nieto Martin, 'Transformationes del ius puniendi en el derecho global' in A Nieto Martin and B García Moreno, *Ius Puniendi y Global Law*, (Tirant lo Blanch, 2019) 17.

[9] LS Borlini, 'Regulating Criminal Finance in the EU in the Light of the International Instruments' (2017) 36 *Yearbook of European Law* (Oxford University Press, 2018) 553.

[10] The financial flows linked to environmental crime and the financing of ethnically or racially motivated terrorism are priorities of the FATF's German Presidency. The summit approached the challenges of digital transformation of AML/CFT, of virtual assets, ethnically or racially motivated terrorism financing, confiscation, and assets recovery via strengthening the FATF standards on beneficial ownership. See: www.fatf-gafi.org/publications/fatfgeneral/documents/outcomes-fatf-plenary-june-2021.html.

[11] M Levi and P Reuter, 'Money Laundering (2006) 34 *Crime & Justice* 297.

In the last 10 years, regulatory aspects have been strengthened with the adoption of the fourth and fifth AML/CFT Directives,[12] whereas the duty on Member States to increase their criminal law toolbox to fight AML/CFT came in 2018 with Directive 2018/1673.[13] Although some of these reforms are still being implemented, it has become clear that the main weakness is mostly a lack of enforcement.

A system conferring only to national authorities the task to detect and prevent illicit money flows proved to fall short in a strongly integrated financial and banking system as the one we have within the EU. Even stronger appears the incapacity of national agencies to counter transnational money laundering phenomena, leaving the Union without a proper response and no recovery of illicit funds. Despite having its epicentre within Europe, the regulatory response for those cases came mainly from overseas. American regulators intervened with severe penalties, some of them so high that they led to the failure of the bank itself.

The appalling failure of European regulators to prevent and detect structural money laundering, as it occurred in the ABLV case, called for an urgent intervention. Neither national authorities nor the European regulators react to phenomena of such an impressive magnitude, where laundering dirty money was described as a core and structural business for some of the European banks involved. In this light, tackling money laundering is also a sensitive issue for the euro area's fledgling banking union. National AML supervisory failures result in reputational risk for the European Central Bank (ECB) in its new capacity of prudential supervisor.[14] And some of the banks involved in main cases were directly or indirectly under the supervision of the European banking regulator, the Single Supervisory Mechanism (SSM) recently introduced within the European Central Bank (ECB). These regulatory gaps generated a firestorm of criticism that forced the ECB-SSM chair to make a public statement in which the lack of a specific competence on AML was highlighted.[15] Nor could the European Banking Authority (EBA) have intervened to prevent the regulatory failure as it lacked the direct powers to coordinate national competent authorities (NCAs).

As many politicians pledged to strengthen anti-money laundering (AML) oversight and enforcement, recent reforms have radically altered financial crime

[12] Directive (EU) 2018/843 of the European Parliament and of the Council of 30 May 2018 amending Directive (EU) 2015/849 on the prevention of the use of the financial system for the purposes of money laundering or terrorist financing [2018] OJ L 156/43.

[13] Directive (EU) 2018/1673 of the European Parliament and of the Council of 23 October 2018 on combating money laundering by criminal law [2018] OJ L 284/22.

[14] J Kirschenbaum and N Véron, 'A better European Union architecture to fight money laundering' Bruegel, Policy Contribution Issue No 19 (October 2018) 2. On the SSM, see S Allegrezza (ed), *The Enforcement Dimension of the Single Supervisory Mechanism* (Cedam Kluwer, 2019).

[15] See in particular the ABLV Bank scandal, in which the credit institution was sanctioned by American regulators for several money laundering incidents. Members of the EU Parliament raised questions regarding the ECB role in information exchange between the detection of money laundering risks and the integration of those risks in prudential supervision; see the answer of D Nouy, Chair of the ECB Supervisory Board, to S Giegold, Member of the European Parliament, of 3 May 2018 avaliable at: www.bankingsupervision.europa.eu/ecb/pub/pdf/ssm.mepletter180503_giegold.en.pdf.

strategies in Europe. They all seem to endorse centralisation of enforcement as their key feature.

As the EU responds to historic money laundering scandals, regional banks and regulators must begin to brace for the impact of stronger AML oversight and enforcement. Some reactions came also at the regional level: in 2019 financial regulators in Denmark, Estonia, Finland, Iceland, Latvia, Lithuania, Norway and Sweden established the Nordic Know Your Customer (KYC), a permanent working group to bolster cumulative efforts to identify, investigate and prosecute money laundering, terrorist financing and other financial crimes.[16]

A first, provisional step toward a centralisation of powers at EU level was taken in December 2019 when the EBA was tasked to lead, coordinate and monitor the fight against money laundering and terrorist financing within the EU, thus becoming a crucial actor.[17]

The latter reform will be soon replaced by a reform package of AML/CFT strategies (Action Plan) announced by the EU Commission in May 2020 and finally published in July 2021.[18] The ambitious plan is composed of four legislative proposals:

(1) a Regulation establishing a new central EU-level AML/CFT Authority (AMLA),[19] to be established in 2023 and operational in 2024;
(2) a Regulation establishing a 'single EU rulebook' for AML/CFT providing for directly applicable rules with no requirement of transposition into national law and common powers and tasks of national supervisors and financial intelligence units (FIUs);[20]
(3) a new – the sixth – anti-money laundering Directive on the mechanisms to be put in place by the Member States for the prevention of the use of the financial system for the purposes of money laundering or terrorist financing and repealing Directive (EU) 2015/849, proposing the adoption of new rules and minimum standards for national supervisors and FIUs, with particular attention to enhanced enforcement, co-ordination and information exchange;[21]

[16] See: dfsa.dk/News/Press-releases/2019/Nordic-and-Baltic-cooperation-to-fight-money-laundering.

[17] See EBA Regulation (Regulation (EU) No 1093/2010 of the European Parliament and of the Council of 24 November 2010 establishing a European Supervisory Authority (European Banking Authority), amending Decision 716/2009/EC and repealing Commission Decision 2009/78/EC [2010] OJ L 331/12), as amended by Regulation (EU) 2019/2175 of the European Parliament and of the Council of 18 December 2019 [2019] OJ L 334/1.

[18] Anti-money laundering and countering the financing terrorism legislative package, available at: ec.europa.eu/info/publications/210720-anti-money-laundering-countering-financing-terrorism_en.

[19] Proposal for a Regulation of the European Parliament and of the Council establishing the Authority for Anti-Money Laundering and Countering the Financing of Terrorism and amending Regulations (EU) No 1093/2010, (EU) 1094/2010, (EU) 1095/2010, COM(2021) 421 final (hereinafter AMLA Proposal COM(2021) 421).

[20] Proposal for a Regulation of the European Parliament and of the Council on the prevention of the use of the financial system for the purposes of money laundering or terrorist financing, COM(2021) 420 final.

[21] Proposal for a Directive of the European Parliament and of the Council on the mechanisms to be put in place by the Member States for the prevention of the use of the financial system for the purposes

(4) a proposal for a Regulation on information accompanying transfers of funds and certain crypto-assets,[22] enhancing the traceability of crypto-asset transfers, obliging all crypto-asset service providers to conduct due diligence on their customers, and prohibiting anonymous crypto-asset wallets.

A milestone in the process of – public driven neo-functional[23] – European integration, the proposed legislative reforms will reshape the entire field of AML/CFT, the revolutionary key element being the new institutional framework focused on centralised enforcement, including direct supervision and sanctioning powers in the hands of the new EU agency.

Largely inspired by the SSM institutional setting and interplay with national agencies,[24] the AMLA will become the centrepiece of an integrated system of European and national AML/CFT supervisory authorities.[25] It aims to improve the current AML/CFT supervisory methodology both in terms of quality and efficiency, especially for cases involving cross-border aspects. The AMLA will adopt regulatory technical standards as well as guidelines or recommendations addressed to obliged entities, AML/CFT supervisors or FIUs, absorbing those functions currently conferred to the EBA.

of money laundering or terrorist financing and repealing Directive (EU) 2015/849, COM(2021) 423 final, available at: ec.europa.eu/finance/docs/law/210720-proposal-amld6_en.pdf. Of particular interest is the Commission's use of the draft AMLD6 to provide for a more robust international dimension to the AML/CFT framework, including by better alignment with the revised FATF Recommendations in relation to third countries. A country that is listed by FATF will also be listed by the EU. There will be two EU lists, a 'black list' and a 'grey list', with the latter reflecting the FATF listing. Following listing, the EU will apply measures proportionate to the risks posed by the country. The EU will also be able to list countries that are not listed by FATF, but which pose a peculiar or specific threat to the EU's financial system. The Commission's stated intention is that both it and the AMLA will have the tools to allow the EU to keep pace with a fast-moving and complex international environment with rapidly evolving risks in this way.

[22] Proposal for a Regulation of the European Parliament and of the Council on information accompanying transfers of funds and certain crypto-assets (recast), COM(2021) 421 final.

[23] T Kuhn, 'Grand theories of European integration revisited: does identity politics shape the course of European integration?' (2019) 26 *Journal of European Public Policy* 1213.

[24] In the Commission proposal, the AMLA organisation and governance are conferred to two collegial governing bodies: (1) an Executive Board of five independent full-time members and the Chair of the Authority that will take all decisions towards individual obliged entities or individual supervisory authorities if the AMLA is carrying out its direct or indirect supervisory functions; and (2) a General Board composed of representatives of Member States. The latter might have two different compositions according to the task to be fulfilled, ie a 'supervisory composition' with heads of public authorities responsible for AML supervision, and a 'FIU composition', with heads of FIUs in the Member States. The General Board will adopt all regulatory instruments, draft technical implementation standards, guidelines, and recommendations. In its supervisory composition, it may also provide its opinion on any decision about directly supervised obliged entities prepared by a Joint Supervisory Team before the adoption of the final decision by the Executive Board. Appeals against binding decisions of the AMLA can be addressed to an Administrative Board of Review that delivers non-binding decisions. They are anyhow appealable before the ECJ.

[25] See Recital 12 Proposal for a Regulation COM(2021) 421: 'the Authority and national AML/CFT supervisory authorities ('supervisory authorities') should constitute an AML/CFT supervisory system'.

10.1.2. The Mission of the New AMLA

But the real added value concerns the enforcement. The new authority will take over the direct supervision of a limited number of selected obliged entities – periodically listed – which operate in a large number of Member States or require immediate action to address imminent risks.[26] In particular, two categories should be considered:

> [H]igh-risk cross-border credit and financial institutions with activity in a significant number of Member States, selected periodically; and, in exceptional cases, any entity whose material breaches of applicable requirements are not sufficiently or in a timely manner addressed by its national supervisor.[27]

To this aim, the AMLA will maintain its system in order to assess the risks and vulnerabilities of the selected obliged entities.

Direct supervision implies strong supervisory powers exercised by the adoption of binding decisions, administrative measures and pecuniary sanctions[28] towards directly supervised obliged entities.[29]

For all the other financial or non-financial entities not subject to direct supervision, the AMLA will exercise indirect supervision, meaning monitoring and coordinating national supervisors that are responsible. FIUs will be coordinated by AMLA in setting up joint investigations, and concretely supported by IT and artificial intelligence services, in efforts to improve expert knowledge on detection, analysis and dissemination methods of suspicious transactions that are necessary to conduct threat assessments.

10.1.3. EPPO

Far from being isolated, the AMLA is the latest step in an extensive strategy of centralisation of enforcement power at the EU level. In the wake of the revolutionary SSM and SRM, centralisation of enforcement in combination with the adoption of sectorial single rulebooks has become the main strategy of the EU integration process. By strengthening its traditional approach in terms of neofunctionalism, the Union fosters centralisation beyond the traditional field of competition law. Similar actions involve both administrative and criminal enforcement: the European Public Prosecutor Office (EPPO), for example, now operates at EU level to fight crimes affecting the EU financial budget. Operative since June 2021, the EPPO will be a game-changer as the first centralised criminal enforcement body,[30] including the field of money laundering.

[26] Art 12(3) AMLA Proposal COM(2021) 421.
[27] Recital 15 AMLA Proposal COM(2021) 421.
[28] See Art 21 AMLA Proposal (2021) 421; for the analyses, see section 10.3.3.
[29] For the list of supervisory powers, see Art 20 AMLA Proposal (2021) 421.
[30] Council Regulation (EU) No 1939/2017 of 12 October 2017 implementing enhanced cooperation on the establishment of the European Public Prosecutor's Office ('the EPPO') [2017] OJ L 283/1.

10.1.4. Aim of this Chapter

This chapter analyses the current and future EU enforcement strategies on AML/CFT adopting an integrated approach where administrative and criminal law enforcement are cooperating to pursue a common goal. It will mostly focus on enforcement structures, including actors, powers and tools. Reference to the regulatory framework on AML/CFT will be limited by the scope of the analysis to those elements having a direct impact on enforcement, whereas more substantive rules on compliance and beneficial owners will be left out.

In order to describe the complex interaction between the two enforcement strategies, I will explore the design of the EU multilevel action in the field of AML/CFT according to a matrix composed of four clusters: time (section 10.3); space (section 10.4); punishment (section 10.5); and rights (section 10.6). Each cluster will include references to the actors and powers at national and European level. A final section will offer suggestions for improving the current framework in light of the Action Plan proposed by the EU Commission in May 2020 and made concrete in July 2021. It will also reflect upon the deeper meaning of the plan for European citizens in terms of liberty and privacy, and how this enforcement whatever-it-takes policy reshapes the balance between control and freedoms of individuals and entities. A European information cloud dominated by many centralised supervisory powers is not counterbalanced by a sufficient level of judicial protection, which remains fragmented at national level.

10.2. The Matrix: Decoding the Complexity of a Multilevel Enforcement Strategy

The numbers are clear in depicting the European failure in fighting money laundering: every year millions of suspicious transaction reports (STRs) are transmitted from the private sector to the national FIUs at EU level, but over 65 per cent of reports are received by just two Member States – the UK and the Netherlands – showing a clear under-enforcement in the majority of the Member States. Moreover, only a fraction of these (around 10 per cent) lead to further investigation by competent authorities. The picture is even more dramatic if we observe the European efficiency in confiscation: Europol estimates that barely one per cent of criminal proceeds in the EU is ultimately confiscated by relevant authorities.[31]

[31] 'From Suspicion to Action, Converting financial intelligence into greater operational impact' European Union Agency for Law Enforcement Cooperation (Europol) QL-01-17-932-EN-N (2017) 4; see for further reference Europol reports 'Does crime still pay? Criminal Asset Recovery in the EU – Survey of Statistical Information', available at europol.europa.eu/newsroom/news/does-crime-still-pay and 'Why is cash still king: a strategic report on the use of cash by criminal groups as a facilitator for money laundering', available at europol.europa.eu/content/why-cash-still-king-strategic-report-use-cash-criminal-groups-facilitator-money-laundering.

The reasons behind such a failure are unclear. Data on FIU activity are opaque: numerous red flags are raised, but regulators are understaffed and unequipped to select the real suspicious transactions. Data on criminal responses are scarce and do not provide a clear picture that goes beyond the obvious: national actors lost their grip on predicate offences, money laundering has often a transnational nature, and implies complex investigations. All these arguments are true, but the way they are presented does not help us to really unpack a complicated phenomenon because they do not adopt a holistic approach in which all the different tracks of enforcement are considered.

Several factors contribute to the complexity of AML/CFT enforcement strategies. First, preventive measures are not coordinated with repressive actions, traditionally the division line between administrative and criminal sanctions.

To better understand this complex interaction between administrative and criminal enforcement, in which international standards are translated into regional (European) and national rules conferring supervisory and investigatory powers to a plethora of agencies – regulators, supervisors, various types of law enforcement agency (LEAs), administrative as well as criminal, public and private – I will below divide this analysis into the four matrix clusters: time; space; punishment and rights.

10.3. The Impact of Time: Prevention versus Repression?

10.3.1. Introduction

The architectural design of the European AML/CFT strategies is based on the coexistence of preventive strategies with repressive measures. Specific compliance measures are mandatory for obliged entities and a network of national and European agencies have the mandate to supervise their enforcement. Finally, failure to comply with preventive measures is mostly conferred to administrative enforcement, the criminal enforcement being up until now relegated to dealing with the intentional criminal behaviours of laundering the money and not covering mere lack of compliance. This traditional distinction between the two sectors is now blurred: on one hand administrative sanctions are often defined as 'punitive in nature' and as such they are treated by supreme European courts as implying a higher standard of protection.[32] Second, the criminal law approach to AML is increasingly expanding in order to cover misconducts previously excluded from that realm. As we will observe later,[33] the choice to include within the sphere of

[32] Case C-489/10 *Łukasz Marcin Bonda*, ECLI:EU:C:2012:319; Case C-373/02 *Öztürk*, ECLI:EU:C:2004:232. See also ch 8 in this volume.

[33] See section 10.6.

criminal law mere attempts or offences committed by negligence has the power to multiply the cases of conflict between the two enforcement structures. However, time becomes a crucial factor for an efficient coordination in order to unpack the complex interaction between the different agencies and powers. I will first present their interplay in terms of information exchange, a prerequisite essential to any coordination effort. The efficiency of the double track between administrative and criminal enforcement relies indeed on the possibility for all the agencies involved to react and to model the level and intensity of reaction in an integrated way.

Recent scandals forced the ECB to recognise the need to take part in the AML common effort despite the lack of a specific mandate. The need for a better cooperation has become clear over in recent years.[34] As Danièle Nouy affirmed in 2018, 'a more European approach to combating money laundering should be considered, for example, through enhanced cooperation and exchanges of information between supervisory and AML authorities'.

In particular, coordination between the preventive and the repressive tiers presents several loopholes in the network of information channels involving the main actors: the EBA; the ECB; the European Anti-Fraud office (Office européen de Lutte Anti-Fraude; OLAF); the EPPO; and the future AMLA.

10.3.2. Information Exchange

Some attempts to improve the network of the information channels, in particular between banking supervisors and the agencies in charge of AML/CFT have taken place in the last two years. Thanks to the amendments to the AML Directive entered into force in 2018,[35] a Multilateral Agreement (hereinafter, the 'Agreement') between the ECB and the AML competent authorities (CAs) was signed in January 2019 indicating the practical modalities for exchange of information in the area of prevention of misuse of financial systems for the purpose of money laundering and terrorist financing. The first remarkable step towards a more effective cooperation is that the Agreement refers to a dialogue between the ECB and the CAs: 'The exchange of information shall take place between the CAs and the ECB, on request or on their own initiative'. The exchange is, however, not limited to the duty to answer to specific requests; still, it does include an autonomous input from one agency to the other.

Several types of information might be 'exchanged'. When the request comes from the ECB to the CAs, it might refer to 'information, which is gathered or created by the CA in the exercise of its AML/CFT functions, that is relevant and

[34] See P Demetriades and R Vassileva, 'Money Laundering and Central Bank Governance in the European Union' (2020) 23 *Journal of International Economic Law* 529.

[35] Art 57a(2) AMLD requires the ECB and the Competent Authorities to conclude, with the support of the European Supervisory Authorities, an agreement on the practical modalities for the exchange of information.

necessary for the exercise of the ECB's tasks under the SSM Regulation, including prudential supervision on a consolidated basis'.[36] It may include AML/CFT sanctions or measures imposed on supervised entities or other information gathered from AML/CFT reports received in line with Article 61(1) AMLD and related to material weaknesses in the supervised entity's AML/CFT governance, systems and controls framework or its exposure to significant AML/CFT risks.[37]

The national CAs are in principle obliged to transmit that information to the ECB when the latter requests them. They can also act on their own initiative, providing 'any other information, which they deem to be relevant and necessary for the exercise of the ECB's tasks'.[38]

As for the opposite movement, CAs

> may submit a request to the ECB for information gathered or created by the ECB in the exercise of its direct supervisory tasks under the SSM Regulation that is relevant and necessary for the performance of their tasks in the area of AML/CFT supervision.[39]

Such a request may include information on sanctions or measures imposed on supervised entities by the ECB for shortcomings in their internal governance arrangements or notifications connected with the exercise of the freedom of establishment and the freedom to provide services, or received by the ECB as part of breach reports. This list is not exhaustive: CAs can ask for any information collected by the ECB on 'business model and governance arrangements gathered during the authorisation process or other information related to AML/CFT gathered for the purposes of the assessment of acquisitions of qualifying holdings and suitability of members of management bodies of the supervised entities'.[40]

The ECB should in principle transmit this information upon request or on its own initiative. The only limitation to this duty to cooperate is the respect of national and supranational legality. Both the ECB and the CAs can decline a request for information where: (1) the request does not conform with the Agreement or the applicable laws; or (2) fulfilling the request would require the office 'to act in a manner that would violate any applicable laws'.[41]

The Agreement indicates the need for all parties to keep the information received 'confidential as required by applicable laws and use or disclose it only as permitted by applicable laws' and to act in compliance with data protection laws.[42]

[36] Information might be 'relevant and necessary for the purposes of the assessment of acquisitions of qualifying holdings, the authorisation of supervised entities, notifications connected with the exercise of the freedom of establishment and the freedom to provide services and the assessment of the suitability of members of management bodies of the supervised entities' (Art 3(2)(a) Multilateral Agreement).
[37] Art 3(2) Multilateral Agreement.
[38] ibid, Art 3(3).
[39] ibid, Art 3(4).
[40] ibid, Art 3(5).
[41] ibid, Art 6(3).
[42] ibid, Art 7.

The described mechanism represents the most advanced model of information exchange between the ECB and national authorities in relation to a criminal offence. The possibility for both participants to act on their own initiative has to be welcomed as a positive improvement in the field of inter-agency enforcement mechanisms. Nevertheless, the information flow as described in the Agreement does not necessarily imply a direct contact between the banking regulator and criminal enforcement: The Agreement is intended to channel the flow to the CAs, ie 'the authority or authorities designated as the competent authorities for supervising and ensuring supervised entities' compliance with the requirements of AMLD'.[43] These authorities may have different statutes and powers according to the specific settings of the Member State.

The Agreement coexists with a more general duty of the ECB to request the relevant NCAs to 'refer the matter to the appropriate authorities for investigation and possible criminal prosecution, in accordance with national law'.[44] This duty arises when the ECB acquires evidence of facts potentially giving rise to a criminal offence, including money laundering or terrorism financing.

This provision excludes any direct contact between the European regulator and national criminal agencies. The traditional argument used to justify such limitation is the lack of previous harmonisation of criminal offences. However, this is not the case of AML/CFT, where a certain degree of harmonisation has been attained, although this is more for money laundering than for terrorism. Furthermore, it is not the national CAs mentioned in Article 136 SSMFR that are in charge of AML/CFT, but rather the national regulators. In the case of money laundering, once the ECB reports to the NCAs, national rules on the transfer of information from the administrative to the criminal authorities apply, with no necessary involvement of the local FIU. The ECB no longer has any duty, and it is up to the NCAs to transmit the information to criminal agencies and ensure follow-up of the case.

10.3.3. Initiatives to Improve Information Management

A second important step to increase interagency cooperation has been the approval of Directive (EU) 2019/1153 on facilitating the use of financial information for the prevention, detection, investigation or prosecution of certain criminal offences, including money laundering. According to Recital 9: 'Member States should assist each other in the widest possible way and ensure that information is exchanged in an effective and timely manner in accordance with

[43] ibid, Art 2(f).

[44] See Art 136 Regulation (EU) 468/2014 of the ECB of 16 April 2014 establishing the framework for cooperation within the Single Supervisory Mechanism between the European Central Bank and national competent authorities and with national designated authorities (SSM Framework Regulation; SSMFR) [2014] OJ L 141/1.

national law and the existing Union legal framework'.[45] The Directive intends to complement the rules on the exchange of information at the preventive level of the fourth and fifth AML Directives with provisions on police cooperation, building a bridge between the two enforcement fields. It provides also contributions to smoothen the exchange of information between FIUs of different Member States, and between a FIU and law enforcement authorities of the same Member States, allowing law enforcement authorities direct access to centralised bank account registries.

At the European level, the EBA is in charge of coordination and strengthening the work of the national CAs,[46] in particular FIUs that hold a central position in the chain of actors responsible for the monitoring of money movements in the EU.[47] Nevertheless, only the reform of December 2019 conferred to the EBA additional coordination powers and – embryonal – enforcement tools in the AML/CFT field.[48] Before its effectiveness could be proved, the Commission proposed to replace the EBA's new powers with the forthcoming new agency, the aforementioned AMLA, designed as a real hub for information management at the EU level, including the sensitive role of global coordinator for international cases involving third countries.[49] The legislative reforms package states clearly that only an expedient access and an efficient use of data can lead to a better enforcement, enabling the Authority to react in a timely manner to potential weaknesses and cases of non-compliance by non-selected obliged entities. To that end, 'the Authority should establish a central AML/CFT database with information collected from all

[45] Directive (EU) 2019/1153 of the European Parliament and of the Council of 20 June 2019 laying down rules facilitating the use of financial and other information for the prevention, detection, investigation or prosecution of certain criminal offences, and repealing Council Decision 2000/642/JHA [2019] OJ L 186/122.

[46] See EBA Regulation (EU) No 1093/2010 of the European Parliament and of the Council of 24 November 2010 establishing a European Supervisory Authority (European Banking Authority), amending Decision No 716/2009/EC and repealing Commission Decision 2009/78/EC, as amended by Regulation (EU) 2019/2175 of the European Parliament and of the Council of 18 December 2019 [2010] OJ L 331/12.

[47] F Mouzakiti, 'Cooperation between Financial Intelligence Units in the European Union: Stuck in the middle between the General Data Protection Regulation and the Police Data Protection Directive' (2020) 11 *New Journal of European Criminal Law* 351.

[48] Art 9b EBA Regulation (EU) No 1093/2010.

[49] See Recital 62 AMLA Proposal COM(2021) 421: Since both predicate offences as well as the crime of money laundering itself often are of a global nature, and given that the Union obliged entities to also operate with and in third countries, effective cooperation with all the relevant third country authorities in the areas of both supervision and functioning of FIUs are crucial for strengthening the Union AML/CFT framework. Given the Authority's unique combination of direct and indirect supervision and FIU cooperation-related tasks and powers, it should be able to take an active role in such external cooperation arrangements. Specifically, the Authority should be empowered to develop contacts and enter administrative arrangements with authorities in third countries that have regulatory, supervisory and FIU-related competences. The Authority's role could be particularly beneficial in cases where the interaction of several Union public authorities and FIUs with third country authorities' concerns matters within the scope of the Authority's tasks. In such cases, the Authority should have a leading role in facilitating this interaction.

supervisory authorities and should make such information selectively available to any supervisory authority within the system'.[50] The Authority will also

> manage, host, and maintain FIU.net, the dedicated IT system allowing FIUs to cooperate and exchange information amongst each other and, where appropriate, with their counterparts from third countries and third parties' ensuring that 'at all times the most advanced available state-of-the-art technology is used for the development of the FIU.net.[51]

The recent Proposal witnesses a change of perspective in terms of cooperation between supervisory, administrative and law enforcement authorities, acknowledging how crucial the latter is for successful combatting of money laundering and terrorism financing.[52] To this aim, the Proposal provides for the possibility for AMLA to establish specific working arrangements or to conclude Memoranda of Understanding.[53] However, specific indications are already provided for by the Proposal, including the horizontal information exchange – ie among EU entities such as OLAF, Europol, Eurojust, and the EPPO – as well as the vertical one, with NCAs.

As for the horizontal transmission of information among EU agencies involving potential criminal offences, the Proposal refers to both administrative and criminal agencies. Hence the AMLA will have the duty to transmit to OLAF without delay any information relating to possible cases of fraud, corruption or any other illegal activity affecting the financial interests of the Union.[54]

Emphasising cross-sectorial cooperation, the Proposal refers explicitly to criminal investigative bodies. What is indeed revolutionary and extremely meaningful in terms of pursuing an integrated enforcement strategy is the provision of a direct link with the EPPO, in charge of criminal investigations of crimes affecting

[50] See Recital 14 AMLA Proposal COM(2021) 421. This data should also cover withdrawal of authorisation procedures, fit and proper assessments of shareholders and members of individual obliged entities as this will enable relevant authorities to duly consider possible shortcomings of specific entities and individuals that might have materialised in other Member States. The database should also include statistical information about supervisory and other public authorities involved in AML/CFT supervision.

[51] See Recital 35 AMLA Proposal COM(2021) 421.

[52] See ibid, Recital 61.

[53] See ibid, Recital 59: 'The Authority should establish cooperative relations with the relevant Union agencies and bodies, including Europol, Eurojust, the EPPO, and the European Supervisory Authorities, namely the European Banking Authority, the European Securities and Markets Authority and the European Insurance and Occupational Pensions Authority. To improve cross-sectoral supervision and a better cooperation between prudential and AML/CFT supervisors the Authority should also establish cooperative relations with the authorities competent for prudential supervision of financial sector obliged entities, including the European Central Bank with regard to matters relating to the tasks conferred on it by Council Regulation (EU) 1024/201314, as well as with resolution authorities as defined in Art 3 of Directive (EU) 2014/59/EU of the European Parliament and the Council and designated Deposit Guarantee Schemes authorities as defined in Art 2(1), point 18 of Directive 2014/49/EU of the European Parliament and the Council.'

[54] See ibid, Recital 14.

the European financial interests.[55] Pursuant to Article 24 Council Regulation (EU) 2017/1939, the Authority 'will without undue delay report to the EPPO any criminal conduct in respect of which it could exercise its competence'.[56]

However, the Proposal is careful in defining the limits of such information exchange: confidentiality obligations as well as data protection might hinder the full disclosure. Confidentiality covering every operational data and professional secrecy restrictions apply even within organs of the Union. However,

> confidential information listed that relates to a supervisory procedure can be fully or partially disclosed to the obliged entities which are parties to such supervisory procedure, subject to the legitimate interest of legal and natural persons other than the relevant party, in the protection of their business secrets.[57]

10.4. One World, a Multidimensional Space to Launder Money

10.4.1. Introduction

The second cluster in the matrix concerns the enforcement space of the AML/CFT strategies. Money laundering – and often terrorism – has a worldwide dimension and a transnational nature. It represents a form of organised economic crime 'grounded in treaty-based obligations that apply between states and impose suppression obligations on domestic jurisdictions'.[58] As a result, the authority to penalise is grounded in national law but the offence often involves several jurisdictions. National agencies are called to indirectly enforce international and regional law, but 'the perpetrator is not treated as an "international criminal"'.[59]

Money laundering is a criminal activity that, more than others, has been able to take advantage of globalised markets. Every single step of the laundering process – be it the placement, the layering or the integration – has evolved englobing new financial opportunities generated by globalisation as well as by new technologies.[60]

[55] S Allegrezza, 'The European Public Prosecutor Office' in K Ambos and P Rackow (eds), *Cambridge Companion to European Criminal Law* (CUP, forthcoming).

[56] See Recital 14, AMLA Proposal COM(2021) 421.

[57] See ibid, Recital 56.

[58] C Stahn, *A Critical Introduction to International Criminal Law* (CUP, 2019) 106. On transnational criminal law, see N Boister, 'Transnational Criminal Law?' (2003) 14 *EJ European Journal of International Law* 953.

[59] ibid.

[60] See the FATF report, 'Opportunities and Challenges of New Technologies for AML/CFT' (July 2021), available at www.fatf-gafi.org/media/fatf/documents/reports/Opportunities-Challenges-of-New-Technologies-for-AML-CFT.pdf; M Campbell-Verduyn, 'Bitcoin, crypto-coins, and global anti-money laundering governance' (2018) 69 *Crime Law Soc Change*, 283; G Dimitropoulos, 'The Law of Blockchain' (2020) 95 *Washingtnoon Law Review* 1117.

Globalisation also concerns the legal framework:[61] international standards, in particular the FATF guidelines, represent the blueprint for every legal reform promoted in Europe in the last decades.[62] Those standards determine the mandatory content of more elaborated regulatory framework proposed by the EU. This has been the case for the fifth AML/CFT Directive as well as for the Directive, dedicated to criminal law,[63] and it represents the basis for the many proposals of the reform package adopted in light of the 2020 Action Plan.[64]

Globalisation of the regulatory standards is unfortunately not reflected in enforcement powers which steadily reside in the hands of national authorities, whose capacity to counter transnational phenomena are limited by existing borders. The problem is particularly acute at international level, where the current scheme of mutual legal assistance has led to extraterritorial actions.[65] This is even more evident when one considers new technologies. The impact of globalisation on parcelled enforcement is also increased by the capacity of financial operators to use every technological innovation made available by the digitalisation of finance. The case of cryptocurrencies as the elective field for money laundering activities shows how quick the blockchain revolution has been metabolised by financial crime.[66]

[61] V Mitsilegas and B Gilmore, 'The EE Legislative Framework Against Money Laundering and Terrorist Finance: A Critical Analysis in the Light of Evolving Global Standards' (2007) 56 *International & Comparative Law Quarterly* 119.

[62] FATF report 'Opportunities and Challenges of New Technologies for AML/CFT' (n 60).

[63] V Covolo, 'The EU Response to Criminal Misuse of Cryptocurrencies: The Young, Already Outdated 5th Anti-Money Laundering Directive', University of Luxembourg Law Working Paper No 2019-015 (6 January 2020) 1–25.

[64] 'Anti-money laundering and countering the financing terrorism legislative package', available at ec.europa.eu/info/publications/210720-anti-money-laundering-countering-financing-terrorism_en.

[65] MK Wright, 'Financing Cr-ISIS: The Efficacy of Mutual Legal Assistance Treaties in the Context of Money Laundering and Terror Finance' (2019) 52 *Vanderbilt Journal of Transnational Law* 299.

[66] S Allegrezza and V Covolo (eds), *Cryptocurrencies and Crime* (forthcoming, 2022); T Wahl, 'AML Package IV: EU Traceability of Funds Legislation to Be Extended to Crypto Assets' eucrim.eu (5 August 2021). EU rules on providing information on money transfers have left aside so far transfers of virtual assets. However, money laundering activities can take place through the transfer of crypto-assets (eg Bitcoin and Ethereum) and damage the integrity of the financial system in the same way as wire funds transfers. In order to close this loophole, the Commission proposed a recast of Regulation 2015/847, which, as an important AML/CFT measure, lays down rules on the information on payers and payees, accompanying transfers of funds. Hence, the Commission proposal will extend the scope of the Regulation to transfers of crypto-assets. This means that crypto-asset service providers will be obliged to provide information on the sender and beneficiary with all transfers of virtual assets, so that the identity of persons who do business with crypto-assets and suspicious transactions in this sector can be identified for AML/CFT purposes. The crypto-asset service provider of the beneficiary must also implement effective procedures, including, where appropriate, *ex post* monitoring or real-time monitoring, in order to detect whether the required information on the originator or the beneficiary is missing. The new provisions would align EU legislation with key standards of the FATF, which recommended the extension of AML/CFT measures to the crypto sector in 2019. The recast of Regulation (EU) 2015/847 is closely connected with the proposal for an EU AML/CFT Regulation. In the future, all crypto-asset service providers will be obliged to conduct due diligence on their customers. In addition, anonymous crypto-asset wallets will be prohibited in the EU. The proposals presented on 20 July 2021 are part of a comprehensive overhaul of the existing EU AML/CFT framework, which will, inter alia, comprise a single EU rulebook against money laundering and terrorist financing.

The use of cryptocurrency is not the only novelty in relation to technologies and digitalisation. Cybercrime has become one of the first predicate offences in terms of relevance. 46 per cent of all business activities have been the victim of cybercrime in 2020 alone. These offences stay often under the radar because the business actors prefer to avoid reporting cyber-fraud to the CAs, instead paying – often in cryptocurrencies – to be very quickly back in business.

No less important is the impact of algorithmic systems on the methods of laundering money. This combination of cybercrime – reluctant to accept geographical barriers of jurisdiction[67] – and algorithmic tools redesigned the traditional scheme of money laundering adding technological complexity to a legal conundrum.

Difficulties in facing transnational offences are manifest even within the EU and unfortunately not limited to money laundering. Most of the financial crimes having a transnational nature have no correspondent opponents, national jurisdictions' action being confined within their territories. Several bodies are involved in the European AML/CFT strategy but none of them has had – until very recently – direct competence throughout the EU, neither in administrative nor criminal law. Not surprisingly, though, the absolute majority of the above-mentioned money laundering cases have been investigated and sanctioned by American regulators that are willing to enforce their jurisdiction without hesitation worldwide.

A different picture might come with the approval of the AMLA Proposal: according to the Commission proposal, the new agency will have full competence throughout the Union, no exception being provided for by the Proposal in terms of the geographic boundaries of the supervisory action. This differentiates the AMLA from its siblings, such as the ECB-SSM mechanism, whose competence of direct supervision is limited to the Eurozone. The discrepancy between the areas of competence brings additional complexity because the EU regulators might have a different level of knowledge – and accordingly a different capacity to promptly coordinate and react – due to the lack of sectorial competence.

10.4.2. Criminal Enforcement Falling Short

Deeper concerns are raised by fragmentation of criminal enforcement in terms of geographical effectiveness. The recent scandals mentioned above offer a depressing but realistic picture: even after the American regulators took concrete actions against European credit institutions, national prosecutors' and enforcement agencies' actions did not lead to any punitive response against individuals or entities.

As for the ABLV case, the Latvian Corruption Prevention and Combating Bureau has found no proof to the claims of the US Department of the Treasury

[67] L Luparia and G Soana, 'Investigating and Prosecuting Crypto-crime: Challenges and Opportunities' in S Allegrezza and V Covolo (eds), *Cryptocurrencies and Crime* (forthcoming 2022) 3–8.

Official Financial Crimes Enforcement Network (FinCEN) on the top management of ABLV Bank's involvement in a large bribery: the case was dropped. As for the role played by Danske Bank in that affair, Danish prosecutors dropped charges against the nine top managers because no individual had shown negligence to such an extent that it could be characterised as gross. In sum, criminal enforcement in these cases has been an almost total failure.

In Germany, two regulatory actions were brought against Deutsche Bank over its controversial relationship with the now notorious Estonian branch of Denmark's Danske Bank. The first fine was imposed by New York regulators in July 2020, with Deutsche Bank agreeing to pay US $150 million in penalties for having failed to take appropriate action to prevent Danske Estonia from transferring billions of dollars of suspicious transactions through Deutsche Bank accounts in New York (over €200 billion).[68]

Only then did the German prosecutor imposed a fine of US $15.8 million on the German bank for its failure to promptly submit reports that would have alerted criminal investigators to suspicious bank transactions.[69]

Even the advent of the EPPO will not radically change this picture, and the reasons are twofold. First, the competence of the European Prosecutor on money laundering is limited to those cases involving property derived from the criminal offences affecting EU financial interests.[70] The latter might evoke the case as a form of ancillary competence only for money laundering cases not directly involving EU dirty money but presenting somehow an inextricable link with a crime falling within the competence of the EPPO.[71] Second, the limited material scope is combined with a limited territorial competence. Not all the Member States participate in the EPPO initiative, approved only thanks to an enhanced cooperation mechanism,[72]

[68] See the report of the International consortium of investigative journalists, available at www.icij.org/investigations/fincen-files/german-prosecutors-drop-probe-into-deutsche-bank-ties-to-estonian-dirty-money-scandal.

[69] ibid.

[70] Art 4 Directive (EU) 2017/1371 of the European Parliament and of the Council of 5 July 2017 on the fight against fraud to the Union's financial interests by means of criminal law.

[71] S Allegrezza, 'A European Public Prosecutor Office to Protect Common Financial Interests: A Milestone for the EU Integration Process' in K Ambos and P Rackow (eds), *Cambridge Companion to European Criminal Law* (CUP, forthcoming); K Ambos, *European Criminal Law* (CUP, 2018), 577; J Öberg, 'The European Public Prosecutor: Quintessential supranational criminal law?' (2021) 28 *Maastricht Journal of European and Comparative Law* 170; F Giuffrida, 'The European Public Prosecutor's Office: King without kingdom?' CEPS Research report (2017) 10–11; A Nieto Martin and M Munoz de Morales Romero, 'The Office of the European Public Prosecutor and Related Offences: Deconstructing the Problem' in P Asp (ed), *The European Public Prosecutor Office – Legal and Criminal Policy Perspective* (Jure, 2015) 120 ff.

[72] The entry into force of the Lisbon Treaty constituted a turning point in the political debate around EPPO, because of the introduction of the enhanced cooperation mechanism under Art 86 TFEU. Art 86(1) of the Treaty of Lisbon substantially reflects the text of Art III-274 of the Constitutional Treaty of 29 October 2004, which was signed but not ratified or entered into force among the Member States of the EU, and expressly introduced a legal basis for the establishment of the EPPO, establishing that in order to combat crimes affecting the financial interests of the Union, the Council, acting by means of regulations to be adopted in accordance with a special legislative procedure, may establish a European Public Prosecutor's Office 'from Eurojust'. The decision must be taken unanimously,

finally accepted by 22 Member States.[73] This means that the EPPO, the ECB-SSM and the future AMLA do not share the same geographical area of competence, and boundaries are impacting the information-sharing and cooperation effort. When the future AMLA will embrace the entire Union, the ECB-SSM will be limited to the Eurozone and the EPPO to the 22 participating Member States, which have not not necessarily adopted the euro: Ireland has the euro as a currency but refused to join the EPPO; Bulgaria and Romania are part of the EPPO but not part of the Eurozone.

This shows the recent tendency of multiplying internal clusters of EU countries to increase the integration process on a sectorial basis. However, the next few years will tell us what are the long-term consequences of having a sort of *chronologie variable* within the Union and what it means in terms of governance and democracy.

Lastly, the recent Directive (EU) 2018/1673, aimed at combating money laundering by means of criminal law[74] and whose definition of 'money laundering' represents the main reference for the entire enforcement system, won't be applicable 'to money laundering involving property derived from criminal offences affecting the Union's financial interests, which is subject to specific rules as laid down in Directive (EU) 2017/1371'.[75] The rationale of such an exclusion is hard to comprehend: as we will see, Member States are called to adapt their criminal law to the Directive requirements, but this reform won't affect the cases of money laundering involving EU frauds.

10.5. Differentiating Sanctions: Limits of a Double-Track System

Sanctions compose the third cluster of this matrix. Two main phenomena might be observed in AML/CFT in recent years: an increase in administrative sanctions

after approval by the European Parliament. In the absence of this requirement, a group of at least nine Member States may establish an enhanced cooperation procedure under Arts 20(2) and 329(1) TEU, informing the European Parliament, the Council and the Commission. In this context, noting the lack of unanimity required by Art 86(1) TFEU, the mechanism of enhanced cooperation has been the main road leading to the approval of the relevant regulation and allowing at least nine Member States to overcome the lack of unanimity of the Council members and to proceed with the establishment of the body.

[73] All EU Member States participated in the initiative except for Ireland, Poland, Denmark, Sweden and Hungary. So far, Hungary, Poland and Sweden have decided not to join the EPPO. Denmark and Ireland have opted out from the area of freedom, security and justice (AFSJ). Working arrangements with these five non-participating Member States are being established to define how the EPPO will cooperate with them.

[74] See section 10.6.

[75] Recital 10 and Art 1(2) Directive (EU) 2017/1371 of the European Parliament and of the Council of 5 July 2017 on the fight against fraud to the Union's financial interests by means of criminal law [2017] OJ L 198/29. According to Recital 10: 'This is without prejudice to the possibility for Member States to transpose this Directive and Directive (EU) 2017/1371 by means of a single comprehensive framework at national level. In accordance with Art 325(2) of the Treaty on the Functioning of the European Union (TFEU), the Member States are to take the same measures to counter fraud affecting the financial interests of the Union as they take to counter fraud affecting their own financial interests'.

established at the EU level as a response to the fragmented and inefficient reactions by NCAs; and the progressive transformation of criminal law intervention. I will first introduce the recent proposal on sanctioning powers conferred to AMLA and then explain in detail the EU action against AML/CFT by means of criminal law.

Administrative pecuniary sanctions are at the epicentre of the reform package presented in July 2021. In a nutshell, the future AMLA will have direct supervisory powers as well as direct sanctioning powers towards the so-called selected obliged entities. When a selected obliged entity 'intentionally or negligently breaches a requirement … under directly applicable acts of Union law …, or does not comply with a binding decision' adopted by the Authority, the latter 'may impose administrative pecuniary sanctions'.[76]

The AMLA body in charge of sanctioning is the Executive Board of the Authority and the material scope will be defined by the Proposal for a Regulation on the prevention of the use of the financial system for the purposes of money laundering or terrorist financing[77] as well as from the Proposal for a Directive on information accompanying transfers of funds and certain crypto-assets.[78]

The sanctions in question have a clear punitive nature according to the well-known Engel criteria: for material breaches of requirements related to customer due diligence, group policies and procedures and/or reporting obligations identified in two or more Member States, the sanction shall amount to at least €1 million and shall not exceed €2 million, or one per cent of the annual turnover. When the breach does not concern transnational activities, the sanction shall amount to at least €500,000 and shall not exceed €1 million, or 0.5 per cent of the annual turnover. For breaches of all other requirements, a higher sanction will be applied in case of transnational activities. For material breaches of the decisions of the Authority, the sanction shall amount to at least €100,000 and shall not exceed €1 million.[79]

For the sake of the proportionality principle, the amount of the penalty 'shall be adjusted, where needed, by taking into account aggravating or mitigating factors'[80] duly listed in an Annex to the Proposal. Where the benefit derived from the breach by the natural or legal person held responsible or the losses to third parties caused by the breach can be determined, they shall be added to the total amount of the sanction, after application of the coefficients.

When the entity is not a selected one, the AMLA retains an indirect supervisory and sanctioning power: the Authority 'may require financial supervisors to open proceedings with a view to taking action in order to ensure that appropriate

[76] Art 21 AMLA Regulation Proposal COM(2021) 421.

[77] AMLR, COM(2021) 420, 2021/0239 (COD).

[78] Directive Proposal for a Regulation of the European Parliament and of the Council on information accompanying transfers of funds and certain crypto-assets (recast) COM/2021/422 final.

[79] Art 21 AMLA Regulation Proposal COM(2021) 421.

[80] ibid.

administrative pecuniary sanctions are imposed'.[81] All the sanctions applied by financial supervisors shall be effective, proportionate and dissuasive.[82]

The first subparagraph shall be applicable to administrative pecuniary sanctions to be imposed on selected obliged entities for breaches of national law transposing the Draft Directive on the prevention of the use of the financial system for the purposes of money laundering or terrorist financing[83] and to any administrative pecuniary sanctions to be imposed on members of the management board of selected obliged entities who under national law are responsible for a breach by an obliged entity.

This extensive sanctioning power covering both intentional and negligent behaviours are a potential source of conflict with criminal law enforcement, radically redesigned by the Directive (EU) 2018/1673, not yet transposed by the large majority of the Member States.

10.6. A Stronger Criminal Law Response for Money Laundering? A Critical Analysis of the Directive on Combating Money Laundering Using Criminal Law

Criminal law enforcement is intended to be a complementary action with the administrative tier of AML. That coordination often proves to be far from optimal.

Solidly in the hands of national systems, criminal sanctions are currently under revision as Member States are called to implement the Directive (EU) 2018/1673, approved in 2018 in relation to money laundering criminal offences. Its transposition into national law was supposed to happen by 3 December 2020, but this process is far from being completed.

Based on Article 83(1) TFEU, conferring to the EU the power to introduce minimum rules on the definition of criminal offences and sanctions in areas of particularly serious crime with a cross-border dimension, this act is the first Directive to tackle money laundering by expanding the scope of criminal law and toughening criminal sanctions. The previous Framework Decision 2001/500/JHS, the very first European act imposing the obligation on Member States to criminalise money laundering based on COE Strasbourg Convention of 1990, fell short in reducing national differences, producing very limited harmonisation of predicate offences and sanctions.[84]

[81] ibid, Art 21(9).

[82] ibid, Art 21(10).

[83] Proposal for a Directive of the European Parliament and of the Council on the mechanisms to be put in place by the Member States for the prevention of the use of the financial system for the purposes of money laundering or terrorist financing and repealing Directive (EU) 2015/849, COM(2021) 423 final.

[84] Art 2 FD 2001/500/JHS on money laundering, the identification, tracing, freezing, seizing and confiscation of instrumentalities and the proceeds of crime. Limited to intentional breaches, the

Furthermore, the Framework Decision (FD) did not include self-laundering as a criminal offence nor foresee any liability of legal persons. As for predicate offences, their harmonisation was very limited: an offence could qualify as predicate offence for money laundering only when it was considered a serious one according to the foreseen penalty,[85] but no list of specific misconducts to be considered as mandatorily 'predicate' was offered. This led to a fragmented picture throughout Member States because of the broad discretion left to national systems, creating inefficiencies in investigating and sanctioning transnational money laundering.

Directive (EU) 2018/1673 increases the scope of application in several ways. First, it confirms the definition of the laundering conducts, but includes an extended definition of self-laundering too.[86] It is now mandatory for Member States to take necessary measures to make sure that the offence described in Article 3(1) is punishable as a criminal offence when committed by the person who committed or was involved in the criminal activity, even if the person is also the one who committed the predicate offence, in the very moment in which the money he/she collected because of his/her crime has been used. Article 5 of the Directive indicates aiding, abetting, inciting and attempting as potential sources of criminal liability. This large sphere might include financial operations carried out by professionals in the field of finance, offering an open door for criminal enforcement to complete regulatory rules imposed on financial professionals to prevent money laundering.

In terms of the definition of illicit properties, the Directive included all different forms of virtual assets or cryptocurrencies,[87] in line with the provisions of the fifth Directive.

The main novelty of the new Directive is the addition of negligence – *culpa* – to intent as the subjective element required to be held liable of money laundering.

Framework Decision already described the main conducts of money laundering: (1) the conversion or transfer of property, knowing that such property is proceeds, for the purpose of concealing or disguising the illicit origin of the property or of assisting any person who is involved in the commission of the predicate offence to evade the legal consequences of his actions; (2) the concealment or disguise of the true nature, source, location, disposition, movement, rights with respect to, or ownership of, property, knowing that such property is proceeds; (3) the acquisition, possession or use of property, knowing, at the time of receipt, that such property was proceeds; (4) the participation in, association or conspiracy to commit, attempts to commit and aiding, abetting, facilitating and counselling the commission of any of the abovementioned offences.

[85] Art 1(b) FD 2001/500/JHS: 'Such offences shall in any event include offences which are punishable by deprivation of liberty or a detention order for a maximum of more than one year or, as regards those States which have a minimum threshold for offences in their legal system, offences punishable by deprivation of liberty or a detention order for a minimum of more than six months'.

[86] Art 3(5) Directive (EU) 2018/1673: 'Member States shall take the necessary measures to ensure that the conduct referred to in points (a) and (b) of paragraph 1 is punishable as a criminal offence when committed by persons who committed, or were involved in, the criminal activity from which the property was derived'.

[87] Definition of 'Property' (Art 2(2) Directive (EU) 2018/1673): 'assets of any kind, whether corporeal or incorporeal, movable or immovable, tangible or intangible, and legal documents or instruments in any form, including electronic or digital, evidencing title to, or an interest in, such assets'. This is repeated in Recital 6.

When the offender *suspected or ought to have known* that the property was derived from criminal activity,[88] in light of the specific circumstances of the case 'such as the value of the property is disproportionate to the lawful income of the accused person and … the criminal activity and acquisition of property occurred within the same time frame', he/she can be charged for money laundering.[89] The inclusion of negligence is a mere option and not an obligation for the Member States. Once again, this is highly relevant for professionals whose criminal liability in relation to money laundering expanded because of the new Directive. The Directive considers as an aggravated circumstance the fact that the offender is an obliged entity that has committed the offence in the exercise of its professional activities. The goal is to sanction the professionals that are using their know-how and competences in the service of money laundering operations.

As for the predicate offences, the Directive adopts a double strategy: first, any offence punishable by deprivation of liberty for a maximum of more than one year (or for a minimum of more than six months) should be considered as a predicate offence, in line with the previous solution offered by the Framework Decision. However, for 22 serious offences the Member States have no choice but to criminalise them as predicate offences, irrespective of the level of the sanction provided under national law. The list includes some obvious offences, such as terrorism, organised crime, tax offences, drug trafficking, but also new ones, such as cybercrime. It is worth noting that the Directive does not define the content of the offences but merely indicates their legal definition. This is left to national legislations, creating major concerns surrounding fragmented rules, penitentiary systems and fixing fines. In terms of enforcement, the Directive does not require a prior or simultaneous conviction for the criminal activity from which the property was derived nor the legal certitude about its criminal origins. It suffices that the property was derived from a criminal activity, without it being necessary to establish all the factual elements or all circumstances relating to that criminal activity, including the identity of the perpetrator. This is highly problematic because it leaves room for enormous discretion by judicial authorities to base the prosecution only on the suspicion of illicit origin of the properties. Consequently, it might entail the shift of the burden of proof on the defendant to state the licit origin of each property.

10.7. The Controversial Relationship between AML Strategies and Data Protection

One major issue in the prevention of the use of the financial system for the purposes of money laundering and terrorist financing concerns the data

[88] Art 3(2) Directive (EU) 2018/1673.
[89] ibid, Recital 13.

protection implications of AML laws. The issue has grown in importance in light of recent globalisation and technological development, which has made financial crimes more complex and harder to prevent. Accordingly, financial institutions are obliged to process and collect increasing amounts of personal data on a daily basis in an effort to prevent such crimes. In particular, the processing of and access to financial data collected by obliged entities could constitute crucial – and sometimes the only – evidence for the purpose of following the monetary transactions in order to detect suspicious money flows.

However, it's unclear how to apply the rules of the GDPR in the context of the AML/CFT legal framework, pursuant to Article 6(3) GDPR. GDPR limits how organisations can use and reuse personal data, while also restricting how long they may retain that data. the collected data can be sensitive, which makes the data protection of individuals extremely important. This has led to the necessity to strike a fair balance between the interest to prevent money laundering and other serious financial crimes, on the one hand, and to protect the interests underlying the fundamental rights to data protection and privacy, on the other. To this aim, specific rules with regard to the general conditions governing the lawfulness of processing of financial data by obliged entities may help to promote compliance and create more legal certainty for obliged entities, without losing the effectiveness of preventing financial crimes.

The question of the compatibility of EU law with requirements concerning the protection of personal data has been extensively dealt with by the ECJ in its existing case law regarding data retention regulation. In several recent cases the Court was called to assess which objective can justify general and indiscriminate retention of traffic and location data and access to these data by NCAs. Records of electronic communication metadata allow detailed conclusions about habits of daily life, such as places of residence, activities carried out, or social relations. Access to this data is necessary to provide evidence and investigative leads on a wide range of financial crimes, such as fraud, insider dealing and market abuse. However, the Court clearly adopted strict requirements for law enforcement access to electronic communications metadata, thus prioritising the necessity to protect privacy. More specifically, in the decisions *La Quadrature du Net ao*[90] and *Privacy International*,[91] the Court ruled that the retention of traffic and location data of all users of electronic communications systems for a limited period of time can be justified when the Member State is confronted with a serious threat to national security. In the subsequent decision *HK v Prokuratuur*,[92] the Court not only confirmed these conclusions, but clarified the circumstances in which access to traffic and location data retained by providers of electronic communications services may, for the purposes of crime prevention, investigation and prosecution,

[90] Joined Cases C-511/18, C-512/18 and C-520/18 *La Quadrature du Net oa*, ECLI:EU:C:2020:791.
[91] Case C-623/17 *Privacy International*, ECLI:EU:C:2020:790.
[92] Case C-746/18 *HK v Prokuratuur*, ECLI:EU:C:2021:152.

be granted to public authorities. In particular, in accordance with the principle of proportionality, the Court holds that only the objectives of combating serious crime or preventing serious threats to public security are capable of justifying access to traffic or location data, and that it is essential that the conditions for access to this data be subject to a prior review carried out either by a court or an independent administrative body. Finally, it is worth noting that the same question has been recently referred to the ECJ also in relation to the conformity of EU law on market abuse with requirements concerning the protection of personal data. In the request for a preliminary ruling lodged on 20 August 2020,[93] the Cour de Cassation (French Supreme Court) has asked the ECJ to assess whether the national legislature must be able to require electronic communications operators to retain connection data on a temporary but general basis in order to enable the administrative authority, in the event of the emergence of grounds for suspecting certain persons of being involved in insider dealing or market manipulation, to require the operator to surrender existing records of traffic data.

Consistently with this case law, the European Data Protection Board (EDPB) has recently expressed its opinion on the European Commission of an Action Plan for a comprehensive Union policy on preventing money laundering and terrorist financing, emphasising how important it is to include specific provisions in the upcoming legislative proposals in order to specify the application of the GDPR in the context of the AML/CFT legal framework, pursuant to Article 6(3) GDPR. Subject to the principle of proportionality, limitations to the right to privacy and data protection for AML purposes may be made only if they are necessary and genuinely meet objectives of general interest recognised by the Union.

10.8. Divergent in Defence: Conclusions

The historic stream of money laundering scandals involving European credit institutions revealed the fragmentation existing among Member States in terms of legal framework and effective response, triggering a harsh political debate within the EU. The absolute urgency for stricter rules and better enforcement at EU level became apparent and was promptly made concrete by a rich package of reforms. From a governance point of view, a strong neo-functionalism dominates recent trends: the EU integration via enforcement is conceived as a 'technocratic, elite-led gradualism, combined with corporatist-style engagement of affected interests'.[94] Efficacy and efficiency are somehow predominant over legitimacy in the political debate. Centralisation as a technique is not necessarily negative. There is a rather strong need for the EU to increase centralisation in emerging fields.

[93] Case C-397/20 *Cilevič*.

[94] PP Craig, 'Integration, Democracy and Legitimacy', Legal Research Paper Series, Paper No 47/2011 (August 2011) 5.

This movement toward the centre should however include all the different aspects of enforcement, whereas the current EU action seems to be limited to the punitive sphere, with the corollary of multiplication of sanctioning tracks and almost no legislative action in terms of judicial review and defence rights of individual and entities involved.

National actors lost their grip – in fact, a grip they never had. But their relegation to a subalternate position has been achieved with sectorial, non-coordinate action and without taking into account all the parts involved, especially in terms of judicial control over such powerful sanctioning powers. This unprecedented increase of direct enforcement powers conferred to EU entities and exercised at a centralised level are not accompanied by a sufficient set of defence rights and procedural safeguards for the entities involved.

The first seven years of the parallel ECB-SSM system shows a very low rate of enforcement at centralised level and some ECJ reprimands on the way the SSM exercises its powers.[95]

When it comes to individuals, they are currently within the scope of direct enforcement of the future AMLA. Hence, their rights might be highly compromised, and their defence action limited when the investigation takes place at the centralised level and the EU regulator requests to NCAs to act against the individuals. Materials collected at the centralised level might be submitted to a strict confidentiality regime, excluding a full disclosure. It is left to national systems to offer a high level of protection, in both administrative and criminal proceedings. This inevitably creates disparities among the Union, where the systems are far from harmonised. Despite the several directives approved in recent years, criminal investigations in particular are still parcelled and diverge from country to country. An increasing number of cases before the ECJ shows how the lack of a previous harmonisation leads to clashes when the systems are called to cooperate.[96] The lack of reflection on several pivotal guarantees in punitive proceedings led to revolutionary decisions of both the ECHR and the ECJ on the need of a public hearing, the right to silence, and *ne bis in idem*.[97]

Geographical and chronological discrepancies in terms of competences have a spill-over effect on building up an area of integrated intervention. Despite political reluctance, the EU could benefit from an overarching reflection on enforcement that overcomes the current non-systematic approach in favour of a choral one, in which the several actors are called to collaborate in shaping future solutions.

[95] Penalties imposed by the ECB within the remit of its supervisory tasks are publicly available at bankingsupervision.europa.eu/banking/sanctions/html/index.en.html.

[96] See eg for the European Arrest Warrant: Case C-479/21 *Governor of Cloverhill Prison and Others*, ECLI:EU:C:2021:919; Case C-221/19 *AV* ECLI:EU:C:2021:278; Case C-414/20 PPU *MM*, ECLI:EU:C:2021:4; for the European Investigation Order, see eg Case C-66/20 *XK*, ECLI:EU:C:2021:670; Case C-584/19 *Aea*, Case C-584/19, *Aeo*, ECLI:EU:C:2020:1002; and Pending Cases C-724/19 *HP*, ECLI:EU:C:2021:1020; and Case C-852/19 *Ivan Gavanozov*, ECLI:EU:C:2021:902.

[97] See ch 9 in this volume.

11

Concluding Remarks on Interdisciplinarity and Fairness in Financial Law

JAN CRIJNS, MATTHIAS HAENTJENS AND RIJNHARD HAENTJENS

11.1. Introduction

In our introduction to this volume, we started from the premise that enforcement is a critical element of law in general and of financial law in particular. In the chapters that follow, a detailed picture is painted of how financial law is enforced through private law, administrative law and criminal law, with a specific focus on the European dimension of financial law and how this dimension influences the enforcement of financial law at a national level. Without striving to do justice to all findings of the previous chapters, in this final chapter we will draw some general conclusions by highlighting two themes that seem to be present in most, if not all, chapters: (1) the interdisciplinary character of financial law as a legal domain; and (2) the delicate balance between effective enforcement and notions of fairness in financial law.

As we will see, both themes are strongly interrelated, since the interdisciplinarity of financial law and its enforcement has significant consequences for the legal position of natural and legal persons involved. Several contributors to this volume have already called attention to this interrelationship, specifically where it regards the legal position of natural and legal persons within administrative law and criminal law and, more specifically, at the intersection of both legal disciplines.[1] In this final chapter we will highlight some problematic aspects of the legal position of natural and legal persons in the context of financial law enforcement, and place them in the broader context of the interdisciplinary character of financial law. We will conclude that the legitimate drive for effective enforcement of financial law needs to go hand in hand with respect for fundamental rights of natural and legal

[1] See eg chs 5, 8 and 9.

persons subject to measures of enforcement, while the balancing of these interests has to be considered as a shared responsibility of the EU and its Member States.

11.2. Interdisciplinarity of Financial Law and its Enforcement

As a primarily functional legal domain, financial law can be characterised as an interdisciplinary legal domain by its nature: as the various contributions to this volume show, all three main legal disciplines, viz private, administrative and criminal law, are involved.[2] Substantive rules of financial law are mainly a matter of administrative law, but when it comes to the enforcement of financial law, this legal discipline is complemented by criminal law and private law, whilst criminal law functions as a capstone for the enforcement of what are considered to be the most serious breaches of financial law.[3] As a consequence, financial law needs to be studied from the perspective of multiple legal disciplines, each with their own character, actors, rules and principles.

This fragmented picture is further complicated by the fact that financial law is mainly EU law or at least originates from EU regulation. This is especially the case for substantive norms of financial law, since the enforcement of financial law is mainly left to national law and to national authorities. Nevertheless, the enforcement of financial law is also significantly influenced by EU law, not only for the goals to be achieved but (sometimes) also for the legal disciplines to be employed and the specific sanctions to be used. Although the EU principle of national procedural autonomy promotes reluctance in prescribing to Member States how to organise their rules of procedure, their court system and their means of enforcement, we have seen various examples of EU financial law with great relevance for the means of enforcement at the national level of the Member States, often boosted by the important principles of effectiveness and equivalence as general principles for the enforcement of EU law.[4] Moreover, and perhaps somewhat contradictory to these latter principles, EU law also influences the enforcement of financial law by formulating fundamental rights for the legal protection of natural and legal person subjected to measures of enforcement.[5] Most of these fundamental rights are laid down in general in the ECHR and the Charter of Fundamental Rights of

[2] See, for an overview, ch 2.

[3] See ch 7 for a critical view on the way the Dutch legislator criminalises breaches of substantive rules of financial law by using blanket legislation. As a result, natural and legal persons are often forced to go to great lengths to find out exactly which rules regulate their activities and whether (and, if so, how) these actions are also subject to criminal sanctions.

[4] See in more detail ch 1.

[5] See eg chs 7, 8 and 9 in which the meaning of fundamental rights as the legality principle (more specifically *lex certa*), the privilege against self-incrimination and the *ne bis in idem* principle for the enforcement of financial law is addressed.

the European Union[6] (as further interpreted and developed by the ECtHR and the ECJ), but some of them are also regulated in more detail in directives of the EU.[7]

This all creates a quite complex matrix with a vertical dimension of a supranational legal domain at the EU level on the one hand and the national jurisdictions of the Member States on the other, and a horizontal dimension of interaction between the three traditional legal disciplines of private law, administrative law and criminal law on the national level. At the same time, the matrix as a whole is aimed at regulating the same financial markets, which are international by definition, and governed by the same set of fundamental rights. This multi-layered and fragmented system of financial law also leads to a shared responsibility for EU institutions and national authorities when enforcing financial law, each using their own means. As a matter of course, this situation also calls for efficient cooperation between all authorities involved, which is not always easy to realise, precisely because of the aforementioned fragmentation. In recent years, this observation has led to a still ongoing development of centralising enforcement powers at the EU level, inter alia culminating in the establishment of European supervisory authorities. However, as the various contributions to this volume show, the responsibility for enforcing financial law continues to be a shared one, in which both the EU and the Member States are responsible for their separate roles. The interdisciplinarity of financial law and its enforcement certainly has major benefits. It is even arguable that such a diverse and varied enforcement toolbox is needed to achieve the policy goals of financial regulation, and may be essential for the efficacy and effectivity of enforcement.[8] Therefore, it is not surprising that the EU and its Member States strive for an integral approach in which EU law and national laws of Member States are aligned, and private law, administrative law and criminal law are complementary as far as possible.[9]

However, this multilevel and interdisciplinary character of financial law and its enforcement also causes several difficult legal questions,[10] as well as certain

[6] See eg ch 5 for the guarantees in case of administrative law enforcement by EU institutions, laid down in Art 41 Charter. And of course, more generally, Title VI on 'Justice' is relevant for law enforcement, providing the right to an effective remedy and to a fair trial (Art 47), the presumption of innocence and the right of defence (Art 48), principles of legality and proportionality of criminal offences and penalties (Art 49) and the right not to be tried or punished twice in criminal proceedings for the same criminal offence (*ne bis in idem*; Art 50).

[7] See eg Directive (EU) 2013/48 of the European Parliament and of the Council of 22 October 2013 on the right of access to a lawyer in criminal proceedings and in European arrest warrant proceedings, and on the right to have a third party informed upon deprivation of liberty and to communicate with third persons and with consular authorities while deprived of liberty [2013] OJ L 294/1; and Directive (EU) 2016/343 of the European Parliament and of the Council of 9 March 2016 on the strengthening of certain aspects of the presumption of innocence and of the right to be present at the trial in criminal proceedings [2016] OJ L 65/1.

[8] See the 'complementary theory' of enforcement as mentioned in section 1.3.

[9] See eg for the interaction between (EU) administrative law and private law chs 3 and 4.

[10] See eg ch 6 on composite procedures in which both national authorities and EU authorities are involved in the decision-making, culminating in a national act or an EU act.

drawbacks and risks for natural and legal persons subjected to measures of enforcement. In other words, whilst violations of financial law may be detected and sanctioned more effectively from an instrumental perspective when a varied toolbox of enforcement measures is available, this varied toolbox may be problematic from a due process perspective. After all, interdisciplinarity may have important consequences for the legal position of natural and legal persons involved, since their position is defined differently in the various legal disciplines. Sometimes this even may lead to a clash of legal principles. For instance, Nan (chapter eight) clearly shows that the enforceable legal duty for natural and legal persons to cooperate with the administrative law enforcement authorities and to provide them with relevant information on the one hand, may clash with the criminal law privilege against self-incrimination (*nemo tenetur*) on the other, which protects the accused to a certain extent against involuntary cooperation with the investigation authorities, inter alia by guaranteeing the right to silence. In the same vein, Doorenbos (chapter seven) warns against incautiously criminalising EU rules of administrative law by using blanket legislation at the national level, since this may raise serious questions from the perspective of the legality principle (*lex certa*).

Perhaps the clearest example of what interdisciplinarity may do, is the danger of breaching the *ne bis in idem* principle in case of cumulating processes of administrative and criminal law enforcement, a danger which to a certain extent has been accepted as justifiable by the ECJ in the context of the enforcement of financial law where it refers to the need for effective, proportionate and dissuasive sanctioning.[11] Concerns regarding the consequences of law enforcement for fundamental rights such as the privilege against self-incrimination, *lex certa* and *ne bis in idem* are definitely not unique for financial law and may always occur when legal domains meet in concrete processes of law enforcement; however, the intrinsic interdisciplinary character of financial law as a functional legal domain makes this domain the more vulnerable to such clashes occurring. This raises the question whether these concerns are sufficiently recognised by legislators and policy-makers at both the EU level and the national level, and how the legal position of natural and legal persons involved, and notions of fairness are taken into account in the ongoing development of financial law.

11.3. Balancing Effectivity and Fairness in Financial Law

The chapters in this volume show that effective enforcement of financial law ranks high on the EU political agenda since the global financial crisis of 2008. In recent years, we have seen an almost continuous stream of EU legislation aimed at regulating the financial markets and preventing them from future disruptions. In many

[11] See in more detail ch 9.

cases this regulation has led to a further centralisation and Europeanisation of the enforcement of financial law, with the centralisation of Eurozone prudential banking supervision at the European Central Bank (ECB) in the Single Supervisory Mechanism (SSM),[12] and the establishment of the three European Supervisory Authorities (ESA) – EBA,[13] ESMA[14] and EIOPA[15] – as most significant achievements. The main goal of these operations has been to improve the effectivity of the enforcement of financial law and, by doing so, contributing to the stability and integrity of financial markets. However, this development towards centralisation and Europeanisation of enforcement of financial law has by no means come to a conclusion.

The way in which AML/CFT regulation has developed in recent years may serve as a good example in this regard,[16] since – as Allegrezza (chapter 10) shows – new AML/CFT legislative proposals are also mainly aimed at improving the effectivity of existing means of enforcement and introducing new means of enforcement. The current state of affairs, where the enforcement of AML/CFT regulations is primarily in the hands of national authorities, has shown to fall short in terms of effectiveness. Although in recent years we have seen several cases of financial institutions being sanctioned by national authorities with substantial fines (eg Danske Bank, ING, Société Générale and ABN AMRO),[17] the *communis opinio* is that these examples – how important these may be from the perspective of deterrence – are only drops in the ocean of the battle against money laundering and terrorism financing, and that (most) national authorities should have done more in enforcing AML/CFT regulations. Therefore, not surprisingly in this specific field of financial law, a development towards centralisation of enforcement to a European level can also be discerned, transferring the responsibility and the powers to enforce AML/CFT regulations partly from the national level of Member States to the EU level. The future Authority for Anti-Money Laundering and Countering the

[12] Council Regulation (EU) 1024/2013 of 15 October 2013 conferring specific tasks on the European Central Bank concerning policies relating to the prudential supervision of credit institutions (SSM Regulation) [2013] OJ L 287/63.

[13] Regulation (EU) 1093/2010 of the European Parliament and of the Council of 24 November 2010 establishing a European Supervisory Authority (European Banking Authority) [2010] OJ L 331/12.

[14] Regulation (EU) 1095/2010 of the European Parliament and of the Council of 24 November 2010 establishing a European Supervisory Authority (European Securities and Markets Authority) [2010] OJ L 331/84.

[15] Regulation (EU) 1094/2010 of the European Parliament and of the Council of 24 November 2010 establishing a European Supervisory Authority (European Insurance and Occupational Pensions Authority) [2010] OJ L 331/48.

[16] See for some recent steps eg Directive (EU) 2018/843 of the European Parliament and of the Council of 30 May 2018 amending Directive (EU) 2015/849 on the prevention of the use of the financial system for the purposes of money laundering or terrorist financing, and amending Directives 2009/138/EC and 2013/36/EU [2018] OJ L 156/43; and Directive (EU) 2018/1673 of the European Parliament and of the Council of 23 October 2018 on combating money laundering by criminal law [2018] OJ L 284/22.

[17] See in more detail ch 10.

Financing of Terrorism (AMLA), with its autonomous power to impose administrative sanctions for breaches of AML/CFT regulations,[18] and the recently established European Public Prosecutor's Office (EPPO) as the first centralised criminal enforcement institution responsible for fighting crimes against the financial interests of the EU,[19] may be the most predominant examples of this development. The proliferation of legal means to exchange information on natural and legal persons horizontally between the national authorities of the Member States and vertically between national and European authorities, may also serve as a clear example of the growing insight that national authorities cannot alone be held responsible for the enforcement of AML/CFT regulations.[20] However, this does not mean that in the near future the Member States will be released from their responsibility regarding the enforcement of AML/CFT regulations; the development of centralisation notwithstanding, national authorities will continue to have to intensify their AML/CFT actions, as will be expressed in a new, already sixth version of the AML/CFT Directive.[21]

In general, we would argue that the seemingly infinite stream of EU financial law regulation must be welcomed, provided it actually contributes to the stability and integrity of our financial markets. However, a holistic view of this body of regulation, as has been undertaken throughout this volume, also seems to show that the EU legislator has primarily been focused on the effectivity and efficacy of regulation, rather than on notions of fairness, despite the aforementioned general sets of fundamental rights which also govern the enforcement of financial law.[22] In our introductory chapter, we suggested that an explanation for this focus may be found in the origins of the EU and its policy goals of creating and regulating the internal market, with as a result a primary focus on economic values.[23] However, the EU also explicitly seeks to be a community of values in which the

[18] Proposal for a Regulation of the European Parliament and of the Council establishing the Authority for Anti-Money Laundering and Countering the Financing of Terrorism and amending Regulations (EU) No 1093/2010, (EU) 1094/2010, (EU) 1095/2010, COM(2021) 421 final.

[19] Council Regulation (EU) 1939/2017 of 12 October 2017 implementing enhanced cooperation on the establishment of the European Public Prosecutor's Office ('the EPPO') [2017] OJ L 283/1.

[20] See in more detail section 10.3.2, referring to the Multilateral Agreement between the ECB and the AML competent authorities (CAs) of the Member States, which is based on Article 57a(2) of the AML Directive (Directive (EU) 2015/849 of the European Parliament and of the Council of 20 May 2015 on the prevention of the use of the financial system for the purposes of money laundering or terrorist financing, as amended by Directive (EU) 2018/843 of the European Parliament and of the Council of 30 May 2018).

[21] Proposal for a Directive of the European Parliament and of the Council on the mechanisms to be put in place by the Member States for the prevention of the use of the financial system for the purposes of money laundering or terrorist financing and repealing Directive (EU) 2015/849, COM(2021) 423 final.

[22] See eg ch 10, in which Allegrezza concludes that efficacy and efficiency are predominant over legitimacy in the European political debate on the enforcement of financial law.

[23] See ch 1. See also ch 9 in relation to the jurisprudence of the ECJ on the *ne bis in idem* principle, which is less strict compared to the jurisprudence of the ECtHR.

fundamental rights of all EU citizens are respected. As the Preamble to the Charter of Fundamental Rights of the European Union states:

> The peoples of Europe, in creating an ever closer union among them, are resolved to share a peaceful future based on common values. Conscious of its spiritual and moral heritage, the Union is founded on the indivisible, universal values of human dignity, freedom, equality and solidarity; it is based on the principles of democracy and the rule of law. It places the individual at the heart of its activities, by establishing the citizenship of the Union and by creating an area of freedom, security and justice.'

Although it would be an exaggeration to state that while designing financial law the EU legislator explicitly sacrifices this mission of safeguarding fundamental rights to the policy goal of improving the effectivity of financial law regulation and its enforcement, it would be fair to say that in the totality of financial law regulation and enforcement measures, fundamental rights may be compromised, especially at the intersection of legal domains where various principles and paradigms may collide. This volume has shown that in concrete processes of administrative and/or criminal law enforcement fundamental rights, such as the right to a fair trial, the legality principle and the right to privacy, may be at risk. As a matter of course, this risk must be prevented, as far as possible, from materialising, since ignoring or neglecting this unintentional effect of interdisciplinarity could ultimately compromise the legitimacy of the enforcement of financial law and thus of financial law itself. This pleads for a holistic approach of financial law in which all relevant legal disciplines are considered, not only with regard to the toolbox of enforcement instruments, but also for the consequences for the legal position and the fundamental rights of natural and legal persons subject to measures of enforcement.

11.4. Conclusion

Financial law and its enforcement have developed rapidly since the global financial crisis of 2007/08. 'Centralisation' and 'Europeanisation' seem to be the key words in this regard. As has been argued above, it will be of critical importance, not only for the stability and integrity of EU financial markets, but also from the perspective of fundamental rights, how this ongoing development of centralisation will materialise in future. Of course, continuing centralisation will have important consequences for the vertical dimension of enforcement, since centralisation directly affects the relation between EU authorities and the Member States regarding their responsibilities for effective enforcement. However, it will also raise new questions regarding the horizontal dimension of enforcement, for instance because enforcement by means of criminal law has traditionally been reserved for the Member States and therefore remained virtually absent at the EU level (with the exception of the recently created powers of the EPPO). Therefore, a development towards centralisation may also rearrange the roles of the traditional legal disciplines where it regards the enforcement of financial law.[24] From the perspective of the *ultima ratio* principle – which prescribes criminal law to be a measure of last resort, also at the EU level[25] – such a rearranging does not necessarily have to be considered negatively, provided that private and administrative law enforcement will be bolstered by adequate procedural safeguards which are at least proportionate to the possible legal consequences or the severity of the sanctions that may be imposed. This brings us to the legal position of natural and legal persons subject to measures of enforcement.

One of the major challenges for regulators and enforcement authorities is to strike a fair balance between effective enforcement on the one hand and respect for the legal position of the natural and legal persons involved on the other. Recent history has shown that financial markets represent critical elements of our present-day societies, which stresses the importance of effective enforcement for achieving key policy goals of financial regulation, such as guaranteeing the stability and integrity of financial markets. However, the overall legitimacy of law enforcement processes and respect for fundamental rights of natural and legal persons involved also need to be upheld. Several chapters in this volume show that in this respect, some work still has to be done,[26] especially where it regards administrative and criminal law enforcement and, more specifically, at the intersection of both legal disciplines where fundamental rights, such as the privilege against self-incrimination and the *ne bis in idem* principle, may be compromised.[27]

Emphasising the importance of legitimacy and fairness in law enforcement may be viewed as pushing at an open door, but several contributors to this volume have convincingly shown that legitimacy and fairness may not always have been the top priorities of legislators in a legal domain which is so strongly focused on safeguarding the stability and integrity of financial markets. The fact that in financial law measures of enforcement are mostly addressed to legal persons instead of natural persons may not be irrelevant, for instance in relation to the question whether fair trial rights have been breached,[28] but this does not constitute in itself

[24] See eg ch 3, showing that centralisation of enforcement powers may also influence the relation between administrative and private law enforcement.

[25] See European Commission, 'Towards an EU Criminal Policy: Ensuring the effective implementation of EU policies through criminal law' COM(2011) 573 final. See also S Melander, 'Ultima Ratio in European Criminal Law' (2013) 3 *European Criminal Law Review* 45; and on processes of decriminalisation in EU criminal law, V Mitsilegas, 'Decriminalisation in the Law of the European Union' in JW Ouwerkerk, J Altena, J Öberg and S Miettinen, *The Future of EU Criminal Justice Policy and Practice. Legal and Criminological Perspectives* (Brill Nijhoff, 2019) 106–18.

[26] See in more detail ch 5, which pleads for the development of a general regulation for administrative law enforcement by European supervisory authorities, such as the ReNEUAL Model Rules.

[27] See chs 8 and 9.

[28] See on differences between the applicability of (certain) fundamental rights to natural persons vs. legal persons ch 8. See also generally on the applicability of fundamental rights to legal persons PHPHMC van Kempen, 'The Recognition of Legal Persons in International Human Rights Instruments: Protection Against and Through Criminal Justice?' in M Pieth and R Ivory (eds), *Corporate Criminal Liability. Emergence, Convergence, and Risk* (Springer, 2011) 355–89.

a persuasive reason to subordinate notions of fairness to the effectivity of law enforcement.

In the end, balancing effective enforcement and respect for the legal position, also of the legal persons involved, is key to the legitimacy of financial law and a shared responsibility of the EU and the Member States. The preceding chapters have confirmed our belief that such a balance can only be achieved when taking an integrated, holistic view on financial law, in which both the vertical dimension and the horizontal dimension of enforcement are taken into consideration. We sincerely hope the contributions in this volume have also been of help to the reader in developing such a holistic view, and may contribute to the discussions on the development of financial law, both at the EU level and at the national level of the Member States.

BIBLIOGRAPHY

S Allegrezza (ed), *The Enforement Dimension of the Single Supervisory Mechanism* (Kluwer Cedam, 2020).

S Allegrezza, 'A European Public Prosecutor Office to Protect Common Financial Interests: A Milestone for the EU Integration Process' in K Ambos and P Rackow (eds), *Cambridge Companion to European Criminal Law* (CUP, forthcoming).

S Allegrezza and V Covolo (eds), *Cryptocurrencies and Crime* (forthcoming).

JGH Altena, *Het legaliteitsbeginsel en de doorwerking van Europees recht in het Nederlandse materiële strafrecht* (dissertation, Leiden) (Wolters Kluwer, 2016).

K Ambos, *European Criminal Law* (CUP, 2018).

F Annunziata, 'European Banking Supervision in the Age of the ECB Landeskreditbank Baden-Wuerttemberg- Foerderbank v ECB' (2020) 21 *European Business Organization Law Review* 545.

J Armour et al, *Principles of Financial Regulation* (OUP, 2016).

TMC Arons, 'Judicial Protection of Supervised Credit Institutions in the European Banking Union' in D Busch and G Ferrarini, *European Banking Law*, 2nd edn (OUP, 2020).

W Aussenegg, R Jelic and R Ranzi, 'Corporate Insider Trading in Europe' (2018) 54 *Journal of International Financial Markets, Institutions & Money* 27.

I van Bael, *Due Process in EU Competition Proceedings* (Wolters Kluwer, 2011).

RW Baker, 'The Scale of the Global Financial Structure Facilitating Money Laundering' in B Unger and D van der Linde (eds), *Research Handbook on Money Laundering* (Edward Elgar, 2013).

R Bax and A Witte, 'The taxonomy of ECB instruments available for banking supervision' (2019) 6 *ECB Economic Bulletin* 85.

S Beiter et al, 'Consequences of Wirecard Scandal: New requirements for corporate governance and audit for German Listed Companies' Gibson Dunn (7 June 2021).

W Blair, R Brent and T Grant (eds), *Banks and Financial Crime. The International Law of Tainted Money*, 2nd edn (OUP, 2017).

N Boister, 'Transnational Criminal Law' (2003) 14 *European Journal of International Law* 953.

GJME de Bont, 'Het pleitbaar standpunt als bijzondere strafuitsluitingsgrond?' (2020) 4 *Strafblad* 219.

LS Borlini, 'Regulating Criminal Finance in the EU in the Light of the International Instruments' (2017) 36 *Yearbook of European Law 2017* (OUP, 2018).

P Boswijk et al, *Transnationale samenwerking tussen toezichthouders in Europa* (WODC, 2008).

F Brito Bastos, 'The *Borelli* Doctrine Revisited: Three Issues of Coherence in a Landmark Ruling for EU Administrative Justice' (2015) 8 *Review of European Administrative Law* 269.

—— 'Derivative Illegality in European Composite Administrative Procedures' (2018) 55 *Common Market Law Review* 101.

—— 'Judicial review of composite administrative procedures in the Single Supervisory Mechanism: *Berlusconi*' (2019) 56 *Common Market Law Review* 1355.

—— 'An Administrative Crack in the EU's Rule of Law: Composite Decision-making and Nonjusticiable National Law' (2020) 16 *European Constitutional Law Review* 63.

M Caianiello, *Right to Remain Silent and not to Incriminate Oneself in the European Union System* (research paper for University of Bologna, 2021).

J Callewaert, 'The Privilege against Self-Incrimination in European Law: An Illustration of the Impact of the Plurality of Courts and Legal Sources on the Protection of Fundamental Rights in Europe' (2004) 5 *ERA Forum* 488.

—— 'The European Convention on Human Rights and European Union Law: A Long Way from Harmony (2009) 6 *European Human Rights Law Review* 768.

D Calvo et al, 'Financial supervisory architecture: what has changed after the crisis?' Bank for International Settlements Report (2018).

M Campbell-Verduyn, 'Bitcoin, crypto-coins, and global anti-money laundering governance' (2018) 69 *Crime Law and Social Change* 283.

G della Cananea, 'The European Union's Mixed Administrative Proceedings' (2004) 68 *Law & Contemporary Problems* 197.

CJ Carrubba and L Murrah, *Legal integration and the Use of the Preliminary Ruling Process in the European Union, International Organization* (CUP, 2005).

OO Cherednychenko and M Andenas (eds), *Financial Regulation and Civil Liability in European Law* (Edward Elgar Publishing, 2020).

J Cnossen and JH Gerards, 'Annotatie bij Europees Hof voor de Rechten van de Mens, 21-10-2013, ECLI:CE:ECHR:2013:1021JUD004275009' in *EHRC Updates* (ECtHR 2020-0160).

Commissie Europeanisering algemeen bestuursrecht, *Europa en het algemeen bestuursrecht, Burger en bestuur in de gemeenschappelijke rechtsorde* (Boom Juridisch, 2021).

V Covolo, 'The EU Response to Criminal Misuse of Cryptocurrencies: The Young, Already Outdated 5th Anti-Money Laundering Directive' University of Luxembourg Law Working Paper No 2019-015 (6 January 2020).

PP Craig, 'The Legal Effect of Directives: Policy, Rules and Exceptions' (2009) 34 *European Law Review* 349.

—— 'Integration, Democracy and Legitimacy' Legal Research Paper Series, Paper No 47/2011.

—— *EU Administrative Law* (OUP, 2018).

S Cras and A Erbežnik, 'The Directive on the Presumption of Innocence and the Right to Be Present at Trial: Genesis and Description of the New EU-Measure' (2016) Eucrim 25.

R D'Ambrosio, 'The Involvement of the NCAs in the ECB's Supervisory Proceedings' in R D'Ambrosio (ed), *Law and Practice of the Banking Union and its governing Institutions (Cases and Materials)* (Quaderni di Ricerca Guiridica, 2012).

P Demetriades and R Vassileva, 'Money Laundering and Central Bank Governance in the European Union' (2020) 23 *Journal of International Economic Law* 509.

S Demková, 'The Grand Chamber's Take on Composite Procedures under the Single Supervisory Mechanism. Comments on Judgment of 27 June 2018, C-219/17 Silvio Berlusconi v Finanziaria d'investimento Fininvest SpA (Fininvest) v Banca d'Italia and others, EU:C:2018:502' (2019) 12 *Review of European Administrative Law* 209.

P Dermine and M Eliantonio, 'Case Note: CJEU (Grand Chamber), Judgment of 19 December 2018, C-219/17, Silvio Berlusconi and Finanziaria d'investimento Fininvest SpA (Fininvest) v Banca d'Italia and Instituto per la Vigilanza Sulle Assicurazioni (IVASS)' (2019) 12 *Review of European Administrative Law* 246.

V Di Bucci, 'Procedural and Judicial Implications of Composite Procedures in the Banking Union' in C Zilioli and K-P Wojcik (eds), *Judicial Review in the European Banking Union* (Edward Elgar, 2021).

G Dimitropoulos, 'The Law of Blockchain' (2020) 95 *Washington Law Review* 1117.

DR Doorenbos, 'Specialisatie en rechtsvinding in het economisch strafrecht' (2010) 7 *Trema* 272.

—— *Schets van het economisch strafrecht* (Wolters Kluwer, 2015).

—— 'Opzet in de Wet op de economische delicten: beter boos dan kleurloos' (2021) 3 *Ars Aequi* 253.

M Eliantonio, 'Judicial Review in an Integrated Administration: the Case of "Composite Procedures"' (2015) 7 *Review of European Administrative Law* 65.

C van der Elst, 'The Belgian Struggle for Corporate Governance Improvements' ECGI – Law Working Paper 114/2008.

C Enoch et al, 'Securing a Safer Financial System for Europe' in C Enoch et al (eds), *From Fragmentation to Financial Integration in Europe* (Report International Monetary Fund, 2013).

G Ferrarini and L Chiarella, 'Common Banking Supervision in the Eurozone: Strengths and Weaknesses' ECGI Law Working Paper No 223/2013.

E Gagliardi and L Wissink, 'Ensuring effective judicial protection in case of ECB decisions based on national law' (2020) 13 *Review of European Administrative Law* 41.

G Gaja, 'Case C-6/99, Association Greenpeace France and Others v. Ministere de l'Agriculture et de la Peche and Others' (2000) 37 *Common Market Law Review* 1427.

F Giuffrida, 'The European Public Prosecutor's Office: King without kingdom?' CEPS Research report (2017).

M Haentjens, 'Private Law in Banking Union Litigation' in C Zilioli and K-P Wojcik (eds), *Judicial Review in the European Banking Union* (Edward Elgar Publishing, 2021).

M Haentjens and P De Gioia Carabellese, *European Banking and Financial Law*, 2nd edn (Routledge, 2020).

RCP Haentjens, *De wederrechtelijkheid in het financiële strafrecht* (Universiteit van Amsterdam, 2016).

RCP Haentjens and M Jurgens, 'De Conceptrichtlijn Marktmisbruik, de Conceptverordening Marktmisbruik en de harmonisatie van handhaving' in R Stijnen en M Jurgens, *Toepassing van Europees Recht* (Kluwer, 2012).

SB Harris, 'Audit industry concentration and potential implications' *Public Company Accounting Oversight Board* (December 2017).

RH Helmholz, 'Origins of the Privilege against Self-Incrimination: The Role of the European Ius Commune' (1990) 65 *New York University Law Review* 962.

HCH Hofmann, 'Composite decision making procedures in EU administrative law' in HCH Hofmann and AH Türk, *Legal Challenges in EU Administrative Law. Towards an Integrated Administration* (Edward Elgar, 2009).

HCH Hofmann, 'Multi-Jurisdictional Composite Procedures. The Backbone of the EU's Single Regulatory Space' Université du Luxembourg Legal Working Paper Series (2019(3)).

KJ Hopt, 'Corporate Governance of Banks and Financial Institutions: Economic Theory, Supervisory Practice, Evidence and Policy' (2021) 13 *European Business Organization Law Review* 13.

JIMG Jahae and TOM Dieben, 'Prejudiciële vragen aan het HvJ EU: liever geen pottenkijkers?' (2015) *Strafblad* 30.

O Jansen and B Schöndorf-Haubold (eds), *The European Composite Administration* (Intersentia, 2011).

BPM Joosen, *Regulatory capital requirements and bail in mechanisms* in M Haentjens and B Wessels, 'Research Handbook on Crisis Management in the Banking Sector' (Edward Elgar Publishing, 2015).

BF Keulen, *Economisch strafrecht* (Guida Quint, 1995).

FGH Kristen, 'Het materieelrechtelijk legaliteitsbeginsel' in FGH Kristen, RMI Lamp, JMW Lindeman, MJJP Luchtman and WS de Zanger (eds), *Bijzonder strafrecht, Strafrechtelijke handhaving van sociaal-economisch en fiscaal recht in Nederland* (Boom Uitgevers, 2019).

K Lackhoff, *Single Supervisory Mechanism. A Practitioner's Guide* (CH Beck-Hart-Nomos, 2017).

A-J Kargopoulos, 'ECHR and the CJEU, Competing, overlapping, or Supplementary Competences?' (2015) 3 *Eucrim* 96.

PHPHMC van Kempen, 'Human Rights and Criminal Justice Applied to Legal Persons. Protection and Liability of Private and Public Juristic Entities under ICCPR, ECHR, ACHR and AfChHPR' (2010) 14 *Electronic Journal of Comparative Law*.

—— 'The Recognition of Legal Persons in International Human Rights Instruments: Protection Against and Through Criminal Justice?' in M Pieth and R Ivory (eds), *Corporate Criminal Liability. Emergence, Convergence, and Risk, Ius Gentium: Comparative Perspectives on Law and Justice 9* (Springer, 2011).

J Kirschenbaum and N Véron, 'A better European Union architecture to fight money laundering' (2018) 19 *Policy Contribution Issue*.

T Kuhn, 'Grand theories of European integration revisited: does identity politics shape the course of European integration?' (2019) 26 *Journal of European Public Policy* 1213.

S Lamberigts, 'The Directive on the Presumption of Innocence: A Missed Opportunity for Legal Persons?' (2016) 1 *Eucrim* 36.

G Lasagni, *Banking Supervision and Criminal Investigation* (Springer, 2019).

K Lenaerts, 'The Rule of Law and the Coherence of the Judicial System of the European Union' (2007) 44 *Common Market Law Review* 1625.

M Levi and P Reuter, 'Money Laundering' (2006) 34 *Crime & Justice* 289.

JMW Lindeman, 'De zwakste schakel, Enkele gevolgen van het stelsel van gelede normstellingen' (2004) 3 *Tijdschrift voor Onderneming en Strafrecht* 78.

MLV López, 'The presumption of innocence in Directive 2016/343/EC of 9 March 2016' (2017) 3 *ERA Forum*.

MJJP Luchtman and RJGM Widdershoven, 'Het Nederlandse strafrecht in de ban van het Unierecht' (2018) 22 *Ars Aequi* 873.

L Luparia and G Soana, 'Investigating and Prosecuting Crypto-crime: Challenges and Opportunities' in S Allegrezza and V Covolo, *Cryptocurrencies and Crime* (forthcoming).

KJ McCarthy, 'Why Do Some States Tolerate Money Laundering? On the Competition for Illegal Money' in B Unger and D van der Linde (eds), *Research Handbook on Money Laundering* (Edward Elgar Publishing, 2013).

S Melander, 'Ultima Ratio in European Criminal Law' (2013) 3 *European Criminal Law Review* 45.

V Mitsilegas, 'Decriminalisation in the Law of the European Union' in JW Ouwerkerk, J Altena, J Öberg and S Miettinen, *The Future of EU Criminal Justice Policy and Practice. Legal and Criminological Perspectives* (Brill Nijhoff, 2019).

V Mitsilegas and B Gilmore, 'The EE Legislative Framework Against Money Laundering and Terrorist Finance: A Critical Analysis in the Light of Evolving Global Standards' (2007) 56 *International and Comparative Law Quarterly* 119.

N Moloney, 'European Banking Union: assessing its risks and resilience' (2014) 51 *Common Market Law Review* 1609.

F Mouzakiti, 'Cooperation between Financial Intelligence Units in the European Union: Stuck in the middle between the General Data Protection Regulation and the Police Data Protection Directive' (2020) 11 *New Journal of European Criminal Law* 351.

JS Nan, *Het lex certa-beginsel* (dissertation, Tilburg) (Sdu Uitgevers, 2011).

E Nelson, J Ewing and L Alderman, 'The Swift Collapse of a Company Built on Debt' *New York Times* (28 March 2021).

I Ņesterova and A Meikališa, 'The right to information about the right to silence as EU procedural guarantee in criminal proceedings and its impact on national legal systems', available at www.law.muni.cz/sborniky/dny_prava_2012/files/pravoEU/NesterovaIrena_MeikalisaArija.pdf.

A Nieto Martin, 'Transformationes del ius puniendi en el derecho global' in A Nieto Martin and B García Moreno, *Ius Puniendi y Global Law* (Tirant lo Blanch, 2019).

A Nieto Martin and M Munoz de Morales Romero, 'The Office of the European Public Prosecutor and Related Offences: Deconstructing the Problem' in P Asp (ed), *The European Public Prosecutor Office – Legal and Criminal Policy Perspective* (Jure, 2015).

SMC Nuijten, 'Rechtsbescherming bij toezicht onder het SSM' (2014) 11 *Tijdschrift voor Financieel Recht* 469.

J Öberg, 'The European Public Prosecutor: Quintessential supranational criminal law?' (2021) 28 *Maastricht Journal of European and Comparative Law*164.

JW Ouwerkerk and PAM Verrest, 'De struisvogel voorbij. Pleidooi voor een actieve participatie in de Europese rechtsontwikkeling inzake fundamentele rechten in de strafrechtspleging' (2021) 7 Delikt en Delinkwent 585.

S Prechal and RJGM Widdershoven, 'Inleiding' in S Prechal and RJGM Widdershoven (eds), *Inleiding tot het Europees bestuursrecht* (Ars Aequi Libri, 2017).

M Prek and S Lefèvre, 'The EU Courts as "National" Courts: National Law in the EU Judicial Process' (2017) 54 *Common Market Law Review* 378.

M Redmayne, 'Rethinking the Privilege Against Self-Incrimination' (2007) 27 *Oxford Journal of Legal Studies* 228.

HC Röhl, 'Procedures in the European Composite Administration' in J Barnes (ed), *Transforming Administrative Procedure* (Global Law Press, 2008).

H Satzger, 'Application Problems relating to "Ne bis in Idem as Guaranteed under Art. 50 CFR/Art. 54 CISA and Art 4 Prot. No.7 ECHR' (2020) 3 *Eucrim* 213.

F Schäfer, '§ 21 Leerverkäufe und Geschäfte in bestimmten Kreditderivaten' in H-D Assmann, RA Schütze and P Buck-Heeb, *Handbuch des Kapitalanlagerechts* (CH Beck, 2020).

F Schauer, *The Force of Law* (Harvard University Press, 2015).

VPG de Serière and BCG Jennen, 'De betekenis van "soft law" in de financiële toezichtwetgeving' (2017) 143 *Ondernemingsrecht* 796.

RA Shiner, 'Corporations and the Presumption of Innocence' (2014) 8 *Criminal Law and Philosophy* 485.

C Stahn, *A Critical Introduction to International Criminal Law* (CUP, 2019).

D Starkman, 'Belgium's biggest banks propose system to share suspected money laundering information' International Consortium of Investigative Journalists (17 November 2020).

G Stessens, *Money Laundering: A New International Law Enforcement* (CUP, 2008).

F Teichmann, 'Recent trends in money laundering' (2020) 73 *Crime, Law and Social Change* 237.

SA Trainor, 'A Comparative Analysis of a Corporation's Right Against Self-Incrimination' (1994) 5 *Fordham International Law Journal* 2139.

'The Spanish imposition: Santander's non-call sets precedent in AT1 bond market' (14 February 2019), available at www.fidelityinternational.com/editorial/blog/santanders-noncall-sets-precedent-in-at1-bond-market-df1531-en5.

TH Tröger, 'The Single Supervisory Mechanism – Panacea or Quack Banking Regulation?' (2014) 15 *European Business Organization Law Review* 449.

AH Türk, 'Judicial review of integrated administration in the EU' in HCH Hofmann and AH Türk, *Legal Challenges in EU Administrative Law. Towards an Integrated Administration* (Edward Elgar, 2009).

P Van Sasse van Ysselt, 'Advies Protocol 16 EVRM inzake de adviesprocedure en wetgevingstechniek van doorverwijzing naar constitutionele normen in het licht van het strafrechtelijk legaliteitsbeginsel' (2020) 4 *NJCM Bulletin* 498.

M Veenbrink, 'The Privilege Against Self-incrimination in EU Competition Law: A Deafening Silence?' (2015) 2 *Legal Issues of Economic Integration* 119.

T Wahl, 'AML Package IV: EU Traceability of Funds Legislation to Be Extended to Crypto-Assets' *eucrim.eu* (5 August 2021).

PJ Wattel, 'Nog vragen?' (2014) 14 *Nederlands Juristenblad* 893.

L Wissink, *Effective Legal Protection in Banking Supervision* (European Law Publishing, 2021).

A Witte, 'The Application of National Banking Supervision Law by the ECB: Three Parallel Modes of Executing EU Law?' (2014) 21 *Maastricht Journal of European and Comparative Law* 89.

K-P Wojcik in H von der Groeben, J Schwarze and A Hatje (eds), *Europäisches Unionsrecht, Art 63 TFEU* (CH Beck, 2015).

—— 'Bankenunion, Brexit und EU-Aufsicht über die Finanzmärkte' (Bonn, 22 January 2018).

K-P Wojcik and M Krauze, 'The use of EU regulations to establish qualitative requirements in the fields of banking supervision and resolution and their impact on civil law and corporate relationships' in BPM Joosen, M Lamandini and TH Tröger, *Capital and Liquidity Requirements for European Banks* (OUP, forthcoming).

MK Wright, 'Financing Cr-ISIS: The Efficacy of Mutual Legal Assistance Treaties in the Context of Money Laundering and Terror Finance' (2019) 52 *Vanderbilt Journal of Transnational Law* 229.

E Wymeersch, 'Noclar or how Accountants deal with Suspected or Occurred Breaches of the Law' Universiteit Gent, Working paper series, Working paper 2016(5).

—— 'Brexit and the equivalence of regulation and supervision' EBI Working Papers 2017(15).

D Zetzsche and M Lehmann '§ 53 WpHG Überwachung von Leerverkäufen; Verordnungsermächtigung' in E Schwark and D Zimmer, *Kapitalmarktrechts-Kommentar* (CH Beck, 2020).

C Zilioli and K-P Wojcik, 'European Banking Union: a giant step towards European integration and a challenge for judicial review' in C Zilioli and K-P Wojcik (eds), *Judicial Review in the European Banking Union* (Edward Elgar Publishing, 2021).

INDEX

Introductory Note

References such as '178–79' indicate (not necessarily continuous) discussion of a topic across a range of pages. Wherever possible in the case of topics with many references, these have either been divided into sub-topics or only the most significant discussions of the topic are listed. Because the entire work is about 'financial law', the use of this term (and certain others which occur constantly throughout the book) as an entry point has been minimised. Information will be found under the corresponding detailed topics.

www.ingramcontent.com/pod-product-compliance
Lightning Source LLC
LaVergne TN
LVHW011751200926
848484LV00003B/673

9781509959747